Communications in Computer and Information Science   1010

Commenced Publication in 2007
Founding and Former Series Editors:
Phoebe Chen, Alfredo Cuzzocrea, Xiaoyong Du, Orhun Kara, Ting Liu,
Krishna M. Sivalingam, Dominik Ślęzak, Takashi Washio, and Xiaokang Yang

More information about this series at http://www.springer.com/series/7899

Mario Piattini · Paulo Rupino da Cunha ·
Ignacio García Rodríguez de Guzmán ·
Ricardo Pérez-Castillo (Eds.)

Quality of Information and Communications Technology

12th International Conference, QUATIC 2019
Ciudad Real, Spain, September 11–13, 2019
Proceedings

 Springer

Editors
Mario Piattini ⓘ
Department of Information Technologies
and Systems
University of Castilla-La Mancha
Ciudad Real, Spain

Ignacio García Rodríguez de Guzmán ⓘ
Department of Information Technologies
and Systems
University of Castilla-La Mancha
Ciudad Real, Spain

Paulo Rupino da Cunha ⓘ
Departamento de Engenharia Informatica
University of Coimbra
Coimbra, Portugal

Ricardo Pérez-Castillo ⓘ
Department of Information Technologies
and Systems
University of Castilla-La Mancha
Ciudad Real, Spain

ISSN 1865-0929   ISSN 1865-0937 (electronic)
Communications in Computer and Information Science
ISBN 978-3-030-29237-9   ISBN 978-3-030-29238-6 (eBook)
https://doi.org/10.1007/978-3-030-29238-6

This Springer imprint is published by the registered company Springer Nature Switzerland AG
The registered company address is: Gewerbestrasse 11, 6330 Cham, Switzerland

Preface

The International Conference on the Quality of Information and Communications Technology (QUATIC) serves as a forum for disseminating advanced methods, techniques, and tools for supporting quality approaches to ICT engineering and management. Practitioners and researchers are encouraged to exchange ideas and approaches on how to adopt a quality culture in ICT process and product improvement and to provide practical studies in varying contexts.

QUATIC 2019 was led by Prof. Dr. Mario Piattini (University of Castilla-La Mancha) and Dr. Paulo Rupino da Cunha (University of Coimbra) as program chairs. The 12th edition of QUATIC was organized by the Alarcos Research Group at University of Castilla-La Mancha with Dr. Ignacio García Rodríguez de Guzmán and Dr. Ricardo Pérez del Castillo serving as organizing chairs. QUATIC 2019 was held during September 11–13, 2019, in Ciudad Real, Spain.

The volume is a collection of high-quality peer-reviewed research papers received from all over the world. QUATIC 2019 attracted a good number of submissions from the different areas spanning over eight thematic tracks in various cutting-edge technologies of specialized focus, which were organized and chaired by eminent professors. These eight special tracks were: Security & Privacy, Requirements Engineering, Business Processes, Evidence-Based Software Engineering, Process Improvement and Assessment, Model-Driven Engineering & Software Maintenance, Data Science & Services, and Verification & Validation.

Technical Papers Summary

The Technical Program Committee of QUATIC 2019 was made up of 192 international academic and industrial domain experts. Based on a rigorous peer-review process by the Technical Program Committee members along with external experts as reviewers, the best quality papers were identified for presentation and publication.

The review process was carried out in a double-blind manner, with a minimum of three reviews for each submission, although most of the submissions were reviewed by four referees. Submitted papers came from countries like Argentina (6), Brazil (30), Ecuador (9), Finland (7), Germany (4), Italy (14), Morocco (7), Portugal (33), Spain (43), among other. Out of the submission pool of received papers (66), only 38% were accepted for these proceedings, 19 full papers and 6 short papers.

Invited Talks

The conference this year included the presence of three outstanding keynote speakers. The first keynote was by Dr. Maria Teresa Baldassarre, who received a degree with honors in Informatics at the University of Bari, Italy, where she has also received her PhD in software engineering. She is currently an assistant professor there. Her talk "From processes to products through research and practice: a perspective on 50 years of software quality," discussed the main roles that quality has covered over the past 50 years with respect to software processes and software products. Relevant results and lessons learned from industrial experiences that point out the need of combining both aspects to deliver high quality software were presented.

The second keynote speaker was Dr. Christof Ebert, managing director at Vector Consulting Services. He supports clients around the world to improve product strategy and product development and to manage organizational changes. He is a professor at the University of Stuttgart and at the Sorbonne in Paris. His talk "Scaling agile for critical systems," provided results from an empirical field study on distributed development with agile practices.

Last but not least, Dr. Antonio Vallecillo is a Professor of Computer Science at the University of Málaga. His research interests include model-based software engineering, open distributed processing, and software quality. His talk "Modeling and evaluating quality in the presence of uncertainty," identified several kinds of uncertainties that have a direct impact on quality and discussed some challenges on how quality needs to be planned, modeled, designed, measured, and ensured in the presence of uncertainty.

Industrial Day

As is tradition, one day of the conference was dedicated to industrial participation. This included some business-oriented, scientific contributions together with some invited speakers such as Domingo Gaitero (Proceso Social), Carlos Manuel Fernández and Boris Delgado (AENOR), Ariel Lunardello (Bip), as well as the already mentioned keynote speaker Christof Ebert.

September 2019

Mario Piattini
Paulo Rupino da Cunha
Ignacio García Rodríguez de Guzmán
Ricardo Pérez-Castillo

Acknowledgements

The proceedings editors wish to thank the dedicated Scientific Committee members and all the other reviewers for their contributions, as well as the University of Castilla-La Mancha (UCLM) for hosting the conference.

Special thanks to the Steering Committee, and the promoters CS03 and Instituto Português da Qualidade.

This conference counted with the generous support of the following sponsors: UCLM, Institute of Technologies and Information Systems (ITSI), Escuela Superior de Informática de Ciudad Real (ESI), Departamento de Tecnologías y Sistemas de Información (TSI), Alarcos Research Group, AQC Lab, Aula Smact (Avanttic), Cojali, DQ Team, and Intelligent Environments (IE); as well as to several collaborators: AENOR, AECDI, COIICLM, COITICLM, and Excmo. Ayuntamiento de Ciudad Real.

Special thanks to the authors and participants at the conference. Without their efforts, there would be no conference or proceedings. Thank you for contributing to the critical mass of researchers that keep this conference alive for what we expect to be many more years to come.

Acknowledgments

Organization

Program Committee Chairs

Mario Piattini   University of Castilla-La Mancha, Spain
Paulo Rupino da Cunha   University of Coimbra, Portugal

Organizing Committee Chairs

Ignacio García-Rodríguez   University of Castilla-La Mancha, Spain
  de Guzmán
Ricardo Pérez-Castillo   University of Castilla-La Mancha, Spain

Organizing Committee

Financial Chair

Aurora Vizcaíno   University of Castilla-La Mancha, Spain

Industrial Day Co-chairs

Moisés Rodríguez   University of Castilla-La Mancha, Spain
María Ángeles Moraga   University of Castilla-La Mancha, Spain

Web Chair

Manuel A. Serrano   University of Castilla-La Mancha, Spain

Publicity Committee

Michael Felderer   University of Innsbruck, Austria
Beatriz Marín   Universidad Diego Portales, Chile

Steering Committee

João Sabbo   CS03, Portugal
Miguel A. Brito   CS03, University of Minho, Portugal
João Pascoal Faria   CS03, FEUP, Portugal
Ana Cristina Paiva   CS03, FEUP, Portugal
Fernando Brito e Abreu   CS03, ISCTE-IUL, Portugal
Vasco Amaral   CS03, FCT-UNL, Portugal
António Moitinho   CS03, Portugal
Carlos Barreiras   CS03, Portugal

Thematic Track Chairs

Quality Aspects in Requirements Engineering

José Luis de la Vara   University of Castilla-La Mancha, Spain

Quality Aspects in Model-Driven Engineering

Juan Manuel Vara Mesa   Rey Juan Carlos University, Spain
Marcos Didonet Del Fabro   Universidade Federal do Paraná, Brazil

Quality Aspects in DevOps Development

Diego Perez-Palacin   Linnaeus University, Sweden

Quality Aspects in Process Improvement and Assessment

Francisco José Pino Correa   Universidad del Cauca, Colombia
Karol Frühauf   INFOGEM AG, Switzerland

Quality Aspects in Verification and Validation

Eda Marchetti   CNR-ISTI, Italy
Javier Tuya   University of Oviedo, Spain

Quality Aspects in Evidence-Based Software Engineering

Marcela Genero Bocco   University of Castilla-La Mancha, Spain
Silvia Abrahão   University Politècnica de València, Spain

Quality Aspects in Security and Privacy

Danilo Caivano   University of Bari, Italy
Ana Cavalli   TéLéCOM & Management SudParis, France

Quality Aspects in Cloud-Based Platforms and Services

Francisco Gortázar   Universidad Rey Juan Carlos, Spain

Quality Aspects in Business Processes

Andrea Delgado   Universidad de la República, Uruguay
Cristina Cabanillas   Vienna University of Economics and Business, Austria

Quality Aspects in Data Science and Artificial Intelligence

Francisco Herrera   University of Granada, Spain

Quality Aspects in Software Maintenance and Comprehension

Francesca Arcelli Fontana   University of Milano Bicocca, Italy
Valentina Lenarduzzi   Tampere University, Finland

Program Committee Members

Adela del-Río-Ortega	University of Seville, Spain
Adriana Marotta	Universidad de la República, Uruguay
Agnieszka Jakóbik	Cracow University of Technology, Poland
Aida Omerovic	SINTEF, Norway
Aiko Yamashita	CoE Advanced Analytics - DNB, Norway
Alberto Silva	Universidade de Lisboa, Portugal
Alejandro Maté	University of Alicante, Spain
Alexander Chatzigeorgiou	University of Macedonia, Greece
Alfonso Rodriguez	Universidad del Bio Bio, Chile
Ambrosio Toval	University or Murcia, Spain
Ana Cristina Ramada Paiva	University of Porto, Portugal
Ana Paiva	Universidade de Oporto, Portugal
Ana Respicio	University of Lisbon, Portugal
Andrea Janes	Free University of Bolzano, Italy
Andreas Nehfort	Nehfort IT-Consulting KG, Austria
Angélica Caro	Universidad del Bio Bio, Chile
Anna Rita Fasolino	University of Naples, Italy
Antonela Tommasel	Universidad Nacional del Centro de la Provincia de Buenos Aires, Argentina
Antonino Sabetta	SAP Labs, France
Antonio Cicchetti	Mälardalen University, Sweden
Antonio Martini	University of Oslo, Norway
António Rito Silva	University of Lisboa, Portugal
Apostolos Ampatzoglou	University of Macedonia, Greece
Bart F. A. Hompes	Eindhoven University of Technology, The Netherlands
Bartosz Walter	Poznań University of Technology, Poland
Beatriz Marín	Universidad Diego Portales, Chile
Boni García	Rey Juan Carlos University, Spain
Breno Miranda	Federal University of Pernambuco, Brazil
Carlos Serrão	ISCTE-IUL, Portugal
Claudia Raibulet	University of Milano Bicocca, Italy
Claudio De la Riva	University of Ovideo, Spain
Damian Andrew Tamburri	Eindhoven University of Technology and JADS, The Netherlands
Daniel Calegari	Universidad de la República, Uruguay
Daniel Grzonka	Cracow University of Technology, Poland
Denis Silveira	Universidade Federal de Pernambunco, Brazil
Dragan H. Stojanovic	University of Nis, Serbia
Elena Navarro	University of Castilla-La Mancha, Spain
Emanuela Gadelha Cartaxo	Federal University of Campina Grande, Brazil
Emilia Cioroaica	Fraunhofer IESE Mannheim, Germany
Emilio Insfran	Universitat Politècnica de València, Spain
Eugene Syriani	University of Montreal, Canada
Fabio Casati	University of Trento, Italy

Fabio Palomba	ETH, Zurich
Fatiha Zaidi	Université Paris-Sud LRI, France
Félix García	Universidad de Castilla-La Mancha, Spain
Ferdinand Gramsamer	INFOGEM AG, Switzerland
Fernando Brito e Abreu	ISCTE-IUL, Portugal
Flavia Santoro	Universidade Federal do Estado do Rio de Janeiro, Brazil
Francesca Lonetti	CNR-ISTI, Italy
Francisco Gortázar	Universidad Rey Juan Carlos, Spain
Francisco Ruiz González	Universidad de Castilla-La Mancha, Spain
Franz Wotawa	Graz University, Austria
Gabriel Alberto García-Mireles	Universidad de Sonora, Mexico
Gabriele Lenzini	Université du Luxembourg, Luxembourg
Geert Poels	Ghent University, Belgium
Gerhard Fessler	Consultant, Germany
Geylani Kardas	Ege University, Turkey
Giuseppe Lami	ISTI-CNR, Italy
Gregory M. Kapfhammer	Allegheny College, USA
Grischa Liebel	Reykjavik University, Iceland
Guilherme Horta Travassos	Universidade Federal do Rio de Janeiro, Brazil
Hajo A. Reijers	Utrecht University, The Netherlands
Hanna Oktaba	Universidad Nacional Autónoma de México, Mexico
Hector Menendez	University College London, UK
Ilaria Pigazzini	Università degli Studi di Milano-Bicocca, Italy
Ioannis Parissis	Grenoble INP LCIS, France
Isabel Lopes Margarido	University of Porto, Portugal
Isabel Sofia Sousa Brito	Instituto Politécnico de Beja, Portugal
Ivano Malavolta	Vrije Universiteit Amsterdam, The Netherlands
J. Andres Diaz-Pace	ISISTAN Research Institute, UNICEN University, Argentina
Jaelson Castro	Universidade Federal de Pernambunco, Brazil
Jennifer Perez	Universidad Politécnica de Madrid, Spain
Jesus Molina	Universidad de Murcia, Spain
Joao Araújo	Universidade NOVA de Lisboa, Portugal
João Ferreira	ISCTE-IUL, Portugal
João Pascoal Faria	Universidade Porto, Portugal
Johnny Marques	Instituto Tecnológico de Aeronáutica, Brazil
Johny Marques	Instituto Tecnológico de Aeronáutica, Brazil
José Antonio Cruz-Lemus	University of Castilla-La Mancha, Spain
Jose Manuel Molina Lopez	Universidad Carlos III de Madrid, Spain
José Merseguer	Universidad de Zaragoza, Spain
Joyce Nabende	Makerere University, Uganda
Juan De Lara Jaramillo	Universidad Autónoma de Madrid, Spain
Juan Pablo Carvallo	Universidad del Azuay, Ecuador
Juha-Pekka Tolvanen	Metacase, Finland

Krzysztof Wnuk	Blekinge Institute of Technology, Sweden
Lidia Lopez	Universitat Politècnica de Catalunya, Spain
Lom Messan Hillah	Sorbonne Université, France
Ludovico Iovino	Gran Sasso Science Institute, Italy
Luigi Lavazza	Università degli Studi dell'Insubria, Italy
Luis Olsina	GIDIS Web, Engineering School, Argentina
Luiz Marcio Cysneiros	York University, Canada
Man Zhang	Institutt for teknologi, Høyskolen Kristiania, Norway
Manfred Reichert	Ulm University, Germany
Manuel Ángel Serrano	University of Castilla-La Mancha, Spain
Manuel Wimmer	Technical University Vienna, Austria
Marcela Ruiz	Utrecht University, The Netherlands
Marcello Thiry	Univali - Universidade do Vale do Itajaí, Brazil
Marco Vieira	University of Coimbra, Portugal
Marcos Sepúlveda	Pontificia Universidad Católica de Chile, Chile
Maria José Escalona	University of Seville, Spain
Maria Lencastre	Universidade de Pernambuco, Brazil
Marielba Zacarias	University of Algarve, Portugal
Martin Höst	Lund University, Sweden
Maurizio Leotta	University of Genova, Italy
Mauro Caporuscio	Linnaeus University, Sweden
Mauro Iacono	Second University of Naples, Italy
Mel Cinnéide	University College Dublin, Ireland
Mercedes Merayo	Universidad Complutense de Madrid, Spain
Michael Areas	University of Costa Rica, Costa Rica
Michael Felderer	University of Innsbruck, Switzerland
Michele Ciavotta	University of Milano Bicocca, Italy
Miguel Ehécatl Morales Trujillo	University of Canterbury, New Zealand
Miguel Goulão	Universidade Nova de Lisboa, Portugal
Moises Rodríguez	AQCLab, Spain
Moises Rodríguez Monje	AQCLab S.L., Spain
Neil Walkinshaw	University of Sheffield, UK
Nelly Condori-Fernández	Universidade da Coruña, Spain
Óscar Pedreira	Universidade da Coruña, Spain
Oum-El-Kheir Aktouf	Grenoble University Valence, France
Patrizio Pelliccione	University of Gothenburg, Sweden
Radu Calinescu	University of York, UK
Rafael Capilla	Rey Juan Carlos University, Spain
Raffaela Mirandola	Politecnico di Milano, Italy
Ralf Kneuper	IUBH Internationale Hochschule, Germany
Ricardo Machado	University of Minho, Portugal
Robert Clarisó	Universitat Oberta de Catalunya, Spain
Roberto Pietrantuono	University of Naples, Italy
Rolf-Helge Pfeiffer	IT University of Copenhagen, Denmark
Rudolf Ramler	Software Competence Center Hagenberg, Austria

Sandro Morasca	Università degli Studi dell'Insubria, Italy
Simeon Veloudis	SEERC, Greece
Stefan Wagner	Institut für Softwaretechnologie, Germany
Steve Counsell	Brunel University, UK
Sylvia Ilieva	Sofia University, Bulgaria
Tanja E. J. Vos	Technical University of Valencia, Spain
Uwe Zdun	University of Vienna, Austria
Vahid Garousi	Wageningen University, The Netherlands
Valentina Casola	University of Napoli Federico II, Italy
Valter V. Camargo	Federal University of São Carlos, Brazil
Vasco Amaral	FCT/UNL, Portugal
Vittorio Cortellessa	Università dell'Aquila, Italy
Wissam Mallouli	Montimage Research & Development, France
Yania Crespo	University of Valladolid, Spain

Additional Reviewers

Bedilia Estrada-Torres
Borce Stojkovski
Enrico Barbierato
Georges Ouffoué
Gian Luca Scoccia
Hadi Jahanshahi

Ignacio Velásquez
Michael Winter
Michele Mastroianni
Sebastian Steinau
Stefano Dalla Palma
Vinh Hoa La

Supporters

Collaborators

Excmo. Ayuntamiento
de Ciudad Real

Promoted by

Contents

Evidence-Based Software Engineering

Process Improvement and Assessment

Model-Driven Engineering and Software Maintenance

Data Science and Services

Verification and Validation

Security and Privacy

GDPR-Based User Stories in the Access Control Perspective

Cesare Bartolini[1] , Said Daoudagh[2,3(✉)] , Gabriele Lenzini[1] ,
and Eda Marchetti[2]

[1] Interdisciplinary Centre for Security, Reliability and Trust (SnT),
University of Luxembourg, Luxembourg City, Luxembourg
{cesare.bartolini,gabriele.lenzini}@uni.lu
[2] Istituto di Scienza e Tecnologie dell'Informazione "A. Faedo" (ISTI),
Consiglio Nazionale delle Ricerche (CNR), via G. Moruzzi 1, 56124 Pisa, Italy
{said.daoudagh,eda.marchetti}@isti.cnr.it
[3] Computer Science Department, University of Pisa, Pisa, Italy

Abstract. Because of GDPR's principle of "data protection by design
and by default", organizations who wish to stay lawful have to re-think
their data practices. Access Control (AC) can be a technical solution
for them to protect access to "personal data by design", and thus to
gain legal compliance, but this requires to have Access Control Policies
(ACPs) expressing requirements aligned with GDPR's provisions. Provisions are however pieces of law and are not written to be immediately
interpreted as technical requirements; the task is thus not straightforward. The *Agile software development methodology* can help untangle
the problem. It has dedicated tools to describe requirements and one
of such them, *User Stories*, seems up to task. Stories are concise yet
informal descriptions telling who, what and why something is required
by users; they are prioritized in lists, called *backlogs*. Inspired by these
Agile tools this paper advances the notion of *Data Protection backlogs*,
which are lists of User Stories about GDPR provisions told as technical
requirements. For each User Story we build a corresponding ACP, so
enabling the implementation of GDPR compliant AC systems.

Keywords: Access Control Policy (ACP) ·
General Data Protection Regulation (GDPR) · User Story

1 Introduction

Nowadays, the Information Technology (IT) domain is moving towards systems
with growing complexity, where digitalization, artificial intelligence, interconnection and mobility are some key factors. Indeed, in their multidisciplinary nature,
they require an extensive deployment of advanced Information and Communication Technologies (ICTs), as well as the adoption of effective measures for
strengthening security, trust, dependability and privacy. These aspects have to

© Springer Nature Switzerland AG 2019
M. Piattini et al. (Eds.): QUATIC 2019, CCIS 1010, pp. 3–17, 2019.
https://doi.org/10.1007/978-3-030-29238-6_1

be considered over the whole Software Development Life Cycle (SDLC), from the gathering of the requirements to the deployment and subsequent maintenance of the system.

Over the last decade, especially for small and medium enterprises, *Agile Software Development (ASD)*, first introduced in the Agile Manifesto [10], and its subsequent evolutions such as eXtreme Programming (XP) and Scrum [14] are becoming commonly-adopted software development processes. Basically, ASD is an iterative approach that focuses on incremental specification, design and implementation, while requiring a full integration of testing and development. In this development process, a common means of capturing the user needs and describing the value that the user would get from a specific functionality is the so-called *User Story* [1]. From a practical point of view, a User Story focuses on a requirement written according to a specific format (see Subsect. 2.1), and guidelines on how to implement it. Usually, depending on the granularity of the story, different names can be used for defining its contents: large ones may be known as *Epics*, and small ones as *Features, User Stories*, and *Tasks* [1].

However, small organisations and software development groups could not expend the effort (in terms of budget and time) needed to collect and implement all the required User Stories prior to release. When the missing stories refer to privacy requirements, the side effect is to release softwares with high privacy risks [3].

With the entering into force of the General Data Protection Regulation (GDPR) (see Subsect. 2.2) this situation is not affordable anymore, because it is changing how *Personal Data* should be processed. Indeed, the GDPR imposes several duties on the *Controller* and the *Processor*, i.e., the data managers, concerning the processing of *Personal Data*, i.e., any information related to an identified or identifiable natural person called the *Data Subject*.

Additionally, the GDPR defines a system of fines to induce controllers and processors to be compliant with its provisions. Thus, the controller and processor need to demonstrate the compliance with the GDPR as required by the *Accountability principle* (Art. 5.2). However, this is not a trivial problem as it involves the definition of specific *purposes*, the management of the *consent* given by the *Data Subject* whose personal data are referring to, and the need to demonstrate compliance with the implemented GDPR's provisions.

Within the Agile development, among the proposed solutions to tackle security issues and vulnerabilities in an efficient way, one that is currently taking place is the possibility of using security backlogs to drive the software development work. In the Agile context, a backlog represents a prioritized features list describing the functionalities to be included in the final product [1]. These backlog items are often provided in the form of User Stories [3]. The set of security backlogs is therefore a list of ready-made specification of security items (requirements and task descriptions) useful for the implementation. An example of a security User Story related to access control is reported in Subsect. 2.1.

Following this tendency, the contribution of this paper consists in three main parts: (i) introduce the concept of *Data Protection Backlog* that contains User

Stories based on GDPR requirements; (ii) map specific provisions of the GDPR to User Stories; and (iii) provide, for each User Story, the corresponding implementation guidance so as to assure a GDPR-compliant design.

Considering in particular this last point, i.e., to ensure the GDPR compliance, it would be helpful to carry out the processing of personal data automatically and in compliance with the obligations imposed by the GDPR.

To this purpose, in this paper we want to move a step towards a compliant implementation of the GDPR, by encoding the User Stories, and consequently the GDPR provisions, as Access Control Policies (ACPs). A valid solution to minimize errors and issues in the GDPR enforcement is to rely on a consolidated, verified and predefined structure of ACPs [28]. In line with this tendency, for each identified User Story, this paper provides a GDPR-based Access Control Policy (ACP) template for each provision related to access control. Indeed, the templates represent meaningful, concrete and predefined blocks for ACP specification, that can be adopted and refined for the different scenarios, so as to overcome possible misinterpretations and reduce security and privacy risks.

As a final result, the set of User Stories, associated with the proper ACP templates, would be a valid starting point for privacy requirements specification, and a generic guidance for who are facing to the problem of GDPR implementation. When a new development starts, the developer could pick up the related predefined User Story and easily implement it.

Outline. We recall User Stories and the GDPR in Sect. 2, where we also give an overview of Access Control (AC). In Sect. 3 we illustrate the related work. The proposed GDPR based User Stories model is described in Sect. 4 and in Sect. 5 we shows the process to the derive the *Data Protection Backlog* containing the User Stories and the associated ACPs. In Sect. 6 we conclude and point out the future work.

2 Background

This section introduces the main concepts used in the rest of this paper: User Stories, the GDPR and AC.

2.1 User Stories

User Stories are an important part of an Agile development process because they represent a valid means to writing simple and understandable requirements [30].

Currently, their adoption is massively growing [13] and several definitions are available [16]. However, most of them agree on the fact that commonly a User Story is a short, simple description of a feature from the perspective of a end user or customer of the system. A User Story typically presents the following structure:

As a *[end user]*, I want to achieve *[goal]* so that *[I realize the following benefit of]*.

An example of a security User Story related to ACP, reported in [1], is as follows:

> As *[an information security manager]* I want *[that it is clearly defined which user accounts are authorised for which activities]* so that *[the effectiveness and correctness of access controls can be checked]*.

One key factor of the widespread use of User Stories is that they can be written at different levels of detail. They can cover large amount of functionalities and in this case are generally known as *Epics*. However, an epic is generally too large for being easily implementable into a single Agile iteration, thus it usually split into multiple smaller User Stories before it is worked on. Thus is for instance the case of features, User Stories, and tasks [1]. In some cases, User Stories are detailed more by adding conditions of satisfaction, i.e., a high-level description of what needs to be true after the Agile User Story is complete.

There is not a specific customer or user role for writing User Stories, but having a common set of product backlog of Agile User Stories is an important factor for a successful development. Indeed, the product backlog can be used to select and prioritize the list of the functionalities that have to be developed in different iterations of the Agile process.

2.2 General Data Protection Regulation

The General Data Protection Regulation (GDPR)[1] defines, among others, several data protection principles and Data Subject's rights. The aim of the new regulation is to strengthen the rights of individuals over their own data, and at the same time to make organizations more accountable with respect to the previous directive. In addition, the GDPR contributes to the harmonization of the previous fragmented data protection laws across the EU, so as to ensure equal right to privacy and to data protection.

The mandatory part of the GDPR is organized in chapters and contains 99 articles. Art. 4 defines *Personal Data* as "any information relating to an identified or identifiable natural person ('data subject')". This means that a *Data Subject* is a natural person (a living human being) whose data are managed by a *Controller*.

The *purpose* of the *processing* of personal data is determined by the controller, and this "processing shall be lawful only if and to the extent that at least one of the" six legal bases "applies" (Art. 6). In particular, one of those legal bases is the consent given by the data subject "to the processing of his or her personal data for one or more specific purposes" (Art. 6.1(a)). *Consent* is defined as "any freely given, specific, informed and unambiguous indication of the data subject's wishes by which he or she, by a statement or by a clear affirmative action, signifies agreement to the processing of personal data relating to him or her" (Art. 4.11).

---

[1] Regulation (EU) 2016/679 of the European Parliament and of the Council of 27 April 2016 on the protection of natural persons with regard to the processing of personal data and on the free movement of such data, and repealing Directive 95/46/EC (General Data Protection Regulation).

However, the GDPR sets the *Conditions for Consent* in Art. 7. On one hand, "the controller shall be able to demonstrate that the data subject has consented to processing of his or her personal data", and this is line with the *Accountability* principle defined in Art. 5.2. On the other hand, "the data subject shall have the right to withdraw his or her consent at any time" and "it shall be as easy to withdraw as to give consent"(Art. 7.3).

The GDPR also sets other fundamental rights of the data subject, such as the right of access (Art. 15) and the right to data portability (Art. 20), and several principles that the controller and processor shall abide to. For instance, the "integrity and confidentiality" principle imposes the controller to use "appropriate technical or organisational measures" to "ensure appropriate security of the personal data, including protection against unauthorised or unlawful processing and against accidental loss, destruction or damage" (Art. 5.1(f)). Paragraph 2 of the same article introduces the Accountability principle, according to which "[t]he controller shall be responsible for, and be able to demonstrate compliance with, paragraph 1".

Finally, the controller shall "taking into account the state of the art [. . .] both at the time of the determination of the means for processing and at the time of the processing itself, implement appropriate technical and organisational measures [. . .] to integrate the necessary safeguards into the processing in order to meet the requirements of this regulation and protect the rights of data subjects." (Art. 25.1). This is the so-called principle of data protection by design.

These brief excerpts from the GDPR show the complexity of the regulation and hint at the subsequent difficulty to introduce such legal concepts into software development environment. A set of User Stories summarizing the main important tasks and features to be implemented in the different contexts can be a valid solution to comply the GDPR requirements. Furthermore, having a formalized representation of the legal concepts and the relations among them could help and facilitate the definition of a more consistent set of policies governing a GDPR compliant data access. Hence, the proposal of this paper: a way to represent GDPR requirements as User Stories organized in a *Data Protection Backlog*, i.e., *Privacy Backlog*, and the associated ACPs in a uniform, simple and processable format.

2.3 Access Control

Access Control is a mechanism used to restrict access to data or systems, based ACPs, i.e., a set of rules that specify who (e.g., Controller, Processor or Data Subject) has access to which resources (e.g., Personal Data) and under which circumstances [24]. One of the emerging AC models is the Attribute-Based Access Control (ABAC) model.

The basic idea of ABAC is to employ attributes (characteristics or properties) of different entities to make access control decisions regarding a subject's (e.g., user o process) access on an object (e.g., file or database) in a system. The AC decisions are evaluated based on authorization policies specified by an administrator using a policy specification language. ABAC authorization policies are a set of rules defined based on the attributes of subjects and objects as well as other attributes, such as contextual attributes.

The National Institute of Standards and Technology (NIST) defines Attribute-Based Access Control (ABAC) as "[a]n access control method where subject requests to perform operations on objects are granted or denied based on assigned attributes of the subject, assigned attributes of the object, environment conditions, and a set of policies that are specified in terms of those attributes and conditions" [12].

This definition lists various key concepts. In particular, *attributes* are characteristics of the subject or object, or environment conditions, containing information given by a name-value pair. A *subject* is a human user, legal entity (e.g., Data Subject or Controller) or an abstract entity, such as a device that issues access requests to perform operations on objects/resource (e.g., Personal Data). Subjects are assigned one or more attributes.

An *object* is a resource for which access is managed by the ABAC system, such as devices, files, records, tables, processes, programs, networks, or domains containing or receiving information. In the context of the GDPR, objects can be either Personal Data or records of processing activities.

An *operation* is the execution of a function upon an object. Operations include read, write, edit, modify and erase. *Environment conditions* represent the operational or situational context in which access requests occur (e.g., current time or location of a user). By referring to the GDPR we assume that the consent is a contextual information. The *policy* is the representation of rules or relationships that allow to determine if a requested access should be allowed, given the values of the attributes of the subject, object, operation and environment conditions.

3   Related Work

In this section, we provide a non-exhaustive overview of the proposals dealing with the main topics of this paper: representing security and privacy by means of User Stories, and how to put in relation AC environment and the GDPR.

3.1   Security and Privacy by Means of User Stories

An important innovation for speeding up the development of software has been the introduction of Agile development and the Scrum methodology. Over the last years, literature has moved an important criticism to these kind of approaches because they mostly ignore the security risk management activity [1,4,23,29]. Thus the concepts of security should be considered during all stages of the software development life cycle, in Agile environment this commonly means integrating security principles in terms of security backlog [3,4]. The security backlog is a set of ready-made User Stories that can be used to cover the security requirements [25]. This new backlog can be used to manage and mitigate the security risks associated with the software [23,29].

The introduction of GDPR requirements in the secure software development adopted into the Agile processes for discovering and solving security threats is not sufficient anymore to guarantee the required privacy level, and few proposal are recently targeting this issue. Among these, in [23] the authors propose a Threat Poker method to exercise both security risks and privacy risks and evaluate the effort needed to remove the corresponding vulnerabilities in the software developed. However, the proposal is mainly focused on the estimation of the seriousness of security and/or privacy risks during software development. Similarly, in [17] the authors present an Agile process for the definition of security and privacy in terms of User Stories, in order to develop a framework to manage Personal Health Information. In particular, the authors highlight the need for suitable policies and procedures for data security and privacy management, so as to make the framework compliant with regulations.

This paper has similar aims, i.e., to contribute to the definition of privacy-related User Stories, but in addition it also provides a practical means for defining concrete privacy policies specification.

3.2   Access Control and the GDPR

Several works use AC as the main means of protecting personal data. For example, an initial proposal [7] for an automatically-enforceable policy language for access and usage control of personal information aims at transparent and accountable data usage. Authors in [27] give a formal definition of the consent as stated in the GDPR, applied in an IoT context.

The work in [11] presents an ABAC model for smart cars ecosystem to take into account the individual user privacy preferences for allowing or denying service notifications, alerts and operations to on-board resources.

Unfortunately, the proposals are fragmented and only consider a few aspects that can be traced back to some of the principles introduced by the GDPR. This paper would like to exploit the ideas proposed by the aforementioned papers towards ACPs specification for GDPR compliance, and to provide a systematic approach to gather as many GDPR requirements as possible, providing corresponding GDPR-compliant ACPs. This paper is inspired by a proposal [26] that describes a new semi-formalized, constrained natural language format for User Stories. The format uses variables to precisely correlate various parts of the story with a predefined format, to express strictly-defined operators in a (almost) natural language. The authors also showed a possible way to extract access control information for role-based access control from this format.

4   GDPR-Based User Stories Conceptual Model

In an attempt to comply with the principle of data protection by design, laid out by Art. 25.1 of the GDPR, we detail a methodology for defining privacy-based User Stories and gathering them to ACPs requirements directly from the GDPR. From a practical point of view, this means first extracting, in an Agile perspective, User Stories that represent atomic privacy or legal requirements to be implemented so as to comply by-design with the GDPR. Then, considering systems that enforce an AC, defining an actionable list of simple AC system specifications which address the core requirements demanded by the GDPR.

The proposal would like to contribute to: (i) an incremental development of the AC system, by guaranteeing that, by design, it maintains compliance with the GDPR; (ii) the Data Protection Impact Assessment (DPIA) along the development of the system; (iii) a mapping between the implemented functionalities and the corresponding GDPR provisions. This will help to create a traceability mechanism useful for demonstrating GDPR compliance, as required by the *Accountability* principle.

The User Stories are built taking in consideration the GDPR concepts of *Data Subject, Controller, Processor, Data Protection Officer (DPO)*, and *Personal Data*.

The conceptual model for User Stories, used for the derivation of the actionable list, is shown in Fig. 1. It is composed of three sub-models: the GDPR Model, User Stories Model and AC Model. The sub-models are combined into the process followed for going from the definition of the User Stories to specification of AC policies.

The sub-models have been voluntarily kept separated to increase the possible generalization of the paper proposal. Indeed, the GDPR Model and AC Model could be replaced by any other legal regulation or legislation which is suited for automatic enforcement.

The remainder of this section provides specific details about these sub-models.

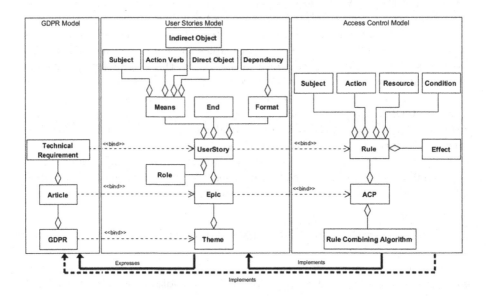

Fig. 1. The conceptual model of GDPR-focused user stories.

4.1   User Stories Model

The User Story used in our model is a modified version of that introduced in [15]. More precisely, we do not consider the *Clarification* and the *Quality* elements of the *End* component; we eliminate the *Adjective* element from the *Means* component; and finally, we introduce the *Theme* component as abstract level to better bind the User Stories to the GDPR.

As depicted in Fig. 1, a User Story always includes one relevant *Role*, which is associated with the stakeholder or legal entity that expresses the need. Currently, due to the complexity of the GDPR text, the number of proposals trying to provide a conceptual model of the regulation [6,21,22] is increasing in literature. Among those available, and in order to relying on a formal base for the role specification, in this paper we rely on the formalization provided by the Privacy Ontology (PrOnto) [19,20]. The details of this ontology are out of the scope of this paper; suffice it to say that the stakeholders that we use in the proposal are *Controller, Processor, Data Protection Officer (DPO), Data Subject* and *Supervisory Authority.*

The *Format* of the User Story is a predefined template in which the role, means, and optional end(s) are specified. As described in Sect. 2 we refer to the most widespread format introduced in [8] which consist of:

As a [type of user], I want [goal], so that [some reason].

Differently, *Means* can have different structures that can be used to represent different types of requirements. Means have three common grammatical elements: (i) a subject with an aim; (ii) an action verb that expresses the action related to the feature being requested; and (iii) a direct object (and optionally an indirect object) on which the subject executes the action.

The End of a User Story explains why the means are requested. However, User Stories often include other types of information, such as dependency on another functionality, i.e., implicit references a functionality which is required for the means to be realized. This is useful in the context of the regulations since legal text often use the cross-reference mechanism between articles.

In the GDPR context, a possible User Story related to Art. 30.4 could be:

As a *[Supervisory Authority]*, I want *[to access the record of processing activities]*, so that *[I can monitor those processing operations]*.

4.2   The GDPR Model

In this study we model the GDPR only from a structural point of view. As described in Sect. 2, the mandatory part of the GDPR is composed of ninety-nine articles organized in chapters; some chapters are then broken in sections. The GDPR's articles present a structure that involves at least other two levels (paragraphs and letters). Finally, each article may include one or more technical requirements.

In order to be aligned with the structure defined in User Stories model, we model the GDPR as an aggregation of articles. More precisely, we do not consider the recitals, and we collapsed all the aforementioned complex structure of the regulation in a more simple one that includes only three levels: *GDPR → Article → Technical Requirement.*

This simple structure helps in binding the GDPR core code with the concept of Theme in Agile terminology; then, the articles represent Epics which contain one or more small and manageable technical requirements, each expressed by means of a User Story.

4.3   The Access Control Model

An ACP defines the AC requirements of a protected system, i.e., a set of AC *Rules* that specify who (e.g., Controller, Processor or Data Subject) has access to which resources (e.g., Personal Data) and under which circumstances [24]. The AC rule is often specified using Natural Language Access Control Policy (NLACP)), that presents the following structure: *[Subject] can [Action] [Resource] if [Condition]* [12].

The Access Control Model used in this proposal is a simplified version of the Policy Language Model provided by the eXtensible Access Control Markup Language (XACML) standard [18]. Even simple, the model captures all the essential concepts for the design of both simple and more complex ACPs.

As in Fig. 1, the model consists of *Rule* class, which represents the most elementary unit of policy enforceable by an Access Control System (ACS). The rule is composed of one single *Subject*[2], one single *Action*, one single *Resource* and one single optional *Condition*. The *Effect* associated with the rule represents the rule-designer's intended consequence of a *True* evaluation for the rule. The usual two values allowed for the rule's effect are: *Permit* and *Deny*. As depicted in Fig. 1, the rule represents an expression of an atomic technical requirement described by a User Story. The ACP class is a composition of rules and *Rule Combining Algorithm* which defines strategy by which the results of evaluating the rules are combined when the ACS evaluates the policy.

5   User Stories Related to Access Control

The process we used to define the set of User Stories, related to the provisions of the GDPR and the AC rules, is composed of three steps (see Fig. 2): (1) *GDPR Articles Selection*; (2) *User Stories Definition*; (3) *GDPR AC Rules Definition*.

GDPR Articles Selection. The input of the process is the GDPR text. Firstly, we selected only the mandatory part of the GDPR which consists of

---

[2] Note that the Subject expressed in this model is different from the one defined in the User Stories Model: the Subject in that model represents a grammatical function in the formulation of the means; while Subject in the AC domain represents an active entity which covers a role. The Subject in this model is an entity that can semantically be correlated with the Role entity in the User Stories Model.

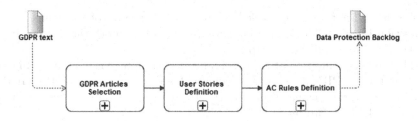

Fig. 2. GDPR-focused user stories definition process.

ninety-nine articles; for each article, we decided whether is related to AC concept, i.e., AC language or AC mechanism, and consequently we created an Epic associated to the current article. The result of this step was the section of forty-one Epics (GDPR articles) related to AC. Specifically, three of them were concerning only AC mechanism; eight were referring only ACPs, and thirty articles related to both ACPs and AC mechanism. For more details about this step we refer to our previous work in [5].

User Stories Definition. For each article identified in the previous phase, we extracted one or more technical requirements and defined a specific User Story for each of them. Thus, the User Stories were added to the Epic associated with the current article. In order to trace the covered GDPR's articles during the Agile development process, we defined a for each Epic an identifier (named EpicID[3]) able to find the GDPR's article the Epic is referring to. Similarly, we defined an identifier for each User Story (called UserStoryID[4]) with the purpose to the specific part of the GDPR's article the User Story related to (e.g., the paragraph or the letter of the article).

GDPR AC Rules Definition. The final step deals with the translation of the technical requirements associated with the AC language, and consequently we defined an AC rule for each User Story conceived in the previous step. It is out of the scope of this paper going into details of the procedure of extracting ACPs. In literature there exist different proposals for the derivation of ACPs from the natural language [2,31] or controlled natural language [9]. In our previous work [5] we defined a systematic approach for deriving ACPs directly from the GDPR, and we refer to it for more details about this step.

As in Fig. 2, the result of this process is a *Data Protection Backlog*, i.e., a Privacy Backlog containing a set of AC rules organized in User Stories, Epics and Theme. This is a ready solution to be used during the Agile development of an ACs system aligned with the GDPR requirements.

---

[3] The identifier EpicID has the following structure: GDPR.Epic.Article.[articleNumber].

[4] The identifier UserStoryID has the following structure: [EpicID].[Paragraph Number].[letter].US.[progressiveNumber].

For space limitation, in Table 1 we present an extract of the defined Data Protection Backlog. The User Stories are reported from both the perspective of the Data Subject and the Controller.

The table is composed of three columns: the column **Article** (first column) contains the GDPR's articles. The column **User Story** contains the GDPR-based User Stories defined. Finally, the third column contains the AC rules related to the User Stories.

Table 1. GDPR-focused user stories: controller and data subject perspectives

Article	User story	AC rule
Art. 6.1(a)	As a [Controller], I want [to process Personal Data only if Data Subject has given consent for one or more specific purpose], so that [the processing shall be lawful].	[Controller] can [Process] [Personal Data] If [PersonalData.purpose = Processing.purpose AND PersonalData.purpose.consent = TRUE]
Art. 7.3	As a [Data Subject], I want [to withdraw my consent], so that [I can exercise my right as stated in Art. 7.3]	[Data Subject] can [Withdraw] [PersonalData.purpose.consent] If [PersonalData.owner = DataSubject AND PersonalData.purpose.consent = TRUE]
Art. 15.1	As a [Data Subject], I want [to access my Personal Data and all the information], so that [I can be aware about my privacy]	[Data Subject] can [Action = access] [PersonalData] AND [Resource = PersonalData.purposes] AND [Resource = PersonalData.categories] if [PersonalData.owner = Data Subject]
Article 15.3	As a [Data Subject], I want [to download a copy of my Personal Data], so that [I can check their correctness]	[Data Subject] can [download] [Personal Data] If [PersonalData.owner = Data Subject]

6   Conclusions and Future Work

This paper presents an Agile methodology to gather access control requirements from the GDPR by using the concept of User Stories. This methodology is a first step towards a formal definition of access control solutions addressing GDPR requirements in Agile environment. To the best of the authors' knowledge, an Agile methodology for the specification of User Stories, organized in Data Protection Backlog, i.e., Privacy Backlog, aimed at extracting legal ACPs from the GDPR is novel. Although grounded in a domain-related implementation (i.e., the GDPR), the Agile methodology yields a more general spectrum, since it can be applied to different data protection legislation that encodes ACPs specification.

In our case, the generation of a set of ACPs aligned with the GDPR was conceived in three phases: the selection of GDPR's articles related to access control; the definition of a Data Protection Backlog containing User Stories extracted from the selected GDPR's articles; and finally, the definition of access control rules, each related to a specific User Story. Having a User Story (and consequently an access control rule) related to a specific GDPR provision helps to detect the rules that need to be updated when the regulation changes.

As a future work, we are planning to consider the GDPR requirements referring access control mechanisms, i.e., requirements from the architectural point of view. Future work includes also the validation of the User Stories by different Agile development teams in the context of an ongoing European project that addresses key regulations such as the GDPR.

References

1. Ahola, J., et al.: Handbook of the secure agile software development life cycle. University of Oulu (2014)
2. Alohaly, M., Takabi, H., Blanco, E.: Automated extraction of attributes from natural language attribute-based access control (ABAC) policies. Cybersecurity 2(1), 2 (2019)
3. Asthana, V., Tarandach, I., O'Donoghue, N., Sullivan, B., Saario, M.: Practical security stories and security tasks for agile development environments, July 2012
4. Azham, Z., Ghani, I., Ithnin, N.: Security backlog in scrum security practices. In: 2011 Malaysian Conference in Software Engineering, pp. 414–417. IEEE (2011)
5. Bartolini, C., Daoudagh, S., Lenzini, G., Marchetti, E.: Towards a lawful authorized access: a preliminary GDPR-based authorized access. In: 14th International Conference on Software Technologies (ICSOFT 2019), Prague, Czech Republic, 26–28 July 2019, pp. 331–338 (2019)
6. Bartolini, C., Giurgiu, A., Lenzini, G., Robaldo, L.: Towards legal compliance by correlating standards and laws with a semi-automated methodology. In: Bosse, T., Bredeweg, B. (eds.) BNAIC 2016. CCIS, vol. 765, pp. 47–62. Springer, Cham (2017). https://doi.org/10.1007/978-3-319-67468-1_4
7. Cerbo, F.D., Martinelli, F., Matteucci, I., Mori, P.: Towards a declarative approach to stateful and stateless usage control for data protection. In: WEBIST, pp. 308–315. SciTePress (2018)
8. Cohn, M.: User Stories Applied: For Agile Software Development. Addison-Wesley Professional, Boston (2004)
9. Fatema, K., Debruyne, C., Lewis, D., O'Sullivan, D., Morrison, J.P., Mazed, A.: A semi-automated methodology for extracting access control rules from the European data protection directive. In: 2016 IEEE SPW, pp. 25–32, May 2016
10. Fowler, M., Highsmith, J., et al.: The agile manifesto. Softw. Dev. 9(8), 28–35 (2001)
11. Gupta, M., Benson, J., Patwa, F., Sandhu, R.: Dynamic groups and attribute-based access control for next-generation smart cars. In: CODASPY 2019, Richardson, TX, USA, 25–27 March 2019 (2019)
12. Hu, C.T., et al.: Guide to attribute based access control (ABAC) definition and considerations [includes updates as of 02-25-2019]. Technical report (2019)
13. Kassab, M.: The changing landscape of requirements engineering practices over the past decade. In: 2015 IEEE EmpiRE, pp. 1–8, August 2015
14. Kniberg, H.: Scrum and XP from the Trenches (2015). Lulu.com

15. Lucassen, G., Dalpiaz, F., van der Werf, J.M.E.M., Brinkkemper, S.: Improving agile requirements: the quality user story framework and tool. Requirements Eng. **21**(3), 383–403 (2016)
16. Lucassen, G., Dalpiaz, F., Werf, J.M.E.M., Brinkkemper, S.: The use and effectiveness of user stories in practice. In: Daneva, M., Pastor, O. (eds.) REFSQ 2016. LNCS, vol. 9619, pp. 205–222. Springer, Cham (2016). https://doi.org/10.1007/978-3-319-30282-9_14
17. McCaffery, F., et al.: A process framework combining safety and security in practice. In: Larrucea, X., Santamaria, I., O'Connor, R.V., Messnarz, R. (eds.) EuroSPI 2018. CCIS, vol. 896, pp. 173–180. Springer, Cham (2018). https://doi.org/10.1007/978-3-319-97925-0_14
18. OASIS: eXtensible Access Control Markup Language (XACML) Version 3.0, January 2013. http://docs.oasis-open.org/xacml/3.0/xacml-3.0-core-os-en.html
19. Palmirani, M., Martoni, M., Rossi, A., Bartolini, C., Robaldo, L.: Legal ontology for modelling GDPR concepts and norms. In: Legal Knowledge and Information Systems: JURIX 2018, vol. 313, p. 91. IOS Press (2018)
20. Palmirani, M., Martoni, M., Rossi, A., Bartolini, C., Robaldo, L.: PrOnto: privacy ontology for legal reasoning. In: Kő, A., Francesconi, E. (eds.) EGOVIS 2018. LNCS, vol. 11032, pp. 139–152. Springer, Cham (2018). https://doi.org/10.1007/978-3-319-98349-3_11
21. Pandit, H.J., Fatema, K., O'Sullivan, D., Lewis, D.: GDPRtEXT - GDPR as a linked data resource. In: Gangemi, A., et al. (eds.) ESWC 2018. LNCS, vol. 10843, pp. 481–495. Springer, Cham (2018). https://doi.org/10.1007/978-3-319-93417-4_31
22. Pandit, H.J., Lewis, D.: Modelling provenance for GDPR compliance using linked open data vocabularies. In: PrivOn@ ISWC (2017)
23. Rygge, H., Jøsang, A.: Threat poker: solving security and privacy threats in agile software development. In: Gruschka, N. (ed.) NordSec 2018. LNCS, vol. 11252, pp. 468–483. Springer, Cham (2018). https://doi.org/10.1007/978-3-030-03638-6_29
24. Sandhu, R.S., Samarati, P.: Access control: principle and practice. IEEE Commun. Mag. **32**(9), 40–48 (1994)
25. Siiskonen, T., Särs, C., Vähä-Sipilä, A., Pietikääinen, A.: Generic security user stories. In: Pekka, P., Juha, R. (eds.) Handbook of the Secure Agile Software Development Life Cycle. University of Oulu, Oulu (2014)
26. Sobieski, Ś., Zieliński, B.: User stories and parameterized role based access control. In: Bellatreche, L., Manolopoulos, Y. (eds.) MEDI 2015. LNCS, vol. 9344, pp. 311–319. Springer, Cham (2015). https://doi.org/10.1007/978-3-319-23781-7_25
27. Ulbricht, M.-R., Pallas, F.: YaPPL - a lightweight privacy preference language for legally sufficient and automated consent provision in IoT scenarios. In: Garcia-Alfaro, J., Herrera-Joancomartí, J., Livraga, G., Rios, R. (eds.) DPM/CBT -2018. LNCS, vol. 11025, pp. 329–344. Springer, Cham (2018). https://doi.org/10.1007/978-3-030-00305-0_23
28. Wachter, S.: Normative challenges of identification in the internet of things: privacy, profiling, discrimination, and the GDPR. Comput. Law Secur. Rev. **34**(3), 436–449 (2018)
29. Wang, W., Gupta, A., Niu, N.: Mining security requirements from common vulnerabilities and exposures for agile projects. In: 2018 IEEE 1st International Workshop on Quality Requirements in Agile Projects (QuaRAP), pp. 6–9, August 2018

30. Wang, X., Zhao, L., Wang, Y., Sun, J.: The role of requirements engineering practices in agile development: an empirical study. In: Zowghi, D., Jin, Z. (eds.) Requirements Engineering. CCIS, vol. 432, pp. 195–209. Springer, Heidelberg (2014). https://doi.org/10.1007/978-3-662-43610-3_15
31. Xiao, X., Paradkar, A., Thummalapenta, S., Xie, T.: Automated extraction of security policies from natural-language software documents. In: Proceedings of the ACM SIGSOFT FSE 2012, FSE 2012, pp. 12:1–12:11. ACM, New York (2012)

Privacy Oriented Software Development

Maria Teresa Baldassarre, Vita Santa Barletta[✉], Danilo Caivano,
and Michele Scalera

Department of Computer Science, University of Bari Aldo Moro, Via Orabona 4,
70125 Bari, Italy
{mariateresa.baldassarre, vita.barletta,
danilo.caivano, michele.scalera}@uniba.it

Abstract. Threats to applications security are continuously evolving thanks to factors such as progress made by the attackers, release of new technologies, use of increasingly complex systems. In this scenario, it is necessary to implement both design and programming practices that guarantee the security of the code on one hand, and the privacy of the data, on the other. This paper proposes a software development approach, Privacy Oriented Software Development (POSD), that complements traditional development processes by integrating the activities needed for addressing security and privacy management in software systems. The approach is based on 5 key elements (Privacy by Design, Privacy Design Strategies, Privacy Pattern, Vulnerabilities, Context). It can be applied forward for developing new systems and backward for re-engineering an existing one. This paper presents the POSD approach in the backward mode together with an experimentation in the context of an industrial project. Results show that POSD is able to discover software vulnerabilities, identify the remediation patterns needed for addressing them in the source code and design the target architecture to be used for guiding privacy-oriented system reengineering.

Keywords: Privacy by design · Secure software development ·
Secure architecture · System reengineering

1 Introduction

Vulnerabilities within code [1] provide the ability for an attacker to access and misuse confidential information. The growth of the attacks implies the need to identify and understand (at least) the most common threats to software security, disseminate security best practices, and address the security problem from the early stages of software development in order to guarantee the confidentiality, integrity and availability of data. Two fundamental aspects come into play in this scenario: *Security* and *Privacy*. Security should be a basic feature of application such as automatically enabling complex password building mechanisms rather than procedures for renewing passwords according to a time frame.

The lack of system security can compromise privacy and for this reason privacy emerges as a proactive, integrative and creative approach to strengthen security requirements starting from the design (Defense in depth) in case of new systems and protect the information assets and data in case of an existing ones (Security Controls).

M. Piattini et al. (Eds.): QUATIC 2019, CCIS 1010, pp. 18–32, 2019.
https://doi.org/10.1007/978-3-030-29238-6_2

It becomes necessary to consider and pursue privacy throughout all phases of the software life cycle. Today several approaches that address security exist, but they often they do not consider the data privacy side of the problem. The same think can be said for the current privacy-oriented approaches. Privacy and security are addressed separately by the already existing approaches. The challenges that companies and the developer communities need to face within this context are many, but to start implementing defenses operatively, three major issues have to be addressed: (i) Translate best practices for both, secure application development and data privacy, into operational guidelines that can be traced back to code structures and software architectures; (ii) Share security and privacy competences within the development team. Privacy and security require specific skills that developers, even talented ones, often do not have. Therefore, it is necessary to share and transfer knowledge; (iii) Integrate new methodologies for data privacy and secure software development into existing business processes. This must be done without affecting the existing processes that are often peculiar to each company and consolidated over time [2]. Coherently, the goal of this work and main contribution is to address these issues by means of: (i) An approach, *Privacy Oriented Software Development* (POSD), that is able to operationally support software development by integrating privacy and security requirements. It works on existing systems as well as on systems to be developed; (ii) *Privacy Knowledge Base* (PKB), a knowledge base that supports decision making in all phases of the software lifecycle. PKB formalizes the relationship between 5 key elements creating a guide navigation throughout them: Principles of Privacy by Design [3], Privacy Design Strategies [4], Privacy Pattern [5], Vulnerabilities [6], Context; (iii) The ability to integrate the approach within the processes used by companies without revolutionizing the latter but strengthening the process of secure development.

The paper is organized as follows. Section 2 discusses related works on the topic of Privacy and Security in software development. In Sect. 3 Privacy Knowledge Base is presented; Sect. 4 describes the approach adopted for the privacy-oriented software development in backward mode; Sect. 5 describes an experimentation carried out on an industrial case study that shows how to apply POSD in Backward mode. Sections 6, 7 and 8, illustrate respectively the discussion of the results, the limitation of the work and conclusions.

2   Related Work

The security of software systems is constantly threatened by the increasing number of attacks. The aim of an attack is to exploit the vulnerabilities within the system's resources such as channels, methods, and data items [7]. The vulnerability is one or more weaknesses that can be accidentally triggered or intentionally exploited and result in a violation of desired system properties [8]. Currently there are more than 140,000 vulnerabilities recorded [9]. Therefore, software development requires security principles to maintain the confidentiality, integrity and availability of the applications and the need to train specialist in this dimension [10]. The concepts of security and privacy in software development are strictly related to each other and in recent years have become of pressing relevance due to the effect of the GDPR [11].

A considerable effort has been made for integrating security principles in software development processes. Some researchers have proposed strategies and frameworks for integrating security practices within the software development life cycle (SDLC) [12], but whatever model is adopted for secure software development, there is still the need for improvements in terms of metrics, penetration testing, developers training in secure development [13], but also to practically integrate security policies for data field into software application transactions during the development phases [14]. For example, [15] proposes a strategy for a clear and engineer like decision making process, and to include security and privacy requirements in software development processes. The model definition specifies what has to be documented and how it has to be documented to avoid misunderstandings, support reproducibility, analysis and formal controls. Furthermore, [16] proposes a Framework of a Software-Defined Security Architecture (SDSA) which can effectively decouple security executions with security controls, reduce the cost of software developments, and enhance the scalability of systems. In [17] an integrated security testing framework for SDLC was proposed to transform activities of SDLC into physical and executable test cases and thus to minimize the vulnerabilities. To quantitatively evaluate the security dimensions during the software production phase and enhance the overall security, [18] adds further steps to SDLC such as follow the organization process, apply peer review, take care about testing and tracking the measure of security on SDCL. However, despite considerable efforts in this direction, many systems are being compromised and vulnerabilities are increasing. As so, the gap between the strategies and frameworks proposed and their actual application is impacted by the growth of attacks.

In terms of privacy, Privacy by Design (PbD) [3] is an approach to address data protection during software development and to integrate privacy throughout the system development lifecycle. The key problem in this approach is the lack of guidelines on how to map legal data protection requirements into system requirements and components. Privacy Design Strategies seek to reduce the gap between "What to do" and "How to do it" [4]. Moreover, in [19] the authors try to correlate and map the available strategies against the "Privacy Patterns" needed to implement them, but the results obtained are limited in scope and far from being used in practice.

Privacy Patterns [20] describe the most important ways in which software systems can offer privacy in software development. A further step in this direction was made by [21] where the proposed design patterns include information about privacy principles addressed as well as relevant software models in the UML notations to be used. In [22] authors propose a set of privacy process patterns for creating a clear alignment between privacy requirements and Privacy Enhancing Technologies [23], and encapsulate expert knowledge of PET implementation at the operational level.

Privacy must be integrated into the design to have strong security [24]. Six protection goals are analyzed in [25] and a common scheme for addressing the legal, technical, economic and social dimension of privacy and data protection in complex IT systems is provided: Confidentiality, Integrity, Availability, Unlikability, Transparency and Intervenability. PRIPARE (Preparing Industry to Privacy by Design by supporting its Application in Research) [26, 27] begins to highlight how privacy requirements can be incorporated into the SDCL. The study introduces systematic methodology for privacy engineering, while Privacy-Friendly Systems Design [28] incorporate privacy through steps: elicitation of privacy requirements; analysis of the impact on the process; identification of supporting techniques. In some of these methodologies or others such as PriS [29], the treatment of privacy occurs during construction or early design activities and not in all the phases.

Privacy by Design in itself lacks concrete tools to help software developers design and implement privacy friendly systems. It also lacks clear guidelines regarding how to map specific legal data protection requirements on the system [30]. In today's environment, privacy needs to be integrated into software development to protect sensitive data in growing systems and to enhance software quality. The principle of Full Functionality of the Privacy by Design [3] underlines this need, as well as the need to integrate the Privacy and Security dimensions.

However, most of the work published deal with a single dimension, integrating either privacy elements or security elements into software development. There are obvious weaknesses in these approaches: the inability to implement solutions to be applied in real contexts as they remain general in the definition and are far from being operative; focus their attention on software systems under development and do not address existing ones; represent new approaches to software development and they can be adopted in place of those already in use.

Starting from these weaknesses, the approach presented in this work (POSD) aims to overcome them: (i) POSD integrates Privacy and Security practices by providing guidelines to developers that can be translated in to operational guidelines, software architecture and software code. (ii) POSD can be used both, during software system development and for reengineering an already existing one. (iii) POSD can be placed alongside the development processes used.

3 Privacy Knowledge Base

Privacy Oriented Software Development is an approach to software development that complements traditional development processes and allows to integrate the elements useful for security and privacy management into any development process. It uses 5 Key Elements to support decisions and choices in all phases of software life cycle. The relationships between the Key Elements (Fig. 1) are formalized in a *Privacy Knowledge Base* (PKB) that can be used by the development team to support decision making, system development and reengineering.

1. **Principles of Privacy by Design.** Privacy by Design may be described through seven principles, each of which specifies actions and responsibilities for evaluating "Privacy by Design Compliance" [2, 3]:

   – *Proactive not Reactive*: It anticipates and prevents privacy invasive events before they happen.
   – *Privacy as the default setting*: Privacy by Design seeks to deliver the maximum degree of privacy by ensuring that personal data are automatically protected in any given IT System or business practice.

- *Privacy Embedded into Design*: Privacy becomes an essential component of the core functionality being delivered, without diminishing them.
- *Full Functionality*: Privacy by Design demonstrates that it is possible to have privacy and security.
- *End-to-End Security*: Strong security measures are essential to privacy, from start to finish. Privacy by Design ensures secure lifecycle management of information, end-to-end.
- *Visibility and Transparency*: Component parts and operations remain visible and transparent to users and providers.
- *Respect for User Privacy*: It requires architects and operators to treat the interests of the individual by offering specific solutions for a strong privacy default, appropriate notice and empowering user-friendly options.

2. **Privacy Design Strategies.** A design strategy describes a fundamental approach to achieve a certain design goal that has certain properties that allow it to be distinguished from other (basic) approaches that achieve the same goal [4]. From this concept, eight privacy design strategies based on the legal perspective on privacy have been derived and are divided in two different categories [31]: *Data Oriented Strategies* and *Process Oriented Strategies*.

Data Oriented Strategies focus on the privacy-friendly processing of the data themselves:

- *Minimize*: Limit the processing of personal data as much as possible.
- *Hide*: Protect personal data or make it unlikable or unobservable. Make sure it does not become public or known.
- *Separate*: Separate the processing of personal data as much as possible.
- *Abstract*: Limit the detail in which personal data is processed.
  Process Oriented Strategies focus on the processes surrounding the responsible handling of personal data:
- *Inform*: Inform data subjects about the processing of their personal data in a timely and adequate manner.
- *Control*: Provide data subjects adequate control over the processing of their personal data.
- *Enforce*: Commit to processing personal data in a privacy-friendly way, and adequately enforce this.
- *Demonstrate*: Demonstrate personal data is being processed in a privacy-friendly manner.

3. **Privacy Patterns.** Security Patterns provide the knowledge collected from security experts in a structured, documented and reusable manner [32] and they contribute to build secure Information System. The solutions offered in the use of these patterns are [33]: detailing the information assets and the level of criticality of these assets; including the deployment details in a real environment, bearing in mind the architecture and the technologies that should be used; carrying out a qualitative

analysis of the most important technological aspects with regard to the proposed solution. Starting from such considerations in the PKB were included the privacy patterns that integrate privacy and security mechanisms [5, 20]. This need was also expressed in [4] which highlights the importance of the patterns in the design phase. Therefore, patterns standardize language in the context of privacy protection document common solutions to privacy problems; help designers identify and address privacy concerns. Each pattern in this context represents an answer to the following questions:

– What privacy design strategies does it implement?
– What vulnerabilities are mitigated/eliminated with the privacy solution?.

4. **Vulnerabilities.** The lack of sufficient logging mechanism or not closing the database connection properly are some examples of vulnerabilities that allow to an attacker to compromise software systems. A list of vulnerabilities classified according to the OWASP Top 10–2017 [6] has been integrated in the PKB. OWASP Top 10 is based primarily on data and information provided by firms specialized in application security or collected by using industry surveys. The goal of OWASP is to provide knowledge and information on the most common and important application security weaknesses.

– *A1-Injection*: Untrusted data is sent to an interpreter as part of a command or query.
– *A2-Broken Authentication*: Authentication and session management not properly implemented allow attackers to compromise data and application.
– *A3-Sensitive Data Exposure*: Sensitive data are not adequately protected in web applications and APIs and the attacker may steal or modify them.
– *A4-XML External Entities (XXE)*: Many XML processors evaluate external entity references within XML documents, so these entities can be used to disclose internal files.
– *A5-Broken Access Control*: Attackers can exploit restrictions on authenticated users not properly enforced. This allows to access unauthorized functionality and/or data.
– *A6-Security Misconfiguration*: Insecure default configurations, incomplete or ad hoc configurations, open cloud storage, misconfigured HTTP headers and verbose error messages contain sensitive information.
– *A7-Cross-Site Scripting (XSS)*: XSS occurs when an attacker executes scripts in the victim's browser which can hijack user sessions, deface web sites, or redirect the user to malicious sites. the underlying flaws are that applications include untrusted data in a new web page without proper validation, updates an existing web page with user-supplied data using a browser API that can create HTML or JavaScript.
– *A8-Insecure Deserialization*: It often leads to remote code execution. Deserializations flaws can be used to perform attacks, including replay attacks, injection attacks and privilege escalation attacks.

- *A9-Using Components with Known Vulnerabilities*: Applications and APIs that used components with known vulnerabilities can facilitate an attack.
- *A10-Insufficient Logging & Monitoring*: The Breach are often caused by insufficient logging and monitoring, coupled with missing or ineffective integration with incident response.

5. **Context.** In PKB Context represents a fundamental element for the system development and/or the reengineering. It consists of:

- *Architectural Requirements* to determine the flow of data within the system, components, roles and responsibilities.
- *Use cases and scenario* to define all interactions with the system. The aim is to protect the information from unauthorized reading and manipulation.
- *Privacy Enhancing Technologies (PETs)* [23], that are a set of tools and technologies that help to protect the personal information handled by the applications such as, just to mention a few, *Data Anonymization,* that consists in making a user's data anonymous and impossible to recompose in order to go back to personal information, or *Pseudonymity Systems*, where the user is identified by a pseudonym and not by his own name.

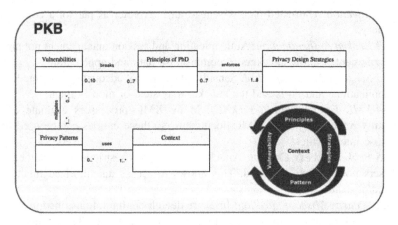

Fig. 1. The relationship between the key elements in PKB

Thus, PKB provides guidelines to developers at all stages of the software lifecycle. These guidelines can be translated into operation by providing the necessary elements for system architecture design and coding. PKB can also be used on existing systems and on systems to be developed. It realizes a guided navigation between the Key Elements starting from any of these (Fig. 2).

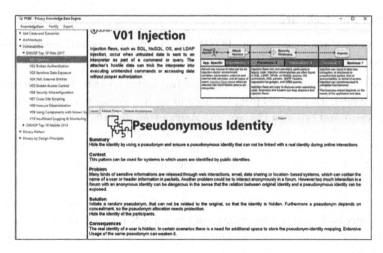

Fig. 2. Privacy knowledge base

4   Privacy Oriented Software Development

POSD approach is inspired to the Software Development Life Cycle framework presented in [12]. It works on existing systems as well as on systems to be developed, allowing to integrate privacy and security elements. This is thanks to PKB that identifies the key elements of the two dimensions and the relationships between them.

In order to overcome the weaknesses identified in Sect. 2 and provide operational guidelines, inputs, tools and techniques, outputs have been identified at each stage of the approach. POSD provides to the development team all the elements and guidelines for development or re-engineer a software system in a secure and privacy-oriented way. It can be used in two ways: *Forward* for developing new systems and *Backward* for reengineering existing systems. In this research work the backward mode is presented.

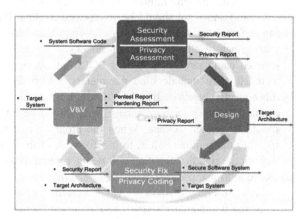

Fig. 3. Privacy oriented software development (backward mode)

4.1   POSD in Backward

In this section al the phases of the POSD will be briefly presented together with the inputs and outputs (Fig. 3).

Analysis. The analysis phase is divided into two parts: *Security Assessment* and *Privacy Assessment*. This derives from the need to analyze the system from both point of views, security and privacy. The *Security Assessment* consists in carrying out a static code analysis of the system to be re-engineered. The output is the Security Report containing the list of vulnerabilities in the system and a list of Recommendation Patterns for each category of vulnerability identified. An example is given below for the "Injection" vulnerability category:

- *Context*: On line 72 of *DIFGetIndirizzo.java*, the method *getIndirizzo()* invokes a SQL query built using input coming from an untrusted source. This call could allow an attacker to modify the statement's meaning or to execute arbitrary SQL commands.
- *Problem*: SQL Injection errors occur when:
  - Data enters a program from an untrusted source. In this case the data enters at *getResultList()* in *DIFGetOrganizationsPartita.java* at line 140.
  - The data is used to dynamically construct a SQL query. In this case the data is passed to *createNativeQuery()* in *DIFGetIndirizzo.java* at line 72.
- *Recommendation*: SQL injection vulnerability is the ability of an attacker to change context in the SQL query, causing a value that the programmer intended to be interpreted as data to be interpreted as a command instead. When a SQL query is constructed, the programmer knows what should be interpreted as part of the command and what should be interpreted as data. Parameterized SQL statements can enforce this behavior by disallowing data-directed context changes and preventing nearly all SQL injection attacks. Parameterized SQL statements are constructed using strings of regular SQL, but where user-supplied data needs to be included, they include bind parameters, which are placeholders for data that is subsequently inserted. In other words, bind parameters allow the programmer to explicitly specify to the database what should be treated as a command and what should be treated as data. When the program is ready to execute a statement, it specifies the runtime values to use for each of the bind parameters to the database without the risk that the data will be interpreted as a modification to the command. Example to use parameterized SQL statements:

  String userName = ctx.getAuthenticatedUserName();
  String itemName = request.getParameter("itemName");
  String query = "SELECT * FROM items WHERE itemname = ? AND owner = ?";
  PreparedStatement stmt = conn.prepareStatement(query);
  stmt.setString(1, itemName);
  stmt.setString(2, userName);
  ResultSet results = stmt.execute();

In the **Privacy Assessment**, the vulnerabilities identified during the static code analysis are provided as input to the PKB in order to identify: (i) the Principle of Privacy by Design violated by the vulnerability, (ii) the privacy Design Strategies to be implemented, (iii) the Privacy Pattern that substantiate the Privacy Design Strategies. The results of this analysis are reported in the Privacy Report.

Design. This phase involves the design of a *Target Archi-tecture* in order to be able to re-engineer the system from a privacy point of view. The input for this phase is the *Privacy Report,* which contains, as previously described, the principles of PbD, privacy design strategies and the list of privacy patterns to use. The relationship between these elements support the team in designing a *Secure Software*

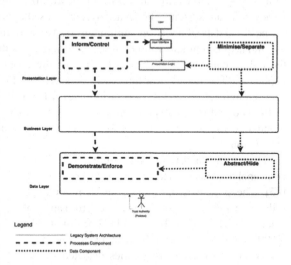

Fig. 4. Privacy design strategies in target architecture

Architecture. The output of the phase is the *Target Architecture,* i.e. the result of the application of the guidelines included in the Privacy Report to the original system. The general strategy followed by POSD is to integrate these guidelines with the minimum impact on the legacy system architecture and by preserving the control logic of the original system. For this reason, all the Privacy Patterns identified by PKB are included in two architectural components (Fig. 4), Data-Oriented and Process-Oriented components, that operationally translate the process flow metaphor of the eight privacy design strategies [4].

Coding. The coding phase, as for the analysis phase, is also divided into parts: **Security Fix** and **Privacy Coding**. Starting from the vulnerabilities and the list of remediation patterns contained in the *Security Report,* the Security Fix will provide the *Secure Software System* in output, where all the vulnerabilities identified have been removed. This reduces the threat of attacks to the system. Instead, the *Privacy Coding* activity, starting from the *Target Architecture* defined in the previous phase and by using the *Secure Software System* obtained, will provide the *Target System* in output.

Verification and Validation. In this phase, before the Target System deployment, *Penetration Test,* to verify the security level of the overall system, and a Hardening phase, to verify the correct setting of the base platform, are carried out. The output of the penetration test activity is the *Pentest Report,* while for the hardening activity the *Hardening Report* is produced. The hardening phase makes use of the CIS Benchmark [34] that consist in best practices for secure system configuration.

5 Case Study

This section presents an ongoing industrial case study that shows the preliminary results of the application of POSD in backward mode for reengineering an existing legacy software system. The legacy system is used by a public company for processing the personal data of about one million users. The two main functionalities of the system are: the acquisition and validation of the data of the subjects requesting the services of the public company and the verification of the economic financial reliability of the applicants. The legacy is a three tiers java system (Presentation, Business and Data). The re-engineering of the system involves a team of 5 people and started in March 2019. The end of the experimentation is scheduled in August 2019 for a total of six months project duration. The preliminary results obtained are presented in the rest of the section.

During the **Security Assessment** phase, static code analysis was carried out by using Fortify SCA [35]. The project meta-information is reported as follows: (i) Number of Files: 371; (ii) Lines of Code: 125,105 (iii) Executable line of Code: 99,997; (iv) Total Vulnerabilities: 1318 (Fig. 5).

The number of vulnerabilities detected by the Fortify SCA analysis were further analyzed to exclude false positives. After false positive removal, the number of vulnerabilities was reduced to 1278.

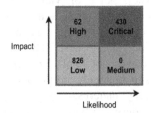

Fig. 5. Vulnerabilities by severity

Table 1. Issues by OWASP top 10 2017 categories.

Vulnerabilities	Severity				Total issues
	Critical	High	Medium	Low	
A1 Injection	373	20	0	695	1088
A2 Broken authentication	0	2	0	0	2
A3 Sensitive data exposure	21	3	0	1	25
A4 XML External Entities (XXE)	0	2	0	1	3
A5 Broken access control	0	33	0	87	120
A7 Cross-Site Scripting (XSS)	38	0	0	0	38
A9 Using components with know vulnerabilities	0	0	0	2	2

Table 1 summarizes the number of remaining vulnerabilities classified according to the OWASP Top 10 2017 categories and severity, i.e. the probability that a vulnerability will be accurately identified and successfully exploited and the impact in terms of damage that an attacker could do by successfully exploiting the vulnerability.

The list of vulnerabilities produced by the Security Assessment activity were analyzed and imported in the PKB in order to identify the violated principles of PbD. The result showed that all 7 principles were violated, and thus the need to implement both Data and Process Oriented strategies in the system. The resulting list of Privacy Patterns to be applied for reengineering the system is shown in (Fig. 6) and the

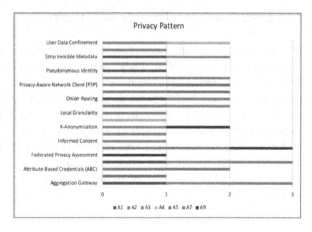

Fig. 6. Privacy patterns to be applied in the system

Target Architecture identified by the development team is available at https://serlab.di. uniba.it/posd.

For what concerns the coding phase that includes a part of Security Fix and a part of Privacy Coding, the team has fixed almost 1200 vulnerabilities by applying the remediation patterns and have already developed about 70% of the target architecture. The remaining remediation patterns will be applied in parallel with the integration of the two privacy components. At the end of this phase, the penetration test and hardening activities will be performed.

6   Discussion

The preliminary results obtained show that POSD was able to address both, security and privacy. It allowed to fix almost 1200 vulnerabilities through the application of the Remediation Patterns provided in the *Security Report* and to addresses the privacy requirements provided by the Privacy Report. The use of PKB across all the phases included in the POSD has allowed to share competences among the development team. The team was able to find vulnerabilities and apply security fixes after having understood the problems arising from the vulnerabilities. At the same time, it allows to support the team during integration of the privacy elements (Principles of PbD, Privacy design Strategies, Privacy Patterns) by supporting its members in design decisions even though they did not have specific privacy skills. Finally, the use of POSD did not impact on the development process used within the organization. All the activities performed by the team, starting from the requirements provided by POSD, were carried out according to the software processes and procedures already used in the company without altering the modus operandi.

7 Limitations and Threats to Validity

The first limitation of the work is represented by the number and size of the software systems used for validation. Only one software system was reengineered; it was however, a real industrial system. A further element of attention is that the coding phase was not completely executed. The reengineering of the system is still ongoing and thus the obtained results are partial and not final yet. Thus, Verification and Validation phase was not carried out. This may represent a serious threat to the validity of the work. The penetration test represents a key point of the POSD in that it definitively certifies the overall effectiveness of the approach. However, the authors are confident that the results obtained so far provide useful insights for the developers for addressing security and privacy.

8 Conclusions

This paper proposes an approach called "Privacy Oriented Software Development" which integrates privacy and security requirements in the software development process. It is based on 5 key Elements for supporting decisions and choices in all phases of software life cycle: Principles of Privacy Design, Privacy Design Strategies, Privacy Patterns, Vulnerabilities, Context. The relationships between the Key Elements are formalized in a knowledge base (PKB) that the developers can use whenever needed during the process execution. POSD can be applied forward for developing a new system and backward for reengineering an existing one. In this work the backward mode was presented together with an industrial case study. The preliminary results obtained show that POSD was able to translate best practices for both, secure application development and data privacy, into operational guidelines, software architectures and code structures to be used. This suggests that the proposed approach may be successfully used for addressing the security and privacy problems. Despite the limitations of the validation carried out, this work has allowed us to start the discussion about this research idea and lay the foundations for future work such as testing the POSD approach in forward mode on systems to be developed especially in the context of software startups; enriching the PKB with new privacy patterns, and implementing a new functionality that allows to export patterns in multiple programming languages.

References

1. Halkidis, S.T., Tsantalis, N., Chatzigeorgiou, A., Stephanides, G.: Architectural risk analysis of software systems based on security patterns. IEEE Trans. Dependable Secure Comput. 5(3), 129–142 (2008)
2. Caivano, D., Fernandez-Ropero, M., Pérez-Castillo, R., Piattini, M., Scalera, M.: Artifact-based vs. human-perceived understandability and modifiability of refactored business processes: An experiment. J. Syst. Softw. 144, 143–164 (2018)
3. Cavoukian, A.: Operationalizing Privacy by Design: A Guide to Implementing Strong Privacy Practices, pp. 1–72 (2012)

4. Hoepman, J.-H.: Privacy design strategies. In: Cuppens-Boulahia, N., Cuppens, F., Jajodia, S., Abou El Kalam, A., Sans, T. (eds.) SEC 2014. IFIPAICT, vol. 428, pp. 446–459. Springer, Heidelberg (2014). https://doi.org/10.1007/978-3-642-55415-5_38

5. Privacy Patterns. UC Berkeley, School of Information. https://privacypatterns.org

6. OWASP, OWASP Top 10 – 2017. The Ten Most Critical Web Application Security Risks. https://owasp.org. Accessed 23 Apr 2019

7. Hatzivasilis, G., Papaefstathiou, I., Manifavas, C.: Software security, privacy, and dependability: metrics and measurement. IEEE Softw. **33**(4), 46–54 (2016)

8. Black, P.E., Badger, L., Guttman, B., Fong, E.: Dramatically Reducing Software Vulnerabilities (2016). https://doi.org/10.6028/NIST.IR.8151

9. IBM: X-Force Threat Intelligence Index 2019. IBM Security. Accessed 24 Apr 2019

10. Baldassarre, M.T., Barletta, V.S., Caivano, D., Raguseo, D., Scalera, M.: Teaching cyber security: the hack-space integrated model. In: Proceedings of the Third Italian Conference on Cyber Security, vol-2315, CEUR Workshop Proceedings (2019)

11. Regulation (EU) 2016/679 of the European Parliament and of the Council of 27 April 2016 on the protection of natural persons with regard to the processing of personal data and on the free movement of such data, and repealing Directive 95/46/EC

12. Kissel, R.L., Stine, K.M., Scholl, M.A., Rossman, H., Fahlsing, J., Gulick, J.: Security Considerations in the System Development Life Cycle. Special Publication (NIST SP) (2008)

13. Jaatun, M.G., Cruzes, D.S., Bernsmed, K., Tøndel, I.A., Røstad, L.: Software security maturity in public organisations. In: Lopez, J., Mitchell, C.J. (eds.) ISC 2015. LNCS, vol. 9290, pp. 120–138. Springer, Cham (2015). https://doi.org/10.1007/978-3-319-23318-5_7

14. Navarro-Machuca, J., Chen, L.: Embedding model-based security policies in software development. In: 2016 IEEE 2nd International Conference on Big Data Security on Cloud (BigDataSecurity), IEEE International Conference on High Performance and Smart Computing (HPSC), and IEEE International Conference on Intelligent Data and Security (IDS), New York, NY, pp. 116–122 (2016)

15. Hilbrich, M., Frank, M.: Enforcing security and privacy via a cooperation of security experts and software engineers: a model-based vision. In: 2017 IEEE 7th International Symposium on Cloud and Service Computing (SC2), Kanazawa, pp. 237–240 (2017)

16. Yanbing, L., Xingyu, L., Yi, J., Yunpeng, X.: SDSA: a framework of a software-defined security architecture. China Commun. **13**(2), 178–188 (2016)

17. Tung, Y., Lo, S., Shih, J., Lin, H.: An integrated security testing framework for secure software development life cycle. In: 2016 18th Asia-Pacific Network Operations and Management Symposium (APNOMS), Kanazawa, pp. 1–4 (2016)

18. Farhan, A.R.S., Mostafa, G.M.M.: A methodology for enhancing software security during development processes. In: 2018 21st NCC, Riyadh, pp. 1–6 (2018)

19. Colesky, M., Hoepman, J., Hillen, C.: A critical analysis of privacy design strategies. In: 2016 IEEE Security and Privacy Workshops (SPW), San Jose, CA, pp. 33–40 (2016)

20. Thomborson, C.: Privacy patterns. In: 2016 14th Annual Conference on Privacy, Security and Trust (PST), Auckland, pp. 656–663 (2016)

21. Suphakul, T., Senivongse, T.: Development of privacy design patterns based on privacy principles and UML. In: 2017 18th IEEE/ACIS International Conference on Software Engineering, Artificial Intelligence, Networking and Parallel/Distributed Computing (SNPD), Kanazawa, pp. 369–375 (2017)

22. Diamantopoulou, V., Argyropoulos, N., Kalloniatis, C., Gritzalis, S.: Supporting the design of privacy-aware business processes via privacy process patterns. In: 11th International Conference on Research Challenges in Information Science, Brighton, pp. 187–198 (2017)

23. van Blarkom, G.W., Borking, J.J., Olk, J.G.E.: Handbook of Privacy and Privacy-Enhancing Technologies. The Case of Intelligent Software Agents. College bescherming persoonsgegevens (2003). ISBN 90-74087-33-7

24. Cavoukian, A.: International council on global privacy and security, by design. In: IEEE Potentials, September–October 2016, vol. 35, no. 5, pp. 43–46 (2016)

25. Hansen, M., Jensen, M., Rost, M.: Protection goals for privacy engineering. In: 2015 IEEE Security and Privacy Workshops, San Jose, CA, pp. 159–166 (2015)

26. García, A.C., et al.: PRIPARE, Privacy and Security by Design Methodology Handook v1.00 (2015). http://pripareproject.eu. Accessed 24 Apr 2019

27. Notario, N., et al.: PRIPARE: integrating privacy best practices into a privacy engineering methodology. In: IEEE Security and Privacy Workshops, San Jose, CA, pp. 151–158 (2015)

28. Spiekermann, S., Cranor, L.F.: Engineering privacy. IEEE Trans. Softw. Eng. 35(1), 67–82 (2009)

29. Kallpniatis, C., Kavakli, E., Gritzalis, S.: Addressing privacy requirements in system design: the PriS method. Requirements Eng. 13(3), 241–255 (2008)

30. Morales-Trujillo, M.E., Matla-Cruz, E.O., García-Mireles, G.A., Piattini, M.: Privacy by design in software engineering: a systematic mapping study. Paper presented at Avances en Ingenieria de Software a Nivel Iberoamericano, CIbSE, pp. 107–120 (2018)

31. Colesky, M., Hoepman, J., Hillen, C.: A critical analysis of privacy design strategies. In: IWPE (2016)

32. Ortiz, R., Moral-Rubio, S., Garzás, J., Fernández-Medina, E.: Towards a pattern-based security methodologiy to build secure information systems. In: Proceedings of the 8th International Workshop on Security in Information Systems WOSIS 2011, pp. 59–69 (2011)

33. Moral-García, S., Ortiz, R., Moral-Rubio, S., Vela, B., Garzás, J., Fernández-Medina, E.: A new pattern template to support the design of security architectures. In: PATTERNS 2010: The 2nd International Conferences on Pervasive Patterns and Applications, pp. 66–71 (2010)

34. Center for Internet Security, CIS Benchmarks. https://www.cisecurity.org/cis-benchmarks/. Accessed 26 Apr 2019

35. Micro Focus: Fortify Static Code Analyze (SCA) (2018). https://www.microfocus.com

Assessing Data Cybersecurity Using ISO/IEC 25012

Javier Verdugo[1,2(✉)] [iD] and Moisés Rodríguez[1,2] [iD]

[1] AQCLab, Camino Moledores, 13071 Ciudad Real, Spain
{jverdugo,mrodriguez}@aqclab.es
[2] Alarcos Research Group, Institute of Technologies and Information Systems,
University of Castilla-La Mancha, Paseo de La Universidad, 4,
13071 Ciudad Real, Spain

Abstract. The importance of data is ever-growing, and it is widely considered to be the most valuable asset of a company. Since data is becoming the main driver of business value, data security is a paramount concern for companies. In recent years, several standards related to security have emerged, most notably those of the ISO/IEC 27000 series. However, they are focused on management systems and security infrastructure, neglecting the security of the data itself. Other standards related to data quality, such as ISO 8000, also fail to address data security in depth. To this end, we propose in this paper a framework for the evaluation of data cybersecurity, consisting of a quality model (based on ISO/IEC 25012), an evaluation process (based on ISO/IEC 25040), and a tool for the visualization of the assessment results. This evaluation framework has been taken as the basis for a data cybersecurity certification scheme, which complements other certifiable standards related to data and security such as ISO/IEC 27001 and ISO 8000.

Keywords: Data cybersecurity · Quality model · Evaluation · Certification · ISO/IEC 25012

1 Introduction

In recent years, and due to the increasing emergence of technologies related to Open Data, Big Data, Business Intelligence, etc., data has become the most important asset of companies that blossom in the digital era. With the growing importance of data as a driver of business value, data security is becoming an even more relevant concern. An example of this is the political agreement on the Cybersecurity Act reached by the European Parliament, the Council and the European Commission. Among other things, The Cybersecurity Act creates a framework for European Cybersecurity Certificates for products, processes and services that will be valid throughout the EU [1].

However, while this EU framework for cybersecurity certification is still being implemented, the focus regarding security has so far been on infrastructure and management systems, but not on the security of the data itself.

© Springer Nature Switzerland AG 2019
M. Piattini et al. (Eds.): QUATIC 2019, CCIS 1010, pp. 33–46, 2019.
https://doi.org/10.1007/978-3-030-29238-6_3

ISO/IEC 27000 [2] is currently the most widespread series of standards for security assessment and certification. Among the security controls proposed by the standards in this series, several are applicable to data, but the purpose of ISO/IEC 27000 is the evaluation and certification of the information security management systems (based on the Deming PDCA cycle), and it does not address specifically the evaluation and certification of data security.

Other standards related to cybersecurity focus on threats and weaknesses over software systems. An example of this is the standard Automated Source Code Security Measure (ASCSM) [3], defined by OMG, which identifies weaknesses that can be detected on the source code of applications through static analysis. As with other approaches to cybersecurity, it does not address data security specifically.

The evaluation of data cybersecurity is currently at a very early stage, and the main global reference standards that are somehow related to the subject, such as ISO/IEC 25000 [4] or ISO 8000 [5] are still under development. On the other hand, there are frameworks for the evaluation of the quality of the software product, the quality of data, the cybersecurity of critical infrastructures, and the certification of information security management systems, but none specific to data cybersecurity.

The main objective of this paper is presenting the data cybersecurity evaluation framework that has been defined, consisting of a quality model, an evaluation process, and a technological environment. The results of data cybersecurity evaluations carried out with the framework presented in this work are the basis for data cybersecurity certification, as part of the scheme defined by AENOR (leading certification body in Spain) for Cybersecurity and Privacy, which consists of several complementary certifiable standards.

The remainder of the paper is structured as follows: Sect. 2 presents the ISO/IEC 25000 series of standards, basis for the model and process proposed in this work. Section 3 presents the data cybersecurity model defined. Section 4 presents the environment for data cybersecurity evaluation and certification. Section 5 presents a case of application of data cybersecurity evaluation. Finally, Sect. 6 presents the conclusions and future work.

2   ISO/IEC 25000 Series of Standards

2.1   Organization of SQuaRE Series of Standards

ISO/IEC 25000 "Software Product Quality Requirements and Evaluation" [6], also known as SQuaRE, is a series of International Standards that stems from and revises the old standards related to software product quality, ISO/IEC 9126 [7] and ISO/IEC 14598 [8]. The ISO/IEC 25000 series was devised with the aim of amending the differences and inconsistencies between those two standards and replacing them, defining a complete framework that establishes, among others, a quality model, a set of metrics and a product quality evaluation process. The standards in the ISO/IEC 25000 family are organized in five divisions, as shown in Fig. 1.

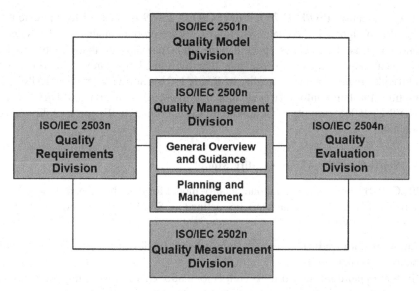

Fig. 1. Organization of the ISO/IEC 25000 series of standards (adapted from [9])

- **ISO/IEC 2500n – Quality Management Division**. The standards in this division define the common models, terms and definitions referred to by all the other standards in the SQuaRE series. This division also provides guidance for supporting functions responsible for the management of software product quality specification and evaluation.
- **ISO/IEC 2501n – Quality Model Division**. The standards in this division provide detailed models for systems and software product quality and quality in use (ISO/IEC 25010 [10]), data quality (ISO/IEC 25012 [4]), and service quality (ISO/IEC 25011 [11]). Guidance on the use of these models is provided as well.
- **ISO/IEC 2502n – Quality Measurement Division**. The standards that form this division include a reference model for systems and software product quality measurement (ISO/IEC 25020 [12]), definitions of quality measures for the different models in the ISO/IEC 2501n division, as well as practical guidance for their application. In this regard, ISO/IEC 25022 [13] provides measures for quality in use, ISO/IEC 25023 [14] for systems and software product quality, and ISO/IEC 25024 [15] for data quality. ISO/IEC 25025, currently under development, will provide measures for IT service quality.
- **ISO/IEC 2503n – Quality Requirements Division**. The standards in this division help to specify quality requirements, which can be used in the process of requirements elicitation for a system or software product to be developed, or as inputs for an evaluation process.
- **ISO/IEC 2504n – Quality Evaluation Division**. The standards that form this division provide a process and requirements for quality evaluation (ISO/IEC 25040 [16]), as well as recommendations and guidelines for developers, acquirers and independent evaluators).

The numeration **ISO/IEC 25050 to ISO/IEC 25099** is reserved for the extension of SQuaRe, designated to contain system or software product quality standards and/or technical reports that address specific application domains or that can be used to complement the standards in the previous five divisions. For example, ISO/IEC 25051 [17] provides requirements for quality of Ready to Use Software Product (RUSP) and instructions for their conformity evaluation, and standards in the range ISO/IEC 25060 to ISO/IEC 25066 provide a Common Industry Format (CIF) for usability-related information.

2.2 ISO/IEC 25012 – Data Quality Model

ISO/IEC 25012 defines a general data quality model for data that is part of a computer system. The fifteen quality characteristics defined in ISO/IEC are categorized according to two points of view:

- **Inherent data quality**: refers to quality characteristics that are measured on attributes of the data itself.
- **System dependent data quality**: refers to quality characteristics that are measured through the capabilities of the computer system retaining the data.

The classification of the fifteen data quality characteristics defined in ISO/IEC 25012 is shown in Table 1. As the table shows, some characteristics are relevant from both points of view.

Table 1. Data quality characteristics defined in ISO/IEC 25012

Characteristics	Data quality	
	Inherent	System dependent
Accuracy	X	
Completeness	X	
Consistency	X	
Credibility	X	
Currentness	X	
Accessibility	X	X
Compliance	X	X
Confidentiality	X	X
Efficiency	X	X
Precision	X	X
Traceability	X	X
Understandability	X	X
Availability		X
Portability		X
Recoverability		X

2.3   ISO/IEC 25024 – Measurement of Data Quality

ISO/IEC 25024 defines data quality measures for quantitatively measuring data quality in terms of the characteristics defined in ISO/IEC 25012 (shown in Table 1).

For each characteristic defined in ISO/IEC 25012, this standard proposes:

- A basic set of data quality measures
- A basic set of target entities to which the quality measures are applied during the data-life-cycle
- An explanation of how to apply the data quality measures
- Guidance for organizations defining their own measures for data quality

3   Model for Data Cybersecurity Evaluation

The data cybersecurity model presented in this work is based on the standards ISO/IEC 25012 (Data quality model) and ISO/IEC 25024 (Measurement of data quality). This model has been incorporated to the evaluation framework of AQCLab, an accredited laboratory that carries out evaluations of software product Functional Suitability [18], software product Maintainability [19] and Data Quality.

3.1   Quality Characteristics

The data cybersecurity model consists of a subset of five characteristics defined in the ISO/IEC 25012 data quality model, selected for their close relation to security aspects:

- **Compliance**: degree to which data adhere to standards, conventions, regulations and similar rules relating to data quality.
- **Confidentiality**: degree to which data is ensured to be only accessible and inter-pretable by authorized users.
- **Traceability**: degree to which an audit trail is provided regarding access and changes made to the data.
- **Availability**: degree to which data can be retrieved by authorized users and/or applications.
- **Recoverability**: degree to which data maintains and preserves a specified level of operations and quality, even in the event of failure.

    As a result of their evaluation, each of these characteristics take a value in the scale 1 to 5. The value in this scale represents the quality level for the characteristic, and it represents the range from deficient quality to excellent quality.

3.2   Quality Properties

The value of each data cybersecurity characteristic is obtained from the values of the several quality properties that intervene in their evaluation. The quality properties defined in the data cybersecurity model have been extracted from the quality measures proposed in ISO/IEC 25024. The specific properties for each of the characteristics of the data cybersecurity model are shown in Table 2.

Table 2. Quality properties for the evaluation of data cybersecurity characteristics and their related point of view (I: Inherent quality: S D: System dependent quality)

Characteristic	Properties	I	S D
		Point of view	
Compliance	Regulatory compliance of value and/or format	X	
	Regulatory compliance due to technology		X
Confidentiality	Encryption usage	X	
	Non vulnerability		X
Traceability	Users access traceability	X	X
	Data values traceability	X	X
Availability	Data availability ratio		X
	Probability of data available		X
	Architecture elements availability		X
Recoverability	Data recoverability ratio		X
	Periodical backup		X
	Architecture recoverability		X

Quality properties of the data cybersecurity model take a quality value in the range [0, 100]. Property values are taken as the basis for the evaluation of the characteristics. Thus, the value for each characteristic is obtained by applying an aggregation function over the values of its related properties. The quality value for properties is obtained by applying measurement functions over some base measures. When these base measures apply at data file level (meaning that the target entity is, for example, a table in a relational database), they are measured for each file in the data repository, and then a categorizing or profiling function is applied to obtain the property value derived from the measurements for all the files in the data repository.

The information on how to obtain the value for each property, as well as any other descriptive information necessary for their evaluation has been defined as part of the data cybersecurity model. In this manner, the model provides the following information for each property: related characteristic, property description, point of view, target entity, target attribute, measurement description, calculation formula, scale, value range, and property measurement function. Table 3 shows an example of how this information is characterized in the model, in this case, for the property Regulatory compliance of value and/or format.

Target entities for the different properties of the model are: data files (tables), elements of data architecture (contextual schema, data models, data dictionary), computer system (as a whole), and elements of system architecture (database management system, documents, forms, presentation devices). Each of these target entities have quantifiable attributes over which the base measurements for each property are defined.

Table 3. Evaluation information for the property Regulatory compliance of value and/or format

Property	Regulatory compliance of value and/or format		
Related characteristic	Compliance		
Description	Degree to which data values and/or format comply with specific standards, conventions or regulations. The organization is responsible for identifying or stablishing which rules the data must comply with in terms of value and/or format. Such rules can be stablished, either internally by the organization owning the data, or by external regulatory bodies.		
Point of view	Inherent		
Target entity	Data file (table)		
Target attribute	Data record (row)		
Measurement description	Regulatory compliance of value and/or format for a data file is obtained as the ratio of records of that file whose value for their fields comply with specific rules, conventions or regulations that have been established.		
Calculation formula	X=A/B X = regulatory compliance of value and/or format for a file A= number of records that have values and/or format that conform to standards, conventions or regulations B= number of records that shall conform to standards, conventions or regulations due to their value		
Scale	Ratio		
Value range	[0.0 - 1.0]		
Property measurement function	Profile function over value of regulatory compliance of value and/or format for each file. Profiling criteria:		
	Level	**Range**	**Description**
	1	[0.0 – 0.6)	Low regulatory compliance of value and/or format
	2	[0.6 – 0.75)	Medium regulatory compliance of value and/or format
	3	[0.75 – 0.95)	High regulatory compliance of value and/or format
	4	[0.95 – 1.0]	Very high regulatory compliance of value and/or format

4   Data Cybersecurity Environment

In order to carry out a data cybersecurity evaluation, a methodologic and technological environment is needed. The evaluation model is the main part of the evaluation environment, but in order to be practical, it must be supported by two elements: a set of processes and activities that stablish the steps that have to be carried out and guide the interaction with the customers, and a set of tools to perform the measurements and evaluations and visualize the results.

Hence, the purpose of the data cybersecurity environment is setting the basis for providing companies and public organisms with data cybersecurity evaluation and certification services.

The methodologic part of the environment consists aims to define the following:

- The set of processes necessary to carry out data cybersecurity evaluations, the specific activities to be carried out, and the artifacts that are handled during the evaluation process (inputs to the process, outputs or deliverables, etc.).
- The set of processes necessary to carry out data cybersecurity certification, based on a previous evaluation.

4.1 Evaluation Process

The evaluation process sets the activities, inputs, outputs, resources and constraints required to carry out a data cybersecurity evaluation, in this case, from the point of view of an independent evaluator. The evaluation process defined in this work has been adapted from the process in the standard ISO/IEC 25040.

The activities and tasks of the data cybersecurity evaluation process are defined as follows. It should be taken into account that the activities are not carried out strictly one after another. Iterations on specific activities or between activities may and usually occur.

Establish the evaluation requirements. This activity consists of the following tasks:

- **Establish the purpose of the evaluation**: The purpose of the data cybersecurity evaluation shall be documented as a basis for the further evaluation activities and tasks.
- **Obtain the data cybersecurity requirements**: The stakeholders of the computer system retaining the data shall identify and provide the requirements according to the cybersecurity model defined by the evaluator. The evaluation model itself also pose a series of specific requirements that the evaluator will provide to the client in order to decide together if the evaluation method meets the client's expectations.
- **Identify data and computer system parts to be included in the evaluation**: All data and computer system parts to be included in the evaluation shall be identified and documented.

Specify the evaluation. This activity consists of the following tasks:

- **Select quality measures (evaluation modules)**: The evaluator shall select quality measures (evaluation modules) to cover all data cybersecurity evaluation requirements. Since the measures of the model are pre-stablished, in this activity the evaluator identifies the mapping between the measures, the data and computer system parts, and the data cybersecurity requirements.
- **Define decision criteria for quality measures**: Decision criteria (numerical thresholds and targets) for the individual measures is already defined as part of the evaluation model.

- **Define decision criteria for evaluation**: The decision criteria for the quality characteristics, whose value is obtained from the combination of values for quality properties, already defined as part of the evaluation model.

  Design the evaluation. This activity consists of the following task:

- **Plan evaluation activities**: The evaluation activities shall be scheduled, taking into account the availability of resources and the data and computer system parts to be evaluated.

Execute the evaluation. This activity consists of the following tasks:

- **Make measurements**: The data cybersecurity measures shall be applied to the data and computer system parts, according to the evaluation plan, resulting in values on the measurement scales.
- **Apply decision criteria for quality measures**: The decision criteria for the measures shall be applied to the measured values, obtaining values for the quality properties. This activity is automated thanks to the technological framework available.
- **Apply decision criteria for evaluation**: The set of decision criteria shall be applied to the characteristics, parting from the property values, and producing the evaluation results.

Conclude the evaluation. This activity consists of the following tasks:

- **Review the evaluation result**: The evaluator and the client shall carry out a joint review of the evaluation results.
- **Create the evaluation report**: The evaluator shall create the evaluation report, detailing the results, and including descriptive information of the evaluation (requirements, evaluation modules, plan, personnel, etc.). The evaluator shall provide the client with the report created.
- **Review quality evaluation and provide feedback to the organization**: The evaluator shall review the results of the evaluation. Feedback from the review should be used in order to improve the evaluation process and evaluation techniques (evaluation modules).
- **Perform disposition of evaluation data**: When the evaluation is completed the data and any other items that may have been provided by the client shall be disposed.

4.2 Certification Process

The data cybersecurity evaluation framework described in this work has been taken as the basis by the Spanish leading certification body, AENOR, for their data cybersecurity certification scheme, which is part of their certification portfolio for Cybersecurity and Privacy, along with other certifiable standards.

The process for obtaining a data cybersecurity certificate consists of the six interaction steps between client, evaluator and certification body shown in Fig. 2.

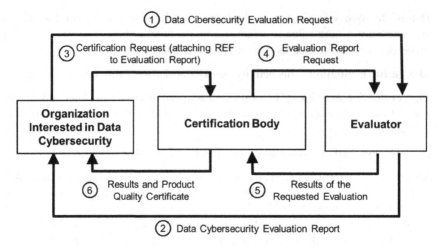

Fig. 2. Steps of the data cybersecurity certification process

4.3   Technological Environment

A technological environment is necessary so that the evaluation of data cybersecurity can be carried out in a practical, efficient and accurate way. This technological environment consists of tools that automate the acquisition, calculation and presentation of the values obtained for the characteristics, properties and measures defined in the evaluation model.

The measurement tools used in the evaluation to obtain the values for base measures depend vastly on the technologies of the computer system of the data product evaluated. For example, for relational databases a query tool can be used to communicate with the DBMS and obtain information needed for some measures of the model.

The evaluation tool of the environment is responsible for applying the decision criteria of the evaluation model. For that, it takes as input the measurement of the base measures defined in the model, once they have been obtained from the target entities. The evaluation tool takes the base measure values specified in an XML file and processes them to obtain the values for quality properties. This processing consists in applying evaluation functions that represent the decision criteria defined in the model as thresholds and profiles. The values for the quality properties are in turned processed to obtain the values for the characteristics of the model. The resulting values for the properties and characteristics after the evaluation are stored in a database.

A visualization tool has been developed in order to consult and represent the results of data cybersecurity evaluations in a clear and concise way. This tool is aimed to be used by both evaluators and clients. The permissions system of the tool allows to control which functionalities and information of which evaluations the user can access based on her role. When the user selects an evaluation (between the ones available to her), its information is displayed (see Fig. 3): name of the data product, version, date of the evaluation, value for characteristics and properties in tabular way, and graphics representing those values (radar chart for characteristics, bar chart for properties).

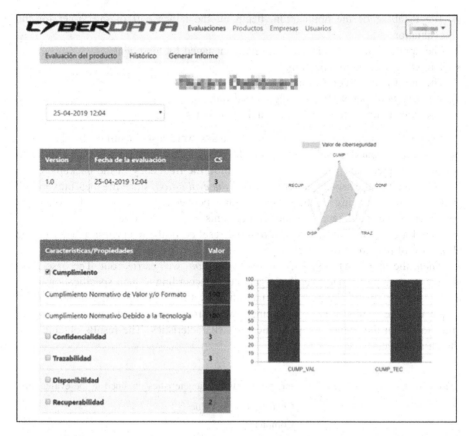

Fig. 3. Snapshot of the visualization tool for data cybersecurity evaluations

The visualization tool provides more functionalities, such as generating downloadable reports for evaluations, showing trends in the values of cybersecurity evaluations, managing companies, data products and users, etc.

5   Example of Application

As a pilot project, the evaluation framework presented in this work has been applied to a commercial product: a business dashboard management tool provided to its users under a SaaS model. This tool uses the balanced scorecard (BSC) approach, allowing the users to define, monitor and control their own KPIs. The evaluation was conducted following the process and using the technological environment defined in the previous section, and applying the model defined in Sect. 3.

As a result of the first activity, *Establish the evaluation requirements*, the cybersecurity model was presented to the client, explaining the characteristics and properties, and the generic requirements related to their measures. The client identified the data and elements of the computer system in the scope of the evaluation:

- The database of the application, being all the tables part of the target for the evaluation.
- The application itself, hosted in a server managed by the client.
- The DBMS of the application.
- The latest backup copies made.
- The results of penetration testing carried out.
- Documentation of the application and computer system.

Specific requirements for some characteristics were also identified by the client, such as rules regarding value or format for some data fields, fields that require to contain encrypted data with a specific algorithm, the frequency of the backups, etc.

As a result of the second activity, *Specify the evaluation*, since the measures for the evaluation were already defined, the mapping between the measures, the data and computer system parts, and specific requirements was carried out.

The third activity, *Specify the evaluation*, resulted in the evaluation plan, with the allocation of resources to activities.

Then, the fourth activity, *Execute the evaluation*, was carried out. The base measurements were performed over the target entities according to their specification in the model and the specific requirements identified by the client for some of the quality properties. The results of the measurement were processed with the evaluation tool in order to obtain the values for properties and characteristics. The results obtained are shown in Table 4.

Table 4. Quality values for the data cybersecurity characteristics obtained in the evaluation

Characteristic	Value
Compliance	5
Confidentiality	3
Traceability	3
Availability	5
Recoverability	2

To finish the evaluation, the last activity, *Conclude the evaluation*, was carried out. First, the results of the evaluation were reviewed, and then the evaluation report was generated with the visualization tool and issued to the client.

6   Conclusions and Future Work

This work presents a first step in a domain that is becoming more and more important, but has not been explored in depth. Although there are many approaches to data quality and cybersecurity, such as standards, models, best practices, etc. none of them actually take into account both at the same time. Data quality approaches usually do not address security aspects comprehensively, and cybersecurity approaches usually focus more on systems infrastructure, software, and networks than on the data.

This work has presented an industrial approach to data cybersecurity based on International Standards. The pilot project conducted has shown that the proposed framework can be used to evaluate and certificate the cybersecurity of the data that companies manage and work with as part of their business mission.

In the future we intend to carry out more evaluations with this framework in order to get more practical knowledge about the feasibility of this type of evaluations, the drawbacks regarding the measures selected and how to apply them in real-life information systems, and in general, make improvements on the data cybersecurity evaluation framework proposed so that it addresses the needs of the market.

Acknowledgements. This research is part of the DQIoT project (INNO-20171086), funded by CDTI; ECD project (PTQ-16-08504), funded by the "Torres Quevedo" Program of the Spanish Ministry of Economy, Industry and Competitiveness; CYBERDATA project (REF: 13/17/IN/013) funded by Consejería de Economía, Empresas y Empleo JCCM and FEDER (Fondo Europeo de Desarrollo Regional); ECLIPSE project (Ministerio de Ciencia, Innovación y Universidades, and Fondo Europeo de Desarrollo Regional FEDER, RTI2018-094283-B-C31); and TESTIMO project (Consejería de Educación, Cultura y Deportes de la Junta de Comunidades de Castilla La Mancha, and Fondo Europeo de Desarrollo Regional FEDER, SBPLY/17/180501/000503).

References

1. European Comission. https://ec.europa.eu/commission/news/cybersecurity-act-2018-dec-11_en. Accessed 16 May 2019
2. ISO/IEC 27000: Information technology – Security techniques – Information security management systems – Overview and vocabulary. International Organization for Standardization/ISO/IEC JTC 1/SC 27 Information Security, cybersecurity and privacy protection (2018)
3. ASCSM 1.0: Automated Source Code CISQ Security Measure. Object Management Group (2016)
4. ISO/IEC 25012: Software Engineering – Software product Quality Requirements and Evaluation (SQuaRE) – Data Quality Model. International Organization for Standardization/ISO/IEC JTC 1/SC 7 Software and systems engineering (2008)
5. ISO/TS 8000-60: Data Quality – Part 60: Data Quality Management: Overview. International Organization for Standardization/TC 184/SC 4 Industrial data (2017)
6. ISO/IEC 25000: Systems and software engineering – Systems and software Quality Requirements and Evaluation (SQuaRE) – Guide to SQuaRE. International Organization for Standardization/ISO/IEC JTC 1/SC 7 Software and systems engineering (2014)
7. ISO/IEC 9126-1: Software engineering – Product quality – Part 1: Quality model. International Organization for Standardization/ISO/IEC JTC 1/SC 7 Software and systems engineering (2001)
8. ISO/IEC 14598-1: Information technology – Software product evaluation – Part 1: General overview. International Organization for Standardization/ISO/IEC JTC 1/SC 7 Software and systems engineering (1999)
9. Zubrow, D.: Measuring Software Product Quality: the ISO 25000 Series and CMMI. SEI (2004)

10. ISO/IEC 25010: Software Engineering – Software product Quality Requirements and Evaluation (SQuaRE) – System and software quality models. International Organization for Standardization/ISO/IEC JTC 1/SC 7 Software and systems engineering (2011)
11. ISO/IEC TS 25011: Software Engineering – Software product Quality Requirements and Evaluation (SQuaRE) – Service quality models. International Organization for Standardization/ISO/IEC JTC 1/SC 7 Software and systems engineering (2017)
12. ISO/IEC 25020: Software Engineering – Software product Quality Requirements and Evaluation (SQuaRE) – Measurement reference model and guide. International Organization for Standardization/ISO/IEC JTC 1/SC 7 Software and systems engineering (2007)
13. ISO/IEC 25022: Software Engineering – Software product Quality Requirements and Evaluation (SQuaRE) – Measurement of quality in use. International Organization for Standardization/ISO/IEC JTC 1/SC 7 Software and systems engineering (2016)
14. ISO/IEC 25023: Software Engineering – Software product Quality Requirements and Evaluation (SQuaRE) – Measurement of system and software product quality. International Organization for Standardization/ISO/IEC JTC 1/SC 7 Software and systems engineering (2016)
15. ISO/IEC 25024: Software Engineering – Software product Quality Requirements and Evaluation (SQuaRE) – Measurement of data quality. International Organization for Standardization/ISO/IEC JTC 1/SC 7 Software and systems engineering (2015)
16. ISO/IEC 25040: Software Engineering – Software product Quality Requirements and Evaluation (SQuaRE) – Evaluation process. International Organization for Standardization/ISO/IEC JTC 1/SC 7 Software and systems engineering (2011)
17. ISO/IEC 25051: Software Engineering – Software product Quality Requirements and Evaluation (SQuaRE) – Requirements for quality of Ready to Use Software Product (RUSP) and instructions for testing. International Organization for Standardization/ISO/IEC JTC 1/SC 7 Software and systems engineering (2014)
18. Rodríguez, M., Oviedo, J.R., Piattini, M.: Evaluation of software product functional suitability: a case study. Softw. Qual. Prof. 18(3), 18–29 (2016)
19. Rodríguez, M., Piattini, M., Fernandez, C.M.: A hard look at software quality: Pilot program uses ISO/IEC 25000 family to evaluate, improve and certify software products. Qual. Prog. **48**, 30–36 (2015)

Requirements Engineering

Data-Driven Elicitation of Quality Requirements in Agile Companies

Marc Oriol[1]([✉]) [iD], Pertti Seppänen[2] [iD], Woubshet Behutiye[2] [iD],
Carles Farré[1] [iD], Rafal Kozik[3,4] [iD], Silverio Martínez-Fernández[5] [iD],
Pilar Rodríguez[2] [iD], Xavier Franch[1] [iD], Sanja Aaramaa[6],
Antonin Abhervé[7], Michal Choras[3,4], and Jari Partanen[8]

[1] Universitat Politècnica de Catalunya, Barcelona, Spain
{moriol,farre,franch}@essi.upc.edu
[2] University of Oulu, Oulu, Finland
{pertti.seppanen,woubshet.behutiye,
pilar.rodriguez}@oulu.fi
[3] ITTI Sp. z o.o., Poznań, Poland
{rkozik,mchoras}@itti.com.pl
[4] University of Science and Technology, UTP, Bydgoszcz, Poland
[5] Fraunhofer IESE, Kaiserslautern, Germany
silverio.martinez@iese.fraunhofer.de
[6] NOKIA, Oulu, Finland
sanja.aaramaa@nokia.com
[7] Softeam, Paris, France
antonin.abherve@softeam.fr
[8] Bittium Wireless Ltd., Oulu, Finland
jari.partanen@bittium.com

Abstract. Quality Requirements (QRs) are a key artifact to ensure the quality
and success of a software system. Despite its importance, QRs have not reached
the same degree of attention as its functional counterparts, especially in the
context of trending software development methodologies like Agile Software
Development (ASD). Moreover, crucial information that can be obtained from
data sources of a project under development (e.g. JIRA, github,...) are not fully
exploited, or even neglected, in QR elicitation activities. In this work, we present a data-driven approach to semi-automatically generate and document QRs
in the context of ASD. We define an architecture focusing on the process and the
artefacts involved. We validate and iterate on such architecture by conducting
workshops in four companies of different size and profile. Finally, we present
the implementation of such architecture, considering the feedback and outcomes
of the conducted workshops.

Keywords: Quality requirements · Non-functional requirements ·
Agile software development · Data-driven requirements engineering

© Springer Nature Switzerland AG 2019
M. Piattini et al. (Eds.): QUATIC 2019, CCIS 1010, pp. 49–63, 2019.
https://doi.org/10.1007/978-3-030-29238-6_4

1   Introduction

Quality management is known to be one of the critical success factors for software projects [1]. There are many examples of software with poor quality (e.g. software with bugs, security issues, technical debt, low quality of service, poor code quality, etc.) that have caused millions of euros of losses. A report conducted by the software testing company Tricentis revealed that software failures caused more than $1.7 trillion in financial losses in 2017 [2].

To be successful, software development companies must understand and manage software quality to ensure that new releases lead to progressive improvement [3]. For such a reason, many approaches have emerged to try to improve the software quality in different phases of the software development lifecycle. In this regard, market studies show a steady increase in the proportion of software development companies' budget being spent on dealing with software quality [4].

It is argued that an optimal approach to ensure a good software quality, should consider and address such quality starting early from the requirements [5]. The artifact that requirements engineers use to state conditions on, and analyse compliance of, software quality are the Quality Requirements (QRs; also known as non-functional requirements) [6].

A QR is defined as *"a requirement that pertains to a quality concern that is not covered by functional requirements"* [6].

QRs play an essential role in the success of software systems, and neglecting or failing to satisfy QRs can lead to critical or even catastrophic consequences [5, 7].

Despite their importance, QRs have traditionally not received the same degree of attention than their functional requirements counterpart [8]. This is also true in trending software development methodologies, like Agile Software Development (ASD), a software development approach that has been widely adopted in the software industry [9].

To address this problem we presented in a previous work an explorative position paper at [10] where we envisaged a conceptual framework, named Q-Rapids, to generate and document QRs using a data-driven approach in the context of ASD. The goal of this paper is to continue such work and present an operational implementation of the approach for generating and documenting QRs in ASD. The contributions of this paper are as follows:

1. A software architecture for a tool implementation, explained with a running example impacting the companies.
2. Workshops to refine and validate the architecture for a tool implementation with prospective end-users.
3. Discussions on the results and current tool support.

The research has been conducted in the context of the Q-Rapids H2020 project (www.q-rapids.eu) which has given us the opportunity to elicit real scenarios and evaluate the results on different company-provided scenarios.

The rest of the paper is organized as follows: Sect. 2 presents the Related Work. Section 3 provides an overview of the overall Q-Rapids Approach. Section 4 describes our proposal, detailing the architecture and artifacts for the QR generation and documentation process. Section 5 evaluates such proposal by means of workshops conducted in four companies. Section 6 reports and discusses the findings of such evaluation, which are then used for the implementation of the tools, described in Sect. 7. Finally, Sect. 8 provides the conclusions and the future work.

2 Background and Related Work

In ASD, the development process is mostly driven by functional requirements. For example, in Scrum [11], requirements are specified as user stories in the product backlog and prioritized based on a customer perspective. This way of eliciting and managing requirements tends to favour functional requirements over QRs [12, 13]. As a result, QRs are not properly documented and only managed in a tacit way [14]. Moreover, despite the numerous sources of information related to product quality that ASD provides (e.g. continuous integration systems and user feedback), there is a lack of methods to support continuous elicitation and management of QRs, throughout the whole software development lifecycle [13].

On the other hand, traditional approaches for eliciting and managing QRs are usually inadequate in the highly-dynamic scenarios in which ASD is more suitable. Traditional techniques to elicit QRs include structured and unstructured interviews, quality models, checklists, prioritization questionnaires, and the like. None of them exploits runtime data. In this context, data-driven requirements engineering [15] is advocated as the proper way to go for eliciting QRs. Some recent proposals in this direction aim at exploiting end-user explicit feedback data [16–18].

Explicit feedback requires user commitment and can be incomplete and/or biased. Implicit feedback can be considered as an alternative/complementary data source for requirements elicitation [15]. As an example, [19] exploits implicit feedback but does not aim at generating QRs but at discovering user preferences and usage patterns. The SUPERSEDE data-driven approach [20] combines both explicit and implicit end-user feedback with other sources like run-time monitors to detect and address different kinds of issues: bugs, new features, QoS violations.

However, none of the aforementioned approaches exploit data gathered from software repositories, project management tools, or code inspectors. Without these other relevant sources, QRs related more directly to "internal" aspects like code quality or the software development process itself could hardly be elicited.

3 The Q-Rapids Approach to Quality Requirements Elicitation and Documentation

Q-Rapids is a quality-aware ASD framework in which QRs are elicited using a data-driven approach. Data from multiple data sources are gathered and evaluated against a Quality Model to generate QRs if an issue is identified.

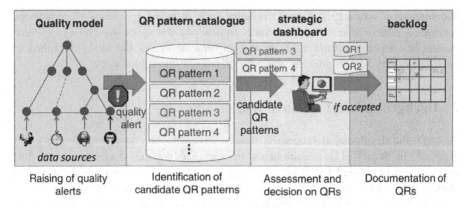

Fig. 1. Main logical components of the Q-Rapids conceptual architecture [10]

Figure 1 depicts the Conceptual Architecture of Q-Rapids with its different phases to generate and document QRs:

- *Raising of quality alerts:* As a first step, data from multiple and heterogeneous *data sources* is gathered (e.g., from Jira, SonarQube, github, runtime monitors, etc.). The collected data feeds a *quality model* that computes the quality of the software. The different elements of the *quality model* represent characteristics of the software quality at different abstraction levels. These elements of the *quality model* have customizable thresholds, that, if violated, automatically raise a *quality alert*
- *Selection of candidate QR patterns:* When a *quality alert* is raised, Q-Rapids identifies *candidate QR patterns* that, after being instantiated to *QRs* and implemented, will restore the value(s) of the element(s) of the *quality model* that raised the alert. A key component used to identify such *candidate QR* is the *QR pattern catalogue* [21]. The *QR pattern catalogue* consists of a set of *QR patterns* that are defined in terms of natural language sentences that include formal parameters (i.e. free variables). The *QR patterns* are bound to *quality model* elements in the schema of the *QR patterns catalogue*. This binding is fundamental in order to match the appropriate *candidate QR patterns* with the raised *quality alert*.
- *Assessment and decision on QRs:* The *candidate QR patterns* are presented to the decision makers—Product Owners, Project Managers or other members of the development team—through a *strategic dashboard*. The decision makers assess the *candidate QR patterns* and instantiates them to particular *QRs* by setting the values of the formal parameters of the *QR pattern*. To support the assessment of the instantiated QRs, the strategic dashboard includes simulation techniques. Such simulations predict the impact that the QRs would have on the values of the different elements of the *quality model* if such *QRs* were implemented.
- *Documentation of QRs:* In case the QR is accepted by the decision maker, such QR is forwarded to the backlog. The strategic dashboard provides the user with a link through which the accepted QR is automatically moved to the organization's requirements repository. The strategic dashboard itself does not depend on any fixed repositories or tools but utilizes the link mechanism to transfer the data content of

the accepted QR to the requirements repository. Building the linkage between the strategic dashboard and the used requirements repository is a task done in the Q-Rapids setting-up actions.

In [10], we introduced the ideas of such QR generation process. We have further elaborated on those ideas and provided a first design, which was evaluated in different companies as part of a co-creation activity for its implementation.

4 QR Generation and Documentation Architecture

4.1 QR Generation and Documentation Process

To design the QR generation and documentation process, we have formalized the different steps and elements required by means of a Business Process Model and Notation (BPMN) process model. The QR generation process are the activities conducted from the raise of an alert until the QR is generated, whereas the QR documentation is the activity to include such QR into the backlog. Such BPMN process model is shown in Fig. 2 and defines the main tasks and artifacts involved. The process starts when a quality alert is triggered. The quality alert is then notified to the decision makers by sending the *«artifact» quality alert*. The decision makers evaluate the quality alert, and request the QR patterns to resolve it. Q-Rapids obtains from the *«repository» QR Patterns Catalogue* the *«artifact» QR patterns* able to resolve the quality alert. The decision makers select and instantiate the QR pattern, generating the *«artifact» QR*, which is finally stored to the *«repository» Backlog*.

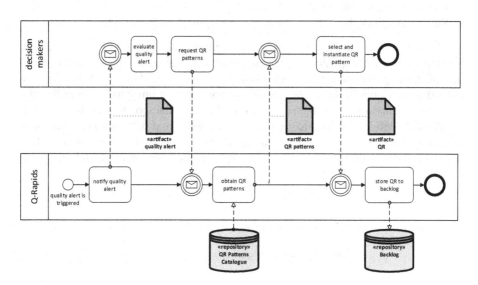

Fig. 2. BPMN process model of the QR generation and documentation process

In the following subsections we describe in detail how we have designed those artifacts. Namely: *quality alert, QR patterns* and *QR*. We also describe and discuss the repositories that we will use for the *QR patterns Catalogue* and *Backlog*.

Finally, the presented artifacts are evaluated in multiple companies (see Sects. 5 and 6). Following the evaluation of the artifacts, we implemented a first prototype of the tools that automate the defined tasks in Q-Rapids (see Sect. 7).

4.2 Quality Alerts

In a previous work, we had defined the quality model based on expert knowledge from the companies of the Q-Rapids consortium [22]. The nodes of the quality model are of different type depending on the abstraction level: at the highest level there are project indicators (e.g. product quality), which are decomposed into quality factors (e.g. code quality), which are decomposed into quality metrics (e.g. duplicated lines of code).

Starting from this quality model, we have defined customizable thresholds on each of the different nodes in order to raise a quality alert if such threshold is violated. We defined the quality alert artifact in JSON with the following metadata:

- **Element id:** a unique identifier for the alert.
- **Name**: name describing the alert.
- **Type**: identifies if the alert is at the quality metric, quality factor or project indicator level.
- **Category**: it is used to bind the alert with the QRs that can solve it. This information is obtained from the node of the quality model that raised the alert and is defined at design time.
- **Date**: Date in which the alert was raised.
- **Status**: Identifies the state of the alert: new, viewed or processed.

The process of raising a quality alert can be illustrated with the following example: A company is using a quality model that includes several quality factors and metrics. One of those quality factors is *Code Quality* that has gone down until reaching the value 0.6 (all values in the quality model are normalized from 0 to 1, where 0 is the worst case scenario and 1 is the best case). In this case, the monitored value is below the threshold defined for this quality factor, which was set to 0.75 (such threshold was defined by the company based on historical data from similar projects and their experience on it). Because of such situation, a quality alert is raised for the *Code Quality* quality factor (see Fig. 3).

Element id	Name	Category	Date	Threshold	Type	Value	Status
prj-codequality-2018-12-17-alert	Code Quality	codequalityCateg	2018-12-17	0.75	FACTOR	0.6	VIEWED

Fig. 3. Example of quality alert in Q-Rapids

4.3   QR Patterns Catalogue

To design and instantiate the QR Patterns Catalogue, we used the PABRE framework [21] and extended it to support the QR generation process. PABRE is a tooled framework that facilitates the reuse in requirement engineering by using requirement patterns. PABRE provides the capability to define a repository with a list of QR patterns that, among other features, can be classified in a schema following a tree-structured form.

In this regard, we defined a schema with the tree structure following the same structure defined in the quality model. In such a manner, there is a clear mapping between the categories of the quality alerts generated and the QRs that can solve them. A generic catalogue of QR patterns is available at the supporting material of this paper [23].

It is worth to remark that such approach enables to have multiple QR patterns for a given quality alert, or that a quality alert at the quality factor level can be solved by the QR patterns bounded to the quality metrics that decompose such quality factor.

For instance, from the previous example, PABRE can retrieve the QRs able to resolve the alert of the *Code Quality* factor. In this case, the QR patterns are: *ComplexFilesReq* (which aims to reduce the ratio of files with a high cyclomatic complexity), *CommentedFilesReq* (which aims to reduce the ratio of files with a high number of commented lines of code) and *DuplicationsReq* (which aims to reduce the ratio of files with a high number of duplicated lines of code). All these QR patterns are bound to the quality metrics *Complex files*, *Commented files* and *Duplications*, respectively; which are quality metrics of the quality model that decompose *Code Quality*.

4.4   QR Patterns

The internal structure of a QR pattern is also based on PABRE [21] and it has been tailored to the specific needs of Q-Rapids. A requirement pattern includes several metadata as described and specified at [24]. But from the point of view of the decision makers, just the following information is visible:

- **Goal**: it describes the objective or problem that the QR pattern aims to solve.
- **Requirement form**: the textual form of the QR pattern. In this textual form, one or more formal parameters can be defined. The formal parameters are free variables that need to be instantiated by the decision makers to produce the QR.
- **Description**: A detailed description of the QR pattern.

An example of the QR pattern *DuplicationsReq* is depicted in Fig. 4.

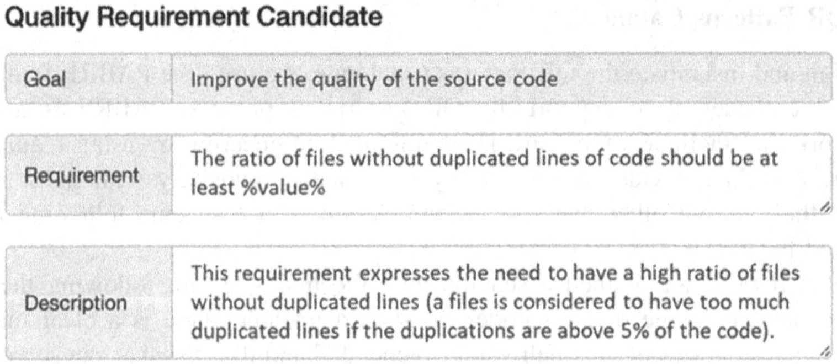

Quality Requirement Candidate

Goal	Improve the quality of the source code

Requirement	The ratio of files without duplicated lines of code should be at least %value%

Description	This requirement expresses the need to have a high ratio of files without duplicated lines (a files is considered to have too much duplicated lines if the duplications are above 5% of the code).

Fig. 4. QR pattern – DuplicationsReq

4.5 Quality Requirements

The QR is an instantiation of the QR pattern. In particular, it is the result produced by the decision maker after instantiating the formal parameter(s) of the QR pattern. To assist the decision maker on instantiating the parameter(s) with appropriate values to solve the quality alert, Q-Rapids will provide simulation techniques that will show the impact that the instantiated QR will have on the elements of the quality model. Such simulation techniques will be based on bayesian networks as proposed in the VALUE framework [25].

Following the example previously described, the decision maker could instantiate the QR patterns provided by Q-Rapids (i.e. *ComplexFilesReq, CommentedFilesReq, DuplicationsReq*) with different values on its parameters and evaluate the impact that those instantiations have on the quality model. During this process of simulation, the decision maker could play with different alternatives and combinations in order to decide the QRs to add. For instance, after playing with different combinations, the decision maker might choose to instantiate the *DuplicationsReq*, setting its value to 85% (leading to the QR "The ratio of files without duplicated lines of code should be at least 85%"), and *ComplexFilesReq*, setting its value to 70% (leading to the QR "The ratio of files with low cyclomatic complexity should be at least 70%"), since, according to the results of the simulation, these two QRs combined would improve the value of *Code Quality* to 0.7, which is above the defined threshold, and hence resolving the quality alert.

4.6 Backlog

In a previous study [26], we identified that companies adopt different practices and tools for documenting QRs. Hence, the Q-Rapids approach for integrating generated QRs in the projects' requirements backlog needs to consider varying documentation practices (e.g., hierarchy level, description, decisions on who documents the generated QR, etc.), as well as multiple requirements management tools (e.g. JIRA, openProject, etc.). To address such heterogeneity, we propose a generic service interface to link the generated QR in Q-Rapids to the projects' backlog. Such service interface can have multiple implementations to meet the needs of each requirements management tool (e.g. JIRA, openProject) and can be tailored to the specific companies' needs. Hence the generated QRs can be added to the project' requirements backlog following specific practices adopted by each company.

5 Evaluation Design, Execution and Analysis

In order to evaluate the artifacts and the process defined, we designed an evaluation that involved the participation of four companies following a structured workshop format. The evaluation was conducted in the four companies of the Q-Rapids consortium, which have different profiles (one large corporation, two large/medium companies and one SME) and produce different types of systems (e.g., from modelling tools to telecommunication software).

The goal of the workshop was twofold. On the one hand, to validate the Q-Rapids QR generation (i.e. the process and its artifacts) and, on the other hand, to conduct an exploratory study of the Quality Requirements documentation process (i.e. the step that documents the QR into the backlogs).

5.1 Workshop Design

The workshop was structured in two parts, following the two goals defined above.

The first part was the validation of the QR generation process. This validation followed a user-oriented perspective involving the representatives of the aforementioned companies. In this regard, the validation focused on the generated artifacts that need to be processed and analysed by the Decision Makers in their tasks of defining and deciding about QRs. Namely: the quality alerts, the QR patterns catalogue and the QR patterns along with the instantiated QRs.

The first part started with a short presentation by the researcher describing the workflow and the structure and contents of each of those artifacts, presenting as well an illustrative example akin to the one presented in Sect. 4, by means of mock-ups. After the description of each artifact, the researcher asked the following questions to retrieve the feedback from the participants. Questions were asked orally to motivate discussion within the company representative participants. The particular questions for each artifact that were investigated are:

- Is the amount of information provided adequate?
- Is the amount of information provided overwhelming?
- Is there any information missing?

The participants were also invited to provide at any time any feedback or comment they wanted to raise.

The second part of the workshop focused on exploring the QRs documentation practice of the companies and identifying important aspects for documenting the generated QRs in the projects' requirements backlogs. Researchers used findings from earlier study with the companies regarding requirements documentation [26] to initiate the discussion. We used requirements documentation templates based on requirements management tool applied in the projects (e.g. JIRA), to guide the discussion and asked the participants to identify aspects they find important while documenting QRs, with a purpose to achieve lightweight and informative QRs documentation.

5.2 Workshop Execution

The workshops were conducted in the four companies of the consortium. The members of the companies who participated in the workshops were involved in the development process or the management of requirements for the software project used as pilot test, and they acted as representatives of their respective development teams. Each workshop had between 1 and 3 members representing the company. Due to the limited amount of participants, analysis was limited to a qualitative assessment and no quantitative study was conducted. Three of the four workshops were conducted in the premises of the company, whereas one workshop was conducted on-line. The workshops were conducted between June 12th 2018 and September 7th 2018. The duration of the workshops range from 124 min to 202 min. Details are summarized in Table 1.

Table 1. Summary of workshops execution.

Company	Bittium	iTTi	NOKIA	Softeam
Country	Finland	Poland	Finland	France
Number of participants	2	1	3	2
Date of the workshop	June 12th 2018	September 7th 2018	June 13th 2018	June 19th 2018
In premises/On-line	in premises	on-line	in premises	in premises
Duration of workshop	196 min	202 min	190 min	124 min

5.3 Data Analysis

The research data were gathered in the workshops by recording the discussions. The recordings were transcribed in a professional transcriptions company in Finland to MsWord documents.

The research data were analyzed by using a combination of thematic synthesis and narrative synthesis [27, 28]. The combination of two synthesis practices was opted because, at a detailed level, the practices of the case companies were very company specific.

The analysis was started by reading through the MsWord documents and dividing the content to sections relevant for the QR generation and QR documentation. The first level division was necessary due to the fact that in the actual discussion the interviewees commented sometimes both viewpoints in parallel.

The documentation-specific sections of the MsWord documents were gathered to Excel tables, one for each case company, the sections were coded and the codes were gathered to higher-order themes according to the thematic synthesis principles [27].

Excel was selected as the tool for the analysis because it is easy to share within an international network of researchers.

The themes identified in the three case companies were summarized and the consistency of the summarized themes were checked by using the principles of the narrative synthesis [28].

6   Results and Findings

6.1   Results on QR Generation

Quality Alerts. All case companies answered that the amount of information provided in the alerts was adequate and not overwhelming. As a respondent summarized, "to me it looks like the most important information". Most companies' representatives provided also valuable feedback and ideas based on their needs in order to improve such quality alert mechanism. All companies pointed out the need for top-down traceability, in order to have "a direct way to access the raw data", or, "the guilty part of the software". Apart from top-down traceability, most participants also required bottom-up traceability. That is, given a quality alert at a lower level (e.g. at the quality metric level), to be able to visualize the values of the upper levels even though their values are not violated.

Finally, one company pointed out the importance of having easy to understand naming on the elements to improve its learnability.

QR Patterns and QRs. All companies answered that the amount of information provided in the QRs was adequate and not overwhelming.

Regarding information missing, some companies' representatives requested to make more explicit the terminology of what is commonly understood as QRs, as a participant requested: "something like stability or security or maintainability". For that, such participant suggested that "non-functional requirement-related keywords could be somehow highlighted in the text. So, that would give clearer understanding that this relates for example to performance issues".

QR Patterns Catalogue. All companies considered the QR patterns catalogue adequate, complete and not overwhelming. As valuable feedback, they pointed out the need to easily "have the ability to add a new quality requirement pattern" as they evolve the quality model. One company, went one step further in this direction, and suggested to be able to extend the QR patterns catalogue on demand. That is, if there is no QR pattern able to solve a particular quality alert there should be the possibility to extend the QR patterns catalogue dynamically.

6.2   Results on QR Documentation

The participants of the workshops raised documentation-related topics important for effective deployment of the QRs generated by the Q-Rapids solution: (1) backwards traceability, (2) information content and end-user value, (3) understandability of QRs, and (4) interfacing to the processes and tools deployed in a company.

While the QRs presented derive from quality issues aggregated from raw quality data by the Q-Rapids quality model, the users of all involved companies highlighted backwards traceability as a key aspect when planning corrective actions for an accepted and documented QR. As one practitioner stated: "So basically if we violate in the development phase something, some quality requirement we already have, we should be able to trace back what requirement we are violating".

The companies had established, well-implemented processes and practices for ASD and quality assurance, and several tools gathering and reporting quality-related information were in use. That sets requirements to the documentation of QRs - the information content of the QRs must be exact and fitted to the processes and practices of the company. The topic was taken up by all companies and is well highlighted in a discussion between the researchers and a practitioner: "But a comment cannot be a mandatory field or is it, will it be used by Q-Rapids?" - "It's not mandatory though, it's…" - "Yeah but okay, do you have a vision that how quality requirements on Q-Rapids could benefit from this comment field information?".

The companies differed from each other in terms of the stability of the deployed processes and tools they used. One had fairly stable processes and requirement repository tools, one was in a middle of change to a new tool, and one company was improving the processes and tools in a continuous manner resulting in a situation where several requirement repository tools were in use in different parts of the organization. Such situation generates challenges to the automatic link for QRs between the Q-Rapids strategic dashboard and the requirement repositories, meaning that there would not be any one-fit-all solution: "But then the question is that which backlog." - "So you have different backlogs following that?" - "Yes…Should we then cover all of, the basic question is that if we are thinking about this mapping and our next step in Q-Rapids, should we select one of those and, omit others?".

7 Tool-Support Implementation

Based on the results of the workshop, we were able to refine the evaluated artifacts and start the implementation of the tools that automate the QR generation and documentation process described in Sect. 4. The modules implemented as a result of those workshops were:

qr-alert module: This module automates the process of evaluating the elements of the quality model and raise an alert if a threshold is violated. Decision makers can specify the threshold for each of these nodes and receive a notification once a violation is triggered. The service can be triggered in time-based manner and configured in terms of running intervals during the day. Moreover, the module allows the user to specify more complex (than simple threshold-based conditions) activation rules that will trigger a quality alert. Users can use any timespan (e.g. range) or a specific date for executing the rule.

qr-generation module: This module automates the process of retrieving the candidate QR patterns that resolve a qr-alert. The module connects to PABRE through its RESTful interface and identifies if a quality alert can be resolved by a QR pattern. If so, it provides the list of QR patterns that can solve the quality alert throughout the tree-based structure.

qrapids-backlog-*: This module is used to store the generated QRs to the backlog. The module defines a common RESTful interface that can have multiple internal implementations, enabling the capability for Q-Rapids to connect to multiple backlogs (e.g. OpenProject, Jira,…).

On top of those components, the workflow was integrated in the Q-Rapids strategic dashboard, which offers to the decision makers an easy-to-use user interface to generate and document QRs, providing also the traceability functionalities requested by the companies through its navigable interface.

Finally, PABRE was also extended to provide the functionality to easily extend the catalogue through import/export functions as well as RESTful methods to dynamically add, update and delete existing QR patterns in the catalogue.

The implementation and documentation of such components is available in github[1].

8 Conclusions and Future Work

In this paper we have presented a data-driven approach for generating and documenting QRs in ASD. Our proposed solution is part of the Q-Rapids framework, which aims at improving QR management in the agile ecosystem. In a nutshell, Q-Rapids collects data from multiple sources of a project (e.g. Jira, SonarQube, github, etc.) and feeds a quality model that computes the quality of the software. Quality alerts are triggered when defined thresholds in the nodes of the quality model are surpassed, which, in turns triggers the QR generation and documentation process. We have formalized such process by means of a BPMN process model where the different tasks, artifacts and repositories involved were defined. To refine and validate our proposal, we have conducted a workshop in four companies of different size and profiles. The results of such workshop have enabled us to iterate on the proposal and implement the tools that automate the activities of the proposed QR generation and documentation process.

As Future work, on the one hand, we plan to improve the current implementation in several directions, such as the simulation techniques to compute the impact of the QRs over the quality model, adding cost functions to estimate the effort to implement such QRs, and improving the overall user experience to facilitate its adoption. On the other hand, we plan to deploy and evaluate the implemented tools in different companies, considering also companies beyond the consortium. For those evaluations, we plan to conduct a quantitative analysis involving a higher number of participants in the study, as well as more complete interviews to obtain additional insights.

Acknowledgments. This work is a result of the Q-Rapids project, which has received funding from the European Union's Horizon 2020 research and innovation programme under grant agreement No 732253.

---

[1] https://github.com/q-rapids (modules qr-alert, qr-generation and qrapids-backlog-*).

References

1. Abbas, N., Gravell, A.M., Wills, G.B.: The impact of organization, project and governance variables on software quality and project success. In: Proceedings of the Agile Conference (2010)
2. Tricentis: Software Fail Watch, 5th edn. White Paper (2018). http://www.tricentis.com/resources/software-fail-watch-5th-edition/. Accessed 19 May 2019
3. Behnamghader, P., Alfayez, R., Srisopha, K., Boehm, B.: Towards better understanding of software quality evolution through commit-impact analysis. In: Proceedings of the QRS (2017)
4. Capgemini: World Quality Report 2015–16. Tech report (2015). www.capgemini.com/resources/world-quality-report-2015-16/. Accessed 19 May 2019
5. Franch, X.: Why are ontologies and languages for software quality increasingly important? In: SERC Talks (2018). http://sercuarc.org/event/serc-talks-why-are-ontologies-and-languages-for-software-quality-increasingly-important. Accessed 19 May 2019
6. Pohl, K., Rupp, C.: Requirements Engineering Fundamentals: A Study Guide for the Certified Professional for Requirements Engineering Exam, 2nd edn. Rocky Nook, San Rafael (2015)
7. Spinellis, D.: Code Quality: The Open Source Perspective. Addison-Wesley, Boston (2006)
8. Wagner, S.: Software Product Quality Control, 2nd edn. Springer, Heidelberg (2015). https://doi.org/10.1007/978-3-642-38571-1
9. Rodríguez, P., Markkula, J., Oivo, M., Turula, K.: Survey on agile and lean usage in finnish software industry. In: Proceedings of the ESEM (2012)
10. Franch, X., et al.: Data-driven elicitation, assessment and documentation of quality requirements in agile software development. In: Krogstie, J., Reijers, H.A. (eds.) CAiSE 2018. LNCS, vol. 10816, pp. 587–602. Springer, Cham (2018). https://doi.org/10.1007/978-3-319-91563-0_36
11. Schwaber, K.: Agile Project Management with Scrum. Microsoft Press, Redmond (2004)
12. Schön, E.-M., Thomaschewski, J., Escalona, M.J.: Agile requirements engineering: a systematic literature review. Comput. Stan. Interfaces **49**, 79–91 (2017)
13. Rodríguez, P., et al.: Continuous deployment of software intensive products and services: a systematic mapping study. J. Syst. Softw. **123**, 263–291 (2017)
14. Bartsch, S.: Practitioners' perspectives on security in agile development. In: Proceedings of the ARES (2011)
15. Maalej, W., Nayebi, M., Johann, T., Ruhe, G.: Toward data-driven requirements engineering. IEEE Softw. **33**(1), 48–54 (2016)
16. Groen, E.C., et al.: A study on how app users report quality aspects in online reviews. In: Proceedings of the RE (2017)
17. Kurtanovic, Z., Maalej, W.: Mining user rationale from software reviews. In: Proceedings of the RE (2017)
18. Lu, M., Liang, P.: Automatic classification of non-functional requirements from augmented app user reviews. In: Proceedings of the EASE (2017)
19. Liu, X., et al.: Deriving user preferences of mobile apps from their management activities. ACM Trans. Inf. Syst. **35**(4), 39 (2017)
20. Franch, X., et al.: A situational approach for the definition and tailoring of a data-driven software evolution method. In: Krogstie, J., Reijers, H.A. (eds.) CAiSE 2018. LNCS, vol. 10816, pp. 603–618. Springer, Cham (2018). https://doi.org/10.1007/978-3-319-91563-0_37
21. Palomares, C., Quer, C., Franch, X.: PABRE-Proj: applying patterns in requirements elicitation. In: Proceedings of the RE (2013)

22. Martinez-Fernandez, S., Jedlitschka, A., Guzman, L., Vollmer, A.M.: A quality model for actionable analytics in rapid software development. In: Proceedings of the SEAA (2018)
23. Oriol, M., et al.: Appendix of: data-driven elicitation of quality requirements in agile companies (2019). http://www.essi.upc.edu/~moriol/qr_elicitation/
24. PABRE API Documentation. http://gessi3.cs.upc.edu/pabre-ws/doc/
25. Mendes, E., Rodriguez, P., Freitas, V., Baker, S., Atoui, M.A.: Towards improving decision making and estimating the value of decisions in value-based software engineering: the VALUE framework. Softw. Qual. J. 26(2), 607–656 (2018)
26. Behutiye, W., Karhapää, P., Costal, D., Oivo, M., Franch, X.: Non-functional requirements documentation in agile software development: challenges and solution proposal. In: Felderer, M., Méndez Fernández, D., Turhan, B., Kalinowski, M., Sarro, F., Winkler, D. (eds.) PROFES 2017. LNCS, vol. 10611, pp. 515–522. Springer, Cham (2017). https://doi.org/10.1007/978-3-319-69926-4_41
27. Cruzes, D.S., Dybå, T.: Recommended steps for thematic synthesis in software engineering. In: Proceedings of the ESEM (2011)
28. Cruzes, D.S., Dybå, T., Runeson, P., Höst, M.: Case studies synthesis: a thematic, cross-case, and narrative synthesis worked example. Empirical Softw. Eng. 20(6), 1634–1665 (2015)

On the Use of Non-technical Requirements for the Evaluation of FOSS Software Components

Juan Pablo Carvallo[1]([✉]), Fabián Carvajal[1], Esteban Crespo[1],
Lucia Mendez[1], María José Torres[2], and Rosalva Vintimilla[1]

[1] Universidad del Azuay (UDA), Av. 24 de Mayo 7-77 y Francisco Moscoso,
Cuenca, Ecuador
{jpcarvallo,fabianc,ecrespo,lmendez,
rvintimilla}@uazuay.edu.ec
[2] Integral IT, La Verbena 26 y Emilio López Ortega, Cuenca, Ecuador
mariajose.torres@integralit.ec

Abstract. Modern enterprises rely on Information Systems specifically designed to manage the increasing complexity of their operation. In the usual case, they are built as hybrid systems which integrate several software components of different nature and origins e.g.; legacy systems, web services, commercial components (typically referred as COTS) and, Free and/or Open Source Software (FOSS). The evaluation of individual software components is highly relevant in this kind of system and is usually conducted with the support of software Quality Models. However, these artifacts usually consider only the evaluation of technical quality requirements, in detriment of non-technical ones (e.g. costs, legal and quality of suppliers) which can be just as critical, particularly in the selection of COTS and FOSS. In this paper, we propose an extension to preexisting software Quality Models, intended to deal with technical and non-technical quality requirements in a homogeneous and holistic way. The relevance of the approach is illustrated in relation to four industrial FOSS adoption processes.

Keywords: Quality model · FOSS · Free and open source software ·
Quality requirements · Non-technical quality requirements

1 Introduction

Modern enterprises rely on Information Systems (IS) specifically designed to manage the increasing complexity of their operation. In the last decades, several alternatives to the traditional development of software from scratch, have emerged in order to construct such IS. In the usual case, they are built as hybrid systems which integrate several software components of different nature and origins e.g., legacy systems, web services, commercial components (typically referred as COTS) and, Free and/or Open Source Software (FOSS). Because of the nature of hybrid systems, proper selection evaluation of software components plays a prominent role. This critical task is usually conducted with the support of *Software Quality Models* (QM) [1], artifacts specifically engineered to support the specification, prioritization and evaluation of requirements, the

© Springer Nature Switzerland AG 2019
M. Piattini et al. (Eds.): QUATIC 2019, CCIS 1010, pp. 64–78, 2019.
https://doi.org/10.1007/978-3-030-29238-6_5

description of software components, and the identification of gaps among their features and requirements.

Several proposals for QM and QM standards have been proposed [1–4], particularly in the case of FOSS several proposals exist e.g. QSOS [5], OpenBRR [6], QualOSS [7], EFFORT [8], most of them as extensions of the ISO/IEC 9126 [9] standard. However, these approaches focus on the evaluation of technical functional and non-functional (internal and external) requirements, forsaking other non-technical aspects which can be just as relevant (e.g. economic, legal and quality of the provider), particularly when acquiring software from third parties e.g. communities and commercial suppliers.

In [12, 13] we found an extension to the ISO/IEC 9126 quality standard, which deals with technical and non-technical quality requirements in a homogeneous and holistically way. 3 characteristics and 15 non-technical characteristics were added to the original ISO/IEC 9126 catalog (which can also extend its successor, the ISO/IEC 25010 standard) for this purpose. This extension is called the extended ISO/IEC 9126 catalog. However, due to its nature, and after conducting an extensive systematic literature review (SLR) to identify critical success factors, potential benefits and risks in the adoption of OSS, we identified that this extension is not enough to deal with non-technical quality requirements in the case of FOSS. In this paper, we propose a new extension to the extended ISO/IEC 9126 quality standard required to support the evaluation and selection of OSS.

In addition to this section, this paper is structured as follows: Sect. 2 introduces previous and related work; Sect. 3 presents the SLR in which this work is based and its main findings; Sect. 4 introduces the new proposal for the extended ISO/IEC 9126 catalog; Sect. 5 evaluates its relevance in relation to four FOSS industrial adoption processes in which we have actively participated; finally, Sect. 6 presents the conclusions and lines of future work.

2 Previous and Related Work

2.1 The ISO/IEC 9126 Quality

The ISO/IEC 9126 software quality standard is one of the most widespread quality standard available in the software engineering community. It proposes quality models as the artifacts that keep track of the quality factors that are of interest in a particular context, i.e. for a software domain of interest. From the 4 parts that compose it, we focus here on the 9216-1 part of the standard [9], which presents a catalogue of quality factors intended for the evaluation of software components.

The ISO/IEC 9126-1 standard fixes 6 top-level characteristics: functionality, reliability, usability, efficiency, maintainability, and portability. It also fixes their further refinement into 27 sub-characteristics but does not elaborate the quality model below this level, making thus the model flexible. Sub-characteristics are in turn decomposed into attributes, which represent the properties that the software products belonging to the domain of interest exhibit. Intermediate hierarchies of sub-characteristics and attributes may appear making thus the model highly structured.

When the domain of interest is complex, building ISO/IEC 9126-based quality models may be tough. We apply the methodology described in [6] for ISO/IEC 9126-based **Quality Model Construction**.

2.2   The Extended ISO/IEC 9126

[12, 13] contain an extension of ISO/IEC 9126 technical characteristics and sub-characteristics with additional non/technical ones arranged in an ISO/IEC 9126-1 tree-like structure, thus the resulting catalogue includes high-level quality characteristics and sub-characteristics, and also lower-level quality attributes. To build the hierarchy we followed the 6 step method presented in [10, 11].

The top-level of the hierarchy has been structured with 3 non/technical character-istics: *Supplier*, *Costs*, and *Product*. These three characteristics group non-technical quality features required to measure the supplier capacity to address and support the project, the implementation costs and the out-of-the-box quality and effort required to get the component running. These non-technical quality characteristics have been further decomposed into 15 non-technical sub-characteristics (see Table 1). Some of them have been decomposed into other sub-characteristics, whenever they were required for structuring or leveling purposes. Following the construction approach, sub-characteristics have been further decomposed into over 160 non-technical quality attributes.

Table 1. Non-technical quality features upper-level hierarchy.

Characterstics/ Sub-charact.	Definition
Supplier	
Organizational structure	Description of the organizational structure of the supplier company.
Positioning and Strength	Description of the position of the supplier company in the market.
Reputation	Capability of the supplier to perform similar projects based on past experiences and certifications.
Services Offered	Description of the services offered by the supplier.
Support	Description of the support mechanisms offered by the supplier.
Cost	
Licensing Schema	Description of the COTS component licensing options.
Licensing Costs	Detail of the costs for the different licensing options
Platform Cost	Estimation of the cost for the required production platform
Implementation Cost	Estimation of implementation costs based on similar past experiences
Network Cost	Estimation of additional cost for network operation.
Product	
Stability	Attributes of the product that bears on the stability of the product.
Ownership	Attributes in relation to intellectual property rights.
Deliverables	Detail of the out of the box and post-implementation deliverables.
Parameterization / Customization	Attributes in relation to the initial effort required for the product to operate.
Guarantees	Detail of the guarantees provided over the product.

Other approaches (please refer to [7, 8] for detailed description) also address the need of non-technical attributes to be considered in evaluation and selection, however, their proposals can be considered non-structured a subset of our approach. We claim that technical and non-technical aspects shall be dealt similarly using a common framework instead of divided assets. To achieve this goal, we propose to extend the ISO/IEC 9126-1 catalog of quality factors with non-technical factors following the same layout than in this standard. In particular, as done in the standard, we fix just the two higher levels of the hierarchy, avoiding excessive prescription of the proposal. We call this catalog the non-technical extension of the ISO/IEC catalog (NT-ISO/IEC catalog for short) to distinguish it from the previous one (Fig. 1):

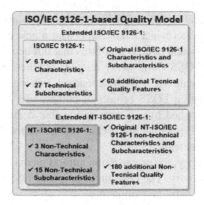

Fig. 1. The different catalogues found.

2.3   OSS Adoption Strategies

The concept of strategy comes from the Greek 'strategos' to denote 'leadership'. An OSS Adoption Strategy is the way in which an organization incorporates OSS as part of its customer offering. In [14], authors describe six different OSS adoption strategies which in the following paragraphs, are presented in ascendant order according to the strength of the relationship between the adopter and its FOSS Developer Community (FOSS-DC). For instance, in Release strategy, there is not relationship with FOSS-DC. In the following bullets, the benefits, and requirements are presented for each strategy.

- **Release:** It implies that the organization releases personalized software as FOSS but does not care whether an OSS community takes it up or forms around it. Additionally, no FOSS-DC is involved. The purpose of this strategy is to develop FOSS (with technical quality) for own use, and offer it to organizations with similar requirements in order to: (a) standardize its subjacent processes; or (b) spread good practices, or (c) reduce cost and risk by avoiding the development. The first two may be related to improving the market, and the third may be focused on strengthening the corporate group companies. In this sense, an example of this strategy can be observed in the public sector, where public entities make their software available to others, releasing it under an OSS license. This strategy demands a minimum involvement with FOSS-DC and the organization does not care for FOSS evolution or maintenance.

- **Acquisition:** This strategy refers to the use of existing FOSS code without contributing to its OSS project/community. Because the adopter organization does not necessarily has, an interest in new releases of the FOSS component, the involvement with the community is minimum after obtains the software and its documentation. In some cases, other companies or freelancers can provide the FOSS component. The specific benefits are that it requires a minimum involvement with FOSS-DC, and does not care about FOSS evolution or maintenance.
- **Integration:** It involves the active participation of an organization in an FOSS community (to share and co-create FOSS) but not necessarily leading or influencing it. The organization establishes a relationship with a new external stakeholder: The Support Forum, from which obtains bug fixes that not necessarily are present in the next version that the FOSS Community releases for the component.
- **Fork:** It means to create an own independent version of the software that is available from an existing FOSS project or community. The FOSS-DC is forked too. This strategy is applied by an organization that decides to continue the (generally critical) FOSS component and FOSS-DC evolution for its own account, to achieve specific requirements.
- **Takeover:** In this strategy, the organization attracts an existent FOSS community to support its business activity. The creation of its own FOSS-DC pursues to 'take the control' of critical software development.
- **Initiative:** It is oriented to initiate an FOSS project and to establish a community around it. The organization creates its own FOSS-DC, because requires to 'take the control' of critical software development.

3 Searching for Relevant NT-Quality Attributes for OSS

Although FOSS has been increasingly used, particularly in the last decade, critical success and failure factors, risks, benefits, and barriers associated with this paradigm have not been deeply analyzed. The lack of knowledge in these relevant issues hampers FOSS adoption both in private and public industries. In 2018, we performed a systematic literature review (SLR) to gain understanding of how these factors affect FOSS implementation. 11 previous SLR where identified, none of them addressing these issues, which endorses our claim that more study is required in the field.

The SRL was conducted following Kitchenham's [15] methodological guidelines. To be rigorous, a protocol was established to search and collect data from the existing FOSS literature. Research question included in the protocol where:

Q1: Which success and failure factors have been documented in the adoption of FOSS in the industry?
Q2: Which are the main risks identified in the adoption of FOSS?
Q3: Which are the perceived benefits in the adoption of FOSS?
Q4: In which software domains has the adoption of FOSS been successful?
Q5: Which are the main factors that prevents organizations from adopting FOSS?

The generic search string was constructed using the words *Open Source Software, OSS, FOSS, FLOSS* and *Freeware* as synonyms; to complete the string we added the words *risk, failure, success, barriers, advantages, benefits* and *application domain*. The search string was built using the "OR" and "AND" logical operators. Search string was constructed to address titles, abstracts and related words: *Title: (Open Source Software OR OSS OR FOSS OR FLOSS OR Freeware) AND Abstract: (Open Source Software OR OSS OR FOSS OR FLOSS OR Freeware) AND (risk OR failure OR success OR barriers OR Advantages OR Opinion OR Impediments OR FLOSS).* The string was properly adapted to the characteristics of the repositories where searches where conducted: IEEE Xplore, ACM, Springer Link, and WOS.

A total of 782 documents were retrieved from the repositories; titles and abstracts where stored in an excel sheet. In a first refinement, only academic articles written in Spanish or English, with methodological basis (e.g. experiment, case study, Systematic Reviews, Systematic Mappings), with at least 5 references in google scholar where included in the study.

Duplicated articles were excluded and we limited the study to written after 1998 of the following types: Journals, Conferences, Magazines, Technical Reports and Books. In a second refinement, all abstracts were reviewed in full, by at least two researchers of the team, to select which were relevant and sound for the study. Documents marked as "relevant" or "maybe relevant" for at least one of the researchers were selected to be full text redden. The documents were extracted, to read the summary, to see if the article could contribute with the investigation, once read, the researchers granted ratings of: "Yes", "No" and "Maybe". Only articles written in Spanish and English where included in the study. At the end, only 155 documents were selected to be full text reviewed. From those, only 92 papers answered, at least, one of the research questions. In addition, backward snowballing techniques allowed for the identification of 33 additional references; only 17 resulted relevant for the study. A table was specifically designed for data extraction and implemented using a spreadsheet editor. Table was refined/extended through the study, to include all information extracted from selected papers, relevant to answer research questions.

The most relevant success factors identified in the study are: (a) Management: software evolution, licensing, project management; (b) Community: community activities and communication; (c) Support: internal and external; (d) training: staff training; (e) Policies: IT enterprise policies.

Regarding failure factors, the most relevant are: (a) Human Resources: IT provider, end users, technical users, development and community; (b) Competitiveness: Market characteristics; (c) Policy: OSS and IT adoption policies absence.

Several risks were also identified, the most relevant are: (a) Laws: assume the responsibility; (b) Software: complexity, processes, tests, support, technology, integration, and architecture; (c) Human resources: developers, community, experts, management, lack of guarantee.

Several benefits have also been identified in the study: (a) Flexibility: source code availability; (b) human resources: community, providers and contributions.

The application domains identified in the study are: (a) system software: Operating systems, server software; (b) application software: mobile apps, office, medical, commercial software, educational, browsers, databases managers, automation and control.

Finally, several barriers for the adoption of FOSS have also been identified: (a) human resources: training, developers, experience, uncertainty, motivation, lack of trained professionals; (b) software: quality, migration, product, version, repositories.

Table 2 presents a relation among the factors and the percentage of papers relating them with the main issues considered in the SLR, namely success and failure factors, risks, benefits, and barriers associated with the FOSS paradigm.

Table 2. Percentages of documents relating factors with categories in the SLR.

Factor	Success	Failure	Risks	Benefits	Domain	Barriers
Management	20%	-	-	-	-	
Community	18%	-	-	-	-	
Support	11%	6.10%	-	-	-	4.60%
Training/learning	10%	-	-	1.80%	-	
Policy	10%	12.10%	-	-	-	5.60%
Costs	8%	-	9.50%	-	-	4.60%
Software	7%	-	23%	8.60%	-	15.70%
System Software	-	-	-	-	53.80%	-
Application Software	-	-	-	-	43.10%	-
Software testing	-	6%	-	-	-	-
Enterprise and organizations	6%	-	-	8.20%	-	9.30%
Control	4%	-	1.40%	-	-	-
Human Resources	4%	39.40%	18.60%	19.50%	-	38.90%
Public sector management	1%	-	-	-	-	-
Information technologies	0.50%	-	-	-	-	-
Perceived values	0.50%	-	-	-	-	-
Competitiveness	-	18.20%	-	-	-	-
Planning	-	9.10%	-	-	-	-
Licensing	-	6.10%	-	0.50%	-	4.60%
Usability	-	3%	-	-	-	-
Laws	-	-	29.70%	-	-	-
Security	-	-	9.50%	5.40%	-	7.40%
Adoption	-	-	4.10%	-	-	-
Model	-	-	1.40%	-	-	-
Scalability	-	-	1.40%	-	-	-
Documentation	-	-	1.40%	-	-	1.90%
Profitability	-	-	-	16.70%	-	-
Flexibility	-	-	-	20.80%	-	-
Development	-	-	-	7.20%	3.10%	-
Time saving	-	-	-	5.40%	-	-
Component Integration	-	-	-	3.20%	-	2.80%
Innovation	-	-	-	1.80%	-	-
Hardware	-	-	-	0.90%	-	-
Compatibility	-	-	-	-	-	4.60%

* Main characteristics from each factor ave been shaded.

4   The Catalogue of NT-Quality Attributes for OSS

Similarly, to the catalogue in [12, 13], the *Extended FOSS NT-ISO/IEC 9126-1* quality catalog (see Table 3), has been structured with a three-levels hierarchical decomposition. At the first level, we have included four main Categories: External Context Actors

Table 3. Extended NT-ISO/IEC 9126-1 quality catalogue.

Code	Hierarchical Categorization	Description	No. Ref.	Meaning	A	I	F	T	I	R
A	COMMUNITY									
A.1	FOSS-DC									
A.1.1	Perceived image	The negative impression about service and future support of FOSS when the payment option is dominant.	3	Barrier		x	x	x	x	
A.2	FOSS-DC SUPPORT									
A.2.1	Feedback	The FOSS-DC feedback implies a set of community practices focused on reinforce the relationships with adopters.	17	Success		x	x	x	x	
A.2.2	Lack of Support	The lack of support that FOSS-DC offer to adopter	5	Barrier		x	x	x	x	
A.2.3	Continuity of project	Loss of interest by part of the developers or FOSS-DC, which causes that FOSS project disappears.	2	Failure		x	x	x	x	
A.2.4	Continuity of community	Loss of interest by part of the developers or FOSS-DC, which causes that FOSS-DC disappears.	2	Failure		x	x	x	x	
A.2.5	Continuity of software development orientation	Loss of interest by part of the FOSS-DC, which conduct the software development in a different direction than the adopter	3	Failure		x				
A.2.6	Version control	The FOSS-DC manages a versioning of FOSS and its documentation	3	Success	x	x	x	x	x	x
A.2.7	Version frequency	The FOSS-DC versioning FOSS with high frequency. It can generate a problem	2	Risk	x	x	x	x	x	x
A.3	FOSS-DC SUPPORT IMPACT ON ADOPTER									
A.3.1	Development effort reduction	The FOSS support contributes to reduce the development time	17	Success		x	x	x	x	
A.3.2	Accessibility to public information	FOSS can benefit to adopters and citizens in general, fostering the access to public information.	2	Success	x	x	x	x	x	x
A.4	UNIVERSITIES, RESEARCH INSTITUTES, AND COMMERCIAL ENTERPRISES									
A.4.1	Cooperation	Cooperation activities between research staff and development staff	17	Success	x	x	x	x	x	x
A.5	EXTERNAL DEVELOPERS									
A.5.1	Participation	Voluntary participation of external developers.	5	Success	x	x	x	x	x	x
B	ORGANIZATIONAL ISSUES									
B.1	RESOURCE MANAGEMENT POLICIES									
B.1.1	Resource optimization	In the vertical application development, the open source models have promote a cost reduction through reuse, collaboration, and shared code.	18	Benefit	x	x	x	x	x	x
B.1.2	No dependence on software providers/vendors	FOSS-DC support to avoid traditional software providers/vendors lock-in (dependencies of negotiation conditions imposed by the supplier)	11	Benefit	x	x	x	x	x	x
B.1.3	Cost management	In order to reduce the costs, the adopter identifies the components of TCO (Total Cost of Ownership) correspondent to FOSS adoption process	5	Risk	x	x	x	x	x	x
B.2	QUALITY POLICIES									
B.2.1	Security strengths	FOSS brings more security than proprietary software because FOSS is audited constantly by external entities.	12	Benefit	x	x	x	x	x	x
B.2.2	Security weakness	Possible vulnerabilities in security schema, which can be originated in the use of libraries of open source, architectural weakness, human errors, incorrect code modifications, among others)	6	Risk		x	x	x	x	
B.2.3	Reliability	FOSS is more reliable than proprietary software because FOSS has the collaboration of developers around the world.	4	Benefit	x	x	x	x	x	x
B.3	INNOVATION POLICIES									
B.3.1	Innovation promotion	The FOSS adoption contributes to increase the innovation	3	Benefit	x	x	x	x	x	x
B.4	LEGAL AND REGULATORY FULFILLMENT									
B.4.1	Lawful knowledge	This knowledge is required to manage adequately some legal and regulatory FOSS issues, mainly related to licensing, Intellectual Property (IP) and Copyright.	---	Barrier	x	x	x	x	x	x
B.4.2	Licensing	Problems of license use and license compatibility	5	Barrier	x	x	x	x	x	x
B.5	TRAINING POLICIES									
B.5.1	Cost of FOSS training	The training investment required by an FOSS project can constitute an entry barrier, if it has not an adequate estimation and management	2	Barrier	x	x	x	x	x	x

(continued)

Table 3. *(Continued)*

B.6	**DECISION-MAKING POLICIES**									
B.6.1	Competitiveness	The FOSS projects must have the minimum competitiveness level in order to make viable them, comparing with proprietary software. The decision about initiate or not an FOSS project considers its competitiveness.	4	Faliure	x	x	x	x	x	x
B.6.2	Strategic Staff Commitment	The support of Strategic Staff to FOSS project constitutes a critical success factor, in particular when the risk or uncertainty levels are high.	2	Success	x	x	x	x	x	x
B.7	**KNOWLEDGE MANAGEMENT POLICIES**									
B.7.1	Organization's experience with OSS	Knowledge and improvements obtained by the organization from previous technical experiences about OSS.	---	Benefit		x	x	x	x	
B.7.2	Staff's OSS experience outside the organization	Knowledge and improvements that the staff has had outside the organization.	---	Benefit		x	x	x	x	
B.7.3	Previous Related Knowledge	This knowledge enables the organization to assimilate and use new outside knowledge. It is both commonality (required to facilitate the communication) and individual (required to foster the diversity).	---	Success	x	x	x	x	x	x
C	**GOVERNMENT POLICIES**									
C.1	**ECONOMIC DEVELOPMENT**									
C.1.1	FOSS Economic Postioning	Refers to the current situation of FOSS in the economic development of the country	6	Benefit	x	x	x	x	x	x
C.1.2	FOSS Economic sustainability	Refers to the trend of FOSS in the economic development of the country	---	Success	x	x	x	x	x	x
C.2	**INNOVATION POLICIES**									
C.2.1	FOSS adoption promotion policies	Policies designed by government to coordinate the innovation development	2	Success	x	x	x	x	x	x
C.3	**PUBLIC POLICIES**									
C.3.1	Incentives to TICs' adoption	The Government encourages organizations to test, adopt, and use new technologies.	3	Support	x	x	x	x	x	x
D	**STAFF CAPACITIES DEVELOPMENT**									
D.1	**CHANGE MANAGEMENT**									
D.1.1	FOSS acceptance	The FOSS adoption is affected by staff level of preparation and motivation to change	6	Barrier	x	x	x	x	x	x
D.1.2	FOSS Skills Development	The inner staff has not the skills required to support the FOSS adoption process (e.g. collaborative teams, crowdsourcing, agile paradigm, etc.)	2	Barrier		x	x	x	x	x
D.1.3	Technical and Business training	The FOSS adoption process requires that the staff has acquired a minimum knowledge (concepts and practices)	6	Success		x	x	x	x	x
D.1.4	Soft Skills	Learning Capacity: to use and renew available knowledge. Absorptive Capacity: to identify, acquire, assimilate, transform, and exploit knowledge. Networking Capacity: to establish, maintain, and expand relationships among actors to exchange knowledge, value, and collaboration. Disseminative Capacity: facilitates the external and internal knowledge and expertise transfering.	---	Success	x	x	x	x	x	x
D.2	**ORGANIZATIONAL CULTURE**									
D.2.1	Openness and Flexibility	Openness to new ideas and approaches to solve problems, facilitates the creative solutions generation, discovering new paths to achieve them, and decreases the change resistance.	---	Success		x	x	x	x	
D.2.2	Risk Tolerance	The organizational risk tolerance implies the willingness to engage in projects that can have uncertain outcomes.	---	Success		x	x	x	x	
E	**FOSS SUPPORT**									
E.1	**SUPPORT AVAILABILITY**									
E.1.1	Inner technical support	The inner staff should be enough to solve user requirements	3 / 4	Barrier / Risk		x	x	x	x	
E.1.2	Source code availability	Availability of source code to review and/or modify.	13	Benefit		x	x	x	x	
E.1.3	Business-IT alignment	Alignment between Information Technologies and Business Model, i.e., to what extent the IT operations support the business goals, business strategy and mission.	---	Success	x	x	x	x	x	x
E.1.4	Strategic commitment for FOSS adoption	Strategic commitment to FOSS: initiative sponsoring and basic requirements (e.g., budget, resources management support, business process management support)	---	Success		x	x	x	x	
E.2	**SUPPORT IMPROVEMENTS**									
E.2.1	Efficiency	The efficient use of resources destined to FOSS adoption	6	Benefit		x	x	x	x	
E.2.2	Integration	Applications with open source code can be used and modified to be integrate according to particular requirements.	4	Benefit	x	x	x	x	x	x
E.2.3	Compatibility	A vertical change from proprietary software to FOSS, can originate compatibility problems with previous formats.	5	Barrier	x	x	x	x	x	x

Relationships, Organizational Issues, Government Policies, Staff Capacities Development, and FOSS Support. We have also proposed a refinement of the *Support* sub-characteristic, categorized under the *Supplier* Characteristic, in the original Extended NT-ISO/IEC 9126-1 quality catalogue, to make it more suitable for the FOSS evaluation context. This sub-characteristic has been renamed FOSS Support when used for FOSS evaluation purposes.

Each characteristic has been further decomposed with two additional hierarchical levels, the first one including sub-characteristics and the second one including attributes, which are observable quality features associated to one or more measures, relevant for the statement of organizational quality requirements and the assessment of FOSS quality, during evaluation.

We have also incorporated additional columns to shape the catalog structure. The first one "Meaning to Adopter", allows for traceability with the main category of factors in the SLR from which the attribute has been identified, namely, Benefit, Entry Barrier, Risk, Success Factor, Fail Factor, or Support. In addition, we have also considered the six OSS adoption strategies proposed in [14] (see Sect. 2.3). These strategies model the strength of the relationship between the adopter and its more representative external context actor: the FOSS Developer Community (hereafter called FOSS-DC). Each attribute has a different relevance (or even no relevance) depending on which adoption strategy is selected by the organization. For instance: if the organization opts for the *Acquisition Strategy*, the attributes *A.2.1 FOSS-DC feedback* and *A.2.2 Lack of FOSS-DC Support* are not applicable, because, in the practice, the FOSS component is used as-is, without modification, and in consequence, FOSS-DC feedback or support is not required. On the other hand, if the adopter opts for the *Fork Strategy*, the active role of FOSS-DC in terms of feedback and support is critical.

The attributes *A.2.6 Version Control*, and *A.2.7 Version Frequency* already appear in the extended NT-ISO/IEC 9126-1 quality catalog (under the product/stability sub-characteristic), but our study has shown that it may have greater impact in FOSS adoption processes, in terms of risks introduced to the project. Version release frequency is usually higher and more flexible in FOSS, since it responds to the dynamics of the FOSS-DC. The increase in version release frequency hampers ability of technical staff to incorporate (parametrize, adapt, modify, test, integrate, and deploy) new versions of FOSS, with significant impact maintainability of IS.

Attributes *B.1.3 Cost Management* and *B.5.1 Cost of Training* are included in the original extended NT-ISO/IEC 9126-1 quality catalogue, but in this work we present a refinement with measures specific for FOOS. In the same way, attributes categorized under Quality Policies (*B.2.1 Security strengths*, *B.2.2 Security weakness*, and *B.2.3 Reliability*) are part of original extended Technical ISO/IEC quality catalogue, but here they are oriented to FOSS adoption support.

In addition, the original extended NT-ISO/IEC catalogue includes a significant amount of attributes intended for the evaluation of licensing schemas. In our context, however, we need to be specific in relation to aspects such as the access, manipulation and redistribution of open source code. Specific measures for each attribute have been defined (not included in this paper due to space limitations, see Table 4 for an excerpt).

Table 4. Except of measures for extended quality catalogue

Code	METRIC				Requires Baseline
	Name	Description	Measurement	Acceptable values	
A	**COMMUNITY**				
A.1	**FOSS-DC**				
A.1.1	Support image perceived	Identifies if adopter has a positive or negative image of FOSS-DC support, in a considering where payed options are the majority.	Image perception identified in adopters	Yes / No	No
A.2	**FOSS-DC SUPPORT**				
A.2.1	Feedback support	The support provided by community in form of patches, documentation, business best practices description, software parametrization, instalation/integration guidelines, and so on.	Effective Support provided by FOOS-DC	Yes / No	No
A.2.2	Lack of support from FOSS-DC	Occasions when the OSS-DC brings insufficient or inexistent support to software products that adopter works with	Responsesw from the FOSS-DC with no sufficient information about FOSS component	Positive integer values	No
A.2.3	FOSS-DC continuity	Identifies if FOSS-DC maintains the support to specific software project	Number of versions released, patches, or effective support activities for the specific FOSS softwar,e in the last period.	Positive integer values	No
A.2.4	FOSS support continuity	Identifies if FOSS-DC maintains its activity	Number of versions released, patches, or effective support activities for any of its FOSS projects, in the last period.	Positive integer values	No
A.2.5	Software development orientation continuity	The FOSS-DC maintain its development and support for the software, with no modifications in relation to the adopter expectation	Continuity verified through the releases, patchs, documentation, and functionalities of FOSS	Yes / No	No
A.2.6	Version control	The FOSS-DC manages its versioning schema for OSS and its documentation	Availability verified in a location referred by FOSS-I	Yes / No	Yes

5   Validating the Catalogue in Practice

In 2008, the Government of "Country Blinded" issued a specific order to enforce the FOSS adoption in the Public Administration. During the first years of the ruling, the efforts for the adoption were isolated and chaotic, causing some disappointment and a kind of misgiving about the regulation.

Table 5. Validation cases.

		DESCRIPTION	TYPE	SIZE/SCOPE	GOAL	REQUIREMENT	ACHIVEMENT
Verification Case	1	VrC1 is a public company. It's scope of action is defined as a strategic public service. Its main purpose is the generation and provision of electrical service and this must respond to the principles of mandatory, generality, universality, responsibility, universality, accessibility, regularity, continuity and quality.	PUBLIC	BIG / NATION WIDE SCOPE	Migrate an mail server plataform from an Exchange Architecture to an Zimbra FOSS architecture	1. Implement a seven nodes plataform for balancing the mail traffic that comes from the the mail domains that are imple-mented in the Ministerio de Electricidad. 2. Fine Tune the plataform in order to protect the mail boxes from no desired messages –SPAM-. 3. Integrate Zimbra FOSS authentication with a Privative Authentication Plataform. 4. Integrate Zimbra FOSS whith an li-censed mail filter solution they already have imple-mented.	After three years, users have adopted the new plat-form successfully. Technicians have learnt to maintain and correct any issues that have come during operation. They don't ask for external support
	2	VrC2 is a public institution whose mission is to "distribute and market electric energy in optimal technical and economic conditions to meet the needs of our customers as a basic foundation of society, in accordance with the current legal framework, seeking social benefit, efficient use of energy and sustained economic equilibrium, through processes of continuous improvement and protection of the environment."	PUBLIC	SMALL / PROVINCE SCOPE	Mail Server's Plataform using Zimbra FOSS implementation and maintenance	1. Implement a single node plataform for the institutional mail service. 2. Configure the DNS based mail authentica-tion registries. 3. Train the insitution's TIC personal about mail service and basic Linux Sys-tem Administra-tion concepts.	After a year and a half, users have adopted the new plat-form; but still have some problems about Mail service's best practices. Technician have some ma-jor problems when trouble-shooting common operating issues. The need for a higher support level is manifested.
	3	VrC3 is an agency in charge of control and regulate the protection and improvement of animal health, plant health and food safety.	PUBLIC	MEDIUM / PROVINCE SCOPE	Implement an Open Source environment for controlling user's workstation software life cycles, centralized authentication, and deploy office software according the job in four different areas	1. Implement an alternative to MS Active Direc-tory for control-ling the domain' workstations. 2. Analyze and Deploy an OSS alternative to MS Windows for the users' workstations. 3. Analyze and deploy an OSS alternative to the user's workstations software accord-ing to the need of the area.	After six months, users have adopted the new operating system, even when there are some applications that are completely new for them. Technician have experi-enced one major problem they couldn't solve by their self. They have an aditional contract for higher support level for one year.
	4	VrC4 is a private company at the service of the Ecuadorian community for 40 years, developing healthy, natural and functional foods for all its consumers.	PRIVATE	BIG / NATION WIDE SCOPE	Mail Server's Plataform using Zimbra FOSS implementation and maintenance	1. Implement a single node plataform for the institutional mail service. 2. Configure the DNS based mail authentica-tion registries. 3. Train the insitution's TIC personal about mail service and basic Linux Sys-tem Administra-tion concepts.	After four years, users have adopted the new plata-form successfully. Some SPAM problems have arised, but they can be solved easily. Technician have earned experience in troubleshooting operating issues after the training sessions. They have an addi-tional support contract for consumed hours.

To address this issue, a group of engineers working in the public sector, conducted a project to develop a set of artifacts to guide the adoption of open technologies in the country. The results of this project include a catalog of templates and guidelines specifically designed for this purpose. With the support of these deliverables, since 2016 the number of projects to migrating to FOSS alternatives in the country has increased both, in the public and private sectors.

Table 6. Impact of NT-quality attributes in validation cases.

Non-Technical Quality Features		Verification Case				Total Impact
		1	2	3	4	
A	**COMMUNITY**					
A.1	**OSS-DC**					
A.1.1	Perceived image	5	5	3	5	18
A.2	**OSS-DC SUPPORT**					
A.2.1	Feedback	5	5	5	5	20
A.2.2	Lack of OSS-DC Support	5	N/A	3	N/A	8
A.2.3	Continuity of OSS-DC	5	3	3	4	15
A.2.4	Continuity of FOSS-DC	N/A	N/A	2	N/A	2
A.2.5	Continuity of Software development orientation	N/A	N/A	N/A	N/A	0
A.2.6	Version control	5	5	5	5	20
A.2.7	Version frequency	2	1	1	2	6
A.3	**OSS-DC SUPPORT IMPACT ON ADOPTER**					
A.3.1	Development effort reduction	2	5	5	4	16
A.3.2	Accessibility to public information	5	5	5	5	20
A.4	**UNIVERSITIES, RESEARCHINST AND COMM ENTERPRISES**					
A.4.1	Cooperation	N/A	N/A	N/A	N/A	0
A.5	**EXTERNAL DEVELOPERS**					
A.5.1	Participation	2	N/A	N/A	N/A	2
B	**ORGANIZATIONAL ISSUES**					
B.1	**RESOURCE MANAGEMENT POLICIES**					
B.1.1	Resource optimization	5	5	5	5	20
B.1.2	No dependence of software providers/vendors	2	4	2	2	10
B.1.3	Cost management	3	N/A	N/A	5	8
B.2	**QUALITY POLICIES**					
B.2.1	Security strengths	5	N/A	5	5	15
B.2.2	Security weakness	5	N/A	5	5	15
B.2.3	Reliability	5	N/A	4	5	14
B.3	**INNOVATION POLICIES**					
B.3.1	Innovation promotion	2	N/A	N/A	N/A	2
B.4	**LEGAL AND REGULATORY FULFILLMENT**					
B.4.1	Licensing	2	5	5	5	17
B.5	**TRAINING POLICIES**					
B.5.1	Cost of OSS training	3	4	2	5	14
B.6	**DECISION-MAKING POLICIES**					
B.6.1	Competitiveness	N/A	N/A	N/A	N/A	0
B.6.2	Strategic Staff Commitment	5	5	5	5	20
C	**GOVERNMENT POLICIES**					
C.1	**ECONOMIC DEVELOPMENT**					
C.1.1	OSS Economic positioning	5	5	5	3	18
C.1.2	OSS Economic sustainability	5	5	5	4	19
C.2	**INNOVATION POLICIES**					
C.2.1	OSS adoption promotion policies	5	5	5	3	18
C.3	**PUBLIC POLICIES**					
C.3.1	Incentives to TICS adoption	5	5	5	2	17
D	**STAFF CAPACITIES DEVELOPMENT**					
D.1	**CHANGE MANAGEMENT**					
D.1.1	OSS acceptance	5	4	4	5	18
D.1.2	OSS Skills development	4	3	2	4	13
D.1.3	Technical and Business training	4	3	2	5	14
E	**OSS SUPPORT**					
E.1	**SUPPORT AVAILABILITY**					
E.1.1	Inner Technical support	3	2	1	3	9
E.1.2	Source code availability	1	1	1	1	4
E.2	**SUPPORT IMPROVEMENTS**					
E.2.1	Efficiency	5	5	5	5	20
E.2.2	Integration	5	5	3	3	16
E.2.3	Compatibility	5	5	5	3	18

In the last two years we got involved in four of such projects, see Table 5 for some details. We use the knowledge gained in these projects to validate the relevance of the attributes included in the catalogue introduced in Sect. 4.

In Table 6, for each verification case, we have assessed the impact of each of the non-technical quality attributes described in the catalogue. Rows include the non-technical quality attributes in the catalogue whilst columns represent} the verification cases. We have used Likert's five levels scale to assess the relevance of each attribute in the projects, (one for the lowest and five for the higher impact).

Last column presents the total impact for each attribute, calculated as the sum of impacts in the four projects. 24 of the 44 non-technical attributes included in the catalogue (54%), were graded with a relevance higher tan of 15 over 20 possible points; 7 (16%) additional attributes, scored between 10 and 15 points, which makes evident the relevance of the attributes in the catalogue for these kind of projects.

It is important to mention that some attributes in the A category were not evaluated. This is due to the fact that, these organizations had already adopted some FOSS and the focus of the project was on upgrading and giving it a better maintenance to the software instead of adopting new software. On the other hand, it is important to consider that, in some cases, public institutions are forced by ministerial decrees to implement specific FOSS products, without chance to evaluate alternatives.

Organizational/Quality Policies attributes have been valuated with the highest scores. It can be argued that OSS products could be more vulnerable due to their open code nature. Consequently, security policies are required to minimize related threats. In contrast, some factors e.g., the *independence of the provider*, are perceived as means to increase protection of personal data, since code can be explored to prevent the existence of "backdoors", used for some manufacturers to introduce remote control codes into the software. In addition, open standards, that grant the freedom of users to exchange information with a FOSS community, are perceived as an important security factor when considering FOSS adoption.

Licensing is another interesting factor to consider. In the context of "Country Blinded", most Chief Technical Officers (CTO) still perceive Open Source as synonym of free software. Therefore, it is evident the lack of accurate economic feasibility and resource allocation studies in the projects.

In three of the four cases presented in Table 5, some consultants tried to sell expensive licensing schemas with the promise of "easiness" in FOSS product's troubleshooting. In fact, lack of technical skills and knowledge has been identified (in the study presented in Sect. 3), as one of the main barriers and risks in the adoption of FOSS. At the end, this fear factor causes some enterprises to purchase expensive licensing for premium functionality.

Despite the fact that attributes in OSS-DC SUPPORT category have the highest impact, it is important to consider attributes in the STAFF CAPACITIES DEVELOPMENT category. Some anthropologic aspects e.g., soft skills, risk acceptance, openness and flexibility ae included in this category. These attributes are highly important in the context of FOSS adoption projects, since successful adoption largely relies in technicians' attitude. Cultural change of technical and end users needs to be carefully addressed in this kind of project.

6 Conclusions and Future Work

The traditional approach to evaluate software components rely on technical requirements widely described in diverse quality models, but does not consider the high relevance of non-technical factors. In this research work, we have proposed a Non-Technical attributes catalogue, which can be used join with Technical ones, to evaluate FOSS Software Components considering the way in which they were adopted by the organization. These requirements are an extension of preexisting software quality models, and were obtained from SLR as a basis to identification success and failure factors, risks, benefits, main software domains, and entry barriers related to FOSS adoption. These requirements were structured in a three level hierarchical catalogue of non-technical attributes, covering from strategic to operative issues in FOSS evaluation context. Finally, the relevance of non-technical attributes was validated in relation to four industrial FOSS adoption cases taken from the experience of our team. Even when some of the attributes couldn't be evaluated, we confirm the suitability of the catalogue when evaluating and selecting a FOSS product. As future work, we will focus on refinement and validation of the measures set for each non-technical attribute in the catalogue, in order to make feasible an objective and systematic evaluation of FOSS component adoption.

References

1. ISO/IEC Standard 25000. Software engineering — Software product Quality Requirements and Evaluation (SQuaRE) — Guide to SQuaRE (2005)
2. Radulovic, F., García-Castro, R.: Extending software quality models - a sample in the domain of semantic technologies. In: SEKE 2011 (2011)
3. Kläs, M., Lampasona, C., Munch, J.: Adapting software quality models: practical challenges, approach, and first empirical results. In: EUROMICRO-SEAA 2011 (2011)
4. Lampasona, C., et al.: Software quality modeling experiences at an oil company. In: ESEM 2012 (2012)
5. Atos: Method for qualification and selection of open source software (QSOS) version 2.0. http://backend.qsos.org/download/qsos-2.0_en.pdf
6. Wasserman, A.I., Pal, M., Chan, C.: Business readiness rating for open source. In: Proceedings of the EFOSS Workshop, Como, Italy, 8 June 2006 (2006)
7. Soto, M., Ciolkowski, M.: The QualOSS open source assessment model measuring the performance of open source communities. In: Proceedings of the 3rd International Symposium on Empirical Software Engineering and Measurement, 15 October 2009 (2009)
8. Aversano, L., Tortorella, M.: Applying EFFORT for evaluating CRM open source systems. In: Caivano, D., Oivo, M., Baldassarre, M.T., Visaggio, G. (eds.) PROFES 2011. LNCS, vol. 6759, pp. 202–216. Springer, Heidelberg (2011). https://doi.org/10.1007/978-3-642-21843-9_17
9. International Organization for Standarization. ISO Standard 9126: Software Engineering – Product Quality, part 1. International Organization for Standarization (2001)
10. Franch, X., Carvallo, J.P.: A quality-model-based approach for describing and evaluating software packages. In: Proceedings 10th IEEE Joint Conference on Requirements Engineering (RE) (2002)

11. Carvallo, J.P., Franch, X.: Using quality models in software package selection. IEEE Softw. **20**(1), 34–41 (2003)
12. Carvallo, J.P., Franch, X., Quer, C.: Managing non-technical requirements in COTS components selection. In: Proceedings of 14th IEEE International Requirements Engineering Conference (RE 2006) (2006)
13. Carvallo, J.P., Franch, X., Quer, C.: Towards a unified catalogue of non-technical quality attributes to support COTS-based systems lifecycle activities. In: Proceedings of 6th IEEE International Conference on COTS-Based Software Systems (ICCBSS 2007) (2007)
14. López, L., et al.: Adoption of OSS components: a goal-oriented approach. Data Knowl. Eng. **99**, 17–38 (2015)
15. Kitchenham, B., Charters, S.: Guidelines for performing systematic literature reviews in software engineering. Technical report EBSE-2007-01 (2007)

Challenges in Requirement Engineering: Could Design Thinking Help?

Ezequiel Kahan[1](✉), Marcela Genero[2](✉), and Alejandro Oliveros[1](✉)

[1] Universidad Nacional de Tres de Febrero, Caseros, Argentina
{ekahan, aoliveros}@untref.edu.ar
[2] Department of Technologies and Information Systems,
University of Castilla-La Mancha, Ciudad Real, Spain
marcela.genero@uclm.es

Abstract. Despite its many successes, requirement engineering (RE) still presents a series of challenges and limitations. Many of the challenges identified almost a decade ago are still present; in some cases, they are accentuated by the increasing complexity, extension and depth of software systems. Design Thinking (DT) is a process that emerged from design areas; due to its effectiveness in solving certain types of problems (wicked problems), its use has spread to other domains. The RE has historically been enriched by the contribution of other domains, theoretical models and frameworks. The contribution of this paper is its reflections on the potential benefits of DT techniques in solving current challenges in the practice of RE. Our contribution is based mainly on our experience as practitioners who train companies in DT, and in the analysis on recent research on the use of DT in RE.

Keywords: Requirement engineering · Requirement elicitation ·
Design thinking

1 Introduction

Information systems are present in every activity of the human being, covering the needs of individuals, organizations and systems; the complex interrelation of these in the political, economic, social and cultural spheres is also addressed by information systems [1]. The main measure of the success of these systems is the degree to which they fulfill their original purpose. We can thus define requirement engineering (RE) as the process of discovering and initially defining that purpose [2] and of recognizing its critical role in both the success and the failure of software development [3, 4]. And we can therefore see that RE is intrinsically difficult [5], and observe that despite the extensive development and widespread use it has experienced over the years, its techniques and processes still present challenges and limitations, many of which are directly related to the evolution of software engineering as a discipline. In 2009, Hansen et al. published an analysis of the state of practice and emerging trends of RE in

M. Piattini et al. (Eds.): QUATIC 2019, CCIS 1010, pp. 79–86, 2019.
https://doi.org/10.1007/978-3-030-29238-6_6

the 21st century [6]. This paper gives continuity to the work of these and other authors, as part of the Design Requirement Workshop held June 3–6, 2007, in Cleveland, OH, USA, "*where leading researchers met to assess the current state of affairs and define new directions*" [7]. The critical requirement issues that were identified are: Business process focus, Systems transparency, Integration focus, Distributed requirements, Layers of requirements, Packaged software, Centrality of architecture, Interdependent Complexity and Fluidity of design. As other authors already stated, there is a direct link between the challenges presented in the requirements and IT project results [8].

We find that concepts like connecting with the space of the problem prior to search for solutions, focus on user needs, and context relevance, closely associated with the discipline of design and Design Thinking (DT) process, could help to reduce or overcome these challenges. DT can be defined as a powerful, effective and widely accessible approach to innovation, which can be integrated into all aspects of business and society, and which individuals and teams can use to generate disruptive ideas that can be implemented and hence generate impact [9]. Born in the world of design, within schools that sought to formalize the processes and ways of thinking typical of designers, their contribution has spread to other areas of knowledge and industries [10]. The distinguishing characteristic of DT is its focus on the needs of the user, its simultaneous work in the problem and solution spaces, and the combined application of a convergent (analytical) and divergent (exploratory) way of thinking. One of the ways to access real needs and requirements is to connect and empathize with the context of the problem to be solved. The DT process assumes the impossibility of fully under-standing the problem, or of rationally deducing an "optimal" solution from it, as an engineering approach would typically imply. By converting ideas into tangible pro-totypes, a more productive communication with stakeholders is enabled; that allows there to be a review and a renewal of the problem space [11]. This, in turn, enables a new solution space to be generated. Regarding the DT process, this consists of a series of stages, which differ from author to author.

Based on some of DT's use tendencies, as well as on our experience as practitioners and specialists in the discipline, our goal in this paper is to carry out a more exhaustive analysis of to what extent DT may potentially address the RE challenges of the 21st century [6]. Although the idea of relating DT with Information Systems (IS) and RE has already been proposed by other authors, [5, 10, 12–21], we consider that the mechanisms by which DT contributes to the problems of RE, along with the impli-cations that this has in the outcome of the projects, have not yet been fully analyzed. Relating the practical experience acquired during the workshops carried out by the first author with the ER problems identified by Hanset et al. can contribute to a better understanding of DT's mechanism [6].

The rest of the paper is organized as follows: Sect. 2 describes the main challenges that RE is facing in the 21st century. Section 3 presents our vision, as practitioners, of the application of DT in different types of companies. Section 3 reflects on the con-tribution of DT to dealing with the RE challenges proposed by Hansen et al. [6]. Finally, Sect. 4 presents conclusions and future work.

2 Our Experience on Applying DT in Industrial Context

Between March and November of 2018, the first author of this paper carried out 24 DT Workshops for different companies in the private sector, as part of his professional and academic activity. Most of these workshops were held in one of the largest telecom companies in South America; participants worked in a variety of roles throughout the company and came from different locations in Argentina. In general, the duration of the workshops was between 1 and 2 days; the main goals of these training activities were: Organizational: Objectives linked to problems that were internal to the organization. For example, problems of collaboration and communication between areas, internal procedures, digitalization of internal processes, etc. Focused on products/services: Objectives linked to the creation and/or evolution of products or services that the organization offers to third parties. The workshops had a two-fold objective: first, to train people in DT process and to instruct them in the use of the DT process to find needs, challenges and/or real business problems and identify possible solutions to them. The structure of the workshops, with theoretical-practical content, was similar in all cases: (1) Presentation of a general theoretical introduction to the DT mindset, (2) DT process presentation and definition, based on the Stanford D. School process [22], (3) Explanation of each of the stages of the DT process, and application of its most representative techniques and (4) Request for feedback from participants about the workshop. In the longer workshops all the techniques were applied, while in the shorter ones those that the instructor considered most appropriate to the goal pursued were chosen (Table 1).

Table 1. DT stages and chosen techniques

Stage of the process	Techniques
Empathize	Exercise about facts vs. Opinion/Inferences; Interviews; Empathy map; Correlations and intuitions about the Map
Define	Archetype of Persona, Journey Map (only in the 2-day Workshops)
Ideate	BrainWriting; Now, How, Wow matrix, dot voting
Prototype	Physical prototypes, Story-boards, Role-Playing
Test	Prototype presentation, feedback collection matrix

Regarding the feedback in each of the workshops (obtained during steps 3 and 4 of the workshop), perceptions and comments of the participants were collected in two different ways: On the one hand, after presenting each stage of the process, and executing the techniques linked to it, the instructor asked the participants for feedback on the results obtained. In the next section, we will set out the feedback obtained, along with some of the insights which emerged from our observations.

3 Linking RE Challenges with DT

In this section we will provide some reflections on the potential contribution of DT to the challenges of RE—as proposed by Hansen et al. [6]—in the 21st century. These reflections were produced using the feedback collected through the workshops mentioned above, first author observations, together with analyses of the contribution of similar studies [5, 10, 12–21].

Business Process Focus: One of the main contributions of DT is to identify the needs of users in the environment of the problem; this helps to capture the business prospects. DT offers the possibility of connecting with experience, transcending what is exclusively technological and incorporating the business perspective. The feedback given by the participants was that the application of the DT process and its techniques allowed them to acquire a large amount of first-hand information regarding the needs and problems of the users on a day-to-day basis; In general, the participants recognized that it was valuable to have the different stages of the DT process connected; this enriched the understanding of the user experience that is associated with the business process. Some examples of these connections were the possibility of validating the prototypes that had been created using the previously-generated Persona archetypes, or an awareness that the solution generated in the ideation stage was adjusted to fit the experience that had been identified in the journey map during the stage of definition. Other studies have found similar applications of DT [16, 18, 21].

System Transparency: One of the contributions of DT to this issue is its integrating vision of the problem to be solved. DT focuses on the user experience, ensuring not only that it reaches a result, but that it does so in the most satisfactory way possible. This involves not only a functional or technical dimension, but also an emotional one. The feedback given by the participants in relation to this issue suggests that DT contributes to the requirements' being more focused on the user experience. After applying the different techniques in the respective stages of the process the participants of the workshops commented that: having discussions and doing exercises prior to the interviews allowed them to have a higher level of awareness about their own biases. Talking about the differences between facts, opinions and inferences helped those taking part to be more attentive to these features during the interviews. As other studies also reveal, the use of techniques that encouraged not only the interviewing of users, but also observation of them, evaluating their thoughts and emotions, gave participants greater depth of understanding both of the problem and of the experience of the client/user [14, 15].

Integration Focus: We did not find a link between DT and this issue. In a systemic mapping on the application of DT to RE that we are carrying out, we have not found any paper thus far that deals with the application of DT to this problem.

Distributed Requirements: On this issue, although these workshops were carried out with participants from nearby locations, in several of those carried out for the Telecomm group, there were participants not only from different companies within the group, for whom the realities of the day-to-day labor varied; there were also employees from different cities throughout the country. In these groups, as people emphasized, there was the chance to develop a shared vision on the different problems, incorporating regional perspectives. This enriched the process, making it possible to have an organizational reality that part of the participants had never known before. The interaction between DT techniques (such as field interviews, construction of different archetypes of personas and journey maps), along with the iterative characteristic of its application and the alternation between divergent and convergent ways of thinking, may allow organizational, group and social characteristics to be captured, enabling them to be incorporated into the creation of distributed requirements. Other studies have found similar applications of DT to distributed requirements [13, 15].

Layers of Requirements: Design efforts today involve multiple layers of requirements, such as abstraction, a focus on user orientation, or timing. This phenomenon of layering includes the transition between business, functional and technical requirements. As we mentioned with respect to the issues of **Business process focus** and **System transparency**, focusing on the user's needs contributes to this perspective. Temporality and volatility of requirements also typically have to do with the user and the application context. DT helps us to understand this temporality and volatility, and to design requirements that support future changes in the system. Our observation of the workshops allowed us to see a diversity of needs that crossed from one layer of the problem to a different one. In one of the workshops in a Telecomm company, one particular challenge that a group of participants found was related to the difficulty users had in finding information scattered in different systems. As this group had both technically-based people and end-users, they were able to explore further and in greater depth the connection between technical necessity (i.e.: the difficulty of building certain interfaces to respond to a certain business architecture) and issues that were functional and business-related. Other studies have found similar applications of DT to layers of requirements [15, 23].

Packaged Software: DT is used today by companies that develop COTS. Companies like SAP use DT as part of their Software development process [24]. Due to the type of objectives of the Workshops carried out, there were not many references to this type of problems. There is nothing specific in DT for that kind of application, although there are indeed aspects that are applicable to its implementation. Many of the elements mentioned in other sections (understanding the context of the problem, identification of different types of users and experiences, etc.) may also be applied to COTS.

Centrality of Architecture: On this point, we have not yet been able to find a clear contribution from DT. In general, it is noteworthy that the focus of the DT process is on understanding the needs of the user in the environment of the problem; it is not about implementing a specific technological solution in a given architecture. Our experience is that DT's contribution, in the best of cases, could rather be related to non-functional requirements to do with the user experience, such as security. Other studies reinforce this idea about security [12].

Interdependent Complexity: The contribution of design in general, and of DT in particular, to wicked and complex problems is something that authors like Rittel and Buchanan, who come from the area of design, established as useful decades ago [25].

Feedback from participants on this point was that DT helped deal with problems that fit the definition of wicked and/or complex problems. According to those taking part, the type of techniques used helped them to have a broader view of the particular user who has the problem, as well as of the environment of application, and the level of interdependence that this problem had with others. Participants also stressed that combining stages and techniques associated with divergent thinking (empathize, devise, prototype) with stages and techniques more associated with convergent thinking (synthesizing, validating) helped reduce some of the complexity. It did so by narrowing the scope of the problem, making it more specific, as well as by validating it through prototyped solutions. This point coincides with findings of several authors, who see in the alternation of ways of thinking one of the characteristic features of DT, namely *mindset* [13–15]. The contribution of DT to wicked problems is something that other authors have already pointed to [18–20].

Fluidity of Design: Since DT is an iterative, incremental and non-linear process, it has the flexibility to continue to enrich existing requirements or to incorporate new ones, depending on the evolution of the problems. To achieve this, DT should be applied continuously and repeatedly throughout the life cycle of the Software project. In this sense, DT is well suited to Agile Software development processes [21]. Something that we saw in the Workshops was that during the validation of the generated prototypes, participants gave feedback which would have made it possible to iterate on the work done, incorporating this new information. Although the duration of the Workshop was limited and did not allow iteration on the process, it is likely that if this had been done, needs that had not been captured initially would have come to light.

4   Conclusions and Future Work

Based on what has been stated on previous sections, we can conclude that the challenges and problems of RE persist. These issues are important, moreover, because they represent a significant percentage of the challenges and failures that IT projects go through. The interest in applying DT to deal with RE challenges has been increasing in recent years; there are several pieces of research work on the use of DT in RE [5, 18–20]. It should also be highlighted that recent tutorials and keynote speeches on the topic have taken place in relevant conferences such as RE 2018 [26] and PROFES 2019 [27], among others.

The current relevance of the topic and our experience with DT in industry motivated us to focus our research on the benefits that DT could provide for requirements elicitation. From the information gained through 24 workshops carried out by the first author of this paper in 2018, alongside the existing literature, in this paper we have been able to elaborate on the potential benefits of DT techniques in solving the main challenges that are currently facing RE. We can conclude that to some extent DT does indeed offer tools to face such challenges. Nonetheless, it is our opinion that if really practical solutions are to be offered there is a need for a specific process of requirement elicitation that will incorporate the most suitable DT techniques.

Future work will therefore be to develop and validate a requirement elicitation process that incorporates DT techniques, in socio-technical IT projects. Regarding the development of the process, we believe that empathy will be extremely valuable, as already demonstrated in the case of privacy requirements [12].

Acknowledgements. The research work presented in this paper has been developed within the following projects: the GEMA project ("Consejería de Educación, Cultura y Deporte de la Dirección General de Universidades, Investigación e Innovación de la JCCM", SBPLY/17/180501/000293), the ECLIPSE project ("Ministerio de Ciencia, Innovación y Universidades, y FEDER", RTI2018-094283-B-C31) and the Software Development Process Research Project at the Universidad Nacional de Febrero (Project lines: Usability of Process and Practice, Agile Practices and Techniques and Requirements Engineering Processes).

References

1. Cilliers, P.: Complexity and Postmodernism Understanding Complex Systems. Routledge, London; New York (2002)
2. Jarke, M., Loucopoulos, P., Lyytinen, K., Mylopoulos, J., Robinson, W.: The brave new world of design requirements. Inf. Syst. **36**(7), 992–1008 (2011)
3. Deb, S.: Information technology, its impact on society and its future. Adv. Comput. **4**(1), 25–29 (2014)
4. Brooks, F.P.: The Mythical Man-Month: Essays on Software Engineering. Anniversary edn. Addison-Wesley, Reading (1995)
5. Vetterli, C., Brenner, W., Uebernickel, F., Petrie, C.: From palaces to yurts: why requirements engineering needs design thinking. IEEE Internet Comput. **17**(2), 91–94 (2013)
6. Hansen, S., Berente, N., Lyytinen, K.: Requirements in the 21st century: current practice and emerging trends. In: Lyytinen, K., Loucopoulos, P., Mylopoulos, J., Robinson, B. (eds.) Design Requirements Engineering: A Ten-Year Perspective. LNBIP, vol. 14, pp. 44–87. Springer, Heidelberg (2009). https://doi.org/10.1007/978-3-540-92966-6_3
7. Lyytinen, K., Loucopoulos, P., Mylopoulos, J., Robinson, B. (eds.): Design Requirements Engineering: A Ten-Year Perspective. LNBIP, vol. 14. Springer, Heidelberg (2009). https://doi.org/10.1007/978-3-540-92966-6
8. Aurum, A., Wohlin, C. (eds.): Engineering and Managing Software Requirements. Springer, Berlin (2005). https://doi.org/10.1007/3-540-28244-0
9. Brown, T.: Design thinking. Harvard Bus. Rev. (2008). https://hbr.org/2008/06/design-thinking. Accessed 22 Sept 2017
10. Waloszek, G.: Introduction to Design Thinking. SAP User Experience Community, 12 September 2012. https://experience.sap.com/skillup/introduction-to-design-thinking/. Accessed 09 Oct 2017
11. Cross, N.: Designerly ways of knowing. Des. Stud. **3**(4), 7 (1982)
12. Levy, M., Hadar, I.: The importance of empathy for analyzing privacy requirements. In: 2018 IEEE 5th International Workshop on Evolving Security & Privacy Requirements Engineering (ESPRE), Banff, AB, pp. 9–13 (2018)
13. Kourtesis, D., et al.: Brokerage for quality assurance and optimisation of cloud services: an analysis of key requirements. In: Lomuscio, A.R., Nepal, S., Patrizi, F., Benatallah, B., Brandić, I. (eds.) ICSOC 2013. LNCS, vol. 8377, pp. 150–162. Springer, Cham (2014). https://doi.org/10.1007/978-3-319-06859-6_14

14. Newman, P., Ferrario, M.A., Simm, W., Forshaw, S., Friday, A., Whittle, J.: The Role of Design Thinking and Physical Prototyping in Social Software Engineering, pp. 487–496 (2015)
15. Sandino, D., Matey, L.M., Vélez, G.: Design thinking methodology for the design of interactive real-time applications. In: Marcus, A. (ed.) DUXU 2013. LNCS, vol. 8012, pp. 583–592. Springer, Heidelberg (2013). https://doi.org/10.1007/978-3-642-39229-0_62
16. Carroll, N., Richardson, I.: Aligning healthcare innovation and software requirements through design thinking, pp. 1–7 (2016)
17. de Carvalho Souza, C.L., Silva, C.: An experimental study of the use of design thinking as a requirements elicitation approach for mobile learning environments. CLEI Electron. J. **18**(1), 6 (2015)
18. Hehn, J., Uebernickel, F.: The Use of Design Thinking for Requirements Engineering, p. 6
19. Hehn, J., Uebernickel, F., Stoeckli, E., Brenner, W.: Designing Human-Centric Information Systems: Towards an Understanding of Challenges in Specifying Requirements within Design Thinking Projects, p. 12 (2018)
20. Hehn, J., Uebernickel, F.: Towards an understanding of the Role of Design Thinking for Requirements Elicitation – Findings from a Multiple-Case Study, p. 10 (2018)
21. Glomann, L.: Introducing 'human-centered agile workflow' (HCAW) – an agile conception and development process model. In: Ahram, T., Falcão, C. (eds.) AHFE 2017. AISC, vol. 607, pp. 646–655. Springer, Cham (2018). https://doi.org/10.1007/978-3-319-60492-3_61
22. Institute of Design at Stanford: An Introduction to Design Thinking PROCESS GUIDE, Stanford (2010)
23. Souza, A.F., Ferreira, B., Valentim, N., Conte, T.: Um Relato de Experiência sobre o Ensino de Múltiplas Técnicas de Design Thinking a Estudantes de Engenharia de Software, p. 14 (2018)
24. Jensen, M.B., Lozano, F., Steinert, M.: The origins of design thinking and the relevance in software innovations. In: Abrahamsson, P., Jedlitschka, A., Nguyen Duc, A., Felderer, M., Amasaki, S., Mikkonen, T. (eds.) PROFES 2016. LNCS, vol. 10027, pp. 675–678. Springer, Cham (2016). https://doi.org/10.1007/978-3-319-49094-6_54
25. Buchanan, R.: Wicked problems in design thinking. Des. Issues **8**(2), 5 (1992)
26. Hehn, J., Uebernickel, F., Mendez Fernandez, D.: DT4RE: design thinking for requirements engineering: a tutorial on human-centered and structured requirements elicitation. In: 2018 IEEE 26th International Requirements Engineering Conference (RE), Banff, AB, pp. 504–505 (2018)
27. Keynote – Prof. Neil Maiden – 20th International Conference on Product-Focused Software Process Improvement, Barcelona, Spain, 27–29 November 2019 (2019)

Business Processes

Understanding Process Models Using the Eye-Tracking: A Systematic Mapping

Vinícius Brito[1], Rafael Duarte[1(✉)], Charlie Silva Lopes[2], and Denis Silva da Silveira[1,2]

[1] Department of Computer Engineering, University of Pernambuco, Recife, Brazil
{vab, rbd}@ecomp.poli.br, dsilveira@ufpe.br
[2] Administrative Sciences Department, Federal University of Pernambuco, Recife, Brazil
charlie1270@gmail.com

Abstract. Business process modeling can involve multiple stakeholders, so it is natural that problems may occur in building and understanding them. One way to perceive these problems is to evaluate the comprehension of these models through the collection of data related to the readers' awareness with an eye-tracking device. This device allows collecting data of specific facial reactions of the people, such as the movement of the eyes and dilation of the pupils and the number of blinks in a specified time interval. The objective of this paper is to provide an overview of researches that evaluate the understanding of process models through eye-tracking techniques. A systematic mapping study was developed to achieve this goal, following the best practices in the area of Software Engineering. This study consolidated 19 papers for the analysis and extraction of data from the 1,161 studies initially found.

Keywords: Business process modeling · Understandability · Comprehension · Eye-tracking · Evaluation · Systematic mapping study

1 Introduction

Establishing efficient processes is the goal that all companies must pursue [1]. Business processes are a set of activities, well determined, coordinated in time and space to achieve goals and organizational objectives [2]. Besides that, they can be represented in models or diagrams composed of visual components [3]. These models are used as an instrument to facilitate the understanding or even to identify points of improvement in an organization [4]. In this perspective, business process models are essential so that the organizations keep control of their flows of activities.

Also, business processes help in specifying the requirements and design of information systems, representing all the data flow of processes. Thus, the path taken by many organizations to produce quality information systems has been to invest in the improvement of business process models. Therefore, processes are expected to result in quality information systems [5]. Studies show that the growth of the models both

© Springer Nature Switzerland AG 2019
M. Piattini et al. (Eds.): QUATIC 2019, CCIS 1010, pp. 89–104, 2019.
https://doi.org/10.1007/978-3-030-29238-6_7

increases the quality of the information systems produced and the productivity of this development [6–8].

Recent and more innovative researches analyze how these models are explained and perceived by their stakeholders [9, 10]. Hereupon, users understand models differently, resulting in different abstractions [11]. Contrary to this statement, in [12], the authors state that one of the main objectives of a process model is to facilitate communication between stakeholders. However, according to these authors, little is known about the factors that influence the understanding of a process model by human agents. Thus, despite the research that has already been done in this field, there are still unanswered questions about the perception of process models. Besides that, cognitive neuroscience and psychology also provide valuable information about this field.

There are several alternatives to evaluating the understanding of business process models. These include experimenting with the collection of data, sometimes with the use of biometric sensors, on the performance of designers and other stakeholders in a given modeling task to know their level of understanding and preferences about the use of a modeling artifact to the detriment of another. Biometric sensors have been explored in recent years as data collection devices become more accessible. Additionally, one of the technologies that have deserved particular attention is eye tracking.

This paper focuses on these pillars (business process, comprehension, and eye-tracking), offering an overview of evaluating the understanding of process models through eye-tracking techniques. We use Evidence-Based Software Engineering (EBSE) to better understand the problem and the field of the research, and to extract and synthesize the results. EBSE provides a rigorous and reliable research methodology, together with auditing tasks to reduce the researchers' bias on the results [13]. Two of the core tools for evidence-based studies are systematic literature reviews (SLR), focusing on identifying the best practices on a given topic based on empirical evidence, and systematic mapping studies, aiming at creating a comprehensive overview of a given research area [14].

The goal of this work is to carry out a systematic mapping study of the existing primary studies and classifying them concerning the information presented. Also, to give an overview of the literature regarding the mediation of terms: business processes, comprehension, and eye-tracking. This paper will provide an adequate position for new research activities in this area; however, it is not its purpose to present a rigid comparison between the studies identified here.

The remainder of this paper is organized as follows: Sect. 2 gives an overview of introductory concepts; Sect. 3 shows the method used in this study describing the planning phase and the research questions addressed; Sect. 4 describes its execution, presenting the selected reviews, the classification scheme adopted and reports the findings; while, Sect. 5 discusses related works; finally, Sect. 6 concludes this paper and summarizes directions for further action.

2   Background

Business process modeling is an interdisciplinary area that has adopted a variety of paradigms and methodologies of different areas such as organizational management theory, computer science, mathematics, linguistics, semiotics, and philosophy [15]. The aim of business process modeling is to build Business Process Model, which are technical drawings that translate abstract representations of processes [16].

In [17], understanding is a criterion that helps to measure whether the information contained in a model can be understood by all stakeholders. The authors also point out that understanding is one of the criteria used to evaluate the quality of a model. This definition implies that the opinion can be investigated from two central angles: personal factors, related to the reader of the model, and the factors that relate to the model itself.

Eye-tracking is a mechanism for collecting cognitive data from its users. This mechanism is used to conduct empirical studies and to study understanding models [18], to realize what can be improved to facilitate, for instance, the interaction of systems with their users. The systems that use this technology are based on theories of the human physiological system, such as the theory of visual perception, and cognitive theories, such as the visual attention theory [19]. Thus, such technology allows analyzing user's performance in reading and interpreting business process models.

3   Method

In [14] the authors describe the process that was used as a starting point for this work. However, the ideas were blended and presented in [14] with the right practices defined for the SLR in [20]. Then, we apply a systematic mapping process, including some good practices used in SLRs. An example of this is the use of a search protocol. This artifact defined a plan, which established the necessary mapping procedures presented here.

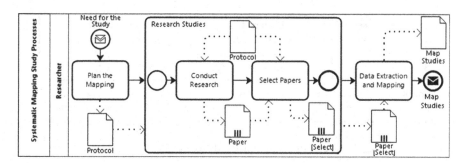

Fig. 1. Typical systematic mapping study processes (The process built using BPMN (Business Process Modeling Notation) [21]). adapted from [14].

Other activities of the process, as proposed in [14], were also altered and/or rearranged in this study. As can be observed in Fig. 1, the process was divided into three main activities: (A) *"Plan the Mapping"*, whose objective is to identify the need for the review, defining the research protocol that will be used to conduct the mapping; (B) "research studies", which aims at collecting the studies (Conduct Research) to select the primary studies (Select Papers), applying the inclusion and exclusion criteria; (C) "Data Extraction and Mapping", which aims at formatting and communicating the results.

3.1 Plan the Mapping

To "Plan the Mapping", it all started by formulating the research questions (Table 1) and the search string to run in the digital libraries (Fig. 2), consequently it was the definition of research sources and, finally, the election of which studies should be selected (included and extracted). (Table 2).

Table 1. Research questions.

ID	Questions
RQ1 (MAIN)	How is eye tracking technology applied in understanding business process models?
RQ2	What metrics are used to measure the visual comprehension of eye-tracking business process models?
RQ3	Which business process model notations are evaluated in the studies?
RQ4	What contributions have been reported about the application of the eye-tracker device to evaluate the understanding of the process models?
RQ5	When and where have the studies been published?
RQ6	How many researchers are using the eye tracking device to evaluate understanding in process models?

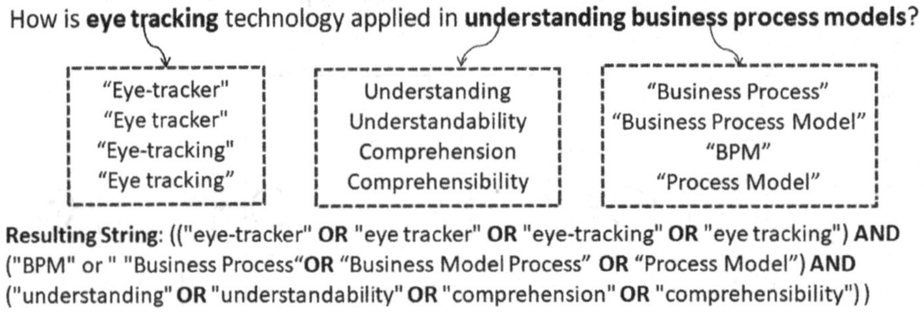

How is **eye tracking** technology applied in **understanding business process models?**

"Eye-tracker" "Eye tracker" "Eye-tracking" "Eye tracking"	Understanding Understandability Comprehension Comprehensibility	"Business Process" "Business Process Model" "BPM" "Process Model"

Resulting String: (("eye-tracker" OR "eye tracker" OR "eye-tracking" OR "eye tracking") AND ("BPM" or " "Business Process"OR "Business Model Process" OR "Process Model") AND ("understanding" OR "understandability" OR "comprehension" OR "comprehensibility"))

Fig. 2. Search string construction based on Silva *et al.* [22].

Regarding the bases of the research, digital databases were chosen to be used, where the results are collected through a search query execution. The research bases selected for this study were: ACM, Engineering Village, IEEExplore, Scopus, Springer Link, Web of Science, and Science Direct (Elsevier).

Based on the study [43], it demonstrates that the use of ocular tracking in Software Engineering has become more common as of 2006. We defined as the search interval the last 13 years, from January 2006 to January 2019. After laying the foundations the next step is identification of keywords. In this mapping, the keywords were extracted from RQ1. Figure 2 illustrates the keywords used in the queries, already grouped with the Boolean operators in the search string.

It is interesting to emphasize the search on all bases. The resulting number of studies can be reviewed through a set of inclusion and exclusion criteria, which aspire to increase the quality of the resulting studies. Table 2 shows the specific criteria, together with different ones which can be applied in any other study.

Table 2. Inclusion and exclusion criteria.

Criteria	Detail
I1 (INCLUSION)	Articles that address in the title and/or abstract the use of eye-tracking technology in the analysis of the understanding of process models
I2 (INCLUSION)	Paper's keywords are among our keywords
E1 (EXCLUSION)	Duplicated papers
E2 (EXCLUSION)	Papers that did not apply to research questions
E3 (EXCLUSION)	Papers with unavailable access
E4 (EXCLUSION)	Papers written in other than the English language
E5 (EXCLUSION)	Papers with only abstract available; extended abstracts or short paper (less than six pages)

3.2   Research Studies

This subprocess consists of two activities: *Conduct Research* and *Select Papers*. The *Conduct Research* activity, which is responsible for performing the searches in digital libraries, required some specific settings during each search in the databases. Here it is worth noting that the databases used have characteristics and limitations themselves and that their search engines work in different ways. Thus, the resulting strand (Fig. 2) was adapted to rotate appropriately in each of the bases. For example, it was considered whether the database accepts a search with plural terms or whether they should be added to the string, or if the database allows searches to be performed considering only parts of the text, or even if searches are always performed considering the full text. In total, 1,161 studies of the automatic search in the digital libraries were found, in which: 75 studies were retrieved from the ACM Digital Library, 15 came from Engineering Village, 23 were retrieved from the Scopus database, 636 from Springer Link, 8 were found in the Web of Science 404 came from Science Direct and no study was retrieved from the IEEE.

In the *Select Papers* activity, the studies were analyzed in two stages: initial selection and final selection. In the initial range, the inclusion and exclusion criteria were applied in all the studies identified, through the evaluation of titles, keywords, and abstracts. However, in some cases, it was difficult to determine whether or not the research was relevant only by reading those data. Thus, whenever there was any doubt about the inclusion or not of a particular study, the recommendation adopted - at this stage - was by its inclusion, being the decision of keeping it postponed to the final selection. In this initial selection, of 1,161, 1,057 studies were excluded because the research question was not applied, 41 of which were duplicated, 1 study was not written in the English, 1 article couldn't be accessed, 31 of them were only a summary and did not criteria of inclusion and exclusion. Based on this first selection, only 30 primary studies were taken to the final selection.

During the final selection, the inclusion and exclusion criteria were applied again in the studies included in the first stage, through the evaluation of their complete texts. This new evaluation resulted in 19 primary studies that fully met all the criteria and would be able to contribute to the results of this work. After each of the two selection stages, initial and final, a review was performed. This review was conducted to increase the reliability and transparency of the selection process, to avoid the exclusion of relevant studies. Here it is interesting to note that the two selection stages were performed independently by two researchers, since the studies can be classified differently. In this happened, a third researcher seeked a consensus between the two previous ones.

4   Data Extraction and Mapping

This section provides an analysis of the results enables us to present the amount of studies that match each research question addressed in this study.

4.1   RQ1 - How Is Eye Tracking Technology Applied in Understanding Business Process Models?

All the studies found used the eye-tracking device to verify comprehension in business process models, each study using the device to evaluate different topics in the understanding of the models. Table 3 presents the categorization of studies by these topics. Studies [28, 33, 39] use the eye tracking device to evaluate different business process modeling notations to determine which is best understood. Studies [28, 35, 41] assess the understanding of structures or specific elements from which they were added in the notation. The remaining studies evaluate how different readers understand business process models in a particular notation.

Table 3. Studies classification.

Application	Studies
In the comparison between notations	[28, 33, 39]
In addition of new artifacts	[23, 35, 41]
In the evaluation of the models	[24–27, 29–32, 34, 36–38, 40]

4.2   RQ2 - What Metrics Are Used to Measure the Visual Comprehension of Eye-Tracking Business Process Models?

Table 4 presents the key metrics used to evaluate the understanding of business process models. The *eyefixation* metric, which consists of the visual attention time of the participant in an area of interest while performing a task [42], it is used in most (84.21%) of the mapped studies. The *scan path* were used in 36.84% consist of the way formed by the balconies, in chronological order, between sets of *eyefixations*. The *saccade* were used in 31.58% and consist of the swift movement that occurs between *eyefixations*, it has a duration of about 40 to 50 ms [42]. Meanwhile, the *duration* represents the time the participant takes to complete a task [43] and was used in 47.37% of studies.

Table 4. Evaluation metrics.

Eye fixation	Saccade	Scan path	Duration	Pupillometry	Comprehension questions	Not specified
[23–28, 30–34, 38–40]	[23, 26–28, 32, 33]	[26–28, 31, 33, 34, 39]	[25–27, 31, 34, 38, 39]	[30, 36]	[28, 34, 38, 39, 41]	[29]

Pupillometry, which consists of measuring pupillary dilatation, is considered an indication of excitation by the participant to a visual stimulus, was present in 2 (10.53%) of the studies. Finally, 26.32% of the mapped reviews use questionnaires with questions about the domain of business process models, and according to the number of correct answers, the participant understands the business process models.

4.3   RQ3 - What Business Process Model Notations Are Evaluated in the Studies?

As it can be seen in the Table 5 the majority of 16 studies evaluate the understanding of business process models in BPMN notation [21]. Study [28] compares the understanding between models in BPMN [23] and EPC [44]. Likewise, the work A11 performs the comparison between the understanding of the models in the notations BPMN [21], EPC [44], Petri Net [45] and eGantt [46]. As well as the study A17 that makes a comparison between the languages CIAN [47] and CIT [48]. Finally, study [24] uses the DCR notation to evaluate the understanding of business process models; and studies [32, 34] did not specify the notation used in the respective studies.

Table 5. Notations assessed by the studies.

BPMN	DCR	EPC	Petri Net	eGantt	CIAN	CTT	Not specified
[23, 25–31, 33, 34, 36–38, 40, 41]	[23]	[25, 33]	[33]	[33]	[39]	[39]	[32, 34]

4.4   RQ4 - What Contributions Have Been Reported About the Application of the Eye-Tracker Device to Evaluate the Understanding of Process Models?

The selected studies present results that show that the application of the eye-tracking device can offer essential contributions to the understanding of the process models. Table 6 presents the contributions of the selected studies.

Table 6. Studies contributions.

Reference	Contributions
[23]	The process models with linked rules are associated with a lower cognitive load, shorter comprehension time and higher accuracy comprehension
[24]	The evaluation of the data allowed the study to classify three distinct reading profiles (Graph, Simulation, and Law text) of process models
[25]	The results suggest that successful error diagnoses are linked to shorter total viewing time and shorter fixation duration, with a significant difference between semantic and syntactic errors
[26]	He identified that both samples of participants, beginners, and experts, have similar strategies to understand a process model in the first iteration. However, they argue that specialists understand process models more efficiently; that is, exploration paths reflect fewer fixations and balances
[27]	It is a work in progress, appearing only the strategy of how a future experiment will run. In the pilot experiment, the visual behavior of 10 participants was analyzed to confirm the theory of the existence of different BPD reading strategies
[28]	The performance of participants decreases as the level of difficulty increases. However, regardless of their level of expertise, all individuals have similar standards when faced with process models that exceed a certain level of difficulty. Participants' overall performance demonstrates a better understanding of business process models in EPC notation compared to the BPMN
[29]	The understanding of the model decreases with the increasing number of nesting and with the size of the model. They point out that the enthusiasm of the reader of the process model disappears with the rising complexity of the model
[30]	It is a work in progress, presenting only a description of the experiment that investigates how designers experience challenges by measuring the cognitive load. The authors did not describe anything in terms of outcome
[31]	There is no influence between the reader's familiarity with business mastery and the proper understanding of the model. They point out that a Visual Cognition Efficiency (measured by Scan Path Precision and Recall) and Visual Cognition Intensity (measured by Total Fixtures and Total Fixture Length) better explain the comprehension performance (higher efficiency, shorter duration) than a model of personal knowledge and model complexity. For them, higher levels of specialization in business process modeling and lower complexity of the model lead to better cognitive efficiency
[32]	The authors pointed out that participants took longer to understand parts of the gateway models, especially XOR and loops

(continued)

Table 6. (*continued*)

Reference	Contributions
[33]	Participants faced difficulties in understanding the models as complexity increased, even with the participant knowing the model scenario. Among the modeling languages, only the eGantts notation obtained a higher level of accuracy as the level of difficulty of the models increased. Regardless of the experience a subject has with process modeling, generally in the first iteration of understanding all follow the same analysis of the model. During the experiments, they found that process models with an explicit start and a final symbol make it easier to understand the process model
[34]	The results indicate that intermediate readers tend to be more effective in terms of understanding the process model compared to beginners. As the level of difficulty increases, the time is taken to understand the process model increases as well. Concerning the less complicated process model, it seems that the newcomers show a weaker performance compared to the intermediaries. In turn, the performance of novices is approaching the same level as that of the intermediaries with an increased level of difficulty. In general, they seem that the BPMN process models can be intuitively understood
[35]	The performance in the understanding of the models was better with the collaborative model than the individual and the layout change of the BPMN models proposed by the experiment
[36]	For a modeler, an increase in the cognitive load was observed whenever it is necessary to name activities of the process model from the text information
[37]	The elements of the area of interest are fixed for longer than other elements of the model by the subjects who provided the correct answer to the question of understanding. More elements of the area of interest are set than other elements of the model by subjects who provided the correct answer to the question of understanding
[38]	It can be observed that the average duration are smaller for the fixations in the task description compared to the fixations in the process model. The perceived lower complexity, once, allows the modelers to consider additional features of the model, such as secondary notation of the process model from the outset. It is noticeable that when the average length of fixings is increased by about 30%, the participants are facing a challenging part of the model
[39]	Inregards to cognitive processing measures, it can be concluded that the layout of the CIAN diagrams generates less efficient searches due to having the highest total number of fixations when the model is explored. Determining the cognitive load during the comprehension task is less in the case of CIAN, which indicates that the participants need more time to understand the individual objects. We can conclude that the use of icons to represent roles facilitates the finding of the answer in the case of CIAN, although the subject needed more time to be sure before responding (they need to visualize more elements). In case of CTT, the location of the response is not so straightforward, but when the subject has located the solution of the comprehension task, he/she is sure of the answer more quickly

(continued)

Table 6. (*continued*)

Reference	Contributions
[40]	The new analysis technique and the exploring of new source data resulted in higher precision at identifying the types of phases in the process of models' creation in relation to the traditional technique. This technique allowed identifying factors such as: problems comprehension, methods discovery, semantic and syntactic validation
[41]	The results of matched post-hoc comparisons show that diagrammatic integration is associated with greater accuracy of comprehension than text annotation and link integration. Obviously, there is no significant difference in mental effort between different integration approaches. The presence and quantity of XOR gateways, AND gateways and issues that require navigation of constructions through loop structures, seems to influence understanding

Among the main contributions of the studies, it was observed that the studies [28, 33, 34] emphasize that the size and complexity of the model influence its understanding. On the other hand, studies [29, 32] affirm that complex structures like loops and nestings diminish the understanding of process models. It was also observed in studies [28, 33] that independently of the level of knowledge, all individuals have similar patterns when faced with process models that exceed a certain level of difficulty. In studies [23, 35], the addition of complementary elements in the models facilitated the understanding of the participants. Only studies [30, 36] evaluate the understanding of process models from the perspective of the designer, and the other studies estimate the understanding from the standpoint of model readers.

4.5   RQ5 - When and Where Have the Studies Been Published?

Figure 3 shows the distribution of the studies considering the year of its publication. The first mapped study is [37] of the year 2012. There is a concentration of publications in the last three years, with the year 2017 demonstrating the highest incidence of papers.

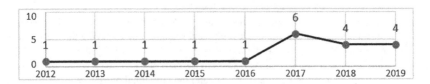

Fig. 3. Distribution of studies per year.

As can it be seen in Fig. 4, the Springer Link research database returned most (78.95%) of the selected studies. Only studies [31, 35] have as source the basis of research Science Direct. No reviews were chosen on the bases: ACM, Engineering Village, IEEE, Scopus and Web of Science.

Among the selected studies 14 (73.68%) were published in conferences. The conferences with the most mapped reviews are International Conference on Business Process Management with three studies [24, 32, 37], Information Systems and Neuroscience also with three mapped studies [25, 30, 36] and Enterprise, Business Process and Information Systems Modeling has 2 mapped reviews [32, 33]. Also, we outlined 4 (21.06%) studies which published papers in journals and only one study [23] (5.26%) was released as a chapter of the book Integrating Business Process Models and Rules.

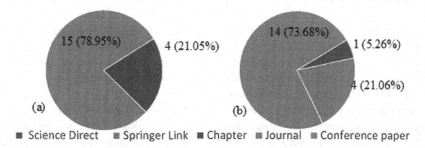

Fig. 4. Studies per database and types.

To understand which studies are most relevant, we observed the number of citations of the selected papers as it can be seen in Fig. 5, from the 19 chosen reviews there are a total of 129 quotes.

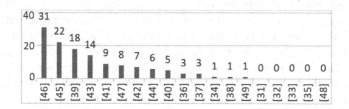

Fig. 5. Number of citations per study.

Papers [31, 35–37] are the most popular accounting for 65.89% of citations. The paper [37] has 31 citations, and this may be due to the pioneering nature of this study, being published in 2012. The works [23–25, 27] have no citation, being less popular perhaps because they were published in more recent years.

4.6   RQ6- How Many Researchers Are Using the Eye-Racking Device to Evaluate Understanding in Process Models?

In the papers there are 42 authors of the 19 mapped studies. Out of the 42 authors, 18 (42.86%) have more than one article included in the mapping. The author with more reviews is Barbara Weber owning five studies. They are followed by the authors

Andrea Burattin, Manfred Reichert, Michael Zimoch, RüdigerPryss and Manuel Neurauter with four studies, these studies are what compose a series of experiments of the same research. Study [26, 35] have the most significant number of authors written by the same seven authors. All the authors of the study [26] are authors of at least one other study of the present mapping, being thus considered the German University Ulm the most influential for the research area of the mapping in question.

5   Related Works

The studies [49, 50] investigate the factors that influence the understanding of process models but do not specifically address the use of do eye-tracking as a way of measuring comprehension. However, there is the study [43] that verifies the use of eye-tracking technology in software engineering. This study conducts a comprehensive survey that does not explicitly address business process models.

Moreover, this research [43] is limited until the year 2014 and with only one search source. After the research by similar studies and in the context already mentioned in work, it was necessary to perform the systematic mapping to know the aspects involved in the understanding of the business process models through techniques and eye-traking.

6   Conclusions and Future Works

The goal of this paper is to provide a comprehensive overview on the evaluation of understanding process models through eye-tracking techniques. To achieve this, a systematic mapping study was performed to find empirical evidence about how the eye-tracking technology has been applied in the understanding of the business process models. The result is an overview of the current practice of eye-tracking in business process models, both industrially and academically. The evidence found indicates that the selected studies are strongly concerned with the understanding of process models, but few of them [30, 35] are concerned with the analysis of DBP understanding in the modeling task. Also, it was possible to verify that there is no standardization about the use of eye-tracking technology in the analysis of the process models. Although there is a standardization of terms used in the use of eye-tracking, e.g. for instance, ocular, sacral, sweep path, duration and attempt-pill [23, 26–28].

These issues identified can be used to offer a research agenda. In works intended for the near future, we will focus our research on the systematization of the manner in which an evaluation with an eye-tracking should be built. Also, we will contribute to improve the state of practice with the conduction of controlled experiments to evaluate the understanding of business process modeling on the fly.

References

1. Vaknin, M., Filipowska, A.: Information quality framework for the design and validation of data flow within business processes - position paper. In: International Conference on Business Information Systems, vol. 8787, pp. 158–168. Springer, Heidelberg (2017)
2. Alotaibi, Y., Liu, F.: Survey of business process management: challenges and solutions. Enterprise Inf. Syst. **11**(8), 1119–1153 (2016)
3. Melcher, J., Seese, D.: Towards validating prediction systems for process understandability: measuring process understandability. In: Proceedings of the 2008 10th SYNASC 2008, Anais, Timisoara. IEEE (2008)
4. Jiménez-ramírez, A., Weber, B., Barba, I., Del Valle, C.: Generating optimized configurable business process models in scenarios subject to uncertainty. Inf. Softw. Technol. **57**(1), 571–594 (2015)
5. Unterkalmsteiner, M., Gorschek, T., Islam, A.K.M.M., Cheng, C.K., Permadi, R.B., Feldt, R.: Evaluation and measurement of software process improvement: a systematic literature review. IEEE Trans. Softw. Eng. **38**, 398–424 (2011)
6. Gibson, D.L., Goldenson, D.R., Kost, K.: Performance results of CMMI-based process improvement. Carnegie-Mellon University, Pittsburgh, PA, Software Engineering Institute (2006)
7. Mohd, N., Ahmad, R., Hassan, N.: Resistance factors in the implementation of software process improvement project. J. Comput. Sci. **4**, 211–219 (2008)
8. Hani, S.U.: Impact of process improvement on software development predictions, for measuring software development project's performance benefits. In: Proceedings of the 7th International Conference on Frontiers of Information Technology, p. 54 (2009)
9. Mendoza, V., Silveira, D.S., Albuquerque, M.L., Araújo, J.: Verifying BPMN understandability with novice business. In: 33rd Symposium on Applied Computing - ACM/SIGAPP, Pau – France, pp. 94–101. ACM (2018)
10. Rodrigues, R.D.A., Barros, M.D.O., Revoredo, K., Azevedo, L.G., Leopold, H.: An experiment on process model understandability using textual work instructions and BPMN models. In: 29th SBES, pp. 41–50 (2015)
11. Figl, K., Recker, J.: Exploring cognitive style and task-specific preferences for process representations. Requirements Eng. **21**(1), 63–85 (2014)
12. Mendling, J., Reijers, H.A., Cardoso, J.: What makes process models understandable? In: Alonso, G., Dadam, P., Rosemann, M. (eds.) BPM 2007. LNCS, vol. 4714, pp. 48–63. Springer, Heidelberg (2007). https://doi.org/10.1007/978-3-540-75183-0_4
13. Kitchenham, B.A., Dyba, T., Jorgensen, M.: Evidence-based software engineering. In: Proceedings of the 26th International Conference on Software Engineering, pp. 273–281. IEEE Computer Society (2004)
14. Petersen, K., Feldt, R., Mujtaba, S., Mattsson, M.: Systematic mapping studies in software engineering. In: Proceedings of the 12th International Conference on Evaluation and Assessment in Software Engineering, EASE 2008, vol. 8, pp. 68–77 (2008)
15. Ko, R.K.L.: A computer scientist's introductory guide to business process management (BPM), XRDS: Crossroads. ACM Mag. Students **15**(4), 4 (2009)
16. Wahl, T., Sindre, G.: An analytical evaluation of BPMN using a semiotic quality framework. In: Advanced Topics in Database Research, vol. 5, pp. 94–105 (2006)
17. Laue, R., Gadatsch, A.: Measuring the understandability of business process models - are we asking the right questions? In: zur Muehlen, M., Su, J. (eds.) BPM 2010. LNBIP, vol. 66, pp. 37–48. Springer, Heidelberg (2011). https://doi.org/10.1007/978-3-642-20511-8_4

18. Sharafi, Z., Shaffer, T., Sharif, B.: Eye-tracking metrics in software engineering. In: Asia-Pacific Software Engineering Conference – APSEC, pp. 96–103 (2015)

19. Moody, D.: The "physics" of notations: toward a scientific basis for constructing visual notations in software engineering. IEEE Trans. Softw. Eng. **35**(6), 756–779 (2009)

20. Kitchenham, B., Charters, S.: Guidelines for performing systematic literature reviews in software engineering. Technical report EBSE 2007-001, Keele University and Durham University Joint Report (2007)

21. OMG BPMN2, Business Process Model and Notation (BPMN) v2.0, Object Management Group (2011)

22. Da Silva, F.Q., et al.: Replication of empirical studies in software engineering research: a systematic mapping study. Empirical Softw. Eng. **19**(3), 501–557 (2014)

23. Wang, W.: The effect of rule linking on business process model understanding. In: Wang, W. (ed.) Integrating Business Process Models and Rules. LNBIP, vol. 343, pp. 42–59. Springer, Cham (2019). https://doi.org/10.1007/978-3-030-11809-9_5

24. Abbad Andaloussi, A., Slaats, T., Burattin, A., Hildebrandt, T.T., Weber, B.: Evaluating the understandability of hybrid process model representations using eye tracking: first insights. In: Daniel, F., Sheng, Q.Z., Motahari, H. (eds.) BPM 2018. LNBIP, vol. 342, pp. 475–481. Springer, Cham (2019). https://doi.org/10.1007/978-3-030-11641-5_37

25. Boutin, K.-D., Léger, P.-M., Davis, C.J., Hevner, A.R., Labonté-LeMoyne, É.: Attentional characteristics of anomaly detection in conceptual modeling. In: Davis, F.D., Riedl, R., vom Brocke, J., Léger, P.-M., Randolph, A.B. (eds.) Information Systems and Neuroscience. LNISO, vol. 29, pp. 57–63. Springer, Cham (2019). https://doi.org/10.1007/978-3-030-01087-4_7

26. Zimoch, M., et al.: Utilizing the capabilities offered by eye-tracking to foster novices' comprehension of business process models. In: Xiao, J., Mao, Z.-H., Suzumura, T., Zhang, L.-J. (eds.) ICCC 2018. LNCS, vol. 10971, pp. 155–163. Springer, Cham (2018). https://doi.org/10.1007/978-3-319-94307-7_12

27. Vermeulen, S.: Real-time business process model tailoring: the effect of domain knowledge on reading strategy. In: Debruyne, C., et al. (eds.) OTM 2017. LNCS, vol. 10697, pp. 280–286. Springer, Cham (2018). https://doi.org/10.1007/978-3-319-73805-5_30

28. Zimoch, M., Mohring, T., Pryss, R., Probst, T., Schlee, W., Reichert, M.: Using insights from cognitive neuroscience to investigate the effects of event-driven process chains on process model comprehension. In: Teniente, E., Weidlich, M. (eds.) BPM 2017. LNBIP, vol. 308, pp. 446–459. Springer, Cham (2018). https://doi.org/10.1007/978-3-319-74030-0_35

29. Pavlicek, J., Hronza, R., Pavlickova, P., Jelinkova, K.: The business process model quality metrics. In: Pergl, R., Lock, R., Babkin, E., Molhanec, M. (eds.) EOMAS 2017. LNBIP, vol. 298, pp. 134–148. Springer, Heidelberg (2017). https://doi.org/10.1007/978-3-319-68185-6_10

30. Weber, B., Neurauter, M., Burattin, A., Pinggera, J., Davis, C.: Measuring and explaining cognitive load during design activities: a fine-grained approach. In: Davis, F.D., Riedl, R., vom Brocke, J., Léger, P.-M., Randolph, A.B. (eds.) Information Systems and Neuroscience. LNISO, vol. 25, pp. 47–53. Springer, Cham (2018). https://doi.org/10.1007/978-3-319-67431-5_6

31. Petrusel, R., Mendling, J., Reijers, H.A.: How visual cognition influences process model comprehension. Decis. Support Syst. **96**, 1–16 (2017)

32. Burattin, A., Kaiser, M., Neurauter, M., Weber, B.: Eye tracking meets the process of process modeling: a visual analytic approach. In: Dumas, M., Fantinato, M. (eds.) BPM 2016. LNBIP, vol. 281, pp. 461–473. Springer, Cham (2017). https://doi.org/10.1007/978-3-319-58457-7_34

33. Zimoch, M., Pryss, R., Schobel, J., Reichert, M.: Eye tracking experiments on process model comprehension: lessons learned. In: Reinhartz-Berger, I., Gulden, J., Nurcan, S., Guédria, W., Bera, P. (eds.) Enterprise, Business-Process and Information Systems Modeling, BPMDS 2017, EMMSAD. LNBIP, vol. 287, pp. 153–168. Springer, Cham (2017). https://doi.org/10.1007/978-3-319-59466-8_10

34. Zimoch, M., Pryss, R., Probst, T., Schlee, W., Reichert, M.: Cognitive insights into business process model comprehension: preliminary results for experienced and inexperienced individuals. In: Reinhartz-Berger, I., Gulden, J., Nurcan, S., Guédria, W., Bera, P. (eds.) BPMDS/EMMSAD -2017. LNBIP, vol. 287, pp. 137–152. Springer, Cham (2017). https://doi.org/10.1007/978-3-319-59466-8_9

35. Petrusel, R., Mendling, J., Reijers, H.A.: Task-specific visual cues for improving process model understanding. Inf. Softw. Technol. **79**, 63–78 (2016)

36. Weber, B., et al.: Measuring cognitive load during process model creation. In: Davis, F.D., Riedl, R., vom Brocke, J., Léger, P.-M., Randolph, A.B. (eds.) Information Systems and Neuroscience. LNISO, vol. 10, pp. 129–136. Springer, Cham (2015). https://doi.org/10.1007/978-3-319-18702-0_17

37. Petrusel, R., Mendling, J.: Eye-tracking the factors of process model comprehension tasks. In: Salinesi, C., Norrie, M.C., Pastor, Ó. (eds.) CAiSE 2013. LNCS, vol. 7908, pp. 224–239. Springer, Heidelberg (2013). https://doi.org/10.1007/978-3-642-38709-8_15

38. Pinggera, J., et al.: Investigating the process of process modeling with eye movement analysis. In: La Rosa, M., Soffer, P. (eds.) BPM 2012. LNBIP, vol. 132, pp. 438–450. Springer, Heidelberg (2013). https://doi.org/10.1007/978-3-642-36285-9_46

39. Molina, A.I., Redondo, M.A., Ortega, M., Lacave, C.: Evaluating a graphical notation for modeling collaborative learning activities: a family of experiments. Sci. Comput. Program. **88**, 54–81 (2014)

40. Burattin, A., Kaiser, M., Neurauter, M., Weber, B.: Learning process modeling phases from modeling interactions and eye tracking data. Data Knowl. Eng. **121**, 1–17 (2019)

41. Chen, T., Wang, W., Indulska, M., Sadiq, S.: Business process and rule integration approaches - an empirical analysis. In: Weske, M., Montali, M., Weber, I., vom Brocke, J. (eds.) BPM 2018. LNBIP, vol. 329, pp. 37–52. Springer, Cham (2018). https://doi.org/10.1007/978-3-319-98651-7_3

42. Santos, M.C.D.F.: Avaliação da Eficácia Cognitiva de Modelos de Requisitos Orientados a Objetivos. Masters Dissertation, Faculdade de Ciência e Tecnologia Universidade nova de Lisboa (2016)

43. Sharafi, Z., Soh, Z., Guéhéneuc, Y.G.: A systematic literature review on the usage of eye-tracking in software engineering. Inf. Softw. Technol. **67**, 79–107 (2015)

44. Scheer, A.-W., Nüttgens, M.: ARIS architecture and reference models for business process management. In: van der Aalst, W., Desel, J., Oberweis, A. (eds.) Business Process Management. LNCS, vol. 1806, pp. 376–389. Springer, Heidelberg (2000). https://doi.org/10.1007/3-540-45594-9_24

45. Petri, C.A.: Kommunikation mit Automaten. Ph.D. thesis, Institut fur Instrumentelle Mathematik (1962)

46. Sommer, M.: Zeitliche Darstellung und Modellierung von Prozessenmithilfe von Gantt-Diagrammen. Bachelors thesis, Ulm University (2012)

47. Lacaze, X., Philippe, P.: Comprehensive handling of temporal issues in tasks models: what is needed and how to support it. In: Workshop 'The Temporal Aspects of Work for HCI (CHI 2004)'. Vienna, Austria (2004)

48. Paternò, F.: ConcurTaskTrees: an engineered notation for task models. In: The Handbook of Task Analysis for Human-Computer Interaction, pp. 483–503 (2004)
49. Dikici, A., Turetken, O., Demirors, O.: Factors influencing the understandability of process models: a systematic literature review. Inf. Softw. Technol. **93**, 112–129 (2018)
50. Figl, K.: Comprehension of procedural visual business process models. Bus. Inf. Syst. Eng. **59**(1), 41–67 (2017)

FakeChain: A Blockchain Architecture to Ensure Trust in Social Media Networks

Iago Sestrem Ochoa[1]([✉]), Gabriel de Mello[1], Luis A. Silva[1],
Abel J. P. Gomes[2,3], Anita M. R. Fernandes[1],
and Valderi Reis Quietinho Leithardt[1,2]

[1] University of Vale do Itajai, Itajai, SC 88302-901, Brazil
{iago.ochoa,gabrieldemello,luis.silva}@edu.univali.br,
anita.fernandes@univali.br
[2] Universidade da Beira Interior, 6200-001 Covilhã, Portugal
valderi.leithardt@ubi.pt
[3] Instituto de Telecomunicações, Covilhã, Portugal
agomes@di.ubi.pt

Abstract. The electoral period has great importance in any democracy, but nowadays, different groups try to get an advantage in the democratic process by posting fake news on social media networks. The use of data mining technique to identify fake news is on development stage, and there is no holistic solution to this problem yet. In our work, we proposed an architecture that uses a centralized blockchain on fake news detection process. The primary characteristic of our architecture is the use of data mining as a consensus algorithm to authenticate the information published on social networks. Using our architecture is possible to identify fake news, alert readers, punish who dissolves this type of information and reward who publish true information on the network.

Keywords: Blockchain · Data mining · Fake news

1 Introduction

The Brazilian 2018 presidential election was one of the most important in the Brazilian history. The political polarization has generated two extremes in the dispute for power. According to the New York Times [13], 44% of the Brazilian population uses WhatsApp as a source of political information. On the eve of the election, the application was used to disseminate an alarming quantity of fake news, in favor of both candidates.

Fake news is an information type that does not represent real facts, and this information is published most of the time on social networks. The purpose of fake news is to generate controversy around a person, aiming to denigrate or benefit his/her image. According to [3], on the 2016 presidential elections of the United States, 8.7 million fake news was shared on Facebook. The negative impact of fake news can be seen from the economic, social, and political point of view.

© Springer Nature Switzerland AG 2019
M. Piattini et al. (Eds.): QUATIC 2019, CCIS 1010, pp. 105–118, 2019.
https://doi.org/10.1007/978-3-030-29238-6_8

With increasing technology evolution, the use of fake news detection techniques becomes necessary to protect users of social networks from being influenced by this kind of news.

In [10] is presented an in-depth study about the definition of fake news and different ways to identify them. Among the techniques presented, the truth-detection method is more consistent with the current scenario, where the main objective is to discover the reliability of the news source and the veracity of the news at the same time. A problem that can restrict the use of this technique is the need for a database to store what sources publish about determined news. For this, it is necessary to use a technique that allows to store the data and keep them continually updated.

In 2008, Nakamoto developed blockchain technology and showed it to the world through bitcoin, a cryptocurrency without a centralizing bank unit [6]. This technology proved to be revolutionary because it ensures users privacy and authenticity in the transactions performed on the platform. Over the years, various applications focused on different scenarios have been developed using this technology.

Considering the scenario of fake news detection, blockchain technology has attracted the attention of researchers because it guarantees the integrity and reliability of the information stored in its block structure. The works presented in [9,11], and [2] show three blockchain architectures focused on the scenario of fake news detection on social networks. However, the solutions presented only address the issue of detecting fake news in social media, dismissing the issue that refers to the reliability of the sources that publish them.

In this way, we intend to use the blockchain technology to detect fake news on social networks and update the reliability level of each source, as shown in [7]. The differential of our architecture is on the consensus algorithm. We used the truth detection technique to guarantee the authenticity of the information published on social networks.

The remainder of this paper is structured as follows. In Sect. 2 is presented the background with the fundamental concepts to understand the proposed architecture. in Sect. 3 is shown the proposed architecture for fake news detection on social networks. Section 4 presents a proof of concept of the proposed architecture and the results obtained through the tests performed. In Sect. 5 is made a comparison between the related works and our architecture, showing the positive and negative features of each work. Finally, Sect. 6 presents the conclusions obtained with this work and the suggestions for future work.

2   Background

Blockchain is a data structure where the blocks are linked together, forming a chain. Inside each block is stored information, this information may vary for each kind of blockchain (i.e., Ethereum and Bitcoin). A cryptographic hash function connects the blocks of the structure, where the hash of the n block is linked with the hash of $n + 1$ block. Some of the characteristics of a blockchain can be defined as type, access, and consensus.

The blockchain type refers to its distribution. Centralized blockchains are stored on a single server, where users have restricted permissions that are set by the network host. In decentralized blockchains, any user can perform operations of writing and reading data. Usually, this type of blockchain is public, allowing access to anyone [5].

The access to a blockchain is characterized by full nodes clients, where the clients who store the blockchain in their device and perform the mining process without relying on other parts. Light clients do not store the blockchain itself and do not participate in the mining process. However, they can access the information contained in the blockchain through the connection with third parties [8].

The consensus is how the blockchain validates the information. The PoW (Proof-of-Work) algorithm ensures consensus in the network by solving a cryptographic problem. The Proof-of-Stake (PoS) algorithm selects the miners of the blocks based on the amount of cryptocurrency the user has, users with higher amount of cryptocurrency has more chances for being chosen to validate the block. The algorithms mentioned above are the most popular ones nowadays, but with the evolution of blockchain technology, new consensus algorithms have been developed to optimize the network and solve existing problems [1].

The truth-discovery algorithm is used to solve conflicts of information that come from different noise sources. This algorithm defines degrees of reliability for a given set of sources, based on the information provided by this sources [4].

Figure 1 illustrates the operation of the truth-discovery algorithm. For an object of interest called *object*, diverse sources s provide an information o in relation to the object. The truth-discovery algorithm processes this information by considering the reliability index of each w source, to get at a conclusion from which sources comes the true information t.

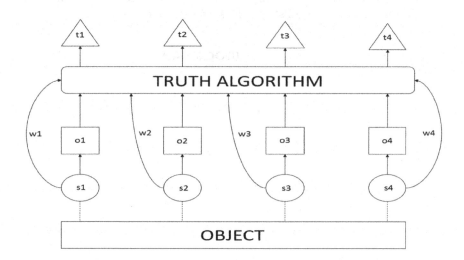

Fig. 1. Truth-discovery algorithm fluxogram.

3   Proposed Architecture

In our architecture, we defined that each news source is considered a network node in the blockchain. Considering that, all sources of news are also miners. The purpose of using this type of architecture is to guarantee the reliability level of each network source since any source that publishes news can be evaluated by what it published.

As the primary goal of our architecture is to prevent fake news spam on social networks, we chose to use a centralized blockchain. News sources are considered full nodes, they are responsible for doing reading and writing operations in the blockchain, in addition to participating in the mining process. The light clients can access the information stored in the blockchain, but they are not able to publish news on it.

As a consensus algorithm, we choose to use the truth-discovery algorithm. When one of the mining nodes defines the veracity of the recorded news of each source, this node earns an increase in its degree of reliability. The nodes that disseminated fake news get their reliability degree decreased as punishment. To be fair to the nodes which have also published real news, even if they can not mine the block, they will also receive a small increase in their reliability degree. In order to not monopolize the network with computational power, our algorithm will use the PoS algorithm concept, where nodes with higher degrees of reliability have more chances to mine new blocks.

Unlike conventional blockchains, we consider in our architecture that every block is an object, so every generated news is considered a blockchain block. Inside each block is stored what each node (source) published about a given object. We choose to define each news as a block to generate transparency to users due to the centralized blockchain architecture, ensuring that the service provider that stores the blockchain does not make changes to it without the consent of the miners. Figure 2 shows the structure described.

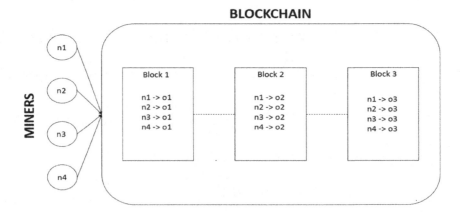

Fig. 2. Blockchain structure.

Storing data in a blockchain is an expensive operation. In this way, the information stored in our blockchain will be metadata abstracted from the published news. Figure 3 shows an example of information stored in the internal structure of a block in our architecture. As can be seen, each block has stored the source, the metadata of the published news, the reliability index of the source after the publication of the news, and the date of publication of the news. Using this type of block structure, we can reduce the storage cost regarding the information.

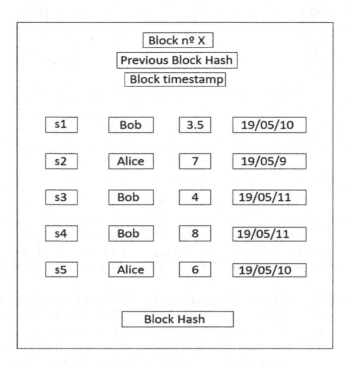

Fig. 3. Blockchain structure.

As can be seen in Fig. 4, our architecture ensures reliability through a degree level given to each source. Even if only one source (node) mines the block the others will gain an increase or decrease in their grade based on what was published, thus guaranteeing democratization in the mining process since the PoS algorithm was chosen to ensure that. We used the Facebook scenario as an example. In (i), the news is published on the social network through a news source. In (ii), the blockchain creates a block and adds what other sources have published on the same object. In (iii), the block is mined, and the reliability levels of each source are updated as calculated by the truth-discovery algorithm.

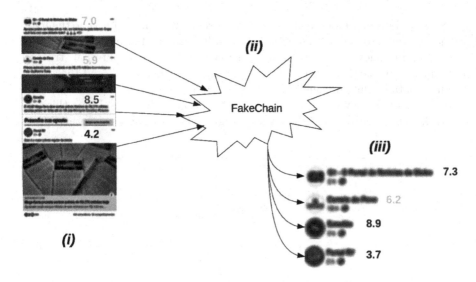

Fig. 4. FakeChain architecture.

4   Proof of Concept and Results

In order to verify the feasibility of using the proposed architecture in a real scenario, we implemented a proof of concept in the Ethereum platform. We used the truffle suite integrated with ganache-cli to create a private network and develop the tests.

We used the smart contracts available in the Ethereum platform to implement the truth finder algorithm. The smart contract developed allowed us to verify and update the reliability levels of each news source. As ganache generates a block for each contract mined, our architecture fit the test environment used.

The tests developed attempted to verify the operation of the contract developed in the Solidity language. We also evaluated the association between the contracts in order to automate the system through the blockchain. Finally, we look at the cost of the contract by varying the number of news publishing sources and checking the overall system operation. We used a desktop computer with Windows 7 OS with 8 GB RAM and AMD FX 6300 3.5 GHz processor. The private network used in the tests had one processing node, with a block size of 12,176,426 gas and 2 Wei gas price.

4.1   Contract Operation

The first test developed corresponds to the operation of the algorithm adapted from Python to the smart contract through solidity programming language. In this test, we attempted to verify the reliability level of the algorithm through the final result of veracity given for each published object. Table 1 shows the results obtained from both algorithms.

Table 1. Precision variation.

Source	Fact	Object	Python algorithm result	Smart contract result
A	Einstein	Special Relativity	True	True
A	Newton	Univ. Gravitation	True	True
B	Einstein	Special Relativity	True	True
B	Galilei	Heliocentrism	True	True
C	Newton	Special Relativity	False	False
C	Galilei	Univ. Gravitation	False	False
C	Einstein	Heliocentrism	False	False

As can be seen in Table 1, the implementation of our algorithm on a smart contract obtained 100 % accuracy result to determine if the presented facts are real or not. We have developed the same test by varying the number of times the contract is executed to verify the accuracy of the results obtained. Figure 5 illustrates the average precision of hits by varying the number of times the contract is executed.

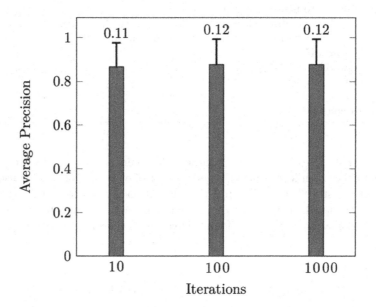

Fig. 5. Average precision and standard deviation varying the number of iterations.

The results presented in Fig. 5 show a small difference in accuracy by varying the number of times the algorithm was executed. The most significant difference considering the number of fact samples is equal to seven, can only be observed between 10 and 100 interactions. From these values, the reliability assignments based on the logarithmic scale do not influence any significant difference in the final execution result of the truth finder algorithm.

4.2   Contract Linkage

To enable the implementation of our architecture, in the smart contract development process, we attempted to link the trustability level of each source in the creation of each new smart contract regarding a new object. We choose to use this type of architecture in order to our application be as much decentralized as possible, eliminating the need for third-party service for storing data regarding the trustability level of each news source. Algorithm 1 illustrates the code function developed to ensure this functionality.

Algorithm 1. Contract Linkage Function

```
 1: procedure GENERATE CHILDREN(address pChildren, address Contract)
 2:     addres nC = new NewsLedger()
 3:     NewsLedger pC = NewsLedger pChildren
 4:     for i=1 to pChildren.size do
 5:         for j=1 to newChildren.size do
 6:             if nC.dataframe[j].source equals dataframe[i].source then
 7:                 nC.dataframe[j].trust = pC.dataframe[i].trust
 8:             end if
 9:         end for
10:     end for
11:     Contract = nC
12: end procedure
```

As seen in Algorithm 1, the function that generates new child contracts belongs to the truth finder contract code. A list of addresses of these subsequent agreements is stored in it. The function, based on the address of the previous contract, generates an instance of the new contract, crossing both contracts, searching similar sources that if found, have their reliability attribute modified.

4.3   Contract Cost

Considering that our proof of concept used the Ethereum blockchain, we evaluated in our tests the contract gas cost for the proposed architecture. For the evaluation of the gas cost of each contract, we vary the functions present in the contract for the standard and pure types. For standard functions, the network allows the storage of data in the blockchain and the use of it as a source of processing. Pure functions use the Ethereum network only as a processing source. Table 2 shows the gas cost of the contract for the two types of function.

As can be seen in Table 2, we developed four contracts versions. In each version, we changed the number of functions of the pure type and the standard

Table 2. Precision variation.

Contract version	Standard functions	Pure functions	Contract cost (gas)
1	18	2	0.241581
2	17	3	0.241581
3	16	4	0.241581
4	15	5	0.241581

type in order to reduce the gas cost of the contract. None of the versions tested presented cost variation. Most of the implemented functions modify states in the contract and have interdependence among them, not allowing a test where all of them were modified to pure. Because of this, there was no difference in the results.

We evaluated the contract cost by the number of sources, and this factor has a significant impact on the contract cost since it is necessary to store what each source reports about a specific object. Therefore, we also evaluated the contract cost by varying the number of sources that publishes a particular news item. Figure 6 shows the results obtained.

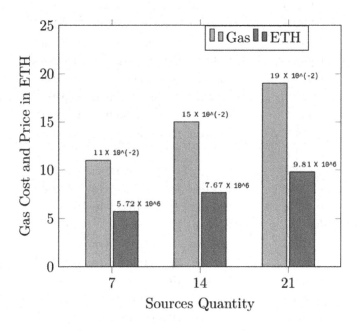

Fig. 6. Gas cost varying sources quantity.

In this test, we varied the number of sources to observe the impact on the gas cost and the price in ETH. The adopted samples were of 7, 14, and 21 news in order to evaluate a possible linear growth based on the tests carried out in Python by [12]. Thus, the results corresponded to the expected values and adopted a continuous growth format.

4.4   Overall System Evaluation

After the performance evaluation of the proposed architecture we did a test to verify the effectiveness of the system for a real situation. We performed the simulation of the proposed architecture by executing three smart contracts, wherein each contract different news items were published. We developed the test with seven, fourteen, and twenty-one news sources. Table 3 shows the values obtained by the tests performed and the expected values.

Table 3. Overall system result.

Source	Trustworthiness	Fact	Object	Fact confidence
A	0.95256	Einstein	Special Relativity	0.95256
A	0.95256	Newton	Univ. Gravitation	0.95256
A	0.95256	Einstein	Special Relativity	0.95256
A	0.95256	Newton	Univ.Gravitation	0.95256
B	0.95256	Einstein	Special Relativity	0.95256
B	0.95256	Galilei	Heliocentrism	0.95256
B	0.95256	Galilei	Heliocentrism	0.95256
B	0.95256	Galilei	Heliocentrism	0.95256
C	0.88077	Newton	Special Relativity	0.88077
C	0.88077	Galilei	Univ. Gravitation	0.88077
C	0.88077	Einstein	Heliocentrism	0.88077
C	0.88077	Galilei	Special Relativity	0.88077
D	0.87954	Newton	Univ. Gravitation	0.95256
D	0.87954	Einstein	Special Relativity	0.95256
D	0.87954	Galilei	Special Relativity	0.88077
D	0.87954	Einstein	Heliocentrism	0.88077
D	0.87954	Einstein	Univ. Gravitation	0.73103
E	0.84334	Newton	Special Relativity	0.88077
E	0.84334	Einstein	Heliocentrism	0.88077
E	0.84334	Galilei	Univ.Gravitation	0.88077
E	0.84334	Newton	Heliocentrism	0.73103

In Table 3, we can observe the results after generating three contracts. We calculated the reliability of each source in the final result according to the grades assigned in previous contracts, and they are in ascending order in Table 3.

In tests done, only ten relationships entered in Table 3 are correct. The results show that the highest grades, considering the reliability of source and fact, were attributed to real facts, propagated mainly by sources A and B, which have a higher reliability index. Considering this, the sites that propagated fake news information, such as C, D, and E, were below the table, even if occasionally they could deliver truthful information.

For the tests, the initial values of Dampening Factor and Influence Related attributes were 0.8 and 0.6, respectively. In the algorithm, Dampening Factor is used as a way to prevent excessively high-reliability indexes. Influence Related, on the other hand, denotes how much information with similar facts can help with reliability. These settings, as well as the samples, were based on the Python language-adapted code.

Regarding the implementation of the Truth Finder algorithm in Solidity, there was only one function of the original algorithm in Python that was not implemented. The Implication function works based on the logic of facts about the same objects that could be conflicting or supportive, which would not cause a significant perturbation in the results, besides an increase in accuracy.

5   Related Work

Song et al. [11] describe the use of blockchain to ensure the authenticity of publications on social networks. The authors mention that blockchain cannot identify the veracity of the data stored in its blocks. Considering this situation, Song et al. suggest the use of a digital signature on information posted by users, thus ensuring the authenticity that someone has verified the information stored in the blockchain. In their model, the social media service provider (i.e., Facebook or Instagram) generates a digital signature through Public Key Infrastructure on each publication done by users and stores the digital signature in the blockchain. In a given moment, when a user wants to check the authenticity of a publication, the public key of the social media service provider is used to verify the authenticity of a publication. The authors report that their system is fraud-proof because only the social media service provider has the private key for the encryption of digital signatures.

Shang et al. [9] present a blockchain architecture to ensure transparency in the process of publishing, disseminating, and tracking news on social media networks. The authors suggest storing information concerning the content of the news, category, and other data about it when the news is published. Regarding the dissemination of the news, the authors indicate storing the information about the time and hash of the news published, thus creating the block structure of the blockchain. When a reader wishes to read a news item, through the information stored in the blockchain, it can verify the origin and path of the news during the publication and dissemination process.

Huckle and White [2] detail an architecture to identify the publication of fake news on social networks. Their solution uses a tool to extract the metadata of an image published in news sites. The metadata is divided into four entities, being copyright, event, object, and agent. Each of these entities is responsible for storing a part of the image metadata. The authors use the blockchain to store the hash of the original image and the metadata of the image. Thus, when a user wants to check if an image is real, it checks in blockchain whether the hash of the image exists.

Table 4 shows a comparison of the related works with our architecture. In the comparison, we listed the year of publication of the paper, the main functionality of the blockchain for the architecture proposed in each of the works, and the advantages and disadvantages of each solution.

Table 4. Related work comparison.

Work	Year	Blockchain functionality	Advantage	Disadvantages
[11]	2019	Digital signature storage	Authenticated information	Centralized architecture
[9]	2018	Information storage	Scratch information	Unauthenticated information
[2]	2017	Hash/metadata storage	Authenticated information	High cost
Our work	2019	Algorithm processing	Reliability e authenticity	Require a significant amount of sources

As can be seen in Table 4, all related works use the blockchain for data storage, but none of the authors mention how to treat the issue of the storage cost of the information in the blockchain since this type of operation has a high cost. In our work, we used blockchain as the processing source for the truth-discovery algorithm, reducing the cost of data storage.

The works presented on [11] and [2] ensure the authenticity of the information, the work of [9] guarantees the readability of the published information. Our architecture guarantees both conditions because the truth discovery algorithm allows to discover the truthfulness of a fact (authenticity) and to update the reliability level of a source based on the news published by it.

Although the work of [11] uses blockchain, it uses a centralized architecture since only one entity can authenticate the information published on the platform. In the work of [9], while ensuring the path of information, the work does not guarantee that the information is correct. In the architecture described in [2], the main disadvantage observed was the cost of the application, since storing an image and its metadata in a blockchain becomes expensive (the solution presented by the authors uses the Ethereum Platform, which has a high cost of information storage). In our work, the main disadvantage observed is the number of news sources to determine the truth of a fact. If there are a small number of news sources, the value of the information's veracity calculation may be false-negative.

6   Conclusion and Future Work

In this paper, we have presented a blockchain architecture focused on fake news detection. Our architecture defines each block as an object, and inside each block is stored what each source knows about this object. Even using a centralized blockchain, our architecture ensures transparency to users through this type of structure, ensuring that the host cannot change the information stored in the blockchain. An advantage of our architecture is the truth-discovery consensus algorithm, which is used to validate and achieve consensus among users, rewarding users who publish real news and punishing those who post fake news.

With the proof of concept developed, we proved the feasibility of implementing the proposed architecture. The smart contract developed proved to be efficient in terms of fake news detection. The simulation of a real situation showed the effectiveness of the proposed architecture. In comparison to related work, our architecture is different because it can show users the reliability index of each news source present in the system through a system of reliability level.

As future work, we intend to improve the smart contract developed to act in a similar way to the PoS algorithm, guaranteeing democratization in the block mining process. We will also develop a data mining module aimed at obtaining the metadata of every social media article. Regarding the blockchain, we intend to develop the same tests on Hyperledger blockchain, considering its focus for business applications. We also intend to develop tests in the NEM blockchain since the advantage of using this blockchain refers to scalability issues.

Although our architecture is promising, it is necessary the study of data mining techniques and blockchain, since both themes are current and lack references that show an implementation focused on the chosen scenario.

Acknowledgment. This work was financed by the Coordenação de Aperfeiçoamento de Pessoal de Nível Superior – Brasil (CAPES) – Finance Code 001 and Fundação de Amaparo à Pesquisa e Inovação do Estado de Santa Catarina – Brasil (FAPESC) – Grant No. 2019TR169. This research has been partially supported by the Portuguese Research Council (Fundação para a Ciência e Tecnologia), under the FCT Project UID/EEA/50008/2019.

References

1. Chalaemwongwan, N., Kurutach, W.: State of the art and challenges facing consensus protocols on blockchain. In: 2018 International Conference on Information Networking (ICOIN), pp. 957–962, January 2018. https://doi.org/10.1109/ICOIN.2018.8343266
2. Huckle, S., White, M.: Fake news: a technological approach to proving the origins of content, using blockchains. Big Data 5(4), 356–371 (2017). https://doi.org/10.1089/big.2017.0071. pMID: 29235919
3. Kshetri, N., Voas, J.: The economics of "fake news". IT Prof. 19(6), 8–12 (2017). https://doi.org/10.1109/MITP.2017.4241459
4. Li, Y., et al.: A survey on truth discovery. CoRR abs/1505.02463 (2015). http://arxiv.org/abs/1505.02463

5. Mukhopadhyay, U., Skjellum, A., Hambolu, O., Oakley, J., Yu, L., Brooks, R.: A brief survey of cryptocurrency systems. In: 2016 14th Annual Conference on Privacy, Security and Trust (PST), pp. 745–752, December 2016. https://doi.org/10.1109/PST.2016.7906988
6. Nakamoto, S.: Bitcoin (2008). https://bitcoin.org/bitcoin.pdf. Accessed 07 May 2019
7. Parikh, S.B., Atrey, P.K.: Media-rich fake news detection: a survey. In: 2018 IEEE Conference on Multimedia Information Processing and Retrieval (MIPR), pp. 436–441, April 2018. https://doi.org/10.1109/MIPR.2018.00093
8. Rouhani, S., Deters, R.: Performance analysis of ethereum transactions in private blockchain. In: 2017 8th IEEE International Conference on Software Engineering and Service Science (ICSESS), pp. 70–74, November 2017. https://doi.org/10.1109/ICSESS.2017.8342866
9. Shang, W., Liu, M., Lin, W., Jia, M.: Tracing the source of news based on blockchain. In: 2018 IEEE/ACIS 17th International Conference on Computer and Information Science (ICIS), pp. 377–381, June 2018. https://doi.org/10.1109/ICIS.2018.8466516
10. Shu, K., Sliva, A., Wang, S., Tang, J., Liu, H.: Fake news detection on social media: A data mining perspective. CoRR abs/1708.01967 (2017). http://arxiv.org/abs/1708.01967
11. Song, G., Kim, S., Hwang, H., Lee, K.: Blockchain-based notarization for social media. In: 2019 IEEE International Conference on Consumer Electronics (ICCE), pp. 1–2, January 2019. https://doi.org/10.1109/ICCE.2019.8661978
12. Takeshi, I.: Truthfinder (2018). https://github.com/IshitaTakeshi/TruthFinder. Accessed 10 May 2019
13. Times, T.N.Y.: Fake news is poisoning Brazilian politics. Whatsapp can stop it (2018). https://www.nytimes.com/2018/10/17/opinion/brazil-election-fake-news-whatsapp.html. Accessed 07 May 2019

An Experience in Modelling Business Process Architecture

Geert Poels[1(✉)] [iD], Francisco Ruiz[2] [iD], and Félix García[2] [iD]

[1] Faculty of Economics and Business Administration,
Ghent University, Ghent, Belgium
geert.poels@ugent.be
[2] Institute of Information Technology and Systems,
University of Castilla-La Mancha, Ciudad Real, Spain
{francisco.ruizg, felix.garcia}@uclm.es

Abstract. We present a mapping of a previously designed Business Process Architecture (BPA) meta-model onto ArchiMate, i.e., the *de facto* standard Enterprise Architecture (EA) modelling language. This construct mapping allows developing process maps, i.e., descriptions of (views of) the business process architecture of an organization. We demonstrate the development of these process maps using the Signavio Business Process Management (BPM) modelling platform. The developed process maps are part of the organization's enterprise architecture model and are linked to BPMN process diagrams that detail the functional, control-flow, data and resource aspects of the business processes included in the process map. Our research contributes to the integration of BPM and EA by researching BPA as a concept common to both disciplines.

Keywords: Process map · Business process architecture ·
Enterprise architecture

1 Introduction

In the Business Process Management (BPM) field, quality is one of four business process performance dimensions, collectively known as the Devil's Quadrangle (i.e., time, cost, quality, flexibility) [1]. Process quality can be internal or external [1], where the former refers to the process participants' perspective (e.g., job satisfaction) and the latter to the process clients' perspective (e.g., satisfaction with the process outcome). Bearing on insights from software quality [2], we contend that *fit for purpose* is another quality viewpoint. This type of quality hasn't received much attention in BPM. In the context of business processes, we see fit for purpose as the fit between an organization's competitive positioning and its internal arrangement [3]. In this perspective, quality of business processes refers to how effective these processes are in implementing an organization's chosen strategy (i.e., strategic alignment). Unlike the other two quality perspectives, this quality dimension cannot be assessed for isolated processes. It requires a holistic view of an organization's collection of business processes as the raison d'être of a process depends on its role in the business (process) architecture of an organization.

© Springer Nature Switzerland AG 2019
M. Piattini et al. (Eds.): QUATIC 2019, CCIS 1010, pp. 119–126, 2019.
https://doi.org/10.1007/978-3-030-29238-6_9

The question of fit for purpose of an organization's business processes is addressed in the field of Enterprise Architecture (EA). Like many BPM quality evaluation and improvement techniques [4–6], many EA analysis techniques are model-based, i.e., require a model of the artefact to be analyzed. For instance, the Process-Goal-Alignment (PGA) method for strategic alignment analysis [7] requires a model of the business architecture representing value chains, their activities, and their relationships with organizational goals and components of the business model.

Models of business process architecture are referred to as process maps [8] or process landscape models [1]. To analyze the fit for purpose of an organization's business processes, the following requirements must be met:

- Being able to systematically develop process maps that represent an organization's collection of business processes;
- Being able to integrate process maps into enterprise architecture models.

Currently, there does not exist a generally used language for modelling business process architectures that allows for integration of process maps into enterprise architecture models. Recently, Malinova [9] designed a modelling language for process maps, based on extensive empirical research into the most commonly used concepts and symbols for representing business process architectures. A related proposal for modelling process landscapes and value chains of core processes is included in the most recent version of the BPM textbook Fundamentals of Business Process Management [1]. These proposals did not address how to integrate the models into enterprise architecture models. To address this gap, we initiated a research project developing a tool-supported language for process maps. We started by designing the Business Process Architecture Meta-Model (BPAM) for describing business process architectures as part of enterprise architectures [10]. Following [11], having a meta-model specification is a requirement for the definition of the abstract syntax of a modelling language. In our current work, we are designing a set of modelling languages for the BPAM. In our search, we came across the Signavio[1] modelling platform for BPM. An interesting feature of Signavio is that it supports, apart from BPMN, also ArchiMate, which is the *de facto* standard EA modelling language. In Signavio, a Business Process element in an ArchiMate model can be linked to the BPMN diagram that models the process represented by this Business Process element.

The ability to link enterprise architecture models (in ArchiMate) with business process models (in BPMN) makes Signavio an interesting case for our research. Therefore, in this paper, we address the research question *How to map BPAM onto ArchiMate such that Signavio can be used as a modelling platform for business process architecture?* To investigate this research question, we designed a mapping of BPAM onto the ArchiMate meta-model such that process maps can be developed in Signavio.

The paper proceeds as follows: Sect. 2 provide background information on the integration of BPM and EA as intended by Signavio and on BPAM. Section 3 then presents our construct mapping. Section 4 concludes the paper and outlines future research.

---

[1] https://www.signavio.com.

2   Background

2.1   Integrating BPM and EA Using Signavio

In academic research, BPM and EA have developed as distinct disciplines with little interaction despite that business process is a key concept in both. Practitioners have, however, felt the need to connect the two fields [12]. For instance, Signavio (the company) has teamed up with Cisco Systems to evolve Signavio (the tool) into a common platform for BPM and EA management. With a combined tool that supports EA modelling with ArchiMate and business process modelling with BPMN, the process landscape can be integrated into the enterprise architecture [13]. The Signavio modelling platform also supports value chain modelling, similar – but not identical – to process landscape modelling as in [1]. Figure 1 shows a screenshot of how elements in a value chain diagram can be linked to BPMN process diagrams. Similar links can be created from within an ArchiMate model.

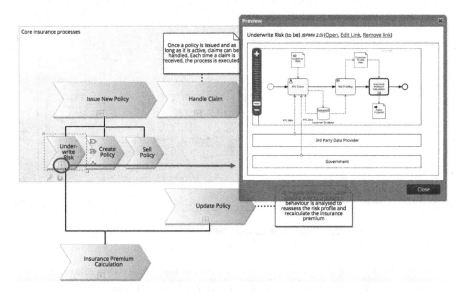

Fig. 1. Signavio screenshot of a value chain diagram with a link to a BPMN process diagram

It seems that the Signavio platform provides the functionality that would be required to describe business process architectures (in ArchiMate or using the tool's native value chain modelling notation) and to link business process architecture elements to BPMN process diagrams that detail the functional, control flow, data and resource aspects of business processes. Knowledge of how to develop process maps (e.g., guidelines, modelling patterns, consistency checking mechanisms) is, however, lacking. By offering a meta-model to represent business process architecture and mapping this meta-model onto ArchiMate, we provide a starting point of a method for developing process maps in Signavio and linking them with business process models.

2.2 Business Process Architecture Meta-Model

The design of BPAM (Fig. 2) was based on a literature review and concept mapping study, where we disentangled the concepts of business process architecture and process map (i.e., a description of (a view of) the business process architecture) [14]. Unlike the work of Malinova [9], BPAM is framed as a meta-model for and complies with the ISO/IEC/IEEE 42010 standard for architecture description, hereby transcending the BPM view of business process architecture as a management tool for large collections of business processes. Furthermore, BPAM includes a placeholder for enterprise architecture elements, allowing them to be related to business process architecture elements in process maps. As such, process maps can be integrated into enterprise architecture models, facilitating EA management techniques like strategic alignment analysis.

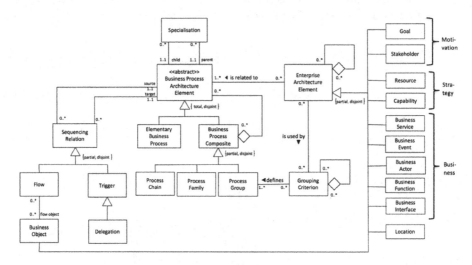

Fig. 2. Business process architecture meta-model [10]

Note that the multiplicity constraints in the meta-model have been relaxed to allow for multiple views of the business process architecture. For instance, one process map for a particular stakeholder/purpose might show a business process as elementary, while another process map for another stakeholder/purpose might show the same business process as composite. Likewise, though a flow is defined by a flow object, it is not required to show this object in the process map. Similarly, for process groups it is not required that the defining grouping criteria are shown in the process map.

Table 1 provides definitions of the BPAM elements. For more details, we refer to [10].

Table 1. Definition of BPAM elements (from [10])

BPAM element	Definition
Elementary business process	An atomic[a] BPA element
Business process composite	A BPA element that is not an elementary business process
Sequencing relation	A relationship between a source BPA element and a target BPA element implying a temporal ordering of source and target
Flow	A sequencing relation in which a business object flows from source to target
Business object	An object that flows between BPA elements (e.g., information, physical items, persons)
Trigger	A sequencing relation in which the source instantiates and starts the target
Delegation	A trigger relation in which the source is dependent on the outcome of the target
Process chain	An aggregate of BPA elements that are related through sequencing relations
Specialization	A relationship between a child element and a parent element implying that the child specializes the parent
Process family	An aggregate of BPA elements that are related through specialization relations where the parent assumes the role of standard process and the children are variants of this standard process[b]
Grouping criterion	A property that defines a process group (e.g., the process owner is the CIO, the process category is core processes)
Process group	An aggregate of BPA elements defined by grouping criteria
Enterprise architecture element	An element that is part of the enterprise architecture and that is related to a BPA element (e.g., a capability realized by a BPA element, a business actor participating in a BPA element)

[a]Atomic means that the internal structure and operation of the business process is hidden. The process map thus provides a black-box view of elementary business processes [15].
[b]Following [15], the standard process represents the process family.

3   Representing Process Maps with ArchiMate

To represent process maps as instantiations of BPAM with ArchiMate in Signavio, the meta-model concepts were mapped onto ArchiMate concepts. Table 2 presents the results of this mapping.

Table 2. Construct mapping BPAM onto ArchiMate and notation in Signavio

BPAM concept	ArchiMate concept	ArchiMate Notation (in Signavio)
Elementary Business Process	Business Process	
Business Object	Business Object	
Business Process Composite	An aggregate of business processes or other such aggregates	
Process Group	Grouping of business processes or aggregates of business processes	
Grouping Criterion	-	Text
Process Chain	An aggregate of business processes or other such aggregates, where aggregated elements are related with triggering or flow relationships.	
Process Family	A business process or aggregate of business processes that is specialized.	
Sequencing Relation	-	-
Trigger	Triggering Relationship between business processes or aggregates of business processes	
Flow	Flow Relationship between business processes or aggregates of business processes	
flow object	Association Relationship from Flow Relationship to Business Object	
Delegation	-	
Specialization	Specialization Relationship between business processes or aggregates of business processes.	
Enterprise Architecture Element	ArchiMate element	ArchiMate standard notation
is related to	ArchiMate relationship	ArchiMate standard notation
is used by	-	Specified as text in the note that describes the Grouping Criterion

When designing the mapping, compromises were made as Signavio strictly adheres to standard ArchiMate and does not support language extension mechanisms. Modelling a BPAM Business Process Composite (or its BPAM Process Chain specialization) as an aggregate of business processes or other such aggregates is clear as long as the aggregated elements are explicitly shown in the process map, which is not required given the high level of abstraction allowed in process maps [10]. If the aggregated elements are not shown, then the mapping is not injective (i.e., the ArchiMate Business Process symbol may represent a BPAM Elementary Business Process or a BPAM Business Process Composite). The same problem holds for BPAM Process Groups and BPAM Process Families, although here the association with a text notation (describing the grouping criterion), even if not mandatory, helps distinguishing between these types of business process composite.

The construct mapping is incomplete for the BPAM Grouping Criterion element and is used by relationship, although both can be represented using text annotations. There is no such solution for the BPAM Sequencing Relation, which is only problematic when BPAM elements are sequenced differently than with trigger, delegation or flow relationships – a case which is rare in practice [10]. The mapping of the BPAM Delegation Relation onto the ArchiMate Serving relationship is unconventional as Serving is not a dynamic relationship (like Triggering and Flow). Therefore we propose to use the ArchiMate symbol for Serving to represent BPAM Delegation in Signavio, while semantically considering it as a Sequencing relation. The source of the Delegation relation is the BPAM element that delegates, while the target is the BPAM element that is delegated to. Visually, however, the source is located at the arrowhead of the Serves relationship, while the target is located at the base of the arrow.

4   Conclusion

The mapping of BPAM onto ArchiMate allows developing process maps in Signavio that are part of the enterprise architecture model of an organization. Signavio allows linking such process maps to process diagrams that detail the processes. Process maps representing (views of) the business process architecture as part of the enterprise architecture can be useful for strategic alignment analysis of an organization's business processes. We see strategic alignment as the fit for purpose of an organization's processes, which is a business process quality dimension that has received little attention in BPM research, despite the recognition of strategic alignment as a key success factor for BPM [1]. This is just one example of a benefit of better integrating the BPM and EA disciplines. Our research on BPAM contributes to the integration of both disciplines.

Further research is required. The linking of enterprise architecture models and business process models in Signavio needs further investigation. For instance, we are developing a consistency checking mechanism for process maps (in ArchiMate) and process diagrams (in BPMN). Further research is also needed to establish a bijective mapping (e.g., by using ArchiMate extension mechanisms). The mapping presented in this paper, specifically aimed at being able to develop process maps in Signavio, results in one of several alternative notations for BPAM we are currently investigating.

Acknowledgements. This work is supported by the projects BIZDEVOPS-Global (ref. RTI2018-098309-B-C31), funded by the Spanish Ministry of Economy, Industry and Competition (MINECO) & FEDER and G3Soft (Engineering of Models for Governance and Management of Global Software Development) funded by "Consejería de Educación, Cultura y Deportes de la Dirección General de Universidades, Investigación e Innovación de la JCCM" of Spain.

References

1. Dumas, M., La Rosa, M., Mendling, J., Reijers, H.A.: Fundamentals of Business Process Management, 2nd edn. Springer, Berlin (2018). https://doi.org/10.1007/978-3-662-56509-4
2. Bøegh, J.: A new standard for quality requirements. IEEE Softw. **2**, 57–63 (2008)
3. Henderson, J.C., Venkatraman, N.: Strategic alignment: leveraging information technology for transforming organizations. IBM Syst. J. **36**(2&3), 472–484 (1999)
4. Delgado, A., Weber, B., Ruiz, F., Garcia-Rodríguez de Guzmán, I., Piattini, M.: An integrated approach based on execution measures for the continuous improvement of business processes realized by services. Inf. Softw. Technol. **56**, 134–162 (2014)
5. Moreno-Montes de Oca, I., Snoeck, M., Reijers, H.A., Rodríguez-Morffi, A.: A systematic literature review of studies on business process modelling quality. Inf. Softw. Technol. **58**, 187–205 (2015)
6. Sánchez-González, L., García, F., Ruiz, F., Piattini, M.: A case study about the improvement of business process models driven by indicators. Softw. Syst. Modeling **16**(3), 759–788 (2017)
7. Roelens, B., Steenacker, W., Poels, G.: Realizing strategic fit within the business architecture: the design of a process-goal alignment modelling and analysis technique. Softw. Syst. Modeling **18**(1), 631–662 (2019)
8. Heinrich, B., Henneberger, M., Leist, S., Zellner, G.: The process map as an instrument to standardize processes: design and application at a financial service provider. Inf. Syst. E-Business Manag. **7**, 81–102 (2009)
9. Malinova, M.: A language for designing process maps: abstract syntax, semantics and concrete syntax. Ph.D. dissertation, Vienna University of Economics and Business (2016)
10. Poels, G., García, F., Ruiz, F., Piattini, M.: Architecting business process maps. Comput. Sci. Inf. Syst. (2019, in press)
11. Guizzardi, G.: Ontological foundations for structural conceptual models. Ph.D. dissertation, University of Twente (2005)
12. von Rosing, M., Hove, M., Subbarao, R.R., Preston, T.W.: Getting Business Transformation right: Combining BPM and EA (2012)
13. Lakhegyi, P., Decker, G., Klauberg, K.: The integration of EAM and BPA (2013)
14. Poels, G., García, F., Ruiz, F., Piattini, M.: Conceptualizing Business Process Maps: Technical report as a complement to Architecting Business Process Maps (2018). https://arxiv.org/abs/1812.05395
15. Van Nuffel, D., De Backer, M.: Multi-abstraction layered business process modelling. Comput. Ind. **63**(2), 131–147 (2012)

Evidence-Based Software Engineering

Empirical Analysis of Object-Oriented Metrics and Centrality Measures for Predicting Fault-Prone Classes in Object-Oriented Software

Alexandre Ouellet and Mourad Badri[✉]

Software Engineering Research Laboratory,
Department of Mathematics and Computer Science,
Université du Québec à Trois-Rivières, Trois-Rivières, Québec, Canada
{alexandre.ouellet,mourad.badri}@uqtr.ca

Abstract. A large number of metrics have been proposed in the literature to measure various structural properties of object-oriented software. Furthermore, many centrality measures have been introduced to identify central nodes in large networks. To the best of our knowledge, only few empirical software engineering studies have explored these metrics in the case of software systems. This paper aims at providing further evidence on the usefulness of centrality measures as indicators of software defect proneness by: (1) investigating the relationships between object-oriented metrics and centrality measures, and (2) exploring how they can be combined to improve the prediction of fault-prone classes in object-oriented software. We collected data from five different versions of one open source Java software system. We used the Principal Component Analysis technique to eliminate metrics (measures) providing redundant information. Then, we built different models to predict fault-prone classes using four machine learning algorithms. Results indicate that: (1) some centrality measures capture information that is not captured by traditional object-oriented metrics, and (2) combining centrality measures with object-oriented metrics improves the performance of fault-prone classes prediction.

Keywords: Object-oriented metrics · Centrality measures ·
Principal Component Analysis · Machine learning algorithms ·
Fault-prone classes prediction · Empirical analysis

1 Introduction

Software metrics have become a key element in several domains of software engineering. Software metrics are used to predict different quality attributes of the software product [5,37]. A large number of object-oriented metrics (OOM) have been proposed in the literature to measure various structural properties

© Springer Nature Switzerland AG 2019
M. Piattini et al. (Eds.): QUATIC 2019, CCIS 1010, pp. 129–143, 2019.
https://doi.org/10.1007/978-3-030-29238-6_10

of object-oriented (OO) software [20]. These metrics are used to assess different software attributes such as size, complexity and coupling. However, many of these metrics are highly related and provide redundant information. In addition, the majority of OOM basically focus on intrinsic properties of classes. Only few OOM quantify some facets of the dependency structure of the software system, capturing mainly information about immediate dependencies.

Furthermore, many centrality measures (CM) have been introduced in the literature to identify central nodes in large networks. These metrics are derived using concepts from Social Network Analysis (SNA) field [9,10,17]. CM can be interpreted as measuring different aspects of a node importance in complex networks and SNA. To the best of our knowledge, only few empirical software engineering studies have explored these metrics. CM, as opposed to most traditional code metrics that only focus on intrinsic properties of singles elements, can be used to better model the control flow and identify the most (relative) important or central components in a software system. This paper aims at providing further evidence on the usefulness of CM as indicators of software defect proneness by: (1) investigating the relationships between OOM and CM, and (2) exploring how they can be combined to improve the prediction of fault-prone classes in OO software. We investigated the three following research questions:

RQ1: Is there a relationship between OOM and CM?
RQ2: Do CM capture information that is not captured by OOM?
RQ3: Does the combination of OOM and CM improve the performance of fault-prone classes prediction compared to using OOM or CM alone?

Some studies have already addressed, but nevertheless summarily, some topics related to our research questions [6,7,13,33,38,39,41,42]. In addition to these, we present in this paper a non-aggregated correlation analysis and an in-depth Principal Component Analysis (PCA). We used some OOM basically related to size, complexity and coupling, and various CM. We also extend the results of previous studies (in terms of fault prediction) by exploring new CM, and investigating various machine learning algorithms.

The rest of the paper is organized as follows. Section 2 gives an overview of the few related studies based on centrality measures in software engineering, and presents some of the important studies that have addressed the prediction of fault-prone classes. Section 3 presents summarily the OOM and CM we used in our study. Section 4 presents the empirical study we performed to investigate the three research questions. Finally, Sect. 5 concludes the paper and gives some future work directions.

2   Related Work

Zimmermann and Nagappan [42] used network analysis on dependency graphs. They investigated different network measures (including degree, betweenness, closeness and eigenvector measures) calculated on low-level dependency graphs (ego network and global network) to predict defects in binaries. The authors found that models predicting faults using network measures have better recall and identify a larger proportion of critical units than models using only simple OO complexity metrics. Tosun et al. [38] replicated the study of Zimmermann and Nagappan on several versions of two open-source projects, one small and one large. They confirmed the results previously obtained. The authors used logistic regression and naïve bayes classifier to predict defects using code metrics and network measures. They found that network measures improve prediction rates for large and complex systems and have no significant impact on small systems. Bettenberg et al. [6] presented a comparison of three different approaches for creating statistical regression models to predict software defects and development effort. Global models were trained on the whole dataset, while local models were trained on subsets of the dataset. Results suggest that local models show a significant increased fit to the data compared to global models. Chen et al. [13] explored the ability of network measures to predict high severity fault-prone modules. The authors used logistic regression to build prediction models, and network measures similar to those used by Zimmermann and Nagappan [42]. Chen et al. concluded that network measures are effective in predicting high severity faults, having comparable explanatory abilities and predictive power to those of traditional code metrics. The authors found, however, that network measures are very unstable for cross-project predictions.

Furthermore, many studies have addressed the prediction of fault-prone classes using OOM. Basili et al. [5] used OOM from the Chidamber and Kemerer (CK) metrics suite [14] to predict fault-prone classes using logistic regression in a C++ system. The authors found that most of OOM from the CK suite are significant to predict fault-prone classes. Gyimothy et al. [19] used OOM mostly from the CK metrics suite to predict fault-prone classes in an open-source C++ system. In addition to the logistic regression, they used some machine learning algorithms. They found that complexity, coupling and size metrics are the most suitable to predict fault-prone classes. Jureczko et al. [25] performed a study on a large number of open-source systems, using twenty metrics, and found similar results to the previous study. Singh et al. [37] also used CK metrics suite to predict fault-prone classes. The authors addressed the prediction of other facets of faults detection as faults severity and number. They compared logistic regression to some machine learning algorithms. Zhou et al. [40] evaluated ten OOM to predict fault-prone classes using logistic regression. They used several versions of the Eclipse system. They found that complexity metrics are suitable to predict fault-prone classes. Scanniello et al. [35] used multivariate linear regression to train fault prediction models on clusters of classes instead of using information from the entire system. Most of the studies cited above are based on the (most frequently used) CK metrics suite. Other studies in the literature have used different metrics, such as MOOD metrics [1,2] or QMOOD metrics [3,4].

3   Object-Oriented Metrics and Centrality Measures

We selected six OOM for the study. We focused on metrics related to three important source code attributes: complexity, coupling and size. The selected OOM, which include a subset of the well-known CK metrics suite [14], have been used in many empirical software engineering studies. We selected deliberately only a few number of widely used OOM [34], related basically to the three important source code attributes mentioned above, since the purpose of our study is to provide in a first step exploratory results on the relationship between OOM and CM, and how they can be combined to improve software defect prediction. Other metrics will be considered in our future works. Furthermore, empirical evidence exists showing that there is a significant relationship between these metrics and fault-prone classes [5,19,37]. We define briefly in Table 1 each OOM we used.

Table 1. Definition of Object-Oriented Metrics (OOM)

Metric name	Definition
Complexity	
Response For a Class (RFC)	The size of methods set that can be executed in response to a message received by an object of a class [14].
Weighted Method Complexity (WMC)	The sum of the complexity of each method of the class. The complexity is evaluated using McCabe cyclomatic complexity [14, 31].
Coupling	
Afferent Coupling (CA)	Number of other classes that the class depends upon [30].
Coupling Between Objects (CBO)	The number of other classes to which the class is coupled [14].
Efferent Coupling (CE)	Number of other classes depending on the class [30].
Size	
Source Lines Of Code (SLOC)	Number of lines of code in a class.

In OO software, static dependencies between classes can be represented by a directed graph (Static Dependencies Graph - SDG). Classes are the nodes of the graph. A directed edge between a node representing a class A and a node representing a class B indicates that class A (origin node) depends on class B (arrival node). We used an unweighted graph to represent static dependencies between classes. Also, we removed the direction of the graph edges for the calculation of some CM as they are not all well defined on directed graphs. Several types of network measures exist. In this paper, we focused on centrality measures (CM). A *centrality measure* is a function assigning every node in the graph a number corresponding to its importance within the graph. High centrality values indicate important nodes. We give in Table 2 a brief description of each CM we used.

Table 2. Definition of Centrality Measures (CM)

Measure name	Definition
Betweenness Centrality (BC)	The number of times the class is part of a geodesic path between two other classes [12].
Closeness centrality (CL)	Sum of the inverse of the distance to all other classes [12].
Density of maximum neighbourhood component (DMNC)	Calculate the ratio of links over the neighbourhood size of the class [29].
Eigenvector centrality (EV)	Sum of the number of dependencies of each class weighted by the distance to the class [32].
Katz (KATZ)	Katz centrality is similar to EV but allows weighting the class [32]. We used the value of the WMC metric as weight as complexity is one of the relevant internal features of the class.
Leverage centrality (LE)	Ratio indicating whether the class is most influenced by its neighbours or received more influence [24].
Lobby centrality (LO)	Largest integer k such as the class has at least k neighbours having each at least k dependencies [28].
Semi-local centrality (SLC)	Counts the number of neighbours, next neighbours to the class's neighbours [12].

4   Empirical Study

4.1   Methodology

Data Collection: The empirical study is based on data collected from five successive versions of a well-known open source Java software system, Ant[1]. We collected data from the following versions of Ant: 1.3, 1.4, 1.5, 1.6 and 1.7. First, we retrieved the different versions of the case study from the Promise repository [25]. We used the CKJM tool[2] to calculate the metrics values. The datasets available on Promise repository indicate classes with faults. For CM, we developed a tool based on the Java library Graphstream[3] and implemented some CM not available in the library. Table 3 gives some statistics on the different versions of Ant we used in the study.

Table 3. Descriptive statistics on the different versions of Ant

Version	Number of classes	KLOC	Number of faulty classes
1.3	126	38	60
1.4	178	54	38
1.5	293	87	106
1.6	352	114	45
1.7	734	208	69
Total	1683	501	318

Research Methodology: For RQ1, we analysed Spearman rank correlation between OOM and CM. We limited the analysis to Spearman rank correlation for two main reasons: (1) the graphical analysis showed a nonlinear (yet monotone) link between the data (in most cases), which allows rank correlation to provide valid results, but not for linear correlation, and (2) we could not analyse in depth the distribution of the OOM and CM (it will have required some extensive analyses, analyses that would have gone beyond the scope of this paper). So, we limited ourselves to a non parametric statistic to avoid making assumptions we could not validate. For RQ2, we used PCA to identify the most significant OOM and CM. For RQ3, we used four machine learning algorithms. The dependent variable is the "class containing a fault." This variable has two modalities: "no" and "yes." In order: (1) to evaluate the prediction models, we used different measures, and (2) to compare the results of the different machine learning algorithms, we used the Friedman statistic test and the Nemenyi post-hoc analysis.

4.2   Relationship Between OOM and CM

To investigate RQ1, we tested the following hypotheses:

H_0: *There is no association between OOM and CM.*
H_1: *There is an association between at least one OOM and CM.*

---

[1] https://ant.apache.org/.

[2] https://www.spinellis.gr/sw/ckjm/.

[3] http://graphstream-project.org/.

We investigated the association for each pair of OOM and CM to understand the associations between selected OOM and CM.

Correlation Analysis: We used the following levels of correlation to evaluate the association between pairs of variables [21]: negligible ($0 \leq r \leq 0.3$), low ($0.3 < r \leq 0.5$), moderate ($0.5 < r \leq 0.7$), high ($0.7 < r \leq 0.9$) and very high ($0.9 < r \leq 1$). We present the correlations between each category of OOM and CM in Table 4. Bold values indicate the correlation coefficients that are significant at the confidence level of 0.95.

The correlations between BC, DMNC, LE and complexity metrics are rather low. WMC is lowly related to CL, EV, LO and SLC. RFC, on the other hand, has a moderate strength relation with the other CM. We explain this by the fact that RFC considers the outgoing coupling. The link between both WMC and RFC and KATZ centrality measure is moderate to high, as KATZ considers complexity OOM (WMC metric) for its own calculation.

Table 4. Spearman correlation coefficients between OOM and CM

Aspect of software	Version	Metric	BC	CL	DMNC	EV	LE	LO	SLC	KATZ
Complexity	1.3	WMC	0.38	0.36	0.23	0.45	0.49	0.47	0.42	0.66
		RFC	0.40	0.65	0.44	0.64	0.38	0.54	0.64	0.76
	1.4	WMC	0.41	0.33	0.33	0.44	0.49	0.49	0.42	0.66
		RFC	0.44	0.57	0.46	0.58	0.37	0.55	0.58	0.73
	1.5	WMC	0.41	0.38	0.36	0.42	0.42	0.49	0.41	0.64
		RFC	0.42	0.61	0.48	0.58	0.35	0.56	0.58	0.72
	1.6	WMC	0.44	0.45	0.39	0.48	0.43	0.53	0.47	0.71
		RFC	0.41	0.64	0.48	0.61	0.35	0.57	0.62	0.76
	1.7	WMC	0.39	0.52	0.39	0.55	0.38	0.59	0.54	0.75
		RFC	0.39	0.65	0.46	0.64	0.36	0.61	0.65	0.79
Coupling	1.3	CA	0.65	-0.16	0.15	0.23	0.60	0.46	0.13	0.29
		CBO	0.61	0.60	0.59	0.86	0.72	0.98	0.80	0.88
		CE	0.37	0.94	0.55	0.75	0.29	0.65	0.78	0.74
	1.4	CA	0.65	-0.13	0.13	0.25	0.60	0.48	0.16	0.31
		CBO	0.65	0.61	0.67	0.88	0.66	0.98	0.83	0.90
		CE	0.45	0.92	0.67	0.76	0.24	0.68	0.79	0.75
	1.5	CA	0.59	-0.14	0.15	0.13	0.62	0.45	0.05	0.21
		CBO	0.62	0.64	0.66	0.82	0.66	0.98	0.77	0.84
		CE	0.46	0.92	0.63	0.78	0.24	0.70	0.80	0.77
	1.6	CA	0.61	-0.05	0.23	0.21	0.60	0.52	0.13	0.29
		CBO	0.66	0.67	0.69	0.83	0.62	0.98	0.78	0.85
		CE	0.48	0.91	0.63	0.79	0.23	0.70	0.81	0.78
	1.7	CA	0.67	-0.13	0.22	0.11	0.66	0.47	0.03	0.18
		CBO	0.63	0.61	0.60	0.77	0.66	0.97	0.72	0.82
		CE	0.39	0.87	0.58	0.78	0.28	0.71	0.80	0.79
Size	1.3	LOC	0.35	0.56	0.34	0.54	0.33	0.45	0.54	0.68
	1.4	LOC	0.40	0.48	0.40	0.51	0.33	0.46	0.51	0.67
	1.5	LOC	0.37	0.48	0.38	0.46	0.30	0.44	0.46	0.64
	1.6	LOC	0.37	0.51	0.38	0.49	0.31	0.45	0.50	0.67
	1.7	LOC	0.36	0.53	0.38	0.54	0.34	0.53	0.56	0.71

For complexity metrics, there is an overall link that we would qualify as moderate (coefficients stand between 0.4 and 0.6). We do not observe important variations among the different versions, which leads us to conclude that software size does not influence the relation between complexity metrics and CM. CA and CBO have a moderate strength link with BC and LE. CA relation to CL, DMNC, EV, KATZ and SLC is very low ($r < 0.3$). CBO has a moderate association with CL, DMNC and SLC, and a high one with EV, KATZ and LO. CE is lowly associated with BC and LE (measure associated with CA), but has a moderate association with DMNC, EV, KATZ and SLC. CE is very highly related to CL.

The centrality measure LO is the only one having a moderate link with both CA and CE. All the other measures are significantly related either to ingoing or outgoing coupling, but not to both. CM are more related to outgoing coupling than ingoing coupling. The association between ingoing coupling and CM is between low and moderate, according to the metrics, and the association between outgoing coupling and CM is between moderate and high. The size metric LOC has a low link with BC, DMNC, LE and LO. For the other measures, CL, EV, KATZ and SLC, the link is moderate. Except for BC, we can observe that LOC and CM, which consider the entire dependency graph, have a stronger relation than LOC with CM considering only local dependencies. According to the results (Table 4), we can reject our null hypothesis and conclude that there is an association between OOM and CM. Consequently, the answer to RQ1 (Is there a relationship between OOM and CM?) is yes.

In addition, from the correlation analysis, we can make two observations. First, the strength of the association between OOM and CM is highly dependent on the type of metric, as coupling metrics show the highest association with CM compared to complexity and size metrics. Secondly, the moderate link observed between complexity metrics and CM might effectively be surprising. Indeed, central classes can be expected to be more complex due to the richness of their connections. According to obtained results, it seems that it is not always the case. This is a motivation for using in our future works other OOM and CM.

Principal Component Analysis: To investigate RQ2, we used PCA. The goal is to decompose the information captured by the metrics (measures) into orthogonal axes. We tested the two following hypotheses:

H_0: *All OOM and CM capture the same information.*
H_1: *There is at least one OOM capturing information that no CM captures or there is at least one CM capturing information that no OOM captures.*

PCA is a technique used to identify the variables explaining most of the data variance among a large set of variables [23]. We applied VARIMAX rotation to ease the selection of significant axes. For each dimensionality reduction, we kept axes explaining between 90% and 96% of the initial variance. We present, in the following tables (Tables 5, 6 and 7), and for space limitation reasons, only the selected variables using each PCA and the cumulative percentage of the variance explained by adding the axis represented by the variables. We applied PCA three times, with three sets of initial variables for each version of the case study: the first time using only OOM (Table 5), the second time using only CM (Table 6), and the third time using the union of selected (best) subsets from the first and second PCA (Table 7).

As it can be seen from Table 5, three major axes are extracted by the PCA, which are size (LOC), afferent coupling (CA) and efferent coupling (CE). The PCA applied on CM (Table 6) identified three characteristics among CM. The first axis is represented by EV. The second and third axis are represented by either LE or CL, depending on the version. Our results are alike those previously

Table 5. PCA applied only to OOM (PCA 1)

Rotated component	1.3	1.4	1.5	1.6	1.7
1	LOC	LOC	LOC	LOC	LOC
	37%	39%	34%	36%	39%
2	CA	CA	CA	CA	CA
	33%	34%	33%	33%	34%
3	CE	CE	CE	CE	CE
	20%	19%	24%	23%	22%
% of variance explained	90%	92%	91%	92%	95%

Table 6. PCA applied only to CM (PCA 2)

Rotated component	1.3	1.4	1.5	1.6	1.7
1	EV	EV	EV	EV	EV
	39%	40%	37%	34%	34%
2	LE	LE	LE	CL	CL
	16%	16%	17%	17%	16%
3	CL	CL	CL	LE	LE
	16%	16%	16%	17%	17%
4	BC	BC	BC	BC	BC
	14%	14%	14%	15%	15%
5	DMNC	DMNC	DMNC	DMNC	DMNC
	11%	11%	12%	12%	13%
% of variance explained	96%	97%	96%	95%	95%

Table 7. PCA applied on selected variables from PCA1 and PCA2 (PCA 3)

Rotated component	1.3	1.4	1.5	1.6	1.7
1	CL	CL	CL	CL	CA
	26%	26%	26%	26%	23%
2	CA	CA	CA	CA	CL
	23%	23%	22%	22%	23%
3	BC	LOC	LE	LE	LOC
	13%	13%	13%	14%	14%
4	LOC	BC	LOC	LOC	LE
	13%	13%	13%	13%	13%
5	LE	LE	BC	BC	DMNC
	13%	13%	13%	12%	13%
6	DMNC	DMNC	DMNC	DMNC	BC
	19%	11%	11%	11%	11%
% of variance explained	99%	99%	98%	98%	97%

established in [6], which indicate that using both local and global information give the best results. As CL and EV are global and LE is local, we consider both sources of information in the selected metrics. The last two axes are respectively represented by BC and DMNC. When PCA is applied to the selected variables (best subsets) from the first two PCA (Table 7), we found that the first axis is represented by a centrality measure, mostly CL. The second axis is represented by the OOM CA. The third and fourth axes are mostly represented by LOC (an OOM) and LE (a CM), depending on the version. The fourth and fifth axes bring significant information and are respectively related to the centrality measures BC and DMNC. In addition to the analysis presented above, we also performed a fourth PCA using this time simultaneously all OOM and CM together. The independent set of variables necessary to explain more than 90% of the variance is composed of the metrics: CA, LOC, CL, LE, DMNC and BC. Due to space limitation reasons, we do not present the detailed results for this last PCA (which are globally similar to those of PCA 3).

From rank correlation and PCA analyses, we can observe that the obtained results support that OOM and CM are somewhere complementary as: (1) not every OOM and CM are associated, and (2) in PCA, some axes are represented by OOM and other by CM. Also, more axes are necessary to explain the same amount of variance when combining OOM and CM. So, for RQ2, we can conclude that there is indeed a part of information that is only captured by OOM and another part only captured by CM. In addition, we also noticed that OOM and CM are not independent either.

4.3   Ability of the Combination of OOM and CM to Predict Fault-Prone Classes

To investigate RQ3, we tested the two following hypotheses:

H_0: *Adding CM does not improve the performance of fault-prone classes prediction.*
H_1: *Adding CM improves the performance of fault-prone classes prediction.*

To perform prediction of fault-prone classes, we used four machine learning algorithms. All these algorithms have been used in many other previous empirical software engineering studies to predict fault-prone classes. We used Artificial Neural Networks (ANN) [26], Logistic Regression (LR) [5,40], Random Forest (RF) algorithm [18,27] and Support Vector Machines, known as SVM [15,36]. We used the R package *mlr* to perform the experimentation [8]. To evaluate the prediction performance we used several indicators, namely, accuracy (acc.) [11], g-mean (Gm) [11] and the area under the ROC (Receiver operating characteristic) curve (AUC) [16]. We also performed a 10-folds cross-validation (CV) [11].

For each version of Ant, we trained three models. The first one is trained by using three OOM: CA, CE and LOC (PCA, Table 5). The second one is trained by using 5 CM: BC, CL, DMNC, EV and LE (PCA, Table 6). The third one is trained by using the selected OOM and CM: BC, CA, CL, DMNC, LE and LOC (PCA, Table 7). We preprocessed the data by scaling each variable to the [0; 1] range. We adjusted the threshold probability to predict a positive observation. We did it because the positive class is under-represented. We calculated the ROC curve [16] on the training set. The ROC curve is a graph of the true positive rate according to the false positive rate. For each threshold, a point of the ROC curve is generated. We found the optimal threshold using the distance to the (0; 1) corner, which indicates a perfect classification. The classification is performed according to the following rule: *if the probability that a class contains a fault is higher than the threshold found, the class is considered fault-prone, otherwise it is considered non fault-prone.* Due to space limitation reasons, we do not present the thresholds found for each algorithm. Classification thresholds tend to be lower for larger versions as the two classes (not fault-prone and fault-prone) are more imbalanced. We present in Table 8 the classification results for each algorithm. We calculated for each learning set three indicators: AUC, the accuracy and the g-mean. Then, we applied CV (10-folds CV). We used the same classification threshold that we found during the initial learning to each learning step of the CV. We evaluated the CV results using only two indicators: accuracy and g-mean.

For ANN, we can see that the models using only OOM tend to have better AUC, but also the lowest accuracy and g-mean, which means that using OOM

Table 8. Evaluation of machine learning algorithms

Algorithm	Version	Set	Learning set			CV		Algorithm	Version	Set	Learning set			CV	
			Auc	Acc.	Gm	Acc.	Gm				Auc	Acc.	Gm	Acc.	Gm
ANN	1.3	1	73%	68%	84%	51%	67%	LR	1.3	1	85%	64%	80%	61%	78%
		2	63%	75%	88%	46%	61%			2	73%	55%	73%	51%	68%
		3	65%	95%	98%	48%	63%			3	84%	65%	82%	58%	75%
	1.4	1	65%	70%	86%	54%	62%		1.4	1	79%	61%	74%	59%	71%
		2	65%	75%	91%	52%	54%			2	66%	59%	70%	56%	66%
		3	61%	94%	96%	55%	57%			3	75%	57%	74%	56%	69%
	1.5	1	80%	62%	80%	57%	73%		1.5	1	77%	53%	71%	53%	72%
		2	68%	69%	85%	51%	66%			2	76%	53%	70%	52%	69%
		3	73%	78%	90%	53%	65%			3	76%	57%	72%	54%	68%
	1.6	1	63%	55%	78%	50%	58%		1.6	1	72%	51%	67%	49%	62%
		2	50%	82%	89%	61%	44%			2	69%	56%	71%	55%	66%
		3	62%	80%	94%	59%	51%			3	68%	52%	68%	49%	61%
	1.7	1	75%	55%	77%	53%	68%		1.7	1	78%	55%	74%	55%	73%
		2	66%	61%	82%	51%	56%			2	77%	51%	71%	50%	68%
		3	70%	65%	82%	57%	57%			3	78%	64%	75%	63%	71%
RF	1.3	1	80%	76%	90%	56%	74%	SVM	1.3	1	74%	64%	80%	55%	72%
		2	78%	84%	94%	49%	66%			2	73%	58%	76%	54%	71%
		3	78%	89%	96%	58%	75%			3	81%	65%	82%	58%	75%
	1.4	1	83%	83%	93%	62%	69%		1.4	1	74%	63%	79%	42%	62%
		2	74%	91%	94%	58%	58%			2	N/A	60%	65%	38%	52%
		3	75%	91%	97%	61%	63%			3	66%	58%	75%	49%	67%
	1.5	1	80%	73%	89%	53%	72%		1.5	1	79%	61%	78%	45%	62%
		2	74%	84%	94%	55%	69%			2	77%	56%	72%	55%	70%
		3	80%	87%	96%	56%	74%			3	72%	64%	81%	47%	65%
	1.6	1	73%	81%	92%	59%	60%		1.6	1	57%	72%	39%	45%	46%
		2	70%	98%	100%	65%	60%			2	46%	73%	21%	60%	41%
		3	71%	91%	97%	63%	60%			3	65%	73%	30%	52%	37%
	1.7	1	77%	84%	93%	67%	61%		1.7	1	63%	48%	65%	42%	53%
		2	74%	99%	99%	73%	42%			2	55%	28%	27%	33%	37%
		3	75%	94%	98%	72%	56%			3	65%	90%	86%	44%	60%

allows a good ordering of the observations. But, when applying a specific threshold the classifiers do not seem to be able to discriminate the real faulty classes well among all classes. The combination of OOM and CM allows the highest accuracy and the highest g-mean values. CM alone have the worst AUC values of the three sets. CM outperform OOM alone but not the combination of OOM and CM in regard to accuracy and g-mean. Regarding CV, the OOM outperform the two other learning sets for the accuracy and the g-mean. It leads us to conclude that the results of the learning set may include some overfitting for the CM set and the OOM & CM set. When using ANN, we can conclude that including CM in the dataset improves the classification results. However, to have a robust model, it must be trained on a larger dataset to reduce the effect of potential overfitting.

The results for LR indicate that the combination of OOM and CM is better than just using either OOM or CM. For the AUC, models trained on OOM are slightly better or equal to models trained on the combination of OOM and CM. For the accuracy and g-mean, the best models are either the ones trained on CM or the ones trained using the combination of OOM and CM. CV results are comparable to those observed on the learning set, which indicates that the models did not overfit the dataset. For CV, the results vary much, making it difficult to identify the best learning set.

For RF, the OOM set is the one having the highest AUC values, but they are generally close to the AUC values for CM and to those of the combination of OOM and CM. For the accuracy and the g-mean, generally the results obtained using only CM are the best, followed by the results of OOM and CM. Using CM improves the classification results when using RF. The CV results indicate, as for ANN, that some overfitting is observed in the learning process, especially for CM. According to accuracy, CM offer the worst performances on small versions (1.3 and 1.4) and the best performances on large versions (1.6 and 1.7). However, the results are lower than those obtained on the learning set. For the g-mean, CM also offer poor performances, and OOM is generally the set offering the best classification rate. The RF algorithm is known to be subject to overfitting, which we clearly observe here. While making prediction with the RF algorithm, using CM improves the classification performance.

The results of SVM indicate, in regard to the AUC values, that the best learning set is the combination of OOM and CM. Similar observations can be made for accuracy and g-mean. G-mean values observed on version 1.6 are really low, but as they are also low for all other algorithms, it leads us to conclude that this dataset is more difficult to learn from than the others. CV results are lower than those obtained with the learning set. For both accuracy and g-mean, the best set is the combination of OOM and CM, but the quality of the prediction is significantly lower than the quality of the other models.

Moreover, we used the Friedman test to perform multiple comparisons [22]. We formed the blocks used in the Friedman test by grouping the results of an algorithm (aggregating versions). We performed the Friedman test for each indicator of the learning set. The test result does not allow us to identify which pairs of blocks have a significant difference if the null hypothesis is rejected; this is why we used the Nemenyi post-hoc analysis. The Nemenyi post-hoc compares each pair of blocks and verifies if they are significantly different [22]. We concluded to significant differences if the p-value is under 10%. We chose to use a higher p-value than is normally used in literature because our sample size is small (five observations only). When using a small size, the type II error is higher. One way to reduce the type II error is to increase the type I error. Allowing some false positive might also allow some situations where H_1 is true, but due to the lack of observations the p-value is high and therefore we would not have rejected H_0.

Table 9. Test on machine learning algorithms (Algo: algorithm, FT: Friedman test p-value, 1: OOM, 2: CM, 3: OOM and CM)

Algo	Indicator	FT	Post-hoc analysis			Algo	Indicator	FT	Post-hoc analysis		
			1 with 2	1 with 3	2 with 3				1 with 2	1 with 3	2 with 3
ANN	AUC	0.074	0.069(1)	0.254	0.802	LR	AUC	0.015	0.012(1)	0.139	0.609
	Acc.	0.015	0.139	0.012(3)	0.609		Acc.	0.504	0.950	0.710	0.510
	Gm	0.015	0.139	0.012(3)	0.609		Gm	0.074	0.802	0.254	0.069(3)
RF	AUC	0.007	0.005(1)	0.254	0.254	SVM	AUC	0.174	0.330	0.930	0.180
	Acc.	0.019	0.047(2)	0.047(3)	1.000		Acc.	0.074	0.856	0.249	0.086(3)
	Gm	0.022	0.031(2)	0.069(3)	0.946		Gm	0.039	0.181	0.759	0.036(3)

Table 9 gives the results of the statistical test applied to results observed in Table 8. In bold font, we indicate the p-values under 10% and indicate between parentheses which one of the sets was the best. We found significant differences for the classification performance indicator in ten cases out of twelve. When the OOM are compared to the CM, we found that OOM outperform significantly

CM regarding AUC three times out of four and CM outperform OOM for accuracy and g-mean once out of four. The two cases where CM outperform OOM are observed on the same algorithm (RF). When we compare OOM with the combination of OOM and CM, we found that the combination outperforms OOM alone in four cases out of twelve, twice for the accuracy and twice for the g-mean, but OOM never significantly outperform the combination. Significant differences are observed on two algorithms (ANN, RF). Finally, CM are outperformed three times by the combination OOM and CM, twice for the g-mean and once for the accuracy. We can conclude that using a combination of CM and OOM provides better results as all tests involving the combination are either better than using only OOM or only CM, or at least similar. Even between them, OOM and CM, we are unable to identify the best set. The two algorithms having the most significant differences are ANN and RF. Overall, we can conclude that combining OOM and CM can improve significantly the performance of fault-prone classes prediction (RQ.3). The AUC does not seem to be affected when using CM as we found no evidence that OOM outperform the combination of OOM and CM in regard to the AUC values. We found many situations when using a combination outperforms the results obtained using either only OOM or only CM in regard to the accuracy and the g-mean indicators.

4.4   Limits and Threats to Validity

Our study contains some threats to validity like any other empirical software engineering studies.

Internal treats: we used two different tools to collect information (metrics) on the classes, one for OOM and one for CM. The two tools use static code analysis, but some information may slightly differ as the two do not have the same representation of the system. Also, the coupling and CM information collected is limited to static dependency analysis. We have not captured the dynamic dependencies. This may be considered in our future works.

External treats: the study has been conducted on only one system which prevents us from generalizing our results. However, Ant system has been widely investigated and is considered as representative of OO software.

5   Conclusions and Future Works

We investigated in this study a new set of measures to describe classes in OO software, the centrality measures (CM). We investigated the relationships between CM and OOM that have been widely used in many empirical software engineering studies. We also explored how they can be combined to improve the prediction of fault-prone classes in OO software. We first investigated the relationships between CM and traditional OOM (RQ1). We divided OOM in three categories: complexity metrics, coupling metrics and size metrics. For each of those categories, we analysed the relationships between OOM and CM using Spearman correlation. We found mainly low and moderate associations between complexity metrics and CM, moderate to high associations between coupling metrics and CM, and moderate associations between size metrics and CM. Then, we analysed the information captured by OOM and CM in order to identify if they share the same information (variance) or if they represent different aspects of the system (RQ2). We found by using an in-depth PCA that as if some OOM and CM are strongly associated, they also capture different information about the system. We identified an independent set of OOM, an independent set of CM and an independent set of OOM and CM combined. Finally, we compared the ability of each (best) subset of metrics (OOM, CM, and OOM and CM combined), identified by PCA, to predict fault-prone classes (RQ3) using four machine learning algorithms. We found that artificial neural network and random forest are the two algorithms providing the best results (in terms of prediction performance). The results have been submitted to a Friedman test and a Nemenyi post-hoc analysis to find significant differences in classification performance. We found that combining OOM and CM can improve significantly the performance of fault-prone classes prediction.

In our future works, we intend to reproduce our experimentations by using other systems to validate the usefulness of CM as indicators of software defect proneness and the gain in software defect prediction performance allowed by their combination with OOM, and including other OOM and CM in order to provide a more extensive understanding of their relationship. We also plan to analyse the capability of CM to predict other aspects of faults prediction such as faults severity and the number of faults in a class (non-binary classification).

Acknowledgement. Part of this work has been supported by NSERC (Natural Science and Engineering Research Council of Canada) and FRQNT (Fonds de Recherche Québec Nature et Technologies) grants.

References

1. Abreu, F.B., Carapuça, R.: Object-oriented software engineering: measuring and controlling the development process. In: Proceedings of the 4th International Conference on Software Quality, vol. 186, pp. 1–8 (1994)
2. Abreu, F.B.E., Melo, W.: Evaluating the impact of object-oriented design on software quality. In: Proceedings of the 3rd International Software Metrics Symposium, pp. 90–99. IEEE (1996)
3. Bansiya, J., Davis, C.: An object-oriented design quality assessment model. University of Alabama, EUA (1997)
4. Bansiya, J., Davis, C.G.: A hierarchical model for object-oriented design quality assessment. IEEE Trans. Softw. Eng. **28**(1), 4–17 (2002)
5. Basili, V.R., Briand, L.C., Melo, W.L.: A validation of object-oriented design metrics as quality indicators. IEEE Trans. Softw. Eng. **22**(10), 751–761 (1996)
6. Bettenburg, N., Nagappan, M., Hassan, A.E.: Think locally, act globally: improving defect and effort prediction models. In: Proceedings of the 9th IEEE Working Conference on Mining Software Repositories, pp. 60–69. IEEE Press (2012)
7. Bird, C., Murphy, B., Nagappan, N., Zimmermann, T.: Empirical software engineering at Microsoft research. In: Proceedings of the ACM 2011 Conference on Computer Supported Cooperative Work, pp. 143–150. ACM (2011)

8. Bischl, B., et al.: mlr: machine learning in R. J. Mach. Learn. Res. **17**(170), 1–5 (2016)
9. Bonacich, P.: Power and centrality: a family of measures. Am. J. Sociol. **92**(5), 1170–1182 (1987)
10. Borgatti, S.P., Everett, M.G.: A graph-theoretic perspective on centrality. Soc. Netw. **28**(4), 466–484 (2006)
11. Boucher, A., Badri, M.: Software metrics thresholds calculation techniques to predict fault-proneness: an empirical comparison. Inf. Softw. Technol. **96**, 38–67 (2018)
12. Chen, D., Lü, L., Shang, M.S., Zhang, Y.C., Zhou, T.: Identifying influential nodes in complex networks. Phys. A: Stat. Mech. Appl. **391**(4), 1777–1787 (2012)
13. Chen, L., et al.: Empirical analysis of network measures for predicting high severity software faults. Sci. China Inf. Sci. **59**(12), 122901 (2016)
14. Chidamber, S.R., Kemerer, C.F.: A metrics suite for object oriented design. IEEE Trans. Softw. Eng. **20**(6), 476–493 (1994)
15. Elish, K.O., Elish, M.O.: Predicting defect-prone software modules using support vector machines. J. Syst. Softw. **81**(5), 649–660 (2008)
16. Fawcett, T.: An introduction to ROC analysis. Pattern Recogn. Lett. **27**(8), 861–874 (2006)
17. Freeman, L.C.: A set of measures of centrality based on betweenness. Sociometry **40**, 35–41 (1977)
18. Guo, L., Ma, Y., Cukic, B., Singh, H.: Robust prediction of fault-proneness by random forests. In: 15th International Symposium on Software Reliability Engineering, ISSRE 2004, pp. 417–428. IEEE (2004)
19. Gyimothy, T., Ferenc, R., Siket, I.: Empirical validation of object-oriented metrics on open source software for fault prediction. IEEE Trans. Softw. Eng. **31**(10), 897–910 (2005)
20. Henderson-Sellers, B.: Object-Oriented Metrics: Measures of Complexity. Prentice Hall, Upper Saddle River (1996)
21. Hinkle, D., Jurs, S., Wiersma, W.: Applied Statistics for the Behavioral Sciences. Houghton Mifflin, Boston (1988)
22. Hollander, M., Wolfe, D.: Nonparametric Statistical Methods, 2nd edn. Wiley, Hoboken (1999)
23. Jolliffe, I.: Principal Component Analysis. Springer, Heidelberg (2002). https://doi.org/10.1007/b98835
24. Joyce, K.E., Laurienti, P.J., Burdette, J.H., Hayasaka, S.: A new measure of centrality for brain networks. PLoS One **5**(8), e12200 (2010)
25. Jureczko, M., Madeyski, L.: Towards identifying software project clusters with regard to defect prediction. In: Proceedings of the 6th International Conference on Predictive Models in Software Engineering, p. 9. ACM (2010)
26. Kanmani, S., Uthariaraj, V.R., Sankaranarayanan, V., Thambidurai, P.: Object-oriented software fault prediction using neural networks. Inf. Softw. Technol. **49**(5), 483–492 (2007)
27. Kaur, A., Malhotra, R.: Application of random forest in predicting fault-prone classes. In: International Conference on Advanced Computer Theory and Engineering, ICACTE 2008, pp. 37–43. IEEE (2008)
28. Korn, A., Schubert, A., Telcs, A.: Lobby index in networks. Phys. A: Stat. Mech. Appl. **388**(11), 2221–2226 (2009)
29. Lin, C.Y., Chin, C.H., Wu, H.H., Chen, S.H., Ho, C.W., Ko, M.T.: Hubba: hub objects analyzer—a framework of interactome hubs identification for network biology. Nucleic Acids Res. **36**, W438–W443 (2008)

30. Martin, R.: OO design quality metrics. An analysis of dependencies, vol. 12, pp. 151–170 (1994)
31. McCabe, T.J.: A complexity measure. IEEE Trans. Softw. Eng. **4**, 308–320 (1976)
32. Newman, M.: Networks: An Introduction. OUP, Oxford (2010)
33. Nguyen, T.H., Adams, B., Hassan, A.E.: Studying the impact of dependency network measures on software quality. In: 2010 IEEE International Conference on Software Maintenance (ICSM), pp. 1–10. IEEE (2010)
34. Radjenović, D., Heričko, M., Torkar, R., Živkovič, A.: Software fault prediction metrics: a systematic literature review. Inf. Softw. Technol. **55**(8), 1397–1418 (2013)
35. Scanniello, G., Gravino, C., Marcus, A., Menzies, T.: Class level fault prediction using software clustering. In: 2013 28th IEEE/ACM International Conference on Automated Software Engineering (ASE), pp. 640–645. IEEE (2013)
36. Singh, Y., Kaur, A., Malhotra, R.: Software fault proneness prediction using support vector machines. In: Proceedings of the World Congress on Engineering, vol. 1 (2009)
37. Singh, Y., Kaur, A., Malhotra, R.: Empirical validation of object-oriented metrics for predicting fault proneness models. Softw. Qual. J. **18**(1), 3 (2010)
38. Tosun, A., Turhan, B., Bener, A.: Validation of network measures as indicators of defective modules in software systems. In: Proceedings of the 5th International Conference on Predictor Models in Software Engineering, p. 5. ACM (2009)
39. Zakari, A., Lee, S.P., Chong, C.Y.: Simultaneous localization of software faults based on complex network theory. IEEE Access **6**, 23990–24002 (2018)
40. Zhou, Y., Xu, B., Leung, H.: On the ability of complexity metrics to predict fault-prone classes in object-oriented systems. J. Syst. Softw. **83**(4), 660–674 (2010)
41. Zhu, L.Z., Yin, B.B., Cai, K.Y.: Software fault localization based on centrality measures. In: 2011 IEEE 35th Annual Computer Software and Applications Conference Workshops, pp. 37–42. IEEE (2011)
42. Zimmermann, T., Nagappan, N.: Predicting defects using network analysis on dependency graphs. In: ACM/IEEE 30th International Conference on Software Engineering, ICSE 2008, pp. 531–540. IEEE (2008)

A Systematic Review on Software Testing Ontologies

Guido Tebes[1], Denis Peppino[1], Pablo Becker[1], Gerardo Matturro[2],
Martin Solari[2], and Luis Olsina[1(✉)]

[1] GIDIS_Web, Engineering School, UNLPam, General Pico, LP, Argentina
`guido.tebes92@gmail.com`, `denispeppino92@gmail.com`,
`{beckerp,olsinal}@ing.unlpam.edu.ar`
[2] Engineering School, Universidad ORT Uruguay, Montevideo, Uruguay
`{matturro,martin.solari}@ort.edu.uy`

Abstract. Undoubtedly, ontologies are a key issue in various areas of Software Engineering (SE), and are widely recognized as a useful approach for representing and managing knowledge. Additionally, one of the SE areas that supports quality assurance is testing. Given that specific methods, processes, and ultimately strategies for software testing involve a large number of specific concepts, it is valuable to have a robust conceptual base, that is, a testing ontology that defines the terms, properties, relationships and axioms explicitly and unambiguously. In order to look for a testing ontology that can be used in a family of testing strategies, in this paper, we investigate, by means of a Systematic Literature Review (SLR), primary studies on software testing ontologies. Following an enhanced SLR process of that proposed by Kitchenham, we analyze the resulting twelve documents in the light of a set of research questions and quality criteria.

Keywords: SLR · SLR process · Software testing ontology · Testing strategy

1 Introduction

Organizations commonly establish and reach business goals for different types of purposes using strategies [15]. Business goals are the main goals that an organization tries to achieve. In the statement of a goal always lies a purpose or intentionality. The purpose of a goal is the reason to achieve it. Purposes can be classified into four categories such as evaluation, testing, development and maintenance. Examples of evaluation purposes may include to understand, monitor, control, improve, select an alternative, etc. while examples of testing purposes can be to review, verify, validate, among others.

Hence, to achieve the purposes of business goals strategies are used. A strategy is a core resource of an organization that defines a specific course of action to follow, i.e., specifies what to do and how to do it. Consequently, strategies should integrate a process specification, a method specification, and a robust domain conceptual base [5]. This principle of integratedness promotes, therefore, knowing what activities are involved, and how to carry them out by means of methods in the framework of a

M. Piattini et al. (Eds.): QUATIC 2019, CCIS 1010, pp. 144–160, 2019.
https://doi.org/10.1007/978-3-030-29238-6_11

common domain terminology. In [15], to achieve evaluation purposes, a family of strategies integrating the three-abovementioned capabilities is discussed. The conceptual framework for this family of evaluation strategies is called C-INCAMI v.2 (*Contextual-Information Need, Characteristic Model, Attribute, Metric and Indicator*) [5, 16].

This conceptual framework was built on vocabularies, which are structured in ontologies. Figure 1 depicts the different C-INCAMI v.2 conceptual components, where the gray-shaded ones are already developed. The ontologies for Non-Functional Requirements (NFRs), NFRs view, Functional Requirements (FRs), business goal, project, and context are defined in [16], while for measurement and evaluation are in [5]. The remainder ontologies (for testing, development and maintenance) are not built yet.

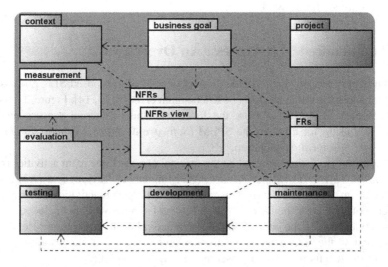

Fig. 1. Conceptual components and their relationships for the C-INCAMI v.2 framework. Note that NFRs stands for Non-Functional Requirements while FRs, for Functional Requirements.

Bearing in mind that there are already integrated strategies that provide support for achieving evaluation purposes, the reader can surmise that strategies that provide support for achieving testing purposes are feasible to be developed as well. Given that a strategy should integrate a well-established domain terminology, therefore, a well-specified testing strategy should also have this capability for the testing domain. A benefit of having the suitable testing ontology is that it would minimize the heterogeneity and ambiguity problems that we currently observe in the different concepts dealing with testing methods and processes. Furthermore, one desirable feature we are looking for is if the existing testing ontologies link their specific terms with FRs and NFRs concepts (as represented in Fig. 1).

In this direction, we conducted a SLR [14, 20] on software testing ontologies in order to establish the suitable top-domain testing ontology to be integrated into the C-INCAMI v.2 conceptual framework. That is, we envision populating the 'testing' conceptual component shown in Fig. 1 and linking it with the FRs and NFRs components. Within the design of the SLR protocol, three research questions are considered: RQ1. *What are the conceptualized ontologies for the software testing domain?* RQ2. *What are the most frequently included concepts, their relationships, attributes and axioms needed to describe the software testing domain?* and, RQ3. *How are existing software testing ontologies classified?* Additionally, a set of quality criteria is formulated which includes that concern of the FRs and NFRs linking.

The rest of the article is organized as follows. Section 2 provides an overview of the followed SLR process. Section 3 illustrates the outcomes of the three main SLR activities: Design the Review, Implement the Review, and Analyze and Document the Review considering primary studies on software testing ontologies. It also discusses main findings. Section 4 addresses related work. Finally, Sect. 5 summarizes conclusions and outlines future work.

2 The Enhanced SLR Process: An Overview

The aim of this section is to provide an overview of our proposed SLR process [20], which enhances the initial proposal of Kitchenham *et al.* [6, 13, 14]. Figure 2 illustrates the augmented SLR process from the functional and behavioral process modeling perspectives using for this end the SPEM (*Software & Systems Process Engineering Meta-Model Specification*) notation.

As seen in Fig. 2, this process like the original one has three main activities (named phases in [6, 13]): (A1) Design Review, (A2) Implement Review, and (A3) Analyze and Document Review. In turn, these activities group sub-activities and tasks. For instance, notice that for the Design Search Protocol sub-activity, the included tasks are shown while not for the rest of the A1 sub-activities. It is expressly done so for communicating the reader that sub-activities have tasks, but at the same time for not giving all the details in order to preserve the diagram legibility.

A1's main objective is to yield the 'SLR protocol' starting from the 'SLR Information Need Goal Specification' artifact. To achieve this, the sub-activities and tasks of Fig. 2 should be performed following the represented flow and the input and output artifacts. Basically, the included activities are: Specify Research Questions, Design Search Protocol, Define Selection and Quality Criteria, Design Data Extraction Form, and Validate the SLR Design. It is worth mentioning that the 'SLR Protocol' document may be in an *approved* or *disapproved* state. In the latter case, a list of 'Detected Problems/Suggested Improvements' must also be produced. This artifact will serve as input to the Improve SLR Design activity, which deals with a set of tasks to introduce changes for improve it. Ultimately, A1 activity ends when the 'SLR Protocol' is *approved*.

The Implement Review (A2)'s main aim is twofold. First, to Perform a SLR Pilot Study (A2.1), if this were necessary. Second, to properly Perform SLR (A2.2) taking now into account all the 'Selected Digital Libraries', not a subset as in A2.1. Note that for first-time cases where a SLR study is not a repeated or replicated one, first performing a pilot test is recommended aimed at fitting the 'SLR Protocol' produced in A1.

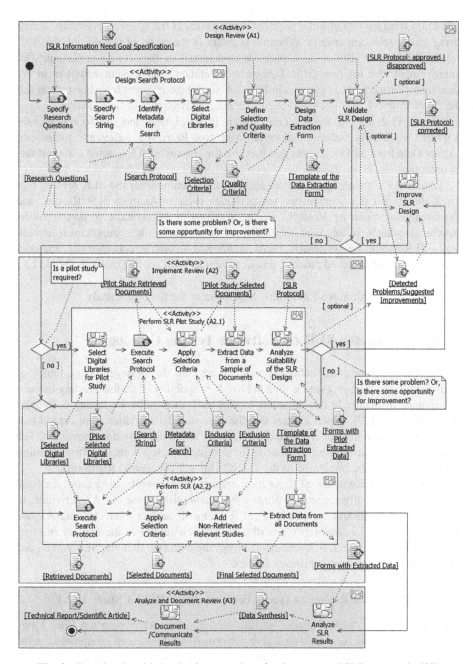

Fig. 2. Functional and behavioral perspectives for the proposed SLR process in [20]

In the last sub-activities of A2.1, considering all the parts that integrate the 'SLR Protocol' artifact and the 'Forms with Pilot Extracted Data', the Analyze Suitability of the SLR Design activity is performed. This analysis permits actually to adjust the data extraction form as well as other protocol aspects such as the research questions, search string and/or selection criteria. When no problem in the protocol is detected, the A2.2 can be carried out. But if do a problem is detected or there is an opportunity for improvement, the Improve SLR Design and Validate SLR Design activities in A1 should be enacted again, as shown in Fig. 2. Once all the changes have been made and the 'SLR Protocol' has been approved, the A2.2 activity should be executed.

Then, A2.2 implies the Execute Search Protocol task and the following sub-activities viz Apply Selection Criteria, Add Non-Retrieved Relevant Studies and Extract Data from all Documents that produce the 'Forms with Extracted Data' artifact as outcome.

Lastly, A3's main objective is to analyze and communicate the SLR results. Figure 2 shows that A3 implies two sub-activities such as Analyze SLR Results, and Document/Communicate Results, which produces the 'Technical Report/Scientific Article' document. In this way, the SLR process concludes. It is important to remark that a SLR should be systematic, reproducible and auditable; consequently, the documentation of the followed process, produced artifacts and applied methods should be a core concern.

In the next Section, we follow this SLR process for the target study.

3   Performing the SLR on Software Testing Ontologies

As commented in the Introduction Section, we are considering developing a family of testing strategies. The first step is then to have the capability of a robust testing-domain terminology available. In this direction, a pilot SLR about software testing ontologies was analyzed in [20], which implies that the A1 and A2.1 activities were carried out. Currently, we have just concluded the whole study so we are fully documenting it. The results allow us to establish the grounds for developing a top-domain software testing ontology that will be integrated to the C-INCAMI v.2 conceptual framework.

This section presents the SLR we have conducted for investigating conceptualized ontologies in the software testing domain by accomplishing the A1-A3 activities. In Subsect. 3.1, we discuss the resulting 'SLR Protocol' artifact after enacting A1 and A2.1. In Subsect. 3.2, we briefly describe the selected studies in the light of enacting A2.2. Finally, in Subsect. 3.3, we analyze from the extracted data the SLR results and findings considering twelve primary studies.

3.1   To Design the Review (A1) and Perform the SLR Pilot Study (A2.1)

Table 1 shows the 'SLR Protocol' artifact yielded after performing the Pilot Study activity. The A1 and A2.1 activities were performed in our research group between the end of May and the beginning of August 2018, and the protocol was also validated by an external group, the same that participated in A2.2. The gray rows in Table 1 document the sub-artifacts of A1 respectively. It follows some descriptions about them.

There are three formulated research questions. RQ1 focuses on the conceptualized ontologies for the software testing domain. Therefore, regarding our stated main goal, we try to capture for the testing domain each ontology that documents a

Table 1. Resulting 'SLR Protocol' produced after performing the Pilot Study (A2.1) activity

Research Questions	
RQ1. What are the conceptualized ontologies for the software testing domain?	
RQ2. What are the most frequently included concepts, their relationships, attributes and axioms needed to describe the software testing domain?	
RQ3. How are existing software testing ontologies classified?	
Search Protocol	
Search String	("Software Testing" OR "Software Test") AND ("Ontology" OR "Ontologies")
Metadata for Search	Title; Abstract; Keywords
Selected Digital Libraries	Scopus, IEEE Xplore, ACM Digital Library, Springer Link and Science Direct
Selection and Quality Criteria	
Inclusion Criteria (IC)	**1.** That the work be published in the last 15 years (from the beginning of 2003 until November 12, 2018); **2.** That the work belongs to the Computer Science area or to the Software/System/Information Engineering areas; and **3.** That the document has the ontological conceptualization of the testing domain (i.e., it is not simply a "lesson learned or expert opinion" or just an implementation)
Exclusion Criteria (EC)	**1.** That the work be a prologue, article summary or review, interview, news, discussion, reader letter, poster, table of contents or short paper (a short paper is considered to that having up to 4 pages' size); **2.** That the work is not a primary study; **3.** That the work is not written in English; **4.** That the work does not document a software testing ontology; **5.** That the ontology presented in the document be an earlier version than the most recent and complete one published in another retrieved document; **6.** That a same document be the result of more than one bibliographic source (i.e., elimination of duplicates); and **7.** That the conceptualized ontology in the current document be a fragment of a conceptualized ontology in another retrieved document
Quality Criteria (QC)	**1.** Is/are the research objective/s clearly identified? **2.** Is the description of the context in which the research was carried out explicit? **3.** Was the proposed ontology developed following a rigorous and/or formal methodology? **4.** Was the proposed ontology developed considering also its linking with Functional and Non-Functional Requirements concepts? **5.** What other terminologies of the software testing domain were taken into account to develop the proposed ontology?

(continued)

Table 1. (*continued*)

Template of the Data Extraction Form with 15 Form Fields (*FF*)
1. Researcher name; **2.** Article title; **3.** Author/s of the article; **4.** Journal/Congress/other; **5.** Publication year; **6.** Digital library; **7.** Name of the proposed ontology; **8.** Specified concepts used to describe software -testing domain; **9.** Methodology used to develop the ontology; **10.** Terminologies or Vocabularies taken into account to develop the proposed ontology; **11.** Classification of the proposed ontology; **12.** Research context; **13.** Research objective/s related to software testing ontologies; **14.** Does the proposed ontology consider its linking with Functional and Non-Functional Requirements concepts? **15.** Additional notes

conceptualization [10] rather than an implementation, conversely to the SLR performed by Souza *et al.* [18], which included both. Inclusion Criterion (IC) 3 deals with this concern.

A robust ontological conceptualization should include not only the terms, attributes (properties), relationships (both taxonomic –*kind_of* and *whole_part*- and non-taxonomic ones) and axioms but also the definition of terms, attributes and non-taxonomic relationships in addition to the specification of axioms. With this in mind, RQ2 tries to get evidence of what are the most frequently included concepts, their relationships, attributes and axioms needed to describe the software testing domain. Regarding that a defined conceptualization requires enough document space, Exclusion Criterion (EC) 1 prevents to include short papers. Additionally, EC5 considers the timeliness and completeness of documented versions of the same ontology while the EC7 prevents that the conceptualized ontology in one retrieved document be a fragment of a conceptualized ontology in another retrieved manuscript.

Lastly, RQ3 tries to get evidence of the ontology classification (e.g., foundational, top-domain, domain or instance ontology) given to a conceptualization by authors.

It is important to remark that Quality Criteria (QC) are considered for extracting required or desirable data in forms but they do not were regarded like exclusion/inclusion selection criteria. For instance, QC4 permits to indicate (by *Yes* or *Not* in the FF14 of the 'Template of the Data Extraction Form') if the selected conceptualized ontology was developed considering its linking with FRs and NFRs concepts (recall Fig. 1).

As a last comment to this sub-section, notice that FF8 in Table 1 allowed us to extract terms, attributes, relationships and axioms following the format: (i) for terms, *TermN* = definition; (ii) for attributes, *TermN(AttributeN.1* = definition,...); (iii) for taxonomic relations, *is_a(TermX_type, TermY_subtype)*, or *part_of(TermX_whole, TermY_part)*; (iv) for non-taxonomic relations, *RelationM_name(TermX, TermY)* with its definition, or even collecting those relations without label whether defined or not; and (v) for axioms, the name and its definition/specification. These form field metadata turned out useful for calculating metrics in the A3 activity, as we analyze later on.

3.2   To Perform the SLR (A2.2)

The A2.2 activity was performed by six members of two research groups between the end of October 2018 and the beginning of March 2019. The workload for carrying out

Table 2. 'Retrieved Documents' per Digital Library after performing Execute Search Protocol

	Scopus	IEEE Xplore	Springer Link	ACM DL	Science Direct	Total
Retrieved Documents	181	88	443	18	1	**731**

Table 3. 'Selected Documents' after performing the Apply Selection Criteria sub-activity

Criteria	Analyzed Content	Initial Studies	Eliminated	Selected Documents	Reduction
IC1, IC2, EC1	Title+Abstract	731	209	522	28.5%
EC6 (Duplicates)	Title+Abstract	522	47	475	6.4%
EC2, EC3, EC4	Full Text	475	456	19	62.3%
IC3, EC5, EC7	Full Text	19	9	10	1.2%
Total		**731**	721	**10**	**98.6%**

the Execute Search Protocol sub-activity (see Fig. 2) was balanced, i.e., two members per each group participated. The remainder two members of GIDIS_Web (the third and last authors) acted as coordinators and consistency checkers throughout A2.2. Table 2 documents the 'Retrieved Documents' per Digital Library totalizing 731 papers, following the specification of the 'Search Protocol' artifact (Table 1).

Table 3 records the number of 'Selected Documents' produced after performing the Apply Selection Criteria sub-activity. This yielded 10 selected primary studies by applying the different inclusion/exclusion criteria over the analyzed content as presented in the 1st and 2nd columns of Table 3. Considering the initial and last states the reduction reached 98.6%. The next activity we carried out was the Add Non-Retrieved

Table 4. Results of using the *Backward Snowballing* method in the Add Non-Retrieved Relevant Studies sub-activity. Retrieved Documents (65) from references were checked for duplicates against the 731 Initial Studies

Backward Snowballing		1st Iteration	2nd Iteration	Total
Retrieved Documents		52	13	65
Eliminated by Criteria	EC6 (Duplicates)	49	13	62
	IC1, IC2, EC1	0	0	0
	EC2, EC3, EC4	1	0	1
	IC3, EC5, EC7	1	0	1
Final Studies		1	0	1

Table 5. 'Final Selected Documents' after performing Add Non-Retrieved Relevant Studies

Selected Documents	Backward Snowballing	Other Method	Final Selected Documents
10	1	1	**12**

Relevant Studies sub-activity as depicted in Fig. 2. For this, we have used two different methods, namely: *Backward Snowballing* and *Prior Knowledge of other Research Work*.

Table 4 records the outcomes of using the *Backward Snowballing* method with two iterations over references performed accordingly. Then, Table 5 shows the number of 'Final Selected Documents' after enacting Add Non-Retrieved Relevant Studies sub-activity, which totalized 12 research primary studies (including the Master thesis [2] retrieved by *Prior Knowledge of other Research Work* from the ResearchGate network by the end of 2017, after surpassing all inclusion and exclusion criteria).

Finally, the Extract Data from all Documents sub-activity should be performed, which has as input the 'Template of the Data Extraction Form' and the 'Final Selected Documents', and as output the 'Forms with Extracted Data' artifact. This sub-activity must be performed in a very disciplined and rigorous way, being also very time consuming. The work distribution for the Extract Data from all Documents sub-activity was as follow. Two members of GIDIS_Web (the 1st and 2nd authors) collected the whole required data of the 12 documents. At random, we selected 4 out of 12 documents which were made available (by Google Drive) for data collection to the two members at Universidad ORT Uruguay, but not shared while gathering the data in order to permit later a more objective checking of consistency. As result of this checking to the instantiated forms of both groups some minor issues were raised and discrepancies consensuated via video chat.

It is worth mentioning that thanks to looking for inconsistencies, we detected that into the collected concepts (i.e., terms, properties, etc.) included in the form for the ROoST ontology [19] there were not only those software testing domain-specific terms, properties and relationships but also those linked and related to the foundational ontology so-called UFO. Hence, we decided to document both in a differentiated way (by colors in the form) so, at analysis time, count only the domain related concepts accordingly. For instance, there are in [19] 77 terms in total, but just 45 software testing domain-specific terms.

Table 6 summarizes aspects of the extracted data for the twelve 'Final Selected Documents' sorted descendingly by year of publication. The acronym PID represents the original paper identification in the whole list of retrieved papers in A2.2. Main information of this SLR's artifacts can be publicly accessed at https://goo.gl/HxY3yL.

Table 6. Summary of extracted data for the twelve 'Final Selected Documents'. PID is the original paper identification (https://goo.gl/HxY3yL) in the 'Forms with Extracted Data'

PID	Conceptualized ontology	Ontological classification	Publ. year	Page size	Development methodology	Used terminology [Glossary, Taxonomy, Ontology]	FR/NFR linking?
347	*RTE-Ontology*, Campos *et al.* [8]	Domain	2017	6	Not specified	PROV-O Ontology	No
383	Vasanthapriyan *et al.* [22]	Domain	2017	8	Grüninger& Fox Method	Glossary by ISTQB; IEEE 829-2008	No

(continued)

Table 6. (*continued*)

PID	Conceptualized ontology	Ontological classification	Publ. year	Page size	Development methodology	Used terminology [Glossary, Taxonomy, Ontology]	FR/NFR linking?
457	Vasanthapriyan et al. [21]	Domain	2017	15	Grüninger& Fox Method	Glossary by ISTQB; IEEE 829-2008	No
468	*ROoST*, Souza et al. [19]	Domain	2017	30	SABiO	Glossary by IEEE 610-1990 & 829-1998; Myers G. J., 2004: "The art of software testing"; SWEBOK; Pressman R., 2006: "Software engineering: a practitioner's approach"; ISTQB; Marthur A. P., 2012: "Foundations of Software Testing"; ISO/IEC/IEEE 29119; SP-OPL; E-OPL; UFO Foundational Ontology by authors	No
1003	Asman et al. [2]	Top Domain	2016	74	Methontology; Ontol.Dev.101	Glossary by ISTQB SWTOI; OntoTest;	No
346	*PTOntology*, Freitas et al. [11]	Domain	2014	8	Ontology Dev.101	Glossary by SWEBOK; IEEE Glossary of SE Terminology; IEEE Standard for Software Test Documentation	No
424	Arnicans et al. [1]	Not Specified	2013	14	ONTO6	Glossary by ISTQB	No
118	Sapna et al. [17]	Not Specified	2011	10	Methontology; Ontol.Dev.101	Glossary by SWEBOK	No
366	Cai et al. [7]	Not Spec.	2009	6	Skeletal	Glossary by SWEBOK, ISO/IEC 9126	No
359	*TOM*, Bai et al. [3]	Domain	2008	8	Not specified	Not specified	No
397	*OntoTest*, Barbosa et al. [4]	Not Specified	2008	6	Not specified	Glossary by IEEE 829; ISO/IEC 12207; The Software Process Ontology by Falbo & Bertollo; STOWS;	No
1000	*STOWS*, Zhu et al. [23]	Not Specified	2005	33	Not specified	Not specified	No

3.3   To Analyze and Document the Review (A3)

A3 includes two sub-activities. The first sub-activity named Analyze SLR Results produces the 'Data Synthesis' artifact. Next, we discuss aspects of data synthesis regarding the three stated RQs, some QC, and also taken into account some quality practices described by D'Aquin *et al.* [9] for ontology design, for which they identify dimensions and features for "beautiful ontologies". Two (out of three) dimensions are formal structure and conceptual coverage, which are characterized by if the ontology is designed in a principled way; it is formally rigorous; it implements also non-taxonomic relations; it has a good domain coverage; it implements an international standard; and it reuses foundational ontologies, among others. Note that Souza *et al.* [18] qualitatively analyze and discuss their SLR findings in the light of these characteristics. We are going to complement this analysis by using direct and indirect metrics as well.

Table 7 conveys the obtained values for direct and indirect metrics for Terms (Tr), Attributes (At) and Relationships (Rh). We have calculated metrics for axioms as well, but are not shown in the table for space reasons.

Table 7. Metrics for Terms, Attributes (Properties) and Relationships. Note that Df stands for Defined; Tx for Taxonomic; NoTx for Non-Taxonomic; and CptuaLvl for Conceptual Level

Ref.	Terms (Tr)			Attributes (At)			Relationships (Rh)						% DfNoTxRh	% TxCptuaLvl
	#Tr	#DfTr	% DfTr	#At	#DfAt	% DfAt	#Rh	#TxRh	#Tx-is_a	#Tx-part_of	#NoTxRh	#DfNoTxRh		
[8]	14	14	100%	0	-	-	16	15	14	1	1	1	100%	93.75%
[22]	50	7	14%	57	0	0%	65	48	30	18	17	0	0%	73.8%
[21]	45	7	15.6%	4	0	0%	46	37	27	10	9	0	0%	80.4%
[19]	45	37	82.2%	4	0	0%	51	27	18	9	24	13	54%	52.9%
[2]	54	54	100%	4	0	0%	131	108	94	14	23	23	100%	82.4%
[11]	14	0	0%	0	-	-	15	7	5	2	8	0	0%	46.7%
[1]	42	0	0%	0	-	-	41	41	41	0	0	0	-	100%
[17]	36	0	0%	0	-	-	50	40	18	22	10	0	0%	80%
[7]	37	0	0%	0	-	-	40	40	40	0	0	0	-	100%
[3]	15	1	6.7%	0	-	-	20	15	2	13	5	0	0%	75%
[4]	52	16	30.8%	0	-	-	50	40	37	3	10	0	0%	80%
[23]	63	19	30.2%	11	8	72.7%	74	67	44	23	7	7	100%	90.5%

Recall that in the last paragraph of Subsect. 3.1, we indicate the format we have extracted terms, attributes, relationships and axioms. Additionally, we have recorded, when available in the primary study, all D̲efined (Df) concepts as well as the definitions for N̲on-T̲axonomic R̲elationships (NoTxRh). Lastly, we have calculated the percentage of T̲axonomic-C̲onceptual-base L̲evel (%TxCptuaLvl). For example, some formulas for indirect metrics are:

$$\%DfTr = (\#DfTr/\#Tr) * 100 \tag{1}$$

$$\#Rh = \#TxRh + \#NoTxRh; \text{ where } \#TxRh = \#Tx\text{-}is\_a + \#Tx\text{-}part\_of \tag{2}$$

$$\%DfNoTxRh = (\#DfNoTxRh/\#NoTxRh) * 100 \tag{3}$$

$$\%TxCptuaLvl = (\#TxRh/\#Rh) * 100 \tag{4}$$

RQ1. *What are the conceptualized ontologies for the software testing domain?*

Table 6 summarizes some data and information extracted from the forms for the twelve primary studies. The six first ontologies obviously did not appear in [18] due to the year of their study was 2013. Moreover, as promised in that paper, they have developed ROoST [19] (see PID 468). Notice that for the Vasanthapriyan *et al.*'s ontology, which appears twice (viz PID 383 [22] and PID 457 [21]), there are two new co-authors in [22]. Moreover, even if both studies share 35 common terms, [22] introduces 15 new terms, while [21] 10 different new terms that are not included in the former. Besides, [22] contributes for instance with 57 attributes while [21] only with 4. Thus, we decided to include both owing that EC5 and EC7 do not apply appropriately for this situation.

Regarding the quality of the formal structure of conceptualized ontologies (i.e., the ontology is designed in a principled way, is formally rigorous, implements also non-taxonomic relations, and reuses foundational ontologies), we observe opportunities of improvement in all the primary studies at different degrees.

So far, the most formally rigorous domain ontology we found is ROoST [19]. It is the unique selected ontology for the software testing domain that is built on a foundational ontology (named UFO). It is well modularized and is well balanced including taxonomic and non-taxonomic relations (%TxCptuaLvl = 52.9). Conversely, the Arnicans *et al.* [1] and Cai *et al.* [7] ontologies have fully taxonomic relations (% TxCptuaLvl = 100), which therefore are taxonomies rather than ontologies. In both cases all relations are kind of, i.e., *is_a*. (Hence, these metric's values confirm quantitatively the qualitative finding made in [18]). Some improvements that ROoST could consider are: to increase the number of attributes (there are just 4, which are not defined), to add the absent definitions of some terms (%DfTr = 82.2), and to add definitions of some non-taxonomic relationships (%DfNoTxRh = 54).

Regarding defined non-taxonomic relations, other three ontologies accomplish this feature in a 100%. However, looking at Table 7, we can say that they are not well balanced since the figure is 15 taxonomic and 1 non-taxonomic relation in [8], 108 and 23 in [2], and 67 and 7 in [23] respectively. On the other hand, for 10 selected ontologies that have non-taxonomic relations, only the quoted 4 ontologies have definitions.

Other relevant aspect for evaluating a conceptualized ontology from the "formally rigorous" characteristic standpoint is the specification of axioms. ROoST has 9 axioms 100% specified. Likewise, STOWS has 6 axioms 100% specified. Specified 50% of them occur for the Vasanthapriyan *et al.*'s ontologies which count with 6 axioms.

Regarding the development (engineering) methodology used for building the ontology conceptualization, 4 out of 12 ontologies do not specify any (see 6th column in Table 6). These are: RTE-Ontology, Campos *et al.* [8]; TOM, Bai *et al.* [3]; OntoTest, Barbosa *et al.* [4]; and STOWS, Zhu *et al.* [23].

Another issue to highlight is that for documenting an explicit conceptualization for any domain ontology in general, and for documenting the inherent complexity of the software testing domain in particular, the manuscript's page size should be a somewhat important indicator to take into account (see values in the 5th column of Table 6). A formal and explicit conceptualization not only should convey the ontological structure by means of well-formed diagrams, but also grouping in tables the semantic (explicit definitions) of terms, properties, axioms, and non-taxonomic relations chiefly. Unfortunately, almost none ontology of the selected set uses tables for communicating definitions. But what is worse, very often definitions of those ontology elements are neglected as can be verified in Table 7. On the other hand, when definitions are available, they are often embedded in the main text of the manuscript. Specifically, from the data collection and measurement point of view, since definitions are not well grouped, it makes these processes more error prone. Ultimately, a simple recommendation for contributing to the clarity and beauty of ontologies is "try to pack all definitions in tables".

RQ2. *What are the most frequently included concepts, their relationships, attributes and axioms needed to describe the software testing domain?*

Considering the conceptual coverage dimension (e.g., the main terms are common in most conceptualized ontologies; the ontology has a good domain coverage; it implements an international standard, among other characteristics), we observe in general opportunities of improvement as well.

Fig. 3. Word cloud (https://www.nubedepalabras.es/) for the recorded Terms from the twelve data extraction forms. Note that Attributes and Relationships names are not included. Also note that the word size is related to the Term frequency, and term colors have no meaning

Regarding the frequency of included terms, Fig. 3 depicts the word cloud for the recorded terms taken from the 12 data extraction forms. 'Test Case' is the most frequently used word with 7 occurrences. Then, it follows decreasingly 'Test Result' (6), 'TestPlan' (5), and other four terms with 4 occurrences. We can see in the figure for example the 'IntegrationTesting' (3) and 'IntegrationTest' (2) terms. Have both terms the same semantic? Looking at the former term, it is not defined in OntoTest [4], but do in ROoST [19] and in Asman *et al.* [2]. While the latter is not defined in Sapna *et al.* [17], but it is in STOWS [23]. Comparing the three existing definitions they differ slightly in the semantic. While in STOWS 'IntegrationTest' is a kind of Context (with semantic of stage, but not a kind of Activity), in ROoST 'IntegrationTesting' has semantic of Level-based Testing that is a kind of Testing Activity, and in Asman *et al.* 'IntegrationTesting' has semantic of Test strategy. In summary, either ontologies have not defined terms or, if defined, the semantic of the same term differs to some extent from each other.

Considering that there are 606 relationships in total, the frequency for #Tx-is_a = 370; for #Tx-part_of = 115, and for #NoTxRh = 121, which represent the 61%, 19% and 20% respectively.

On the other hand, taking into account if the ontology has a good domain coverage, some of them such as RTE-Ontology, Campos *et al.* [8], and PTOntology, Freitas *et al.* [11] are devoted for specific testing sub-domains, i.e., Regression Test and Performance Testing respectively (see #Tr in Table 7, which are just a few). Conversely, the domain scope and coverage of, for example, ROoST [19], Asman *et al.* [2], and STOWS [23] are broader (see #Tr, #At and #Rs in Table 7, and their research objectives in the extraction forms at https://goo.gl/HxY3yL accordingly). However, ROoST does not cover concepts related to 'Static Testing' and 'NonFunctional Testing', while the Asman *et al.* ontology does. For instance, note that the 'NonFunctional Testing' term has 2 occurrences in the word cloud, so only 2 out of 12 ontologies deal with this aspect.

Lastly, regarding the reuse of terminologies of international standards and other conceptual bases, Table 6 summarizes this information in the 7th column. Only two ontologies viz. TOM, Bai *et al.* [3] and STOWS did not specify any.

RQ3. *How are existing software testing ontologies classified?*

Regarding this RQ, we collected the ontology classification (viz foundational –top-level-, top-domain, domain or application/instance ontology) given to the conceptualization by authors. Table 6 summarizes this information in the 3th column. Note that 4 out of 12 conceptualized ontologies did not specify any category. The remainder are domain ontologies, and just Asman *et al.* named it top-domain ontology, justifying in [2] this classification. As above mentioned, ROoST relies on a foundational ontology so-called UFO.

4 Related Work and Discussion

To the best of our knowledge, there are two secondary studies previously performed for software testing ontologies, so the SLR presented in this paper becomes the third. The first study performed in 2013 is documented in [18], while the second one conducted in 2015 is documented in [2]. Additionally, in 2016 a tertiary study was published by Garousi *et al.* [12] titled "A systematic literature review of literature reviews in software testing", whose goal was to systematically classify the secondary studies in software testing. In Table 15 of [12], for the "Testing-related terminology" mapping sub-category, authors indicate they "did not expect to find studies on this topic". So neither [18] nor [2] were included, surely due to the inclusion/exclusion selection criteria used in that study.

Considering our stated main goal, we try to capture software testing domain ontologies that document a conceptualization for this domain. Conversely, Souza *et al.* included both conceptualized and implemented ontologies. Their findings for those included conceptualizations are in line with our findings for the same six primary studies [1, 3, 4, 7, 17, 23]. However, we have augmented the qualitative analysis made by Souza *et al.* by using metric's values quantitatively (see the specification of metric formulas in Eqs. 1 to 4). This has allowed to confirm not only their findings but also to broaden our analysis and better justify the results. Furthermore, the SLR process we have followed foster a more systematic, reproducible and auditable approach.

On the other side, the main goal of the Asman *et al.* [2] research work was to build a top-domain software testing ontology. In this context, they used the SLR approach as a research methodology for getting prior evidence on testing ontologies. Authors found eight software testing ontologies, which most of them were included in our present work, while a couple of them were excluded owing to our established inclusion/exclusion selection criteria. However, a rigorous documentation of the followed SLR process (i.e., activities and artifacts) is rather missing in [2], which it represents a threat of repeatability and auditability.

5 Concluding Remarks and Future Work

As stated in the Introduction, a general benefit of having the suitable software testing ontology is that of minimizing the current heterogeneity, ambiguity and incompleteness problems in concepts, i.e., mainly in terms, properties and relationships. We have initially confirmed that there exists heterogeneity, ambiguity and incompleteness for concepts dealing with testing activities, artifacts and methods. Consequently, we are looking for the suitable software testing ontology for populating the 'testing' conceptual component (Fig. 1), which in turn should appropriately relate some of its concepts with FRs and NFRs components' concepts. Note that an additional finding recorded in the last column of Table 6 is that none conceptualized ontology links its testing conceptual component or module with FRs and NFRs components.

In this study, we have documented the conducted SLR (as part of the A3's second sub-activity) following a well-established SLR process. This process specification promotes the validation of the 'SLR Protocol' artifact not only in the A1 activity but also in A2.1 by performing a pilot test. In addition, we have paid thorough attention to consistency checking in the A2.2 sub-activity. Hence, we have tried to minimize the threats of validity for getting evidence that this type of research methodology entails.

As an ongoing work in this line of research, we have just started to develop the suitable top-domain testing ontology to be integrated into the C-INCAMI v.2 conceptual framework. Obviously, we are going to adopt or adapt those explicit terminologies coming from not only some of the existing primary studies but also from official and *de facto* international standards (e.g., ISO/IEC/IEEE 29119-1:2013 https:// www.iso.org/standard/45142.html, and ISTQB https://www.istqb.org/downloads.html respectively), which are widely adopted by professional testers.

Acknowledgments. This work and line of research are supported by Science and Technology Agency of Argentina, in the PICT 2014-1224 project at UNLPam.

References

1. Arnicans, G., Romans, D., Straujums, U.: Semi-automatic generation of a software testing lightweight ontology from a glossary based on the ONTO6 methodology. Front. Artif. Intell. Appl. **249**, 263–276 (2013)
2. Asman, A., Srikanth, R.M.: A top domain ontology for software testing. Master Thesis, Jönköping University, Sweden, pp. 1–74 (2016)
3. Bai, X., Lee, S., Tsai, W.T., Chen, Y.: Ontology-based test modeling and partition testing of web services. In: IEEE International Conference on Web Services (ICWS 2008), pp. 465–472 (2008)
4. Barbosa, E.F., Nakagawa, E.Y., Riekstin, A.C., Maldonado, J.C.: Ontology-based development of testing related tools. In: 20th International Conference on Software Engineering and Knowledge Engineering (SEKE 2008), pp. 697–702 (2008)
5. Becker, P., Papa, F., Olsina, L.: Process ontology specification for enhancing the process compliance of a measurement and evaluation strategy. CLEI eJnal **18**(1), 1–26 (2015)
6. Brereton, P., Kitchenham, B., Budgen, D., Turner, M., Khalil, M.: Lessons from applying the systematic literature review process within the software engineering domain. J. Syst. Softw. **80**(4), 571–583 (2007)
7. Cai, L., Tong, W., Liu, Z., Zhang, J.: Test case reuse based on ontology. In: 15th IEEE Pacific Rim International Symposium on Dependable Computing, pp. 103–108 (2009)
8. Campos, H., Acácio, C., Braga, R., Araújo, M.A.P., David, J.M.N., Campos, F.: Regression tests provenance data in the continuous software engineering context. In: 2nd Brazilian Symposium on Systematic and Automated Software Testing (SAST), Paper 10, pp. 1–6 (2017)
9. D'Aquin, M., Gangemi, A.: Is there beauty in ontologies? Appl. Ontol. **6**(3), 165–175 (2011)
10. Fernández-López, M., Gómez-Pérez, A., Juristo, N.: METHONTOLOGY: from ontological art towards ontological engineering. In: Spring Symposium on Ontological Engineering of AAAI, pp. 33–40. Stanford University, California (1997)
11. Freitas, A., Vieira, R.: An ontology for guiding performance testing. In: IEEE/WIC/ACM International Joint Conferences on Web Intelligence (WI) and Intelligent Agent Technologies (IAT), (WI-IAT 2014), vol. 1, pp. 400–407 (2014)
12. Garousi, V., Mäntylä, M.: A systematic literature review of literature reviews in software testing. Inf. Softw. Technol. **80**, 195–216 (2016)

13. Kitchenham, B., Charters, S.: Procedures for Performing Systematic Reviews, EBSE T.R., Software Engineering Group, School of Computer Science and Mathematics, Keele University and Department of Computer Science University of Durham, UK, vol. 2.3 (2007)

14. Kitchenham, B.: Procedures for Undertaking Systematic Reviews, Joint TR, Computer Science Department, Keele University (TR/SE-0401) and National ICT Australia Ltd. (0400011T.1) (2004)

15. Olsina, L., Becker, P.: Family of strategies for different evaluation purposes. In: XX CIbSE 2017, CABA, Argentina, pp. 221–234. Curran Associates (2017)

16. Olsina, L., Becker, P.: Linking business and information need goals with functional and non-functional requirements. In: XXI CIbSE 2018, Bogotá, Colombia, pp. 381–394. Curran Associates (2018)

17. Sapna, P.G., Mohanty, H.: An ontology based approach for test scenario management. In: Dua, S., Sahni, S., Goyal, D.P. (eds.) ICISTM 2011. CCIS, vol. 141, pp. 91–100. Springer, Heidelberg (2011). https://doi.org/10.1007/978-3-642-19423-8_10

18. Souza, E.F., Falbo, R.A., Vijaykumar, N.L.: Ontologies in software testing: a systematic literature review. In: CEUR Workshop Proceedings, vol. 1041, pp. 71–82 (2013)

19. Souza, E.F., Falbo, R.A., Vijaykumar, N.L.: ROoST: reference ontology on software testing. Appl. Ontol. J. **12**(1), 1–30 (2017)

20. Tebes, G., Peppino, D., Becker, P., Olsina, L.: Specifying the process model for a systematic literature review (In Spanish). In: XXII CIbSE 2019, La Habana, Cuba, pp. 1–14. Curran Associates (2019)

21. Vasanthapriyan, S., Tian, J., Xiang, J.: An ontology-based knowledge framework for software testing. In: Chen, J., Theeramunkong, T., Supnithi, T., Tang, X. (eds.) KSS 2017. CCIS, vol. 780, pp. 212–226. Springer, Singapore (2017). https://doi.org/10.1007/978-981-10-6989-5_18

22. Vasanthapriyan, S., Tian, J., Zhao, D., Xiong, S., Xiang, J.: An ontology-based knowledge sharing portal for software testing. In: IEEE International Conference on Software Quality, Reliability and Security Companion (QRS-C 2017), pp. 472–479 (2017)

23. Zhu, H., Huo, Q.: Developing a software testing ontology in UML for a software growth environment of web-based applications. In: Software Evolution with UML and XML, pp. 263–295. IDEA Group (2005)

Hamcrest vs AssertJ: An Empirical Assessment of Tester Productivity

Maurizio Leotta$^{(\boxtimes)}$(iD), Maura Cerioli(iD), Dario Olianas, and Filippo Ricca(iD)

Dipartimento di Informatica, Bioingegneria,
Robotica e Ingegneria dei Sistemi (DIBRIS), Università di Genova, Genova, Italy
{maurizio.leotta,maura.cerioli,dario.olianas,filippo.ricca}@unige.it

Abstract. *Context.* Extensive unit testing is worth its costs in terms of the higher quality of the final product and reduced development expenses, though it may consume more than fifty percent of the overall project budget. Thus, even a tiny percentage of saving can significantly decrease the costs. Since recently competing assertion libraries emerged, we need empirical evidence to gauge them in terms of developer productivity, allowing SQA Managers and Testers to select the best.

Objective. The aim of this work is comparing two assertion frameworks having a different approach (matchers vs. fluent assertions) w.r.t. tester productivity.

Method. We conducted a controlled experiment involving 41 Bachelor students. AssertJ is compared with Hamcrest, in a test development scenario with the Java language. We analysed the number of correct assertions developed in a tight time frame and used this measure as a proxy for tester productivity.

Results. The results show that adopting AssertJ improves the overall tester's productivity significantly during the development of assertions.

Conclusions. Testers and SQA managers selecting assertion frameworks for their organizations should consider as first choice AssertJ, since our study shows that it increases the productivity of testers during development more than Hamcrest.

Keywords: Hamcrest · AssertJ · Empirical study

1 Introduction

In the last two decades, automated software testing has gained the spotlights of software development. Indeed, starting from the *agile revolution*, tests have been an important part not only of quality assessment, but of code development itself, with practices like *test first*[1], *test driven development* (see e.g. [3]) and *behaviour driven development* (see e.g. [28]). Writing tests before developing the corresponding functionalities increases the requirement understanding, reduces the number and impact of defects in final products, and decreases the costs of bug

---

[1] http://www.extremeprogramming.org/rules/testfirst.html.

© Springer Nature Switzerland AG 2019
M. Piattini et al. (Eds.): QUATIC 2019, CCIS 1010, pp. 161–176, 2019.
https://doi.org/10.1007/978-3-030-29238-6_12

fixing, letting them be spotted in the early phases of development (see e.g. [19]). It provides also *living documentation* (see e.g. [1,20]), where tests clarify the expectations about the system and inherently document the current version of the system if they pass. Finally, comprehensive test suites, used as *regression tests*, let the system evolve with confidence that no undesired effects will take place.

Though many different types of functional testing exist, the more widespread[2] among them is the basic unit testing, used to validate that each unit of the software (a method/class in the context of object-oriented programming) performs as designed. There is no doubt that extensive unit testing is worth its costs in terms of the higher quality of the final product and reduced development expenses. However, as stated in [11], "studies indicate that testing consumes more than fifty percent of the cost of software development". Thus, even small percentage savings on the testing process can significantly improve the project budget.

The first standard step toward saving on the testing process is to automate it through testing frameworks (e.g. JUnit or TestNG), which run the test method(s) and report successes/failures to the testers. The expected results are described by *assertions*, that are methods checking values (the result of the call under test, or the final status of some part of the system) against given conditions, and raising an exception in case of failure. Both testing frameworks and assertion libraries are currently a hot topic, with their numerous (mostly open-source) development projects showing a high number of commit and downloading, and their choice is far from obvious.

Nowadays, the most popular assertion libraries for the Java language are Hamcrest[3] and AssertJ[4]. The former hit the market first, is more well-established, and still attracts more attention, as for instance shown by Google Trend[5], where for the period from April 2018 to April 2019 on the average AssertJ scores forty-five and Hamcrest scores seventy-three over a maximum of a hundred. AssertJ, on the other hand, has a more active development community, provides more assertion methods out of the box, and adopts a *fluent style*, based on the dot notation, which is supposed to make writing assertions easier and the results more readable.

To investigate the claimed advantages of one of the frameworks w.r.t the other for what concerns the productivity of assertion writing, we applied Evidence-Based Software Engineering [13] to this context. In particular, we conducted a controlled experiment [27] involving forty-one Bachelor students to compare their capabilities in writing assertions in AssertJ and Hamcrest, taking into account both correctness and effort. We also devised a method to select the

---

[2] https://www.mountaingoatsoftware.com/blog/the-forgotten-layer-of-the-test-automation-pyramid.

[3] http://hamcrest.org/.

[4] https://joel-costigliola.github.io/assertj/.

[5] https://trends.google.com/trends/explore?q=Assertj,Hamcrest.

most practically essential assertion methods, so to restrict our experiment to writing tests involving those methods.

The paper is organized as follows: Sect. 2 briefly describes the assertion libraries used in this study: AssertJ and Hamcrest. The selection process for singling out the assertion methods more used in practice fills Sect. 3. The description of the empirical study and the preliminary results are in Sects. 4 and 5 respectively. Finally, related works are discussed in Sect. 6 while conclusions are given in Sect. 7.

2   Assertions: Dot Notation vs. Matchers

JUnit[6], being the leading unit test framework for Java programming[7] is the natural choice as reference testing framework for our experiment. Indeed, its most recent version, JUnit 5, has built-in support for different assertion libraries, including those we want to compare: Hamcrest and AssertJ.

The *first generation* style of assertions used to be simply stating a boolean expression to be `true`. But that approach had a couple of major limitations: the expression to be evaluated is in most cases complex or a variable initialized by non-trivial code (in both cases making the test difficult to understand), and in case of failure, the error message is not much help, because it only says that the evaluation of the expression is `false`, while `true` was expected.

Thus the *second generation* of assertions has been introduced, with methods to state specific properties about the objects under test and the state of the overall system. For instance, `assertEquals` takes two arguments and states that they are equals. If they are not, the automatic error message captures the values of the parameters, giving more informative feedback. The problem with the second generation style is that numerous different methods would be needed to cover several common uses. But if all were provided, the users would have to memorize a plethora of assertion methods, to be able to select the needed one. Therefore, this approach cannot succeed, taken between lack of expressivity and steep learning curve.

More recently a *third generation* assertion style has appeared on the scene. It has just one (overloaded) assertion method, `assertThat`, and uses different mechanisms to provide the needed flexibility depending on the specific library. In the following, we will discuss the basics of Hamcrest and AssertJ approaches.

Hamcrest. The first release of Hamcrest dates back to 2006, and the name is an acronym of *matchers*, from its key concept. In Hamcrest, the `assertThat` method takes two parameters: the object of the assertion, in most cases the result of the call under test, and a matcher, a boolean function *matching* the first parameter against the expected property. For instance, if c is a collection of strings `assertThat(c, hasItems("cd","ef"))` succeeds if c contains both `"cd"` and `"ef"`.

---

[6] https://junit.org.

[7] https://redmonk.com/fryan/2018/03/26/a-look-at-unit-testing-frameworks/.

Technically the matchers are just objects of classes implementing the `Matcher` `<T>` interface, but seldom they are directly created by a `new`. Good practices suggest providing, together with matcher classes, *factories* for them. Thus, we can use method calls to create new objects getting much more readable assertions. Indeed, the method names in factories, like the `hasItems` call in the previous example, are carefully chosen so that their invocations mimic natural language sentences.

Moreover, using methods to build objects paves the way to a language to compose simple matchers to get more complex ones. For instance, `everyItem` takes a matcher on the type of the elements and produces a matcher on a collection; thus, if `c` is a collection of numbers, `assertThat(c, everyItem(greaterThan(10)))` succeeds if all the elements in `c` are greater than 10. Other useful matcher composition methods are `allOf` and `anyOf`, to state that all/any matcher of a collection of matchers must succeed, and `not`, to negate matchers. Composing matchers greatly improves the expressive power of Hamcrest without dramatically increasing the number of matchers to memorize. However, the standard library defines a non-negligible number of basic matchers (about 90), and users are encouraged to define their own at need. Thus, users have to memorize many matchers to proficiently use Hamcrest and, though the matcher names are in most cases easy to remember/guess, still this need put a burden on the testers.

AssertJ follows a different approach w.r.t. Hamcrest. Indeed, its `assertThat` has a unique parameter, the element under test, and yields an object of a class providing methods to express conditions on values of the type of the parameter. For instance, if `f` is an `InputStream`, then `assertThat(f)` has type `AbstractInputStreamAssert`, with methods like `hasSameContentAs(InputStream expected)`. As for Hamcrest, choosing apt names for the assertion methods allows writing assertions reminiscent of English sentences, like for instance the following[8]: `assertThat(fellowshipOfTheRing).hasSize(9);` Moreover, as the result type of assertion methods is again a class of assertions, assertions can be naturally chained, like in

```
assertThat(fellowshipOfTheRing).hasSize(9)
                    .contains(frodo, sam)
                    .doesNotContain(sauron);
```

providing a logical conjunction, as the assertion passes if all its parts do.

More sophisticated logical manipulations can be expressed using the `is`/`are` and `has`/`have` assertion methods, that take a `Condition` as argument and match it against the element under test. All methods have the same semantics, but using the most appropriate from a linguistic point of view greatly improves readability (the plural forms are for collections and apply the condition to all their elements). Methods like `not`, `allOf`, `anyOf` can be used to create complex `Condition` expressions, as well as `areAtLeast`, `areAtMost`, `areExactly` on collections, taking a further integer argument and verifying that the number of the collection elements satisfying the condition matches the requirement. Hamcrest

---

[8] This example, as the following ones, is taken from https://joel-costigliola.github.io/assertj/.

matchers can be used to create AssertJ conditions thanks to small adapters. Thus, AssertJ fully matches Hamcrest expressive power with a similar syntactic approach, besides providing other assertion methods.

But the real hit of AssertJ is that testers do not have to remember the names of the assertion methods, because writing `assertThat(_)` and following it with a dot they get help from the IDE (*code completion facility*), listing all the methods in the assertion class, that is, all the assertion methods applicable to the given type. Moreover, as the assertion methods are clustered by the type of the actual value to be tested, their number for each given type is manageable (though the overall collection is impressively large, with about 380 methods, and hence expressive), and static correctness reduces the risk of errors.

3   Practical Usage of Hamcrest Matchers and AssertJ Methods

Both the Hamcrest and AssertJ frameworks are highly expressive, providing, respectively, many matchers and assertion methods. But some of them are more used/popular than others. Hence, to make a fair and significant comparison of the two frameworks, we need to determine which assertion methods/matchers are the most used in practice and focus the experiment mainly on them. With this aim, we applied the following mining procedure to repositories on GitHub, the world's leading repository hosting service:

1. we collected the list of all the Hamcrest matchers and AssertJ assertion methods;
2. we defined the repositories inclusion/exclusion criteria for our analysis;
3. we devised an automated procedure to count instances of the matchers/assertion methods in our lists from the repositories satisfying our inclusion criteria;
4. finally, we ran the procedure and reported the results in percentage.

In the following subsections, a detailed explanation of the various steps is provided.

Collecting the Lists of Hamcrest Matchers and AssertJ Methods. To find all the available matchers of Hamcrest (version 2.0.0.0) and the assertion methods of AssertJ (3.9.0), we used reflection on the respective packages. In particular, for Hamcrest, we extracted all the public static method names from the classes in the sub-packages of `org.hamcrest`. For AssertJ, we extracted all public method names from classes whose name ends in "Assert" in the package `org.assertj.core.api`.

Defining Repositories Selection Criteria. Following the work of Kalliamvakou et al. [12] and Vendome et al. [26], to exclude too simple or personal repositories we selected only the ones matching the following criteria: ① at least six commits, ② at least two contributors, ③ at least one star[9] or watcher[10],

---

[9] On GitHub users star other users' repositories to express appreciation.

[10] Watchers are users who asked to be notified of repository changes.

and ④ not a fork. Indeed according to Kalliamvakou et al. the 90% of projects have less than 50 commits, the median number of commits is six (criterion ①), and the 71.6% of the projects on Github are personal projects (criterion ②). Moreover, criterion ③ guarantees that at least a user besides the owner is interested in the project. Finally, as in the work of Vendome et al., we excluded forks to avoid over-representation of matchers and methods used by highly forked projects (criterion ④).

Mining Assertions Data from GitHub. To find usages of AssertJ and Hamcrest assertions, we queried the Searchcode[11] API, that returns a list of files in public repositories containing the required text. The API allows filtering for language (Java in our case) and code repository hosting platform (we selected GitHub). Since results are limited to the first 1000 hits, to increase the number of results we searched matcher (method) by matcher (method). We constructed search queries concatenating the following elements:

- Import name for the considered framework (`org.hamcrest` or `org.assertj.core.api.Assertions.assertThat`)
- `@Test` (to be sure to include only occurrences in test scripts)
- Matcher (method) name

For each result (a file), after checking if the corresponding repository matches our criteria[12], the script downloads it and memorizes its Searchcode ID, to avoid downloading it again in case it contains other assertions and so appears in further queries. Then, our script analyses the file, identifies its assertions as the text between an `assertThat(` and a semicolon, cleans them from their parameters, and counts the occurrences of each matchers/methods appearing in them. To correctly identify matcher/method names and avoid false positive due to substring collision, like for instance `isNot` in `isNotIn` for AssertJ, we search using a regular expression that matches strings:

- starting and ending with any string (the name may appear anywhere in the assertion)
- containing at least one non-alphanumerical character (the separator before the name)
- then the matcher/method name
- then an open round parenthesis (for the matcher/method call)

Results. Analysing the source code of the two frameworks, we found a total of 87 Hamcrest matchers and 376 AssertJ methods available to developers. Then,

---

[11] https://searchcode.com/.

[12] The information needed to apply the selection criteria is not completely accessible via the GitHub API. For example, it is not possible to directly ask for the number of commits, but only for a list of commits that may be divided into different pages, thus requiring several calls to the API. So, we retrieved the required information from the repository GitHub home page, using Requests-HTML for Python (https://html.python-requests.org/).

Table 1. Usage of Hamcrest matchers and AssertJ methods in real GitHub repositories.

Matcher	Hamcrest frequency	%	cumulative	Method	AssertJ frequency	%	cumulative
✗ equalTo	22438	50,32%	50,32%	✗ isEqualTo	5555	43,41%	43,41%
is	9269	20,79%	71,10%	✗ isFalse	833	6,51%	49,91%
✓ notNullValue	2858	6,41%	77,51%	✗ isTrue	818	6,39%	56,31%
nullValue	1656	3,71%	81,23%	as	593	4,63%	60,94%
✓ instanceOf	1470	3,30%	84,52%	✓ isSameAs	507	3,96%	64,90%
✓ containsString	1258	2,82%	87,35%	✓ isNotNull	504	3,94%	68,84%
✓ not	845	1,89%	89,24%	✓ isNotEqualTo	459	3,59%	72,43%
✓ sameInstance	612	1,37%	90,61%	isNull	438	3,42%	75,85%
✓ greaterThan	512	1,15%	91,76%	get	356	2,78%	78,63%
✓ closeTo	510	1,14%	92,90%	✓ hasSize	341	2,66%	81,29%
✓ hasItem	411	0,92%	93,83%	containsExactly	247	1,93%	83,22%
✓ hasSize	269	0,60%	94,43%	isLessThanOrEqualTo	217	1,70%	84,92%
anyOf	241	0,54%	94,97%	✓ contains	154	1,20%	86,12%
hasItems	229	0,51%	95,48%	isAfterOrEqualTo	140	1,09%	87,22%
contains	227	0,51%	95,99%	isBeforeOrEqualTo	138	1,08%	88,30%
greaterThanOrEqualTo	210	0,47%	96,46%	isGreaterThanOrEqualTo	133	1,04%	89,33%
✓ allOf	205	0,46%	96,92%	isBefore	129	1,01%	90,34%
lessThanOrEqualTo	136	0,30%	97,23%	✓ isGreaterThan	128	1,00%	91,34%
✓ startsWith	126	0,28%	97,51%	isAfter	124	0,97%	92,31%
✓ lessThan	126	0,28%	97,79%	✓ isEmpty	119	0,93%	93,24%
✓ hasEntry	123	0,28%	98,07%	✓ isLessThan	117	0,91%	94,16%
arrayWithSize	107	0,24%	98,31%	✓ isInstanceOf	110	0,86%	95,01%
✓ empty	99	0,22%	98,53%	containsOnly	48	0,38%	95,39%
✓ hasKey	83	0,19%	98,72%	✓ containsEntry	48	0,38%	95,76%
✓ endsWith	69	0,15%	98,87%	isNotZero	44	0,34%	96,11%
containsInAnyOrder	53	0,12%	98,99%	size	44	0,34%	96,45%
arrayContaining	48	0,11%	99,10%	✓ isNotEmpty	43	0,34%	96,79%
arrayContainingInAnyOrder	47	0,11%	99,20%	isZero	37	0,29%	97,08%
hasToString	44	0,10%	99,30%	✓ exists	34	0,27%	97,34%
hasItemInArray	40	0,09%	99,39%	overridingErrorMessage	31	0,24%	97,59%
isIn	28	0,06%	99,46%	✓ startsWith	25	0,20%	97,78%
isEmptyString	26	0,06%	99,51%	containsKey	23	0,18%	97,96%
typeCompatibleWith	25	0,06%	99,57%	hasMessage	22	0,17%	98,13%
isOneOf	24	0,05%	99,62%	isExactlyInstanceOf	20	0,16%	98,29%
either	24	0,05%	99,68%	doesNotContain	20	0,16%	98,45%
emptyArray	21	0,05%	99,72%	isNotSameAs	19	0,15%	98,59%
hasXPath	21	0,05%	99,77%	asList	17	0,13%	98,73%
isEmptyOrNullString	17	0,04%	99,81%	✓ endsWith	14	0,11%	98,84%
emptyIterable	16	0,04%	99,85%	✓ containsValues	14	0,11%	98,95%
both	14	0,03%	99,88%	✓ isNotNegative	11	0,09%	99,03%
✓ everyItem	13	0,03%	99,91%	isEqualToComparingFieldByField	9	0,07%	99,10%
✓ hasValue	9	0,02%	99,93%	isNullOrEmpty	8	0,06%	99,16%
hasProperty	8	0,02%	99,94%	✓ containsKeys	8	0,06%	99,23%
isA	7	0,02%	99,96%	matches	7	0,05%	99,28%
emptyCollectionOf	4	0,01%	99,97%	containsExactlyInAnyOrder	7	0,05%	99,34%

searching such matchers and methods in GitHub, we found 44592 hits in 2279 files for Hamcrest and 12798 hits in 770 files for AssertJ from 210 repositories overall (other 592 matching repositories did not satisfy the criteria, and were discarded).

Table 1 lists the 45 more frequent Hamcrest matchers and AssertJ methods. It is interesting to note that they achieve a cumulative frequency of 99.97% and 99.34% for Hamcrest and AssertJ, respectively. Moreover, about the 50% of the assertions use `equalTo` or `isEqualTo`, and only 51 out of 87 Hamcrest matchers and 75 out of 376 AssertJ methods are used at least once in the code found on GitHub repositories matching our criteria. These numbers suggest that developers mostly use a small fraction of the available constructs. Moreover, the most used assertion methods in AssertJ have semantic equivalent Hamcrest matchers in the top popular list and vice-versa.

Summary: Even if both frameworks provide many matchers and assertion methods, **in practice developers use only a few of them**. This result permits us to narrow the comparison only to a subset of assertions without significant loss of generality or fairness.

4 Experiment Definition, Design and Settings

Based on the Goal Question Metric (GQM) template [2], the main goal of our experiment can be defined as follows: "*Analyse the use of two different assertion frameworks for Unit Testing of Java programs with the purpose of understanding if there is an impact w.r.t. the production costs of test cases from the point of view of SQA Managers and Testers in the context of Junior Testers executing tasks of assertion development.*"

Thus, our research question is:

RQ. Does the tester productivity vary when using AssertJ instead of Hamcrest (or vice-versa)?

To quantitatively investigate the research question, we measured the productivity of the participants as the number of correct assertions developed in a limited amount of time (i.e., the number of correct assertions is a proxy for measuring the productivity construct).

The *perspective* is of *SQA Managers* and *Testers* interested in selecting the better framework for improving productivity. The *context* of the experiment consists of two collections of assertions (respectively *Obj1* and *Obj2*, i.e., the *objects*) both to be implemented in both frameworks and of *subjects*, 41 Computer Science bachelor students.

We conceived and designed the experiment following the guidelines by Wohlin *et al.* [27]. Table 2 summarizes the main elements of the experiment. For replication purposes, the experimental package has been made available: http://sepl.dibris.unige.it/HamcrestVsAssertJ.php.

Table 2. Overview of the experiment

Goal	Analyse the use of Hamcrest and AssertJ during test assertion development tasks to understand if there is a difference in terms of productivity
Quality focus	Correctness of the developed assertions
Context	Objects: two collections of Assertions (*Obj1*, *Obj2*)
	Subjects: 41 BSc students in Computer Science (3rd year)
Null hypothesis	No effect on productivity (measured as number of correct assertions developed in a limited time slot)
Treatments	Hamcrest and AssertJ frameworks in JUnit
Dependent variable	Total number of correctly developed assertions

In the following we present in detail: treatments, objects, subjects, design, hypotheses, variable and other aspects of the experiment.

Treatment. Our experiment has one independent variable (main factor) and two treatments: "H" (Hamcrest) or "A" (AssertJ). Thus, the tasks require adopting, in the former (latter) case, the Hamcrest (AssertJ) framework, that is, developing the assertions by Hamcrest matchers (AssertJ assertion methods).

Objects. The objects of the study are two collections of seven *assertions descriptions* (*Obj1* and *Obj2*) included in a test suite for a simple JSON to CSV converter[13]. These assertions require working with lists, hash-maps, and other Java non-trivial types. The object design strives at balancing complexity as much as possible. For this reason, each assertion description in an object has a correspondent one in the other object with the same complexity, that is the same linguistic complexity and comparably straightforward to implement using our target assertion methods/matchers in both treatments.

In details, starting from the list of the most used Hamcrest matchers and AssertJ methods (see Table 1) we conceived 14 assertions descriptions whose implementations are expected to use at least one of them. Indeed, our *reference implementation* of the 14 assertions descriptions in Hamcrest (AssertJ) uses 18 matchers (17 assertion methods) in the top-45 list (some assertion descriptions require more than one matcher (method) to be implemented), and a couple of less popular (`equalToIgnoringCase` and `anExistingFile` in Hamcrest; `isCloseTo` and `isEqualToIgnoringCase` in AssertJ). In Table 1 the green ✓ marks the specific matchers/methods expected to be used by the subjects participating in our experiment. Vice versa, red ✗ marks the matchers/methods forbidden unless expressly allowed in the development of the assertions. We added this constraint to the experiment to force the students to use the specific matchers (assertion methods) provided by the frameworks, preventing them from using complex expressions and `equalTo`/`isEqualTo` (always a viable, though in many cases low-quality, solution adopted by testers in about 50% of cases, as shown by our analysis).

Assertion Examples. Let us see an example of the tasks given to our subjects. The provided code includes the test setup and comments both to clarify the setup and to specify the assertion to be implemented by the students. For the sake of understandability, we have translated the comments in English, that in the experiment were in the student mother tongue (i.e., Italian).

```
@Test
public void testCsvContentAtIndex() {
  // Load a JSON file in the Hashmap f
  List<Map<String, String>> f =
    JSONFlattener.parseJson(new File("f/mysmall.json"), "UTF-8
      ");

  // Assert that the forth element of flatJson:
  // (1) has a field named "user" with the value "John"
  // (2) has some field with 26462 as value
```

For the above example, for instance, we expected something like the following solutions.

```
// Hamcrest reference implementation
assertThat(f.get(4), allOf(hasEntry("user", "John"),
  hasValue("26462")));
```

---

[13] https://github.com/Arkni/json-to-csv.

```
// AssertJ reference implementation
assertThat(f.get(4)).containsEntry("user", "John")
    .containsValues("26462");
}
```

Subjects. The experiment was conducted in a research laboratory under controlled conditions (i.e., online). Subjects were 41 students from the Software Engineering course, in their last year of the BSc degree in Computer Science at the University of Genova (Italy). They had a common Java programming knowledge, matured through a course of the previous year with significant project activity. Automated testing was explained during the Software Engineering course (i.e., the course in which the experiment was conducted), where detailed explanations on both Hamcrest and AssertJ were provided. Students participated into our experiment on a voluntary base, after five mandatory labs about software engineering, including one about unit test automation using basic JUnit assertions. Before the experiment, all the subjects have been trained on Hamcrest and AssertJ assertions with a one-hour presentation including assertions development (similar to the ones required in the experiment).

Experiment Design. The experiment adopts a counterbalanced design planned to fit two Lab sessions (see Table 3). Subjects were split into four groups balancing as much as possible their ability/experience, as ascertained by the previous mandatory software engineering labs. Each subject worked in Lab 1 on an object with a treatment and in Lab 2 on the other object with the other treatment.

Table 3. Experimental design (H = Hamcrest, A = AssertJ)

	Group A	Group B	Group C	Group D
Lab 1	*Obj1* A	*Obj1* H	*Obj2* H	*Obj2* A
Lab 2	*Obj2* H	*Obj2* A	*Obj1* A	*Obj1* H

Dependent Variables and Hypothesis Formulation. Our experiment has only one dependent variable, on which treatments are compared measuring the productivity construct for which we defined the relative metric (as done, e.g., in [21]). The number of correct assertions was used as a proxy to measure productivity. For each subject and lab, the *TotalCorrectness* variable was computed by summing up: *one* if the developed assertion is correct and *zero* if wrong, incomplete, or missing. Thus, the *TotalCorrectness* variable ranges from zero to seven, where seven corresponds to seven correct assertions.

Since we could not find any previous empirical evidence that points out a clear advantage of one approach vs. the other, we formulated H_0 as non-directional hypothesis:

H_0. *The use of a framework w.r.t. the other does not improve the total correctness of the produced assertions*

The objective of a statistical analysis is to reject the null hypotheses above, so accepting the corresponding alternative one H_1 (stating instead that an effect exist).

Material, Procedure and Execution. To assess the experimental material and to get an estimate of the time needed to accomplish the tasks, a pilot experiment with two BSc students in Computer Science at University of Genova was performed. The students finished both tasks in 118 and 127 min (also producing some incorrect assertion implementations) and gave us some information on how improving the experimental material, in particular concerning the description of the assertions to develop. Given the times of the students and the time constraint of the labs, we set the total time of the entire experiment to 2 h (1 h for treatment).

The experiment took place in a laboratory room and was carried on using Eclipse. The subjects participated in two laboratory sessions (Lab 1 and Lab 2), with a short break between them.

For each group (see Table 3), each lab session required to develop seven assertions adopting Hamcrest or AssertJ respectively, and the subjects had 60 min to complete it. For each Lab session, we assigned a specific Eclipse project to each subject, and for each assertion to be developed, subjects: (a) recorded the starting time; (b) developed the assertion using the online documentation; (c) recorded the ending time.

Analysis Procedure. Because of the sample size and the non-normality of the data (measured with the Shapiro–Wilk test [23]), we adopted non-parametric tests to check the null hypothesis. This choice follows the suggestions given by [18, Chap. 37].

In particular, after computing descriptive statistics, we used a two-step analysis procedure. First, we calculated a contingency table displaying the frequency distribution of the variable *TotalCorrectness* for the two treatments. The table provides a basic picture of the interrelation between the treatment and the obtained correctness and provides a first rough insight into the results. To investigate the statistical significance, we applied the Fisher test.

Second, since subjects developed assertions of two different objects with the two possible treatments (i.e., Hamcrest and AssertJ), we used a paired Wilcoxon test to compare the effects of the two treatments on each subject. While the statistical tests allow checking the presence of significant differences, they do not provide any information about the magnitude of such a difference. Therefore, we used the non-parametric Cliff's delta (d) effect size [10]. The effect size is considered small for $0.148 \leq |d| < 0.33$, medium for $0.33 \leq |d| < 0.474$ and large for $|d| \geq 0.474$.

Since we performed two different analyses on the *TotalCorrectness* dependent variable, we cannot use $\alpha = 0.05$; we need to compensate for repeated statistical tests. While several techniques are available, we opted for the most conservative one, the Bonferroni correction [7]. In a nutshell, the conclusion will be taken by comparing the p-value to a corrected significance level $\alpha_B = \alpha/nt$, where nt is the number of statistical tests performed. Thus, in our case, $\alpha_B = 0.05/2 = 0.025$.

5 Results

Let us start with a short description of the results from the experiment, analysing the effect of the main factor on the dependent variable. Table 4 summarizes the essential descriptive statistics (i.e., median, mean, and standard deviation) of *Correctness*.

Table 4. *Correctness*: descriptive statistics per Treatment and Results of paired Wilcoxon test

Subjects	Hamcrest			AssertJ			p-value	Cliff's delta
	Mean	Median	SD	Mean	Median	SD		
41	2.600	2.000	1.172	3.325	3.000	1.289	0.0036	−0.3131 (S)

Table 5 presents the contingency table of *Correctness*, considering the tasks performed by the same subject as independent measures.

Table 5. *Correctness*: contingency table

		Correct	
		Yes	No
Treatment	**Hamcrest**	107	180
	AssertJ	133	154

Comparing the results, it is evident that adopting AssertJ the participants were able to develop a greater number of correct assertions: 133 vs. 107. We applied the Fisher test on the contingency table that returned a p-value = 0.017. From these results emerges a preliminary statistically significant influence of the treatment on the capability to develop correct assertions.

Figure 1 summarizes the distribution of *TotalCorrectness* by means of box-plots. Observations are grouped by treatment (Hamcrest or AssertJ). The y-axis represents the Total correctness achieved on the seven assertions to develop: score = 7 represents the maximum value of correctness and corresponds to developing seven correct assertions. The boxplots confirm the previous analysis: the participants achieved a better correctness level when developing the assertion using AssertJ (median 3) than Hamcrest (median 2). By applying a Wilcoxon test (paired analysis), we found that in this case too, the difference in terms of correctness is statistically significant, as p-value = 0.0036, see Table 4. The effect size is small d = -0.3131. Therefore, we can reject the null hypothesis H_0 and accept H_1.

Summary: The adoption of AssertJ instead of Hamcrest significantly increase the number of correct assertions developed in a limited amount of time (60 min in our experiment).

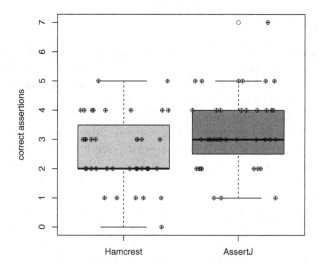

Fig. 1. Boxplots of correctness (number of correct assertions developed in 60 min)

Threats to Validity. This section discusses the threats to validity that could affect our results: *internal, construct, conclusion* and *external* validity threats [27].

Internal validity threats concern factors that may affect a dependent variable (in our case, *TotalCorrectness*). Since the students had to participate in two labs (seven questions each), a learning/fatigue effect may intervene. However, the students were previously trained and the chosen experimental design, with a break between the two labs, should limit this effect.

Construct validity threats are related to the evaluation of correctness, that is the only manual part of the data processing. Indeed, we used a script to extract from the student projects the assertions and their timing and did a spot-check of the script results. Then we run the student tests on the reference implementation and considered wrong the failing ones. Two of the authors independently manually evaluated the successful tests to identify those unable to spot bugs as required by their specifications, and a third author compared the evaluations. The controversial assertions were further analysed to reach a consensus. The overall scores have been automatically computed using a spreadsheet.

Threats to *conclusion validity* can be due to the sample size of the experiment (41 BSc students) that may limit the capability of statistical tests to reveal any effect, and the object size, that could be insufficient to significantly cover the assertion spectrum.

Threats to *external validity* can be related to the use of students as experimental subjects. We cannot expect students to perform as well as professionals, but we expect to be able to observe similar trends. Further controlled experiments with different sets of assertions and/or more experienced developers (e.g., software practitioners) are needed to confirm or contrast the obtained results.

6 Related Work

Since, as [6] states "*Where the creation, understanding, and assessment of soft-ware testing and regression testing techniques are concerned, controlled experi-mentation is an indispensable research methodology*", the empirical studies aim-ing at the reduction of testing costs are many. However, the approaches most studied to save effort during testing are (1) writing only those tests with max-imum expectations of capturing a bug, (2) limiting regression testing to the tests with higher probability of finding errors (see e.g. [25]), and (3) improv-ing automatization of testing (see e.g. [4,15–17]). For the first two categories, researches focus on empirically assessing the probability of capturing bugs for given tests (see e.g. [8,24,25]), while papers in the last category compare the efficacy of automatic and manual testing techniques or of different automatic approaches (see e.g. [4,15,22]). Our study addresses an independent issue: (4) the influence of the choice of assertion style on the costs of developing tests. Thus, our work helps optimizing test development and adds to the optimization in category (3) and (1), as it applies to automated tests that have already been deemed necessary.

Another research topic somehow related to this paper is studying the under-standability of tests. Most works in this area compare different categories of tests, like for instance Grano et al. [9] and Dak et al. [5], discussing readability of human-produced tests vs. automatically generated ones. A few papers, like for instance [14], and many web pages and posts[14] compare and discuss different styles of assertions. In particular, in [14] AssertJ, the same library used in our empirical study, is compared with JUnit Basic assertions, in a test comprehen-sion scenario.

Understandability, though extremely important, is relevant mostly when *reading* tests as part of the code documentation or for their maintenance. Here, we focus instead on the costs of *developing* tests.

7 Conclusions and Future Work

In this paper, we have presented a controlled experiment comparing Hamcrest and AssertJ assertion styles from the point of view of development costs in practice. We analysed the number of correctly implemented assertions in a given time to gauge the overall productivity in completing the assignments. Even if the experiment has been conducted with two specific frameworks and with the Java language, we believe that our results can be generalized to other programming languages and other assertions frameworks belonging to the same categories of AssertJ and Hamcrest (i.e., able to provide fluent assertions and matchers). To get our comparison as fair and as useful in practice as possible, we first studied

---

[14] https://www.blazemeter.com/blog/hamcrest-vs-assertj-assertion-frameworks-which -one-should-you-choose,
https://www.ontestautomation.com/three-practices-for-creating-readable-test-code/,
https://www.developer.com/java/article.php/3901236/.

the usage distribution of Hamcrest matchers and AssertJ assertion methods, to be able to focus our experiment only on the most widely adopted (and not trivial).

The results indicate that adopting AssertJ significantly increases the number of correct tests so that AssertJ is a better choice over Hamcrest when development productivity is sought. This piece of empirical evidence can be exploited by Testers and SQA managers for a better selection of assertions frameworks for JUnit in their organizations. Even if we have no data supporting it, we believe that the aspect more relevant of AssertJ is its code completion facility that has simplified the activity of participants outperforming, in this way, Hamcrest. We intend to study this aspect in future works. Moreover, we plan to replicate this experiment with professional subjects to confirm our results; of course, we will use more challenging assertions as tasks, given the greater knowledge of the participants.

References

1. Adzic, G.: Specification by Example: How Successful Teams Deliver the Right Software, 1st edn. Manning Publications Co., Shelter Island (2011)
2. Basili, V.R., Caldiera, G., Rombach, H.D.: The goal question metric approach. In: Encyclopedia of Software Engineering. Wiley (1994)
3. Beck, K.: Test-Driven Development: By Example. Addison-Wesley, Boston (2003)
4. Berner, S., Weber, R., Keller, R.: Observations and lessons learned from automated testing. In: Proceedings of 27th International Conference on Software Engineering, ICSE 2005, pp. 571–579. ACM (2005)
5. Daka, E., Campos, J., Fraser, G., Dorn, J., Weimer, W.: Modeling readability to improve unit tests. In: Proceedings of 10th Joint Meeting on Foundations of Software Engineering, ESEC/FSE 2015, pp. 107–118. ACM (2015). https://doi.org/10.1145/2786805.2786838
6. Do, H., Elbaum, S., Rothermel, G.: Supporting controlled experimentation with testing techniques: an infrastructure and its potential impact. Empirical Softw. Eng. **10**(4), 405–435 (2005). https://doi.org/10.1007/s10664-005-3861-2
7. Dunn, J., Dunn, O.J.: Multiple comparisons among means. ASA **56**, 52–64 (1961)
8. Garousi, V., Özkan, R., Betin-Can, A.: Multi-objective regression test selection in practice: an empirical study in the defense software industry. Inf. Softw. Technol. **103**, 40–54 (2018)
9. Grano, G., Scalabrino, S., Oliveto, R., Gall, H.: An empirical investigation on the readability of manual and generated test cases. In: Proceedings of 26th International Conference on Program Comprehension, ICPC 2018. ACM (2018)
10. Grissom, R.J., Kim, J.J.: Effect Sizes for Research: A Broad Practical Approach, 2nd edn. Lawrence Earlbaum Associates, New York (2005)
11. Harrold, M.J.: Testing: a roadmap. In: Proceedings of 22nd International Conference on Software Engineering, ICSE 2000, pp. 61–72. ACM (2000)
12. Kalliamvakou, E., Gousios, G., Blincoe, K., Singer, L., German, D.M., Damian, D.: The promises and perils of mining github. In: Proceedings of the 11th Working Conference on Mining Software Repositories, MSR 2014, pp. 92–101. ACM (2014)
13. Kitchenham, B.A., Dyba, T., Jorgensen, M.: Evidence-based software engineering. In: Proceedings of 26th International Conference on Software Engineering, ICSE 2004, pp. 273–281. IEEE (2004)

14. Leotta, M., Cerioli, M., Olianas, D., Ricca, F.: Fluent vs basic assertions in Java: an empirical study. In: Proceedings of 11th International Conference on the Quality of Information and Communications Technology, QUATIC 2018, pp. 184–192. IEEE (2018). https://doi.org/10.1109/QUATIC.2018.00036

15. Leotta, M., Clerissi, D., Ricca, F., Tonella, P.: Capture-replay vs. programmable web testing: an empirical assessment during test case evolution. In: Proceedings of 20th Working Conference on Reverse Engineering, WCRE 2013, pp. 272–281. IEEE (2013). https://doi.org/10.1109/WCRE.2013.6671302

16. Leotta, M., Clerissi, D., Ricca, F., Tonella, P.: Approaches and tools for automated end-to-end Web testing. Adv. Comput. 101, 193–237 (2016). https://doi.org/10.1016/bs.adcom.2015.11.007

17. Leotta, M., Stocco, A., Ricca, F., Tonella, P.: PESTO: automated migration of DOM-based Web tests towards the visual approach. J. Softw.: Test. Verif. Reliab. 28(4), e1665 (2018). https://doi.org/10.1002/stvr.1665

18. Motulsky, H.: Intuitive Biostatistics: A Non-mathematical Guide to Statistical Thinking. Oxford University Press, Oxford (2010)

19. Nagappan, N., Maximilien, E.M., Bhat, T., Williams, L.: Realizing quality improvement through test driven development: results and experiences of four industrial teams. Empirical Softw. Eng. 13(3), 289–302 (2008). https://doi.org/10.1007/s10664-008-9062-z

20. Ricca, F., Torchiano, M., Di Penta, M., Ceccato, M., Tonella, P.: Using acceptance tests as a support for clarifying requirements: a series of experiments. Inf. Softw. Technol. 51(2), 270–283 (2009). https://doi.org/10.1016/j.infsof.2008.01.007

21. Ricca, F., Torchiano, M., Leotta, M., Tiso, A., Guerrini, G., Reggio, G.: On the impact of state-based model-driven development on maintainability: a family of experiments using UniMod. Empirical Softw. Eng. 23(3), 1743–1790 (2018). https://doi.org/10.1007/s10664-017-9563-8

22. Shamshiri, S., Just, R., Rojas, J.M., Fraser, G., McMinn, P., Arcuri, A.: Do automatically generated unit tests find real faults? An empirical study of effectiveness and challenges (t). In: Proceedings of 30th International Conference on Automated Software Engineering, ASE 2015, pp. 201–211. IEEE (2015)

23. Shapiro, S.S., Wilk, M.B.: An analysis of variance test for normality (complete samples). Biometrika 3(52), 591–611 (1965)

24. Soetens, Q.D., Demeyer, S., Zaidman, A., Pérez, J.: Change-based test selection: an empirical evaluation. Empirical Softw. Eng. 21(5), 1990–2032 (2016)

25. Suri, B., Singhal, S.: Evolved regression test suite selection using BCO and GA and empirical comparison with ACO. CSI Trans. ICT 3(2–4), 143–154 (2015)

26. Vendome, C., Bavota, G., Penta, M.D., Linares-Vásquez, M., German, D., Poshyvanyk, D.: License usage and changes: a large-scale study on github. Empirical Softw. Eng. 22(3), 1537–1577 (2017). https://doi.org/10.1007/s10664-016-9438-4

27. Wohlin, C., Runeson, P., Höst, M., Ohlsson, M., Regnell, B., Wesslén, A.: Experimentation in Software Engineering - An Introduction. Kluwer Academic Publishers, Dordrecht (2000)

28. Wynne, M., Hellesøy, A.: The Cucumber Book: Behaviour-Driven Development for Testers and Developers. Pragmatic Bookshelf (2012)

Process Improvement and Assessment

Do We Rework? A Path to Manage One of the Primary Cause of Uncertainty in Software Industry

Satriani Giuseppe[✉] and Urretavizcaya Imanol[✉]

Tecnalia Research and Innovation, Parque Tecnologico Ed. 700,
48160 Derio, Spain
{Giuseppe.Satriani,Imanol.Urretavizcaya}@tecnalia.com

Abstract. With the advent of the information age and more intense competitions among IT companies, the differentiation factors must be found in the capability of the organization to fit its purpose and consequently to continuously manage uncertainty. Rework is the most important cause of uncertainty in the IT industry and consequently it is one of the major factors that negatively affect the organizations capability to fit customer expectations. For this reason, rework must be dealt with rigorously and in a structured way by any organization that wants to survive and win the competition. The approach to be used should necessarily use quantitative management and assessing the quality of software development processes and products not only by measuring outcomes, but also predicting outcomes and making a trade-off between benefits and costs. On the basis of our very long experience in leading and implementing improvement initiatives on this matter in less mature or very mature organizations in Europe and Latin America, we summarize in this article the pragmatic and staged path to be implemented to be successful in controlling and reducing rework.

Keywords: Uncertainty · Rework · Predictive model · Cost model · Errors · Montecarlo simulations · Testing · Peer-Reviews

1 Introduction and Contextualization

Love Peter provided a very appropriate definition of rework in his article "Forensic Project Management" [8]: an exploratory examination of the causal behavior of design-induced rework". Rework is "the unnecessary process of redoing a work activity that was incorrectly carried out the first time".

In software industry, rework derived from change requests and errors corrections is the most important cause of uncertainty in achieving projects results in terms of delivered quality, schedule and effort deviation. Redoing things, costs! Redoing things generates delays! Redoing things forces people to extra time! Only 29% of the projects were fully successful with respect to time and budget and the 52% of projects costs overcome in 189% their original estimates [1]. The 5th edition of the Software Fail Watch by the testing company Tricentis estimates the global impact of software failure in $1.7 trillion in financial losses [2].

© Springer Nature Switzerland AG 2019
M. Piattini et al. (Eds.): QUATIC 2019, CCIS 1010, pp. 179–192, 2019.
https://doi.org/10.1007/978-3-030-29238-6_13

In the last twelve years we had the opportunity to provide consultancy or execute process improvement projects in more than two-hundred organizations from different areas (Public Administrations, Banks, Defense, Engineering, Railway, IT Service Providers, etc.), by using different methodologies: more traditional maturity models, 6 sigma projects, agile transformations and others. Normally our improvement projects start with an initial analysis and with a quick cause analysis session, to find the root-causes of rework. After more than 10 years of data collection, we can have accurate and reliable data from 58 companies from different countries from Europe and Latin America; with these data we are able to consolidate the following one-level fishbone diagram; the % associated to each of the five most important root causes is the weight provided to the category by applying a Delphi approach among project managers belonging to the 58 companies (Fig. 1).

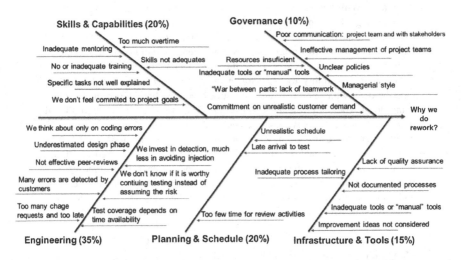

Fig. 1. Fishbone diagram of typical rework causes in IT companies. Data derived from our own data collection based on 58 European and Latin American companies

2   Error Analysis: The Element that Shines by Its Absence

In all these cases, error management is a controversial issue; in less mature organizations (those organizations that do not have an institutionalized improvement program) we normally listen to things like that: "we do not have errors; tests cost us too much; functional or system test find a lot of errors; we do not have time for thinking on rework, etc.". These are typical excuses of what we have called "resistant to change"; these organizations are typically afraid that inefficiencies will be seen, afraid that someone could use data to control personal work and evaluate personal performances. In the last few years, there is another argument used by the "resistant", another excuse that began to take big importance within organizations: "we do Agile". When this happen, normally, those persons have not read at all the Agile manifesto or they make an "integralist" interpretation: they extrapolate from the concept of self-managed teams the rule of no needs to register anything and no retrospectives based on data analysis, because recording is considered a useless bureaucracy.

Why the software industry does not have the same "obsession" so well deployed within the most cutting-edge industry to always look for the cause of any failure however small to try to avoid it? Machine wear, vibrations, operating modes, manufacturing times; all the dimensions are analyzed to establish the causes of the errors and thus be able to avoid them before they re-appear. In the IT world, the most advanced thing that many companies have achieved is to automate the test phase (the new trending topic): "we make continuous integrations and automate the tests in those cases where the cost justifies it". The situation is falling back into the error that automation of whatever (management processes, testing, development, …) is the panacea that heals everything. Test automation, is obviously an important part of the solution because it allows increasing the number of errors found, but the crucial question is not really addressed in this way. The questions to be answered are: what do I have to test? What are the most effective testing strategies? In order to answer to these crucial questions, it is mandatory to collect data: record the errors, but not only the error itself and its cost, record what type of error is, record where it is found and where it comes from in terms of elements that are affected by that error, as well as the life cycle phase where the error has been injected.

In more mature organizations (those that have already faced the problem and have overcome the resistance to change, coming to appreciate the benefits of the systematic approach to quality), we normally listen to this other kind of things: "we have problems in error registration, high variability in data collection, we do not register the source of error, we are not able to quantify the factors affecting error detection/injection, we still discover errors too late from the phase in which have been generated, etc". These are the real problems of those who have decided to begin the long road of understanding what mistakes are made making and how to fix them.

In this article we are not going to explore the ways in which we can avoid these failures or solve these root causes; we provide you with empirical tools to quantify this problem in your organization, predict and consequently, act to minimize its impact, by using a real case. The novelty contribution of this article is the pragmatic application of the statistical process control and the development of a predictive model based on Montecarlo simulation that combine defect density and resolution costs. In this way we could provide to the organizations a powerful tool that informs about the economic risk impact of their decisions regarding the verification activities to include during the project life-cycle to balance error detection and costs. The current available model is still under evolution; our intention is to identify for each verification activity, a set of factors that directly affect their effectiveness; in this way, project managers can decide the better combination of these factors to optimize the result, combining detection and cost results for quality and non-quality activities.

3 Real Case Solution

3.1 Description and Context

Our real case solution has been developed based on the data available in two IT companies; both of them are IT service type of companies in the outsourcing market. The main characteristic of their business is that they have to process "request of work" derived by the customer by maximizing the efficiency. The request of work that are part of this real case are exclusively evolutionary maintenance type. Both organizations adopted CMMI as the reference model for creating a common and homogeneous baseline of processes and for stabilizing their performances. They started with CMMI in 2006 and they got LVL 5 for the first time in 2011. We think that starting with an high maturity level, strongly helps the speed with which a stable and accurate predictive model can be got, but this is not a mandatory requirement. We also think that a CMMI LVL2 consolidated solution not done just to have the "certification" but to approach real performance problems is mandatory. The management of our two organizations asked us to make an analytical study with the aim to provide them with a tool to helps project management in the decision making process; they were no longer willing to accept, the lack of quality in deliveries and therefore the rejection of many of them; this situation generates an huge amount of rework with an enormous negative impact in projects profitability, as well as a very strong loss of credibility by their customers.

This situation led to defining an initial indicator to measure the effectiveness of the internal verification process: the CIE (Error Injection Coefficient); this lag indicator measures the relationship between the errors found by customers during the validation and operation phases and those detected internally before starting the UAT; however, the definition of this indicator is not enough, although it became (and still is) one of the main objectives of the companies to ensure the quality of delivery and customer satisfaction.

At the beginning, the CIE indicator turned out to be inefficient; this situation was due to the fact that a clear and systematic error register process was not in place, especially during internal verification activities; the values shown by this indicator were always very low. This situation led to the start of an improvement project that was divided into 2 clearly identified phases:

1. Address and resolve problems in error detection activities: "what kind of mistakes we make and where"; to achieve this goal is mandatory to put in place a verification mechanism that is able to detect errors as soon as possible within the life-cycle and not just limited to the functional/system test
2. Establish a mechanism to avoid error repeatability; this mechanism must be based on the detection process defined in the previous point, as well as on a continuous learning process of the development team.

3.2   Solution Path

In order to make the overall problem solution easier to manage, the incremental improvement path has been structured in six stages to be built incrementally one-by-one and by allowing enough time for consolidating the result of a stage before implement the following one.

Stage N. 1 (Error Recording). The mandatory foundation for obtaining a solution to prevent and control rework is a simple but often forgotten action: any error, any incident, any anomaly must be registered together with a set of appropriate data, to maximize the information exploitation.

Well-recorded errors speak to us, tell us stories, allow us to learn, allow us to act so as not to commit them again. Unfortunately, there is a strong resistance to adopt these good practices because many persons consider them as a "bureaucratic" task without added value; sometime, people feel these practices as a way to evaluate the quality of their own work.

According to our real experience, the data to be recorded to obtain an appropriate errors registration are: in which detection activity has been identified; in which activity has been injected (source); correction cost, which are the affected components. The cost of correction may not be necessary at this time at the level of individual error, but could be done at the level of error types, to provide priority criteria to select the different improvement actions, according to the cost of the types of error recorded; however, at a later stage it will be necessary to identify the individual cost of each error.

The importance of this first stage is so essential that once established, we must not spare the necessary activities that help its deployment to be quickly become a systematic and homogeneous lifestyle for everybody. Audit activities are then crucial, as well as training, mentoring and measurement. A good practice in use in some organization is the establishment of a monthly meeting to quantitatively evaluate the degree of data quality related to errors among the different projects; this is a brilliant way to stimulate healthy competition to achieve a common goal.

The data available in the historical records of the 2 companies in this real case are the following:

- 451 development projects for a total of 5332 request of works.
- These requests of work have 47,465 errors found in different internal detection filters or in UAT.
- For every request of work we have: data related to every verification filters applied; for every error found: the origin phase of the error (analysis, technical design or implementation), the verification filter that found it; the correction cost of every error and the functional task witch were generated the error.
- The distribution of request of work by project can be observed in Fig. 2, as well as the distribution of errors established in each of these development tasks.

Stage N. 2 (Error Analysis and Act Accordingly). If data are collected, they must be appropriately analyzed and the consequence of this analysis must generate corrective actions for negative results and opportunity actions, in case of especially good results.

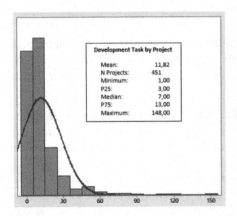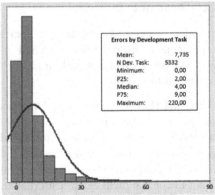

Fig. 2. Development task by project and errors by development task distribution

- Analyze which types of errors are the most frequent to facilitate the identification of which tests could be automated or to better focus test plans definition and/or activities to review/audit.
- Analyze which components, modules, programs or classes are more susceptible that in them "an error" arises; it allows to: improve which are the tests on which more attention, rigor and details in the definition must be put; make very focused peer reviews and thus minimize the distance between injection and detection.
- Analyze where errors are injected compared to where they are detected to shorten this distance: this can be easily established with an error injection table. This "distance" is strategically important because it is closely related to the cost of correcting errors.

Stage N. 3 (Develop and Evolve an Error Injection Table). This is a very powerful tool that, based on historical data, provides to the organization very useful data on where and how many errors are detected, where and how many they are injected, based on the verification activities (we called errors filters) in place during the life-cycle. Moreover, with the available data in an error injection table is easy to quantify the yield of each verification activity. An error injection table:

- it allows to quantify the degree of rework and a first sniff of its cost: the further away the injection phase is from the detection phase, the higher the associated cost (exponential curve) are; the reason is because things already done must be thrown away (cost of waste); if there is an error in the functional analysis and it is detected in user tests, there are many tasks that need to be even repeated: functional analysis, technical analysis, coding, testing and regression; all this adds a great cost to the error correction and it also disables the ability to carry on new tasks (cost of lost opportunities).
- it allows to discover which error detection activities are inefficient: verification activities such as tests and peer reviews are expensive and there is a temptation to be the first to be eliminated in the project; normally when peer reviews start, the

detected errors are almost always 0, so the temptation to eliminate these activities is very strong since they are expensive to execute; the error injection table allows us to see if there are errors in those phases that have not been detected, and in those cases it may be necessary to modify the peer-review strategy to be more efficient in its detection; with this tool, we can see if these activities are effective and if we must act in some of them so that the benefits provided exceed the costs of their execution.

- if a control of yield variability was established for each detection phase, for example through a control chart [3], a further very powerful element of analysis and decision is added. In this case we could know when to act on that phase, by analyzing the out-of-control points and trends and activating root cause analysis sessions to identify factors that cause exceptional executions both in positive and negative terms. If the yield of each of the detection phases is equal to or greater than 65%, it is mathematically proved that with 3 consecutive filters the global yield will be greater than 95%.

- a further step forward in the evolution of the error injection table is to identify those factors that mostly impact each detection phase, to know in a preventive manner where we must act when the process yield is not in line with expectations. If the factors are quantified, we could obtain a regression equation to quantify the benefit in terms of yield based on the factors values (Fig. 3).

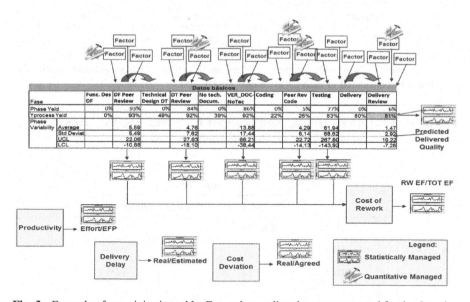

Fig. 3. Example of error injection table. For understanding the acronyms used for the detection activities identification, please refer to the glossary at the end of this article

Stage N. 4 (Develop a Cost Model Associated to the Error Injection Table). This model is necessary to provide priority criteria for evaluating the actions to be carried out by the organization. It provides the economic dimension to the project manager decision making process to optimize the overall composition of detection activities to maximize the trade-off between number of detected errors and detection costs. The model could be more or less complicated: average cost per type of error, establishing a confidence interval for a mean or median (depending on whether there are very extreme values that can influence the mean), a cost most likely established by type of error or even a modeling of cost types.

The problem in this case is the amount of data needed and their breakdown, to obtain something useful; each type of error injected has to be compared with the types of activity that detect them; consequently, the more filters we have, the more cost types we must have. A way to identify which data are necessary to establish the cost model is provided in Fig. 4.

		Injection Phases		
		Analysis	Technical Design	Implementation
Verification filters	PR_DF	Main Purpose	*Not applicable*	*Not applicable*
	PR_DT	Possible	Main Purpose	*Not applicable*
	PR_COD	Possible (but difficult)	Possible (but difficult)	Main Purpose
	PRU_FUN	Possible	Possible	Possible
	PRU_INT	Possible	Possible	Possible
	REV_ENTR	Possible	Possible	Possible

Fig. 4. Example of all possible combinations between detection activities and injection activities that should be considered to derive a error cost model.

The models performed have been executed by establishing the average cost of errors obtained from historical data; the data used are those shown in Fig. 5:

		Injection Phases		
		Analysis	Technical Design	Implementation
Verification filters	PR_DF	0,30	-	-
	PR_DT	0,50	0,30	-
	PR_COD	1,00	0,60	0,50
	PRU_FUN	2,10	1,30	0,98
	PRU_INT	4,50	3,45	2,25
	REV_ENTR	5,70	4,18	3,15
	CLIENT	7,35	5,65	3,96

Fig. 5. Average cost of errors in hours of effort, according to historical data by type of filter and origin of the error.

Stage N. 5 (Develop a Predictive Model). The definition of predictive model is provided in the glossary, at the end of this article [4, 5].

To implement this stage is mandatory to have stable yields of each detection activity; this is the result of a systematic improvement activity to eliminate the root causes of errors injection in the most typical errors. For achieving this situation, the organization continuously works to understand and eliminate (by implementing improvements) special cause of process variation and gradually it will get stable processes related to verification activities. This is a mandatory requirement to model both the errors injected in each phase and the effectiveness of the established verification filters, by establishing a predictive model that will support project managers to take an informed decision on which detection activities (filters) is important to execute in the project to be more effective both at the compliance level of the CIE, and at the cost level of the subsequent verification and correction activities.

This model is based on a Montecarlo simulation [6], that allows to evaluate and understand the impact of risk and uncertainty. The steps to get to the Montecarlo simulation are the following:

1. Model the behavior of the injection of errors in the different phases.
2. Modeling the detection behavior of the different filters considering the different sources of the errors.
3. Integrate in the predictive model the costs of correcting errors according to their origin and filter detection
4. Establish enough simulations of all parameters (here, 10,000 simulations)
5. Obtaining the behavior curves of the simulation to obtain the form of the process followed by the indicators to be estimated (CIE and Cost) and their variability (by considering that in the process there are big differences between projects, the percentiles of 25%, 50% and 75%) (Figs. 6 and 7).

SIMULATION INPUTS:

Project Size (person-days)	1000
Actual Project Lifecycle Phase:	Estimation
REAL DEFECTS FOUNDS:	
Functional Analisys	0
Technical Analisys	0
Code	0

Filters to be executed

PR_DF	No
PR_DT	No
PR_COD	No
PRU_FUN	Si
PRU_INT	Si
REV_ENTR	Si

Fig. 6. Inputs for the Montecarlo simulation model

Currently we are working to obtain a more advanced version of the previous predictive model that include in the error injection table the projection of the error

SIMULATION RESULTS:

	CIE (%)	Cost (hours)
Objective	85%	15000
% greater than Objective	74,44%	26,82%
% less than objective	25,56%	73,18%

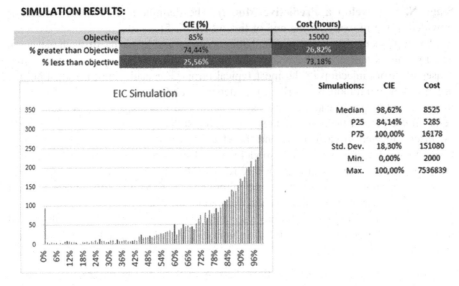

Simulations:	CIE	Cost
Median	98,62%	8525
P25	84,14%	5285
P75	100,00%	16178
Std. Dev.	18,30%	151080
Min.	0,00%	2000
Max.	100,00%	7536839

Fig. 7. Results obtained by applying the Montecarlo simulation model

injection and the performance of the filters based on factors, some of them controllable. A typical path of usage of this predictive model could be the following:

The Project Manager will initiate the simulation during the estimation phase making assumptions about the available profiles and the execution of the different quality filters depending on the availability of said profiles, the estimated dates, etc.

In each phase transition, the number of total errors found depending on the origin must be included, to modify the modeling of the errors found (different types of injection modeling have been found depending on the number of errors found). At the end of each verification phase you can also review the next detection activities composition to make the best possible decision regarding the execution of verification filters.

Example of Use of the Predictive Model. The following is an example of application of the model that we obtained with the data set of the two companies; project managers use this model if the project size is more or equal than 1000 person-hours; the goal is to define the most appropriate verification strategy to be taken at the early stages of the project and by adjusting it once each verification activity included in the model has been executed. In this situation we should also considering the main "temptations" to which the project manager is subjected and that we have already commented previously:

- The methodology asks to carry out all phases and all verification filters.
- Peer reviews are very expensive and detect few errors, so I eliminate Peer Review from the project: PRU_INT + PRU_FUN+REV_ENTR
- I do not do internal tests (Functional and Integration) I only establish the review by the external group before the delivery: PR_DF+PR_DT+PR_COD+REV_ENTR

- There is a risk that the external group cannot prove on time, so I only do the internal tests and the Peer Review: PR_DF+PR_DT+PR_COD+PRU_INT+PRU_FUN (Figs. 8 and 9).

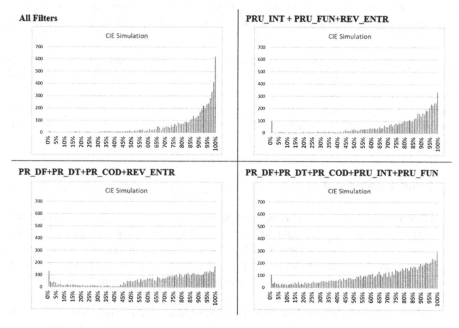

Fig. 8. Scenarios for CIE simulations obtained by applying the predictive model

	CIE Value (objective >85%)			Cost value (hrs: QA + No QA Activities) (objective <15,000)			% loss goals	
Scenario	P25	Median	P75	P25	Median	P75	CIE	Cost
All PR and Test applied (all filters)	91%	99%	100%	4953	6806	13237	18%	22%
PRU_INT + PRU_FUN+REV_ENTR (NO PR)	85%	98%	100%	5317	8463	16116	26%	27%
PR_DF+PR_DT+PR_COD+PRU_INT+PRU_FUN	51%	75%	91%	4160	6285	13025	65%	22%
PR_DF+PR_DT+PR_COD+REV_ENTR	72%	97%	100%	4659	7152	15303	37%	25%

Fig. 9. CIE and cost for every scenario.

Analysis of the different scenarios:

- PRs are efficient to detect early errors and eliminate huge rework costs, as we can see in the comparison between "all filters" and "no PR"; however, their contribution to the CIE is not as important, because most of the errors are injected in the coding phase, but the rework they generate far exceeds the cost of execution of the Peer Review that would detect them in early phases.

- If it is necessary to choose between the types of tests, the probability of not complying with the objective of the CIE is greater when we do not do the external tests; however, the cost of quality + rework activities are triggered by doing only external tests (due to the need for more external testing cycles and the necessary regression).

There is no clear scenario when establishing which phases need to be executed and which are not; the model makes it very clear that all the PRs cannot be eliminated and that it is highly recommendable to do the tests by the independent team (REV_ENTR); but beyond this there is no ideal situation; it is the Project Manager who has to make the decisions based on the profiles available at the time and based on what is offered by the predictive model.

4   Final Considerations

For IT companies, rework is an issue to be addressed to improve delivered quality and other strategic and economic goal both for projects and for the overall organization. We have provided a five stages approach to define a successful path to manage uncertainty. The no-execution of these stages leaves the organization in a "happy ignorance" about the effectiveness of the detection activities they are executing, as well as about the cost of errors correction. Moreover, organizations that do not start the virtuous path we are suggesting, will indefinitely think that error recording, testing and more in general, detection activities are pure bureaucracy: "we have to do because the methodology asks for it and the auditors will identify no-conformances" or, even worst, could appear undesirable temptations such as "I do not do Peer Reviews", "I do not have time, so I avoid testing", etc.

The suggested path to manage uncertainty is a valuable way to understand the problem and to quantify the benefits; the initial data collection (stage 1) and the consequent data analysis (stage 2) offer a first insight into the magnitude of the problem and its effects; the subsequent transformation into an error injection table (stage 3) provides a first approach in detecting where to change the current approach to be more efficient; once the process is stable a predictive model can be established (stage 5) to help project manager to decide (based on quantitative data) where and which detection activities should be established to maximize the process yield; if error correction costs are appropriately collected and included in the predictive model (stage 4) a further, valuable data is provided for a better decision taking to find the optimal trade-off between process yield and detection costs. The final and unique goal every organization must have is what David Anderson calls "fit for purpose" [7].

5 Glossary of Terms

CIE
Relationship between errors found internally versus total errors; The total errors are the sum of the errors found internally and those that are found by the client in the acceptance tests or during the guarantee phase.

PREDICTIVE MODEL
Is a statistical technique to predict future behavior based on historical and current data. Normally the model has input factors, whose values and whose combinations, determines a result that the model proposes with a certain confidence interval. The power of a predictive model derives from the possibility to make a "what-if" analysis, to determine the optimal combination of factors that maximize the result achievement. Consequently, the more controllable input factors you have, the more chance we will have to "change the future"

PR_DF
Peer Review for the documentation established during the functional analysis phase. It is not a revision of the format referring to what the methodology demands, but a thorough functional review as to what the client demands and what has been developed as an analysis based on those needs. This Peer Review allows detecting both errors in the functional analysis, as well as lack of definition or ambiguities in the client's requirements.

PR_DT
Peer Review for the documentation established during the technical analysis phase. Analogously to the previous Peer Review, the functional analysis is taken as reference and the congruence of the technical analysis is reviewed.

PR_COD
Peer Review for the code established during the implementation phase. This is a functional review for code; the format review is done automatically by tools.

PRU_INT
Integration test that are made by the development team.

PRU_FUN
Functional test that are made by the development team.

REV_ENTR
Internal Acceptance Test that are made by an independent team before the deliver to the client for User Acceptance Test.

References

1. The Standish Group: Chaos Report 2017 (2017)
2. Software Fail Watch is an analysis of software failures. The 5th Edition of the Software Fail Watch identified 606 recorded software failures, impacting half of the world's population (3.7 billion people), $1.7 trillion in assets, and 314 companies. https://www.tricentis.com/software-fail-watch/
3. Wheeler, D.J.: Understanding Variation: The Key to Managing Chaos, 2nd edn. SPC Press, Knoxville (2000)
4. Gartner IT Glossary: Predictive modeling and its uses. https://www.gartner.com/it-glossary/predictive-modeling/
5. Hao, Y., Zhang, Y.: Statistical prediction modeling for software development process performance. In: IEEE 3rd International Conference on Communication Software and Networks (2011)
6. Bandy, H.B.: Modeling Trading System Performance: Monte Carlo Simulation, Position Sizing, Risk Management, and Statistics, 1st edn. Blue Owl Press, Incorporated (2011)
7. Anderson, D.J., Zheglov, A.: Fit for Purpose: How Modern Businesses Find, Satisfy and Keep Customers. Blue Hole Press (2017)
8. Love, P.E.D., Edwards, D.J.: Forensic project management: the underlying causes of rework in construction projects. https://www.tandfonline.com/doi/abs/10.1080/10286600412331295955

Studying Continual Service Improvement and Monitoring the Quality of ITSM

Sanna Heikkinen[1] and Marko Jäntti[2](✉)

[1] Istekki Oy, P.O Box 2000, 70601 Kuopio, Finland
`sanna.heikkinen@istekki.fi`
[2] School of Computing, University of Eastern Finland,
P.O Box 1627, 70211 Kuopio, Finland
`marko.jantti@uef.fi`

Abstract. Through Continual Service Improvement (CSI), IT service providers aim at identifying, documenting, evaluating and prioritising improvement areas in services and service processes. CSI plays a crucial role in managing service and process quality as well as transforming improvement suggestions and ideas into concrete actions and product features. Unfortunately, many companies lack the systematic CSI approach and tools. This may lead into lost business opportunities, long processing times in implementing customers' change requests and finally losing key customers. Additionally, digital transformation creates a need for more agile and flexible CSI. Therefore, CSI is an actual and interesting research target from service quality perspective. In this paper, CSI practices of a Finnish IT service provider company are studied. The research problem is: How IT service provider organizations perform Continual Service Improvement methods as part of daily service operation management? The main contribution of this paper is to present findings from a case study with a ISO/IEC 20000 compliant service organization. We focus on exploring how the quality of CSI targets is monitored, how CSI is organized and deployed into practice and how service-related improvements are managed.

Keywords: Continual Service Improvement · Service quality · Service management

1 Introduction

Continual Service Improvement (CSI) enables IT service providers to identify, document, evaluate and prioritize improvement areas in services and service processes leading to increased quality in service provision [5]. CSI plays a crucial role in transforming improvement suggestions and ideas into concrete actions and product features. Especially in today's digital service business, customers have

Supported by Digiteknologian TKI-ympäristö project A74338 (ERDF, Regional Council of Pohjois-Savo).

M. Piattini et al. (Eds.): QUATIC 2019, CCIS 1010, pp. 193–206, 2019.
https://doi.org/10.1007/978-3-030-29238-6_14

high expectations regarding delivery time of new service features and customer experience [10]. Together with service design [6], CSI is able to identify improvements to service solutions and thus helps to meet better changing business needs of customers.

Unfortunately, many companies lack the systematic CSI approach and tools. This may lead into lost business opportunities, long through put times in implementing customers' wishes and even losing key customers. Therefore, CSI is an actual and interesting research target in the context of service management and service science [32]. Best practices of service management and continual service improvement can be applied by not only IT providers but any service company from any industry such as hospitality, healthcare, energy [3] or legal services [22] to manage, operate and improve services more systematically. In this paper, we focus on CSI performed by IT service providers.

CSI requires continuous monitoring of customer satisfaction, services and processes, staff performance, competences, and service efficiency. By processing improvement suggestions systematically, the organization is able to improve the quality of provided services, effectiveness of service operations, and cost efficiency. Communicating improvement suggestions and the actions required by them the organization strengthens the positive attitude towards the culture of continual improvement.

Continual improvement can be found in several service quality management standards and frameworks such as:

- ISO 9001:2015. The organization shall determine and select opportunities for improvement and implement any necessary actions to meet customer requirements and enhance customer satisfaction [14].
- ISO/IEC 20000-1:2011. There shall be a policy on continual improvement of the Service Management System (SMS) and the services. The policy shall include evaluation criteria for the opportunities for improvement [15].
- ISO/IEC 15504-8. The purpose of the improvement process is to continually improve the SMS, services and processes. Base practices involve identifying and evaluating improvement opportunities, planning and implementing approved improvements, and communicating results of improvement actions [16].
- IT Infrastructure Library (ITIL). Continuous improvement of services is performed through Continuous Service Improvement Programmes (CSIP). CSIP is an ongoing formal programme undertaken within an organisation to identify and introduce measurable improvements within a specified work area or work process [25].
- Control Objectives for Information and related Technology (COBIT) PO8: Manage Quality. Continuous improvement is achieved by ongoing monitoring, analysing and acting upon deviations, and communicating results to stakeholders [7].

Previous studies on continual service improvement have focused on business-driven continual service improvement [23], establishing a continual service improvement model [12], continual improvement in the context of Kaizen [2] and success factors on ITSM implementations [26]. Shrestha et al. [28] use a combination of Balanced Scorecard and SERVQUAL [31] (a model of service quality) to assist service improvement. They aim at proposing a tool that would help IT organizations to select targets (ITSM processes) for process improvement with evidence-based information. The automation of process assessment activities with a tool reduces the effort in determining IT service management process capability levels [29].

Gervala [11] states that IT governance (through use of ITIL) can contribute to better business performance, for example, in the form of performance evaluation of services and identification of performance problems. Similarly, Jäntti and Hotti [18] explore interface between IT service governance and IT service management and propose that it is valuable to recognize the differences between these two. Effective IT service governance would ensure that all ITSM processes are considered equal in terms of receiving resources for continual improvement. A Service Management Office function with ITSM process owners would be a good example of a governance function while process managers and practitioners operate perform daily operative service management.

Additionally, many of existing service improvement studies have focused on improving a specific IT service management process such as incident management [17], problem management [20] and release management [19].

There are various monitoring targets for CSI such as services, processes and infrastructure. Lima et al. mention in their study [23] staff behavior (how staff follows processes), project budgets, and automatic monitoring of IT infrastructure [23]. Some targets (elements of IT infrastructure) can be monitored automatically through monitoring tools while other areas might require manual observation by service staff. Pollard and Cater-Steel [26] report that IT service management (ITSM) implementations need a project champion. Therefore, organizational CSI programme also requires a strong champion in order to succeed.

Van Aartsengel and Selahattin [1] propose establishment of a systematic performance measurement framework to assist CSI. They comment that a good performance measurement framework enables organization to receive more visibility how local performance measures fit with enterprise level global performance measures. Thus, everybody in the organization is able to see how individual performance measurements are related to each other.

Gacenga and Cater-Steel [9] have studied performance measurement of ITSM in an Australian university. They found that there were both internal factors (meeting the need for improved governance, alignment of IT strategy with organisation strategy, and having a mechanism to provide feedback to IT customers) and external factors (benchmarking against others in the same industry, and availability of metrics in the ITSM tool) that influenced selection of performance metrics. In addition to performance measurement, there are studies that have focused on improving IT Service Management evaluation [24] and creating measurement systems to improve monitoring of IT service management [21].

In this paper, CSI practices and quality monitoring methods of a Finnish IT service provider company are studied. The results of the study might be used by quality managers, CSI managers, and any service staff responsible for continual improvement. The results can be applied for speeding up the establishment of a CSI programme and CSI activities. The remainder of the paper is organized as follows. Section 2 describes the research methods. Section 3 presents the results of the study. Section 4 provides an analysis, and conclusions are given in Sect. 5.

2   Research Methods

This study aims at answering the following research problem: How IT service provider organizations perform Continual Service Improvement as part of daily service operation management? The study was started by dividing this broader level research problem into three research questions:

- How the quality of services, service processes and service management system are monitored?
- How Continual Service Improvement has been organized and deployed?
- How service-related improvement suggestions (CSI items) are managed?

According to Yin [30], a case study is "an empirical inquiry that investigates a contemporary phenomenon within its real-life context". The real life context refers to daily service management of an IT service provider organization.

This study focused on continual service improvement methods in the context of IT service management. The case organization was selected because the main author of this paper was working for the case organization, thus having an easy access to data. Additionally, we considered the case as a representative case because its service operations and processes are compliant with ITSM standards (ISO/IEC 20000) and service management frameworks (ITIL). Finally, the research team has had long term collaboration with the case organization which helps in receiving relevant data on ITSM. This study can be considered as exploratory case study with process improvement aspects [27].

2.1   Case Organization

The case organization Alfa has 570 employees and provides information, communication and medical technology services to its customers in Finland. Alfa also operates in a service integrator role for social and healthcare organizations and municipalities.

The turnover in 2018 was 112 million euros with facilities in three cities. Alfa's service management system is based on ISO/IEC 20000 and ISO 9001. Service process assessment and reviews are carried out systematically in Alfa to enable continual improvement. Alfa had recently replaced the service management tool with a new one.

2.2   Data Collection Methods

Data for this study was collected by using multiple sources of evidence from the case organization Alfa between 2018-2019. The data was captured by the first author while the second author participated in documenting the case study.

- Documentation (case documentation such as quality handbook, ITSM process descriptions, standards: ISO 9001 and ISO/IEC 20000, monthly steering board infoletters, personnel info presentations, intranet information letters, and CSI guidelines documentation)
- Archives (CSI records in the service management system)
- Interviews/discussions (CSI process owner, quality manager, process managers, financial manager, HR manager, HR specialists, development manager, group managers, Service Management Office SMO)
- Participative observation (observations on monitoring methods in case Alfa, participation in SMO meeting in a CSI process manager role)

Each interviewee was asked to provide his/her own perspective or opinion on CSI, for example, Financial Manager was asked to provide a list of monitoring and measurement methods and information how they analyze data and which metrics they use. Service Management Office is a function inside Alfa aiming at meeting monthly to dicuss the progress of process improvement tasks, to receive support from other process managers, to solve process related problems in a bigger group, and to prepare for forthcoming changes and audits.

2.3   Data Analysis

A within case analysis technique [8] was used to analyze case study data from a single case organization. Authors performed data collection and data analysis as a joint effort. Main analysis techniques included tabularization and categorization of data from case Alfa. The analysis was performed by pattern matching technique and tabulating the most relevant findings.

Patterns in our case were: 1. quality monitoring and measurement (monitoring and measurement of services, service management processes and service management system), 2. organization and deployment (organization and deployment of Continual Service Improvement, including roles, responsibilities, model of introducing CSI in the organization) and 3. management of improvements (management of improvement suggestions within CSI covering tools, processes and methods for identification, management and implementation of improvement/development ideas). Patterns 1 and 3 were major elements of CSI [6] that can be seen as predicted patterns [30]. The pattern 2 was based on the authors' own experiences referring to the fact that organizing CSI is a complicated set of tasks and requires more investigation.

3   Results

The results of this study have been presented in this paper according to three research questions.

3.1 How the Quality of Services, Service Processes and Service Management System Are Monitored?

Figure 1 shows quality monitoring mechanisms for services, service management system and service management processes in the case organization Alfa. Elements that we identified included customer and service management aspects, monitoring and measurement actions, schedules, and roles responsible for the measurement actions.

		Actions	When	Role
Monitoring and measurement aspects	Service and customer satisfaction	Customer survey	1 x year	Business relationship management's process manager
		Customer feedback	After closing incident/service request	Group manager
		Customer satisfaction survey (Text message survey after service Desk call)	1 x month	Service Desk group manager
		Pos./neg. feedback and complaints	Continuous	Service manager & customer manager
		Project feedback	After each project	Project manager
		Service meetings	2-4 x year	Service manager& customer manager
		Service manager and Group manager meetings	Every 1,5 month	Service manager & group manager
	Maintenance and development of the service management system (SMS)	Actions	When	Role
		Internal audit	1 x year	Quality manager/specialist
		External audit	1 x year	3 part
		Service Management Office (SMO) meetings with process managers	1 x month	Quality manager
		Process improvement plan and tasks	In the first quarter (Q1)	Process owner
		Process metrics	1 x month	Process manager
		Process maturity assessment (Tudor IT Process Assessment, TIPA)	1 x year	Quality specialist
		Management review	2 x year (spring and fall)	Quality manager
		Quarterly meeting to plan SMS task	4 x year	Quality manager & quality specialist

Fig. 1. Quality monitoring mechanisms of services, SMS and service processes in case Alfa.

We observed that quality monitoring covers various aspects (service and customer satisfaction, maintenance and development of a SMS, economy, and staff satisfaction, competence and performance). The case organization monitors the provided services in order to verify that customer requirements are fulfilled. At the same time, one may observe flaws or improvement suggestions identified by customers. According to case Alfa's quality manual, every employee of case Alfa is responsible for continous monitoring and evaluation of daily work routines and identification as well as sharing information of bottlenecks and improvement suggestions.

Staff satisfaction and competence level is defined by personnel surveys and career development discussions. Various types of customer satisfaction monitoring was found, such as collecting service and customer satisfaction data with annual customer satisfaction surveys, ticket resolution surveys after closure of each service request or incident and text message surveys in case of service desk phone calls. In order to monitor success of project management, the organization uses project feedback surveys.

3.2   How Continual Service Improvement Has Been Organized and Deployed?

According to case study observations, Continual Service Improvement in case Alfa was organized around organization-wide service management where two quality management standards (ISO 9001, ISO 20000) were directly linked to maintenance and development of the service management system. In addition to standards, project management frameworks (PRINCE2), IT service management best practices (ITIL), IT service process assessment frameworks (Tudor IT Process Assessment Model [4]), Lean frameworks and Service Integration and Management (SIAM) were identified to have relations to the service management and continual improvement of case Alfa.

The case Alfa had established a CSI manager role in order to boost continual improvement of services and service management as well as a CSI specialist role that focused on documenting improvement practices to ensure compliance with requirements of standards and to introduce the CSI model to staff and perform the CSI process manager role.

For every process, there is a dedicated process owner (member of Alfa management board) that is responsible for defining annual goals for process aligned with the organization's strategy. Additionally, for each service management process, there is a process manager that is responsible for continual process improvement of his/her own process area.

Moreover, there are development managers who are responsible for unit development according to tasks assigned by the director of the unit. Development managers also develop service offerings for business units in the context of processes, customers and products and services.

Our next step was to study how CSI had been introduced in case Alfa. The introduction of formal CSI in Alfa started and proceeded with following steps. The first step was to clarify the CSI-related process description text and make it more unified. A new section (Chap. 6) was created describing how data is collected by measurements, how it is analyzed and evaluated and how improvement areas are identified.

The second step was to create unified process templates and create version control and acceptance procedures for them. Third, intranet (file management) was deployed to serve as a centralized datastore for process documentation. Fourth, service management office meetings were started with process managers.

Fifth, service management tool Beta (name changed from anonymity reasons) was introduced in 2016. It enabled monitoring various types of tickets and improved specialists' understanding on various service management processes (change tickets, incident tickets, problem tickets) because before this all the requests had been classified as service requests. Sixth, metrics were prepared for service management processes and these were monitored from ppt presentation (in Service Management Office meetings).

Finally, Continual Service Improvement manager participated in monthly meetings of service groups and informed staff on continual improvement and management of improvement suggestions. Discussions with CSI process owner revealed the benefits that CSI had provided to organization (March 21st, 2019). According to comments from these discussions, CSI makes communication easier, gives a better overview of big picture, provides a diagram that is easy to present to interested parties, and should perhaps have swimlanes in order to address and clarify action requests coming from management.

3.3   How Service Related Improvement Suggestions (CSI Items) Are Managed?

Among first tasks of the new CSI manager had been to define a process for identifying and managing improvement suggestions. Next, an overview of that process is presented in Fig. 2.

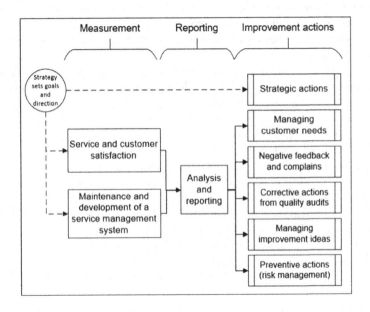

Fig. 2. Types of improvement actions in case Alfa.

Figure 2 shows how the CSI items (improvement actions) fall under 5 main categories: managing customer needs, dealing with negative feedback and complaints, corrective actions from quality audits such as ISO/IEC 20000 followups, improvement ideas related to services, and preventive actions from the risk management process. Additionally, there are strategic actions addressing the strategic goals of Alfa. Concerning tools and systems, our findings from the case organization showed that tools served two main purposes in CSI: (1) identifying improvements and (2) managing the improvement suggestions.

– IT service management system (communicated as an enterprise resource planning system within the case organization and to its customers)

- Survey tool to capture feedback on resolved tickets
- File management system to store CSI-related documentation
- Intranet involving information letters, process sites and instructions
- Wiki system involving production instructions
- Reward management tool. Based on implemented improvement suggestions, one can suggest reward for a specialist or a specialist group.

The final step in our study was to conduct interviews with process managers (April 2019) to identify how they see the Continual Service Improvement Model. Next, findings from these interviews are presented:

Release, Deployment and Change Management Process Manager: "The model includes descriptions, data and inputs that have been collected together under the umbrella of CSI. In the process manager role, one can take a part of CSI and start improving that particular part of it. Thus in the future, the next potential developer has a more complete picture of the process upon which to continue improving it."

Quality Specialist and Knowledge Management Process Manager: "The model benefits and supports the continual improvement required by standards. Continual improvement is not only processing improvement suggestions. In the process manager role, the model enables improvement of operations (core activity). There are also deficiencies related to CSI. The staff does not recognize improvement model and thus shall complain instead. They do not recognize that there are persons to whom ideas could be delivered. The staff is not able to identify how ideas could be logged or managed."

Incident and Service Request Management Process Manager: "The challenge is that we have too few people to promote and work in Continual Improvement. We should have a working group. Our management should participate and sell Continual Improvement further. I am thinking whether measurement results are stored in a fragmented way. Additionally, challenges are caused by diversity of data. We should describe the process of implementing improvement targets. Evaluation and analysis of results should be clarified in the next release. The selection of appropriate implementation method requires understanding on organizational processes.

Configuration Management Process Manager: "The CSI model creates good basis for a process visualization tool. I got good feelings from the presentation. Strategy, vision, mission in logical order. There are metrics that lead to identification of improvement targets. From the process manager perspective, it makes my own role/share in CSI clearer and clarifies tasks. It describes inputs for continual improvement."

4   Analysis

Table 1 shows the analysis of results according to three research questions. Data source has been described by using abbreviations: IN = Interviews/discussions,

Table 1. Analysis of key findings

RQ	Observation (Source)	Conclusion
RQ1	Every employee responsible for improving (DO)	Joint responsibility for CSI
-"-	SMO/audits in key role in improv. SMS (PO, DO)	SMS under CSI
-"-	ITSM maturity assessed by TIPA (PO)	From compliance to maturity
-"-	Customer feedback from many points (PO, DO)	Customer focus visible
-"-	Meas. results easier to find (PO, DO, IN)	Evidence available
RQ2	CSI workgroup needed (IN)	More discussion on CSI
-"-	CSI gives a big picture (IN)	Clear view as a benefit
-"-	Define responsib. for IAs (PO)	Ensure implem. of IAs
RQ3	Staff not aware where to record impr. (IN)	Continue CSI awar. work
-"-	Manag. should participate in CSI (IN)	Engage top management
-"-	Speed up processing time of ideas (PO)	Go or No go decision

DO = Documentation, PO = Participative observation, DOB = Direct observation, PA = Physical artefacts. Other abbreviations: IA = Improvement action.

The process of Continual Service Improvement had a clear interface to quality improvement of services, products and service management processes in the case organization Alfa. We found processes, metrics, roles and several tools supporting directly continual service improvement including quality monitoring, reporting and management of improvement ideas.

We observed that monitoring targets were clearly defined and also communicated to employees. One of the key reasons or a trigger for developing a systematic CSI approach seemed to be establishment of ISO 20000 compliant service management system and its follow up work on ITSM maturity assessment.

Implications for Practice: We found a rich set of evidence how CSI and 7-step improvement model had been introduced in Alfa: (1) identifying and documenting the 7-step improvement model from the perspective of ITSM processes, (2) recording annual development tasks of ITSM processes and monitoring them in SMO meetings, (3) gathering process documentation to the organization's intranet and quality management system, (4) implementing ITSM process assessment (for 9 processes), (5) enabling logging improvement ideas from a self-service portal (ITSM tool) for staff, (6) communicating the procedure of logging and processing improvement ideas in Intranet, conducting information sessions for staff, providing guidance for recording improvement ideas in monthly group meetings, and CSI workshop, (7) selecting specific management board persons to process owners, (8) documenting the monitoring and measurement methods, (9) including Continual Improvement to management review (status of external and internal audits, TIPA assessments, and improvement ideas, (10) developing an improvement suggestion record with new features (automated routing to the group responsible for evaluating the idea, functionality regarding prioritization and evaluation of ideas), and (11) planning the deployment of process visualization tool to support better process transparency, interfaces between processes and inputs to improvement actions.

Regarding implications for practice, data constructed from this study may help other service organizations to establish their own continual improvement methods and metrics within a shorter timeframe and to decrease change resistance towards continual improvement programmes.

Concerning the management of improvement suggestions, we identified five different types of improvements (e.g. managing customer needs, negative feedback, improvement ideas, corrective actions, preventive actions) that had their own specific workflow and source. We observed that the new ITSM tool had been adjusted to serve also needs of CSI and allowed easy collection, reporting and management of improvements.

Implications for Theory: The development of our Continual Service Improvement model started from an ITSM theory-based model approx. ten years ago. While CSI subprocesses have been written in quite a generic way in ITIL publications, there is definitely more room for innovative theory-based CSI models that challenge the traditional (and rather generic) Measurement - Reporting - Manage improvements process structure or literature reviews that would focus on continual service improvement but would utilize the findings of existing ITSM-related literature reviews [13]. ITSM theories can also introduce new tools to increase productivity of ITSM. This study supports the findings of Shrestha et al. [28] regarding continual service improvement of ITSM. They reported that ITIL framework and the international standard ISO/IEC 20000 of ITSM fail to provide guidelines or requirements for selecting target processes that should be improved. In our study, the case organization's process managers select improvement targets in the beginning of the year and record improvement actions to a joint document. Additionally, we made a general observation that most employees in Alfa were quite positive towards CSI concept and willing to share their opinion on CSI model.

We agree with Lewis and Brown [22] that service operation quality may depend very much on how well service package design and process design have been made. Poorer the design of service, more improvement efforts needs to placed to the service in service operation phase. Very few of existing academic articles discuss how CSI is visible in each service lifecycle stage: strategy, design, transition, operation. More research is needed to address this. Gacenga and Cater-Steel [9] reported an interesting finding that availability of the metrics in ITSM tool affected the selection of performance metrics. We observed that reporting capabilities of the tool was one of the key reasons, besides better customization opportunities and tool performance issues, why case organization Alfa had started to replace their old ITSM tool with a new one. The new tool enabled quick creation of dashboards (personal and public) and metrics.

Regarding implications for theory, we consider this study valuable for academic community because it provides deep insights and increased understanding of a service organization's CSI tools, methods, metrics, roles and practices. We highly recommend engaging ITSM practitioners to participate in writing academic IT service management case studies. This would better generate discussion on real world ITSM problems.

5 Conclusions

This study aimed at answering the research problem: How IT service provider organizations perform Continual Service Improvement methods as part of daily service operation management? The main contribution of this paper was to present findings from a CSI-related case study with a ISO/IEC 20000 compliant service organization.

This research problem was divided into the following three research questions: (1) How the quality of services, service processes and service management system are monitored? (2) How Continual Service Improvement has been organized and deployed? and (3) How service-related improvement suggestions (CSI items) are managed?

Regarding the first research question, Alfa aimed at increasing transparency and utilization of data by documenting monitoring and measurement methods (what, when, who is responsible, what is the output). This also enables Alfa to evaluate usefulness and effectiveness of metrics, for example, whether they produce data to support decision making. When implementation date of metrics is known, it helps allocating resources to measurement, data analysis and improvement actions (for example, annual customer survey in the end of year, monitoring process improvement targets monthly in SMO meetings).

Related to the second research question, we presented steps how CSI and 7-step improvement model were introduced in case Alfa. Introduction methods included a rich set of activities such as workshops, information seminars, interviews, implementing changes to the ITSM tool and the improvement suggestion record.

Concerning the third research question, we identified that when timelines of measurement and monitoring methods are known and resources have been allocated for them, the organization can focus better on analyzing results from measurements and planning improvement actions. For example, identified improvement actions (customer need, negative feedback, preventive actions) based on a customer survey are taken into account in the service improvement plans; and it is possible to implement corrective actions (quality exceptions, improvement ideas) from internal audits before external audits. Thus, improvement actions can be planned in a smarter way (paying attention to the big picture of parallel improvements instead of single improvement actions) to be able to implement them. This may lead to more transparent, systematic and managed improvement actions.

The following limitations are related to this case study: First, research data was collected from one service company in Finland by one researcher. Using researcher triangulation could have provided additional insights into case organization. Second, case study does not enable us to generalize results to other companies. However, findings that we found were valuable add on to the existing service science including detailed information on service monitoring mechanisms and types of improvement actions that can be used to extend the theory of IT service management and Continual Service Improvement. Third, regarding internal validity, there may be bias caused by the fact that one of the authors was working in the case organization. However, this also increased the quality of inferences because the author's work role included improvement of CSI and thus, the research team gained a deep understanding of the research subject. Fourth, we did not categorize results according to different organizational levels such as management and service operations. These levels could be taken into account in further case studies. Additionally, most of our interviews focused on managers. Interviews with staff might have revealed new insights on CSI. Further research could be related, for example, managing improvement records systematically with an ITSM tool.

References

1. van Aartsengel, A., Selahattin, K.: A Guide to Continuous Improvement Transformation - Concepts, Processes, Implementation. Springer, Heidelberg (2013). https://doi.org/10.1007/978-3-642-35904-0
2. Abdulmouti, H.: The role of Kaizen (continuous improvement) in improving companies' performance: a case study. In: Proceedings of the 2015 International Conference on Industrial Engineering and Operations Management (IEOM), pp. 1–6, March 2015
3. Allen, S.: Development of a work monitoring, evaluation and improvement process. Eng. Manag. J. **10**(3), 135–141 (2000)
4. Barafort, B., et al.: ITSM Process Assessment Supporting ITIL. Van Haren Publishing, Zaltbommel (2009)
5. Cabinet Office: ITIL Continual Service Improvement. The Stationary Office, UK (2011)
6. Cabinet Office: ITIL Service Design. The Stationary Office, UK (2011)
7. COBIT 4.0: Control Objectives for Information and Related Technology. ISACA (2005)
8. Eisenhardt, K.: Building theories from case study research. Acad. Manag. Rev. **14**, 532–550 (1989)
9. Gacenga, F., Cater-Steel, A.: Performance measurement of it service management: a case study of an Australian university (research in progress). In: PACIS 2011–15th Pacific Asia Conference on Information Systems: Quality Research in Pacific, AIS Electronic Library (2011)
10. Gentile, C., Spiller, N., Noci, G.: How to sustain the customer experience: an overview of experience components that co-create value with the customer. Eur. Manag. J. **25**(5), 395–410 (2007)
11. Gervalla, M., Preniqi, N., Kopacek, P.: IT infrastructure library (ITIL) framework approach to IT governance. IFAC-PapersOnLine **51**(30), 181–185 (2018)
12. Heikkinen, S., Jäntti, M.: Establishing a continual service improvement model: a case study. In: Winkler, D., O'Connor, R.V., Messnarz, R. (eds.) EuroSPI 2012. CCIS, vol. 301, pp. 61–72. Springer, Heidelberg (2012). https://doi.org/10.1007/978-3-642-31199-4_6

13. Iden, J., Eikebrokk, T.: Implementing it service management: a systematic literature review. Int. J. Inf. Manag. **33**, 512–523 (2013)
14. ISO: ISO 9000:2005 Quality management systems - Requirements. ISO Copyright Office (2005)
15. ISO/IEC 20000:1: Part 1: Service management system requirements. ISO/IEC JTC 1 Secretariat (2011)
16. ISO/IEC TS 15504-8:2012: Information technology - Process assessment -Part 8: An exemplar process assessment model for IT service management. ISO/IEC TC JTC1/SC7 Secretariat (2012)
17. Jäntti, M.: Lessons learnt from the improvement of customer support processes: a case study on incident management. In: Bomarius, F., Oivo, M., Jaring, P., Abrahamsson, P. (eds.) PROFES 2009. LNBIP, vol. 32, pp. 317–331. Springer, Heidelberg (2009). https://doi.org/10.1007/978-3-642-02152-7_24
18. Jäntti, M., Hotti, V.: Defining the relationships between it service management and it service governance. Inf. Technol. Manag. **17**(2), 141–150 (2016)
19. Jokela, K., Jäntti, M.: Challenges and problems in product portfolio release and deployment management. In: Proceedings of the 9th International Conference on Service Systems and Service Management (ICSSSM12). IEEE, Shanghai (2012)
20. Kajko-Mattsson, M.: Corrective maintenance maturity model: problem management. In: ICSM 2002: Proceedings of the International Conference on Software Maintenance (ICSM 2002), p. 486. IEEE Computer Society, Washington, DC (2002)
21. Lahtela, A., Jäntti, M., Kaukola, J.: Implementing an ITIL-based IT service management measurement system. In: Proceedings of the 4th International Conference on Digital Society, pp. 249–254. IEEE Computer Society, St. Maarten, February 2010
22. Lewis, M., Brown, A.: How different is professional service operations management? J. Oper. Manag. **30**(1), 1–11 (2012)
23. Lima, A., deSousa, J., Oliveira, J., Sauve, J., Moura, A.: Towards business-driven continual service improvement. In: 2010 IEEE/IFIP Network Operations and Management Symposium Workshops, pp. 95–98. IEEE, NJ (2010)
24. McNaughton, B., Ray, P., Lewis, L.: Designing an evaluation framework for IT service management. Inf. Manag. **47**, 219–225 (2010)
25. OGC: ITIL Planning to Implement. The Stationary Office, UK (2002)
26. Pollard, C., Cater-Steel, A.: Justifications, strategies, and critical success factors in successful ITIL implementations in U.S. and Australian companies: an exploratory study. Inf. Syst. Manag. **26**(2), 164–175 (2009)
27. Runeson, P., Höst, M.: Guidelines for conducting and reporting case study research in software engineering. Empir. Softw. Eng. **14**, 131–164 (2009)
28. Shrestha, A., Cater-Steel, A., Tan, W., Toleman, M.: A model to select processes for IT service management improvement. In: ACIS 2012 : Proceedings of the 23rd Australasian Conference on Information Systems, pp. 1–10. ACIS (2012)
29. Shrestha, A., Cater-Steel, A., Toleman, M.: Virtualising process assessments to facilitate continual service improvement in IT service management. In: ACIS 2015 Proceedings - 26th Australasian Conference on Information Systems. ACIS (2015)
30. Yin, R.: Case Study Research: Design and Methods. Sage Publishing, Beverly Hills (1994)
31. Zeithaml, V., Parasuraman, A., Berry, L.: Delivering Quality Service: Balancing Customer Perceptions and Expectations. The Free Press, Nariman Point (1990)
32. Zhang, L.J., Zhang, J., Cai, H.: Services Computing. Springer, Heidelberg (2007). https://doi.org/10.1007/978-3-540-38284-3. Tsinghua University Press, Beijing

Strategies for Developing Process Reference Models: An Analysis of Selected Cases from the Product Development and Management Domain

Fritz Stallinger[✉]

University of Applied Sciences BFI Vienna,
Wohlmutstrasse 22, 1020 Vienna, Austria
fritz.stallinger@fh-vie.ac.at

Abstract. Reference models available for process assessment and improvement in various domains are often criticized to be too generic or unable to capture industry, domain, or company specific requirements. Although typically a plethora of process reference-like models and other best practice resources are available to potentially close the criticized gaps, companies are reluctant to move towards the implied multi-model-based process management approaches or to customize or extend existing models according their proprietary needs. Approaches and methods to develop, enhance or customize available models or to integrate multiple models are often not satisfactorily understood and far away from being industry practice. The goal of the research underlying this paper is thus to support the development and enhancement of process reference models for complex industry contexts. As a sample domain the area of product development and management in the software and systems engineering domain is used. The paper analyses the development of four industry-driven model development cases to identify their model development contexts and goals as well as development strategies, approaches, and related rationales. The aim of the paper is to contribute to the understanding of how process reference models are developed and how they can be enhanced or adapted to broader and more complex contexts in order to deliver value and competitive advantage to the respective businesses.

Keywords: Process assessment · Process improvement ·
Process reference model · Reference model development ·
Product development and management

1 Introduction, Goals, and Overview

The work presented here is part of a research endeavor (cf. [1]) to provide methodological support for systematically developing Process Reference Models (PRMs) in the domain of developing and managing software-intensive products. The models resulting from application of the envisioned methodology are typically intended to support the migration to or the improvement of product-oriented engineering of such systems.

© Springer Nature Switzerland AG 2019
M. Piattini et al. (Eds.): QUATIC 2019, CCIS 1010, pp. 207–221, 2019.
https://doi.org/10.1007/978-3-030-29238-6_15

A main trigger for the work and also for the PRM development cases analyzed therein emerged from the observation in the core software engineering domain that traditional PRMs and underlying life cycle models for *Software Process Improvement* (SPI) (e.g. [2, 3]) are generally not fully suitable for application to the improvement of product-oriented software engineering. Particularly Rautiainen et al. [4] state that these approaches to SPI focus rather on the software process for customer projects in large organizations, while product-oriented organizations require a view to software engineering and management – and consequently SPI – that combines business and development considerations based on a clear product focus. The goal of general applicability to any type of software development and the often implicitly assumed project context of these models further imply a lack of consideration of product-specific engineering and reuse paradigms and a lack of integration with management activities [5].

The resulting needs to develop PRMs for further focus areas as well as more complete and integrated models, to integrate such models with existing models, or to specialize them for specific paradigms, etc. requires methodological support for PRM development beyond generic methods for from-scratch development (cf. e.g. [6]), customization (cf. e.g. [7]) or harmonization (cf. e.g. [8]).

The objectives of the overall research endeavor encompass (cf. [1]): to analyze a series of PRM development cases in order to distill their overall goals, engineering strategies, used methods, etc.; to assess these method elements with respect to their generic applicability and include them in a pool of method elements; to establish an architecture and meta-model describing and putting into relation these methodology elements; to distill guidelines to support the combination and orchestration of the methodology elements; and to evaluate the resulting methodology.

The steps to achieve these objectives are outlined in Sect. 3 below. The work presented in this paper mainly covers approach and results related to the initial analysis of PRM development cases. The scope of the work is in a first step restricted to PRMs conformant to the meta-model for PRMs as defined in ISO/IEC 15504 (SPICE) [9].

The proposed overall work builds on rather spare existing works with respect to systematic methodological support for developing generic processes for reference model development, customizing reference models to specific domains, or harmonizing multiple reference models (cf. e.g. assessments of the state-of-the-art in [7, 10] or [11]).

The rest of the document is structured as follows: Sect. 2 sketches the research areas involved in the work and major related work; Sect. 3 provides an overview on the approach and research methods envisioned for the overall research endeavor and for the first step of the overall work subject to this paper; Sect. 4 presents key characteristics of the selected model development cases; Sect. 5 presents the results obtained from an analysis of these cases; Sect. 6 summarizes and concludes the paper.

2   Involved Research Areas and Related Work

The major involved research areas comprise *'assessment-based process improvement'* as the overall area dealing with the conceptual frameworks underlying the work as well as the application of its results, in particular setting the scene and determining the requirements for PRMs; *'reference models for product-oriented software or systems engineering'* dealing with the scope, characteristics, challenges, and best practices of the targeted application domain; and *'Process Reference Model Engineering'* as the emerging discipline of how to systematically develop, maintain, and enhance PRMs.

ISO/IEC 15504 (SPICE) [9] distinguishes between PRMs and Process Assessment Models (PAMs). While a PRM defines a set of processes in terms of their purpose and outcomes, a compatible PAM extends the PRM's process definitions through the identification of a set of indicators of process performance and process capability.

PRMs for product-oriented software or systems engineering are expected to provide best practices for the engineering and management of software and/or system products and to address the particular characteristics and challenges of the respective business.

Particularly 'Process Reference Model Engineering' as the discipline of how to systematically engineer and enhance process reference – and in a wider sense process capability and process maturity – models has recently gained attention as an emerging topic in literature (cf. [10, 12]). Despite the variety of models being developed and customized Wangenheim et al. [10] assert a lack of methodological support. According [12] 'most published models are based on practices and success factors from projects that showed good results in an organization or industry, but which lack a sound theoretical basis and methodology'. Similarly, [7] with reference to [13] states that literature detailing how such models are developed, evolved, and adapted is extremely rare.

Specific related work in the field of method provision for process capability and maturity model development comprises in particular the following:

De Bruin et al. [14] propose a generic, i.e. application domain independent, phase-oriented, six-step framework for the development of maturity assessment models. The generic phases comprise: scope; design; populate; test; deploy; and maintain. The framework also characterizes the decisions involved in the scope and design phases.

Mettler [15] analyses the fundamentals of process maturity models in information systems and the typical phases of maturity model development and application by taking a design science research perspective. The work is based on the phases proposed by [14] and assumes that development and application of maturity models are inherently connected. Consequently a phase model for both, development and application of such models is proposed and the relevant decision parameters for each phase in respect to rigor and relevance of the maturity model are discussed.

Salviano et al. [6] propose a generic framework for the development of process capability models that is based on their previous experiences in experimenting different processes to develop diverse models. The framework is composed of seven sequential practices, customization rules applied to these practices, examples of utilization and examples of techniques. The seven sequential practices comprise: initial decisions; sources analysis; strategy for development; model design; draft model development; draft model validation; and model consolidation.

Larsson et al. [16] report a case study-based synthesis of five reference models in the area of software product integration and comparison with activities performed in seven product development projects. The authors conclude that none of the descriptions of best practices available in the different reference models covers the problem situations for the investigated product developments and that these reference models need to be merged into one set of practices. The applied procedure for combining the reference models is only shortly sketched and relying on the experience of the authors

Wangenheim et al. [7, 10] propose a method for the customization of process capability/maturity models to specific domains/sectors or development methodologies that is based on ISO/IEEE standard development processes and the integration of knowledge engineering techniques and experiences about how such models are currently developed. The method is structured into five phases: (1) Knowledge Identification; (2) Knowledge Specification; (3) Knowledge Refinement (including draft model validation and community approval); (4) Knowledge Usage; (5) Knowledge Evolution.

Pardo et al. [8] present an ontology for harmonization projects of multiple standards and models. The ontology is intended to provide the main concepts and a consistent terminology for supporting and leading the implementation of improvement projects where multiple models have to be harmonized. It is complemented by a guide to support the determination of the harmonization goals, a process for driving multi-model harmonization, and a set of methods and techniques. Based on preceding research [17], the authors also note that beside the terminological differences existing between models, the inconsistencies and terminological conflicts also appear in the techniques, methods and related concepts established to support harmonization of multiple models. The process for driving the harmonization is presented in more detail in [11].

3 Approach and Method

To achieve the objectives of the overall research endeavor as described under Sect. 1 above the following 4-step approach is applied following a design science-approach [18, 19] (cf. [1] for a more details):

Step 1 – Identification and Analysis of PRM Development Cases. A series of PRM developments from the software/system product engineering domain are analyzed post-mortem in order to distill the overall goals of these model developments, pursued engineering strategies, used methods, applied validation approaches, etc.

Step 2 - Development of Methodology Architecture. In this step, the architecture of the methodology for the development of PRMs in the software/system product engineering domain together with meta-models for relevant methodology elements will be defined and preliminarily validated.

Step 3 - Population of the Methodology. In this step, the methodology will be populated with methodology elements identified in the analysis of model developments in step 1. For that purpose these elements have to be assessed with respect to their generic applicability and adapted accordingly. This step also comprises distilling guidelines to methodologically support the combination and orchestration of the methodology elements based on the goals and requirements of a model development endeavor.

Step 4 - Evaluation of the Methodology. The objective of this final step is to initially validate the proposed PRM development methodology for the software/system product domain, particularly by application to a further model development endeavor within that domain and respective evaluation and by expert reviews.

In Step 1 above encompassing the focus of this paper several PRM development cases are identified and analyzed with respect to the goals of model development, the specific application domain, involved source models, key stakeholders of the target model, pursued model engineering and model creation strategies, linkage with and/or positioning against established standards, key challenges of model development, used model engineering methods and techniques, applied validation approaches, etc.

The PRM development cases have been identified out of the set of PRM model developments in which the author has been personally involved and which fulfilled the criteria of (1) using the ISO/IEC 15504 (SPICE) PRM meta-model and (2) of providing a PRM in the software/system product engineering domain. Main analysis methods were content analysis of development artifacts and documentation as well as clarifying interviews with persons involved in the model development cases.

4   Model Development Cases

The four PRM development cases analyzed in the context of this paper are briefly described and characterized in the following sub-sections.

4.1   OOSPICE PRM for Component-Based Software Engineering

The OOSPICE PRM [20, 21] has been developed within the EU-funded project OOSPICE (IST-1999-29073) by a consortium of academic partners and industry partners like Computer Associates, Volvo Information Technology, and others.

Originally starting from object-oriented software development contexts, the project aimed at contributing to overcome the shortcomings experienced when applying standard software process assessment approaches (e.g. predecessors of [2, 22]) to component-based software development contexts, e.g. inadequate terminology, inadequate granularity of processes, lack of paradigm-specific processes and process requirements.

The OOSPICE project targeted at providing ISO/IEC 15504 [9] conformant reference processes for component-based, domain- and reuse-oriented software development, thus clearly leaving the implicit project context of relevant standard PRMs available at the time of project execution. Beside the goal of providing an ISO/IEC 15504 conformant PRM, major further goals included the provision of a conformant assessment model and assessment methodology as well as the provision of a methodology for component-based development.

4.2   GDES-Reuse PRM for Reuse in Industrial Engineering

The GDES-Reuse PRM [23] has been developed within the GDES (Globally Distributed Engineering and Services) project series in cooperation between Siemens AG Corporate Technology and a university partner plus associated research institution.

The project series aimed at developing concepts and methods to exploit the improvement potentials of engineering organizations and to increase engineering maturity in general and converged at developing a model-based methodology for assessing and improving an organization's reuse practices and exploiting respective reuse potentials.

The project results encompass an ISO/IEC 15504 [9] conformant PRM and an organization-focused reuse maturity model, both intended to foster reuse and product-oriented engineering according multiple reuse paradigms (component-based, platform-based, prefabricates, product-lines, etc.) in industrial engineering as a specialization of systems engineering. These core models are accompanied by a process assessment model capable to 'feed' both core models, a reuse potentials analysis method, and an improvement measurement planning method.

4.3   INSPiRE PRM for Software Product Management

The INSPiRE PRM [5, 24] has been developed within the INSPiRE (INtegrated and Sustainable PRoduct Engineering) project in cooperation between a software engineering research institution and an industry partner from the automation domain.

Model development focused on linking and integrating business and product related goals as typically pursued by the software product management function with core software engineering activities, based on the observations that (1) the various frameworks available for software product management lack integration with or addressing of core software engineering activities and that (2) traditional SPI approaches generally lack the provision of explicit or detailed software product management activities.

The project's key results encompass an ISO/IEC 15504 [9] compliant 'standalone' PRM for software product management comprising key outcomes of software product management activities from selected software product management frameworks and an 'add-on' model for software product management intended for use in combination with the software life cycle processes of ISO/IEC 12207 [3].

4.4   SPiRE PRM for Reuse and Product-Orientation in Systems Engineering

The SPiRE PRM [25–28] has been developed within the context of the SPiRE (lightweight Software Product and pRocess Evolution) project based on the results of the GDES project (cf. 4.2 above) under involvement of the GDES industry partner.

The aim of this reference process model development was to support the transformation of system engineering from the project-based development of highly customerspecific solutions to the reuse and customization of so-called 'system products'.

Development work emerged in several steps, covering the integration of the GDES-Reuse PRM (cf. 4.2 above) with a process model for product-oriented industrial engineering provided by the GDES industry partner, extension of the INSiRE PRM (cf. 4.3 above) from software-level to software and system-level product management, and synthesis of these two resulting models into an add-on reference model to enhance ISO/IEC 15288 [29] on system life cycle processes with product- and reuse-oriented engineering and product management practices as an integrated framework for process assessment and improvement in contexts where systems are developed and evolved as products.

5   Analysis Results

The PRM development cases have been analyzed in order to get an overall understanding of the major development constraints, steps and strategies followed.

5.1   Analysis of Selected Development Case Characteristics

As a starting point, Table 1 provides an overview of selected key characteristics of the respective PRM development cases.

Table 1. Selected characteristics of analyzed PRM development cases.

Development case	OOSPICE PRM	GDES-Reuse PRM	INSPiRE PRM	SPiRE PRM
Main stakeholder	EU, Internat. Project Consortium	Siemens AG Corp. Tech.	SW-Company (SME)	Research center
Target community	Europe/Software	Corporate/Systems	Company/Software	Global/SW +Systems
Overall goal	Support transition to CBSE	Systematize, exploit reuse	Support transition to product-SW	Support transition to reuse and 'system products'
Scope	PRM PAM PIM AM -	PRM+OMM PAM - AM IM	PRM PAM - - -	PRM - - - -
Meta-model	ISO 15504	ISO 15504 +Extension	ISO 15504	ISO 15504
Meta-model selection	Project Constraint	Evaluation & selection	Implied by target model	Implied by source/target models
Validation approach	Expert reviews; Pilot assessments	Expert reviews; Pilot assessments	Expert review; Pilot assessment	Expert review

PRM ... Process Reference Model
PAM ... Process Assessment Model
PIM ... Process Implementation Model
OMM ... Organizational Maturity Model
AM ... Assessment Methodology
IM ... Improvement Methodology

The development cases differ significantly with respect to the main stakeholders driving the PRM development. These range from consortium members of a an European Union funded R&D project pursuing competitiveness and similar goals on behalf of the European Union, to the Corporate Technology Department of a global player like

Siemens AG, down to internationally operating medium sized software companies, or research centers that pursue such PRM developments as part of their strategic research.

The target communities – the main intended beneficiaries of the model development results – largely correspond with or can be derived from the single developments' stakeholders. They encompass the European software industry as a whole, the corporate systems engineering divisions or the sponsoring company's software development departments, as well as potentially any company in the software/system engineering domain.

Details on the overall goals of the PRM developments as summarized in Table 1 can be found in the short descriptions of the model development cases under 4 above.

Of more importance is the pursued scope of the model developments. All analyzed cases had the development of a process reference model (PRM) and a process assessment model (PAM) – providing the indicators for measuring the requirements of the PRM – on their agenda, except of the SPiRE PRM case that did not target the development of a PAM primarily for resource constraints.

In addition to these two core model types, the OOSPICE project also provided a methodology for component based development, indicated as process implementation model (PIM) in Table 1 and a proprietary assessment method (AM) which among others serves the purpose of mapping real world process instances to the respective processes of the PAM and respectively PRM for assessment purposes. – In the case of OOSPICE, a major development constraint was to construct the PRM, PAM, and PIM in a way that ideally all three models would use the same process structure, considered to represent a main competitive advantage compared to potential other PAMs and PIMs implementing the OOSPICE PRM.

Alternatively, the GDES-Reuse model development started with the initial vision to develop a maturity model for reuse in systems engineering similar to an existing maturity model for reuse in software engineering (cf. Table 2 below, line on GDES-Reuse). Beside this organizational maturity model (OMM), the development of a PRM had been added to the development agenda in the conceptualization phase as a consequence of a meta-model evaluation and selection for the overall model suite. Also in line with the original vision of producing an OMM, an assessment method (AM) and a dedicated improvement prioritization and planning method (IM) have been developed.

With respect to the meta-model used for representing the PRM all four PRM development cases used the ISO/IEC 15504 [9] approach. In case of the GDES-Reuse model-suite development, this meta-model has been extended in order to allow the representation of the identified reuse practices and results in a staged reuse maturity model.

The selection of the ISO/IEC 15504 PRM (and PAM) meta-model was a pre-set project constraint in case of the OOSPICE development, a result of the identification and evaluation of a series of potential meta-models in case of GDES-Reuse, and implied by either the target model in case of the INSPiRE model development (integration of the software product management model with ISO/IEC 12207 using that meta-model) or both the target (i.e. ISO/IEC 15288 [29]) and the source models in case of the SPiRE model development case.

Table 2. Main sources and engineering strategies of analyzed PRM development cases.

Development Case	Main Source(s)	Stage 1	Stage 2	Stage 3
OOSPICE PRM	• Propr. CBD PIM • CBD Best Practices • ISO 15504 PRM	PRM-Abstract. Lit. research -	PRM-Enrichment -	PRM Interface Identification
GDES-Reuse PRM	• Proprietary SW-Reuse OMM • Reuse Best Pract.	Meta-model transformation Lit. research	PRM-Enrichment	
INSPiRE PRM	• Product Mgmt Best Practices • ISO 12207 PRM	Lit. research -	PRM-Construction -	PRM Integration
SPiRE PRM	• GDES Reuse PRM • Prod.-Or. Eng. PIM • INSPiRE PRM • ISO 15288 PRM	PRM-Merging Domain Extens. -	PRM Integration	PRM Interface Identification

Primary means of model validation are similar across all development cases and were typically realized by pilot applications in real-world situations of the PAM and underlying PRM plus accompanying evaluations and by means of expert reviews during and at the end of model development, enhanced by presentation of the models to the respective scientific communities in the form of conference or journal publications.

5.2   Identification of Main Sources, Steps, and Methods for PRM Development

The analysis provided here focuses on identifying the high level strategies and major inputs used for the development of the PRM of the respective model development cases. Approaches applied for developing other model or method elements, i.e. PAMs, PIM, OMM, AMs, IM (cf. line 'Scope' in Table 1 above) are not dealt within this paper.

Table 2 identifies the main sources and PRM engineering stages for the selected PRM development cases. They are shortly explained in the following sub-sections.

The OOSPICE PRM for Component-Based Software Engineering. Development of this model [20, 21] initially focused on the challenge of substituting the generic, waterfall-like engineering processes of the original ISO/IEC 15504 standard with component-based software engineering – i.e. paradigm-specific – reference processes. The major sources for this undertaking were a proprietary process model for component based development (CBD) in use by one of the major industry partners in the consortium and literature research in order to identify best practices for CBD.

The proprietary CBD process model provided the major structures for the resulting PRM, but – in terms of ISO/IEC 15504 representing a PIM – had to be elevated to the abstraction level of a PRM, mainly expressing process purposes and process outcomes and defining meaningful process groupings. The resulting initial PRM was then further enriched with results from literature best practice research.

Later in the project – triggered by decisions on the upcoming revisions of ISO/IEC 15504 and ISO/IEC 12207, particularly on ISO/IEC 12207 becoming the PRM for ISO/IEC 15504 for software lifecycle processes – the decision was taken within the consortium to use the upcoming ISO/IEC 12207 management processes as management processes for the OOSPICE PRM, resulting in the need to identify (and adapt or explain with notes) at PRM level the major interfaces between the newly developed CBD engineering processes and the newly standardized software engineering management processes.

From a process reference model engineering perspective this PRM development case thus indicates the need for method support for:

- abstracting/generalizing PRMs out of 'lower-level' models like PAMs or PIMs,
- identifying PRM elements (process purposes, process outcomes) in existing literature or similar best practice documentation,
- relating/consolidating such PRM element candidates with existing PRMs,
- identifying interfaces between PRMs or process groups/categories within a PRM.

The GDES-Reuse PRM for Reuse in Industrial Engineering. The development of this model [23] started with the challenge to transform the meta-model of an existing proprietary organizational maturity model for SW-Reuse towards the continuous meta-model as used in ISO/IEC 15504, while maintaining the model's content.

The resulting initial PRM had then to be further enriched with reuse best practices emerging from literature research, whereby this enrichment particularly had to cover the handling of and interplay between the various additional reuse approaches and paradigms not covered by the original OMM. Further development stages providing other elements of the GDES-Reuse model suite like the resulting OMM or IM are not shown in Table 2 due to the focus on PRM development here.

From a process reference model engineering perspective this PRM development case adds the need for method support for:

- transforming the meta-model underlying a PRM while maintaining its model content, particularly from various organizational/staged towards continuous representations as used by ISO/IEC 15504 [9].

The INSPiRE PRM for Software Product Management. This model development [5, 24] started from scratch with a best practice identification for software product management in existing literature that identified several frameworks, but all of them either far away of being a PRM-like model or being such a model, but being far away of satisfactorily covering the software product management function.

This led to the situation that a PRM for software product management, particularly its structure had to be constructed from scratch. In a subsequent step this model was integrated with the ISO/IEC 12207 [3] PRM for software life cycle processes.

From a process reference model engineering perspective this PRM development case adds the need for method support for:

- constructing PRMs from scratch out of identified PRM element candidates (process purposes, process outcomes, etc.), particularly supporting structuring of the emerging PRM into processes and process groups, handling redundancies between element candidates, and traceability of element and element candidates to their sources,
- integrating PRMs in the sense of combining two PRMS into one resulting PRM while maintaining major parts of the structure and contents of both.

The SPiRE PRM for Reuse and Product-Orientation in Systems Engineering. This model development [25–28] started with two key activities: firstly, merging the GDES-Reuse-PRM with a proprietary process model for product-oriented systems engineering, intended to cover the engineering aspects of reuse and product-orientation in systems engineering; secondly, extending the concepts of product management from the software domain to the domain of 'system products' by creating a respective PRM.

The resulting PRMs were integrated into a PRM for reuse-based engineering and management of 'system products'. Finally, for the resulting PRM, the interfaces and minor overlaps with ISO/IEC 15288 [29] on system life cycle processes were identified.

From a process reference model engineering perspective this PRM development case adds the need for method support for:

- merging PRMs in the sense of combining two PRMS into one resulting PRM where both input PRMs widely 'disappear' and a new PRM structure emerges.

Method support for 'extending' a PRM from one domain to another as described above does not appear meaningful at this stage as this appears to be rather an expert-based 'invention' of a PRM (expert-based filling of 'white spots').

6 Summary and Conclusions

The focus of the present paper was on capturing, distilling and systematizing major insights and experience from four selected PRM development endeavors in the domain of developing and managing software and software-intensive products and to identify major method elements as part of the envisioned PRM development methodology.

The case-based identification of specific tasks to be performed in PRM developments comprises:

- abstracting/generalizing PRMs out of 'lower-level' models like PAMs or PIMs,
- capturing PRM elements (best practices in form of process purposes, process outcomes) in existing literature or similar best practice documentation,
- consolidating such PRM element candidates with existing PRMs,
- constructing PRMs from scratch out of identified PRM elements, supporting structuring of the emerging PRM, handling redundancies between element candidates, and traceability of element and element candidates to sources,
- identifying interfaces between PRMs or between process groups within PRMs,

- integrating multiple PRMs into one resulting PRM while maintaining major parts of their structure and contents,
- merging PRMS into one resulting PRM where a new PRM structure emerges, and
- transforming the meta-model underlying a PRM while maintaining model contents.

These results will be used in the continuation of the research as an initial set of candidate methodology elements. The approaches used in the model development cases to implement these tasks will be analyzed in order to distill respective method descriptions and guidance. The results will also be used in Step 2 and Step 3 of the overall research approach outlined under Sect. 3 above for definition of the architecture and meta-model of the envisioned PRM development methodology, as well as for the population of the methodology with a meaningful set of methodology elements.

The four PRM development cases were selected from cases where the author has been personally involved. The potential concern of a certain bias with respect to the obtained results might be narrowed by the fact that the implementation of these PRM development cases has been carried out in the context of consortia and project settings with multiple partner organizations not overlapping across cases, and involving a huge number of development and research staff.

A major reason for this selection has been the access to in-depth development documentation and artifacts, particularly with respect to performance of the subsequent research steps as outlined above. At a later stage, extension of the analysis to other PRM developments in the software/system product development domain and to PRM developments for other contexts and domains is envisioned as part of future work.

The four analyzed model development cases – although limited in number – covered paradigm-specific engineering (reuse, component-based development) as well as management aspects (engineering management, product management) and the combination and integration of these aspects in PRMs. They can be judged as representative with respect to involved PRM development challenges and complexity.

As a consequence, from an organizational perspective the resulting PRMs 'by nature' go beyond the scope of a single project. This imposes – although not explicitly dealt with in the paper – additional requirements and needs for adaptations of assessment methodologies potentially associated with PRMs used as input models. In general, process assessment and improvement as well as process development methods have been considered as out of scope of the present paper.

The scope of the work presented here as well as of the underlying overall research endeavor has been limited to PRM developments based on or at least resulting in PRMs compliant with ISO/IEC 15504 (SPICE), which itself has evolved through several development steps within the timeframe covered by the selected PRM development cases. ISO/IEC 33001 [30] is a revision of ISO/IEC 15504 and the resulting ISO/IEC 330xx family of international standards is intended to supersede the ISO/IEC 15504 standards family. Nevertheless, the implied changes are not envisioned to significantly impact the validity or usability of the results of this research as the latter build on the very fundamental concepts of PRMs.

Overall, the proposed work is expected to contribute to overcoming the problem with respect to a lack of systematic understanding and methodological support of how PRMs are developed. The results obtained from analyzing PRM development cases in the software/system product engineering domain and the resulting PRM development methodology are expected to be transferable to other domains.

Acknowledgements. The work on this paper was supported by the project *Multi-Project Management and Integrated Management* funded by the *City of Vienna*.

References

1. Stallinger, F., Plösch, R.: Towards methodological support for the engineering of process reference models for product software. In: Mitasiunas, A., Rout, T., O'Connor, R.V., Dorling, A. (eds.) SPICE 2014. CCIS, vol. 477, pp. 24–35. Springer, Cham (2014). https://doi.org/10.1007/978-3-319-13036-1_3
2. CMMI Product Team: CMMI for Development, Version 1.3 (CMMI-DEV, V1.3). http://resources.sei.cmu.edu/asset_files/TechnicalReport/2010_005_001_15287.pdf
3. International Standards Organisation: ISO/IEC 12207:2008 - Systems and software engineering — Software life cycle processes (2008)
4. Rautiainen, K., Lassenius, C., Sulonen, R.: 4CC: A framework for managing software product development. EMJ – Eng. Manag. J. **14**, 27–32 (2002)
5. Stallinger, F., Neumann, R.: Extending ISO/IEC 12207 with software product management: a process reference model proposal. In: Mas, A., Mesquida, A., Rout, T., O'Connor, R.V., Dorling, A. (eds.) SPICE 2012. CCIS, vol. 290, pp. 93–106. Springer, Heidelberg (2012). https://doi.org/10.1007/978-3-642-30439-2_9
6. Salviano, C.F., Zoucas, A., Silva, J.V.L., Alves, A.M., Wangenheim, C.G., von Thir, M.: A method framework for engineering process capability models. In: EuroSPI 2009, The 16th EuroSPI Confernece, European Systems and Software Process Improvement and Innovation, Industry Proceedings, pp. 6.25–6.36 (2009)
7. Hauck, J.C.R., von Wangenheim, C.G., Mc Caffery, F., Buglione, L.: Proposing an ISO/IEC 15504-2 compliant method for process capability/maturity models customization. In: Caivano, D., Oivo, M., Baldassarre, M.T., Visaggio, G. (eds.) PROFES 2011. LNCS, vol. 6759, pp. 44–58. Springer, Heidelberg (2011). https://doi.org/10.1007/978-3-642-21843-9_6
8. Pardo, C., Pino, F.J., García, F., Piattini, M., Baldassarre, M.T.: An ontology for the harmonization of multiple standards and models. Comput. Stand. Interfaces **34**, 48–59 (2012)
9. International Standards Organisation: ISO/IEC 15504-1:2004 - Information technology - process assessment - part 1: concepts and vocabulary (2004)
10. von Wangenheim, C.G., Hauck, J.C.R., Zoucas, A., Salviano, C.F., McCaffery, F., Shull, F.: Creating software process capability/maturity models. IEEE Softw. **27**, 92–94 (2010)
11. Pardo, C., Pino, F.J., Garcia, F., Baldassarre, M.T., Piattini, M.: From chaos to the systematic harmonization of multiple reference models: a harmonization framework applied in two case studies. J. Syst. Softw. **86**, 125–143 (2013)
12. García-Mireles, G.A., Ángeles Moraga, M., García, F.: Development of maturity models: a systematic literature review. In: Baldassarre, T., Genero, M., Mendes, E., Piattini, M. (eds.) EASE 2012, 16th International Conference on Evaluation & Assessment in Software Engineering. Proceedings, pp. 279–283. IEEE, Piscataway (2012)

13. Matook, S., Indulska, M.: Improving the quality of process reference models: a quality function deployment-based approach. Decis. Support Syst. **47**, 60–71 (2009)
14. De Bruin, T., Rosemann, M., Freeze, R., Kulkarni, U.: Understanding the main phases of developing a maturity assessment model. In: Campbell, B., Underwood, J., Bunker, D. (eds.) Australasian Conference on Information Systems (ACIS) (2005)
15. Mettler, T.: A design science research perspective on maturity models in information systems. https://www.alexandria.unisg.ch/Publikationen/214531
16. Larsson, S., Myllyperkiö, P., Ekdahl, F., Crnkovic, I.: Software product integration: a case study-based synthesis of reference models. Inf. Softw. Technol. **51**, 1066–1080 (2009)
17. Pardo, C., Pino, F.J., García, F., Piattini Velthius, M., Baldassarre, M.T.: Trends in harmonization of multiple reference models. In: Maciaszek, L.A., Loucopoulos, P. (eds.) ENASE 2010. CCIS, vol. 230, pp. 61–73. Springer, Heidelberg (2011). https://doi.org/10. 1007/978-3-642-23391-3_5
18. March, S.T., Smith, G.F.: Design and natural science research on information technology. Decis. Support Syst. **15**, 251–266 (1995)
19. Peffers, K., Tuunanen, T., Rothenberger, M.A., Chatterjee, S.: A design science research methodology for information systems research. J. Manag. Inf. Syst. **24**, 45–77 (2007)
20. Stallinger, F., Dorling, A., Rout, T., Henderson-Sellers, B., Lefever, B.: Software process improvement for component-based software engineering: an introduction to the OOSPICE project. In: Fernandez, M., Crnkovic, I. (eds.) 28th Euromicro Conference. Proceedings, 4–6 September 2002, Dortmund, Germany, pp. 318–323. IEEE Computer Society, Los Alamitos (2002)
21. Henderson-Sellers, B., Stallinger, F., Lefever, B.: Bridging the gap from process modelling to process assessment: the OOSPICE process specification for component-based software engineering. In: Fernandez, M., Crnkovic, I. (eds.) 28th Euromicro Conference. Proceedings, 4–6 September 2002, Dortmund, Germany, pp. 324–331. IEEE Computer Society, Los Alamitos (2002)
22. International Standards Organisation: ISO/IEC TR 15504-5:1998 - Information technology —Software process assessment—Part 5: An assessment model and indicator guidance (1998)
23. Stallinger, F., Plösch, R., Pomberger, G., Vollmar, J.: Integrating ISO/IEC 15504 conformant process assessment and organizational reuse enhancement. J. Softw. Maint. Evol.: Res. Pract. **22**, 307–324 (2010)
24. Stallinger, F., Neumann, R., Schossleitner, R., Zeilinger, R.: Linking software life cycle activities with product strategy and economics: extending ISO/IEC 12207 with product management best practices. In: O'Connor, R.V., Rout, T., McCaffery, F., Dorling, A. (eds.) SPICE 2011. CCIS, vol. 155, pp. 157–168. Springer, Heidelberg (2011). https://doi.org/10. 1007/978-3-642-21233-8_14
25. Stallinger, F., Neumann, R., Vollmar, J., Plösch, R.: Towards a process reference model for the industrial solutions business: integrating reuse and product-orientation in the context of systems engineering. In: Rout, T., Lami, G., Fabbrini, F. (eds.) Process Improvement and Capability Determination in Software, Systems Engineering and Service Management. Proceedings of: 10th International SPICE Conference 2010, Pisa, Italy, 18–20 May 2010, pp. 129–139. Edizioni ETS, Pisa (2010)
26. Stallinger, F., Neumann, R., Vollmar, J., Plösch, R.: Reuse and product-orientation as key elements for systems engineering: aligning a reference model for the industrial solutions business with ISO/IEC 15288. In: Raffo, D.M., Pfahl, D., Zhang, L. (eds.) ICSSP 2011. Proceedings of the 2011 International Conference on Software and Systems Process, 21–22 May 2011, Waikiki, Honolulu, HI, USA, pp. 120–128. Association for Computing Machinery, New York (2011)

27. Stallinger, F., Neumann, R.: Enhancing ISO/IEC 15288 with reuse and product-orientation: key outcomes of an add-on process reference model proposal. In: EuroSPI2 2012. European Systems, Software & Service Process Improvement & Innovation, Industrial Proceedings, 19th EuroSPI2 Conference, 25–27 June 2012, pp. 8.1–8.11. DELTA, [Hørsholm] (2012)
28. Stallinger, F., Neumann, R.: Enhancing ISO/IEC 15288 with reuse and product management: an add-on process reference model. Comput. Stand. Interfaces **36**, 21–32 (2013)
29. International Standards Organization: ISO/IEC 15288:2008 - Systems and Software Engineering—System life cycle processes (2008)
30. International Standards Organization: ISO/IEC 33001:2015 - Information technology – Process assessment – Concepts and terminology (2015)

Model-Driven Engineering and Software Maintenance

Concern Metrics for Modularity-Oriented Modernizations

Bruno Santos$^{(\boxtimes)}$ ⓘ, Daniel San Martín ⓘ, Raphael Honda,
and Valter Vieira de Camargo ⓘ

Universidade Federal de São Carlos, São Carlos, SP, Brazil
{bruno.santos,daniel.santibanez,raphael.honda,valtervcamargo}@ufscar.br

Abstract. A known problem in legacy systems is the presence of cross-cutting concerns in their architecture hampering and increasing the maintenance costs. A possible solution for that is the conduction of modularity-oriented modernization aiming at restructuring the legacy software system in order to improve its artifacts (source code, database, others) quality. Architecture-Driven Modernization (ADM) is focused on modernizing legacy software systems by using the concepts of model-driven architecture, software reengineering and standard metamodels. Knowledge Discovery Metamodel (KDM) is a standard from ADM that is able to represent software systems by means of KDM instances that are going to be modernized. An intrinsic part of the modernization process is to measure both KDM versions, the legacy and the modernized one. The measurement of legacy KDM instances enables the software engineer to quantify the existing problems while the measurement of the modernized one enables to verify whether the problems have been solved or not. Structured Metrics Metamodel (SMM) is a metamodel that can be used to specify metrics to be applied on KDM instances. However, even though most of the well known metrics are supported by SMM, there is no study that investigate how SMM could be used to specify concern metrics. We present how SMM can be used to specify concern metrics and a tool to support this measurement process, enabling the conduction of modularity-oriented modernizations to help ensuring the quality of the modernization process. Furthermore, we also discuss some challenges to be overcome involving the quality measurement process in ADM blueprint.

Keywords: Software modernization · Metrics ·
Architecture-Driven Modernization · Structured Metrics Metamodel ·
Knowledge Discovery Metamodel

1 Introduction

Software systems become legacy when their maintenance and evolution cost increasingly rise to unbearable levels, but they still deliver great and valuable benefits for companies [12]. An alternative to the aforementioned problem is

© Springer Nature Switzerland AG 2019
M. Piattini et al. (Eds.): QUATIC 2019, CCIS 1010, pp. 225–238, 2019.
https://doi.org/10.1007/978-3-030-29238-6_16

software reengineering. Nowadays, we have a more updated methodology to deal with software reengineering that is Architecture-Driven Modernization (ADM), where the software goes through a reengineering process by using models as can be seen in Model Driven Architecture (MDA). ADM was started in 2003 by the ADM-Task Force (ADMTF), an OMG initiative to use MDA concepts in the legacy software modernization context. The ADM's main goals are to provide a set of standard metamodels to support software modernization and to support software engineers while performing modernization projects by means of enabling the creation of reusable and interoperable modernization tools (MTs) [3]. MTs support the automation of at least one of the modernization tasks by following ADM concepts [10].

Among the metamodels proposed by OMG are both Knowledge Discovery Metamodel (KDM), and the Structured Metrics Metamodel (SMM). By Means of KDM it is possible to represent all software artifacts present in a legacy system, such as source code, graphic user interface (GUI), databases, configurations files, architecture and higher level abstractions [7]. On the other hand, The SMM Metamodel can be used to represent both metrics and metrics results and its advantage is to facilitate the reuse of metrics definitions, tool interoperability and sharing of metrics results that helps in the process of software quality assurance while using models/metamodels instances. KDM and SMM are platform and language independent so modernization tools that consider them can be reused in different modernization projects.

In a modernization process, normally, there are the "as-is" and the "to-be" software, e.g. the legacy and the target software. Performing measurements is important to plan and estimate how to deal with the modernizations refactorings. The Aspect-Oriented Programming (AOP) is an existing alternative when the goal is to conduct a modernization process to deal with crosscutting concern modularization. Crosscutting concerns are software concerns which could be scattered and tangled over the legacy software code, like persistence, logging, security and others. Thus, this research deals with metrics and a measurement approach to collect data about crosscutting concerns in a modernization process that uses ADM approach. To do this, KDM models need to be annotated/marked by concern mining tools, like Crosscutting Concern KDM (CCKDM) tool [8]. The main goal of this research is to measure the legacy software searching for relevant information about the diffusion of the crosscutting concerns and also to measure the target software, to investigate if the target software quality is in conformance with the planning.

As a motivation, we can mention the scarcity of approaches for measuring KDM models using SMM models [4], that is, the usage of existing metrics translated to be used in ADM context by means of SMM. Another motivation was the feasibility study of the definition and computation of concern measures in SMM instances to be applied in KDM instances.

To achieve the main goal of this research, we used the approach of Santos et al. that enables the representation of aspect-oriented systems in KDM models [11]. Once we could represent both the legacy and the target software in AOP we used concern metrics to measure them and collect important information to the software engineer. This process is performed with help of a modernization tool that is able to measure KDM and/or KDM-AO (Aspect-Oriented KDM) models and generate metrics results. To perform the measurements, we used two known metrics; Concern Diffusion over Operations (CDO) and Concern Diffusion over Components (CDC) [9].

An important step of the approach here presented is the implementation of a parameterization system for the users in order to set which crosscutting concerns are going to be measured, for instance: Persistence, Logging, Security, and others. Another important point is to understand how these concerns had been annotated by the previously used concern mining tool, since a KDM model could be marked/annotated with tags that might look like "concern=persistence" or "cc=persistence", thus, this parameters need to be informed [8]. All the process, measurements and tools used in this paper are detailed in the following sections.

Summing up, the goal of this paper is to study the feasibility of the concern measurements in the ADM context and to define a tool support to apply concern measures over KDM Metamodel instances. To achieve this goal, we performed the following activities: Reuse an approach that could represent AOP in KDM models, define a SMM Metrics Library that represents concern measures, and implement a tool for applying SMM metrics in KDM and aspect-oriented KDM (KDM-AO) instances.

The main contribution of this paper is a research about concern measurement and its feasibility in the ADM context, a SMM Concern Metrics Library, and a tool that applies the quality metrics approach in KDM and KDM-AO instances.

This paper is organized as follow: Sect. 2 describes the background about ADM and its metamodels (SMM and KDM). In Sect. 3, Modularity-Oriented Modernization is presented. Section 4 describes the specification Concern Metrics for ADM. Section 5 shows the Tool Support. Section 6 presents an Execution Engine and Metrics Library case study. Section 7 presents related works. Finally, Sect. 8 presents the conclusion about this research.

2 Architecture-Driven Modernization

Architecture-Driven Modernization (ADM) is an approach where the software goes through a reengineering process using models. The main ADM goal is to develop a set of standardized metamodels to represent all the information existing in a modernization process. KDM and SMM are two of a set of standard metamodels of ADM.

According to the OMG the most important artifact provided by ADM is the KDM metamodel, which is a multipurpose standard metamodel that represents all aspects of the existing information technology architectures. The idea behind the standard KDM is that the community starts to create parsers from different languages to KDM. As a result everything that takes KDM as input can be considered platform and language-independent. For example, a refactoring catalogue for KDM can be used for refactoring systems implemented in different languages [11]. The current version of the KDM is 1.4 and it is being adopted by ISO as ISO/IEC 19506 [7].

SMM is the ADM Metamodel responsible to provide metaclasses to define metrics. A SMM Model could represent a metric definition or a measurement result. Because SMM is a standard, metrics definition and measurements results can be exchange between engineers and can be reused in several projects. The main SMM terms are: measures (metrics) and measurements (models that contains metrics application results). A SMM Measure Model is a model that contains metrics definitions. A SMM Measurement Model is a model that contains the results of a specific measurement instance. To apply SMM Measure Model into KDM Model, we need a tool that receives as input: a XMI File that contains SMM Measures and XMI (one or more) Files that contains KDM instances.

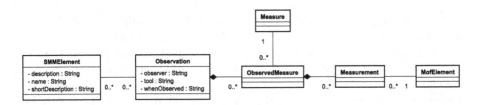

Fig. 1. The approach of the SMM metamodel

To work with SMM metamodel you need to instantiate some important SMM metaclasses, as you can see in Fig. 1, the minimum requirement to use SMM in a modernization process is to instantiate a Measure, an Observation (Metaclass that represents measurements information, like data, engineer name and tool name), and a measurement, that will be performed in KDM models or any model based on meta object facility OMG metamodel. All metrics instantiation have some attributes: Name, Description, Scope, Characteristic, Operations, etc. Scope is the name of the Metaclass that will be measured. Characteristic is for example: Size, when the goal of the measure is to calculate index related to system size and Operation contains the operation that will be applied in the target model to collect indexes, for example, an OCL Code or XPath code.

3   Modularity-Oriented Modernization (MOM)

KDM-AO is a heavyweight extension for KDM that contains new metaclasses, like AspectUnit, AdviceUnit and PointCutUnit [11]. These and others new metaclasses that were introduced into the KDM Metamodel allow the creation of instances of AOP Software. Thus, it is possible to use this programming paradigm in ADM.

Figure 2 presents the modernization scenario, entitled as Modularity-Oriented Modernization. The main goal is to convert a legacy system (**A**), which

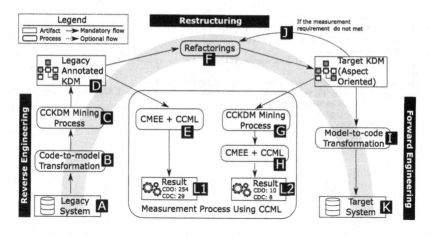

Fig. 2. Modularity-Oriented Modernization Scenario (MOM)

contains bad modularized concerns, into a new aspect-oriented version (**K**) where the concerns are then well modularized by using proper abstractions.

In order to perform this modernization process, two requirements must be met. The first one is to have a way of making the concerns evident in the KDM models representing the legacy system. That means pinpoint which model elements (classes, methods, attributes, etc) are affected or contribute to the implementation of given concerns - this process is known as concern mining [8]. To make them evident, we can use annotations, stereotypes, etc. The second requirement is to have a way of representing aspect-oriented concepts in KDM models. This is necessary for the target model, as it should be able to represent a solution for the crosscutting problem. There are basically two ways of doing that, by employing lightweight extensions or heavyweight ones. In our case, we opted for reusing a heavyweight aspect-oriented KDM extension [11].

Once these two requirements are met, we are able to conduct the whole process. That is, firstly we can apply a measurement process in the legacy annotated KDM to figure out the current modularity problems. Secondly, once we have an aspect-oriented KDM instance representing the target system we can mine it again, annotating and measuring it in order to check whether the modularity problems were solved.

In Fig. 2, this process is explained in more details. It starts with the automatic transformation of a legacy source code into a KDM instance (**B**). This process is performed automatically by MODISCO [1]. As the Legacy KDM contains information about the legacy system, it's necessary to discover what components, operations and attributes contribute to the implementation of a concern. To carry out this mining process (**C**), we use CCKDM (Concern Mining KDM) [8], a mining tool that annotates KDM model elements that contribute to the implementation of certain concerns. Listing 1.1 shows an example of an annotated KDM model where the annotation is highlighted.

```
<codeElement concern="Persistence" xsi:type="code:MethodUnit" name="connectionDB"...>
.    <attribute %tag="export" value="private"/>
.    <source language="java">
.        <region file="/0/@model.2/@inventoryElement.16" language="java"/>
.    </source>
.    <codeElement xsi:type="code:Signature" name="ConnectionDB">
.    .    <parameterUnit type="/0/@model.o/@codeElement.0/@codeElement.0/@codeEle...">
.    .        <source language="java">
.    .            <region language="java"/>
.    .        </source>
.    .    </parameterUnit.
.    </codeElement>
...
</codeElement>
```

Listing 1.1. Snippet of an annotated KDM model

In this case, CCKDM identified a MethodUnit that is affected by the persistence concern. Notice that the way CCKDM adopts for annotating the models is by using the annotation "concern". In this example, there is a MethodUnit annotated with <concern="Persistence">. Therefore, since the models are annotated we can measure based on these annotations and answer questions as "How many operations implement something about persistence?".

After the code-to-model transformation (**B**), the CCKDM mining (**C**) produces a Legacy Annotated KDM (**D**) to be measured by Concern Metrics Execution Engine (CMEE) and Crosscutting Concern Metrics Library (CCML) approaches (**E**). CMEE is an eclipse plug-in for applying metrics in a KDM instance. The metrics must be specified by using a SMM model.

Table 1 presents an example of crosscutting concern metrics library with the name of the measure, its scope and unit. CDO and CDC are described in the next section. Concern diffusions over LOC (CDLOC) is the number of transition points for each concern; transition points are points in the code where there is

Table 1. Crosscutting Concern Metrics Library (CCML)

CC_MetricsLibrary.smm (physical file)			
Model			
MeasureLibrary			
Measure	Scope	Unit	
CDO	AdviceUnit/MethodUnit	Affected Operations	...
CDC	Aspect/Class/InterfaceUnit	Affected Components	...
CDLOC	SourceRegion	Affected SourceRegion	...
Disparity	Aspect/Class/InterfaceUnit	Affected Components	...
Concentration	Aspect/Class/InterfaceUnit	Affected Components	...
...	...	...	

a "concern switch". Disparity and Concentration metrics quantifies the closeness between program components (such as files or functions) and features.

The result of this step is a set of metrics calculated (**L1**). Based on these results, the modernization engineer needs to decide what refactorings (**F**) should be applied in order to improve the crosscutting concerns modularization. Then, after the refactorings, the KDM-AO Models (since now they also represent aspect-oriented concepts) needs to be mined (**G**) and measured again (**H**), to collect new information about the modularization (**L2**). If the engineer agrees with the results, then the KDM-AO Models will be transformed into source-code (**I** and **K**). If the engineer is not satisfied with the results (**J**), the process returns to the step (**F**) again.

4   Specifying Concern Metrics for ADM

In this section the goal is to present how SMM can be used to specify concern metrics. We chosen CDO (Concern Diffusion over Operations) and CDC (Concern Diffusion over Components) metrics because they are specific to measure separation of concerns [9]. CDO purpose is to measure the diffusion of a concern over operations, like methods and advices. CDC measures the diffusion of a concern in the system's components, like Classes, Interfaces and Aspects. These two metrics give to the modernization engineer an overview about concern diffusion over the system. In the following, we will explain how to define these metrics in SMM models.

The fields that you need to fill in the SMM Editor to define the CDO Metric are the following: name, label, description, trait (what characteristic this metric measures?), Scope (what is the target of the metric?), label format, Categories, Operation (the code that will be applied in the target KDM Model), Unit (what the Unit is used in this metric? For example: meters, kilometers, kilo, etc).

The element Operation is one of the most important. This element contains the code that will be applied in the target KDM Model. Thus, it is very important to know how to develop an Operation. All Operation has a name, a description, a language (what language you will use to define the operation?) and body (the body of the operation, where you need to put the code). In this case, we decide to use XPath to write CDO and CDC Operation code. SMM Specification by OMG uses OCL in their examples. In this paper, the choice of XPath for implementing the Operation Code (rather than using OCL) has been made by the author because of their XPath expertise. XPath is a directory language that you can use to query KDM or any MOF-Based Model (A model that is based on the meta-metamodel MOF).

Table 2 depicts the body of CDO and CDC Operations. The goal of these codes is to query the target KDM Model in order to collect data about concern diffusion. CDO retrieves instances of methods and advices of a KDM model that were annotated with a specific tag name and tag value. Similarly, CDC retrieves

Table 2. CDO and CDC operation definition

Metric	Language	Body
CDO	XPath	//codeElement='code:MethodUnit' and [@tagName='tagValue'] or //codeElement='code:AdviceUnit and [@tagName='tagValue']

CDC	XPath	//codeElement='code:ClassUnit' and [@tagName='tagValue'] or
		//codeElement='code:InterfaceUnit and [@tagName='tagValue'] or
		//codeElement='code:AspectUnit and [@tagName='tagValue']

instances of classes, interfaces and aspects of a KDM model that were annotated with a specific tag name and tag value. Note that tag names and tag values are parameters which can be settled through CMEE in order to capture a specific concern.

For instance, it is possible to set "tagName" and "tagValue" with "concern" and "Persistence" respectively, then CMEE will replace these parameters and apply the operation. Listing 1.2 shows the case for the CDO operation and Fig. 3 depicts the Object Diagram that is an instance of KDM that represents CDO Metrics [9].

```
//codeElement="code:MethodUnit" AND [@concern="Persistence"] OR
//codeElement="code:AdviceUnit" AND [@concern="Persistence"]
```

Listing 1.2. Replaced parameters CDO Operation

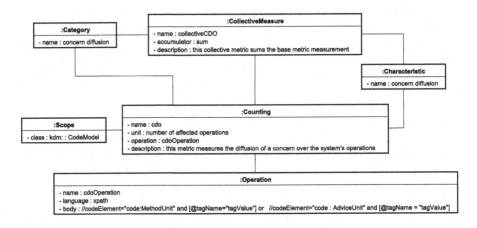

Fig. 3. CDO object diagram

In the Object Diagram we have instantiated some important metaclasses, like *Counting*. *Counting* is a specialized measure class that serves to define metrics for counting, such as the number of operations affected by some specific cross-cutting concern. If we decide to measure more than one target model, we could instantiate *CollectiveMeasure* metaclass, that applies an operation (sum, average, maximum value, minimum value, etc) to a Counting measurement results.

It is not always possible to define concern metrics faithfully using the ADM metamodels. This is the case of the CDLOC [9]. This metric measures the implementation alternation of concerns between lines of code, but in KDM, there is no element that represents a line of code, but there is an element that represent a region of the source code.

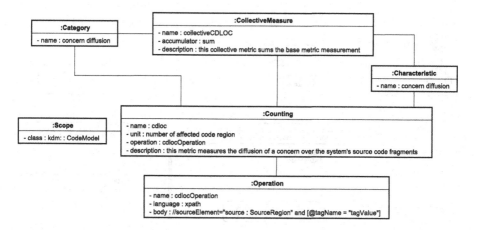

Fig. 4. CDLOC object diagram

Thus, it was necessary to adapt this metric to measure SourceRegion elements instead of Lines of Code. This adaptation can be seen in Fig. 4, where we can see that the code makes mention for an Operation element that searches for SourceRegion elements. To define our Concern Metrics Library we have used MoDisco SMM Editor. This editor is part of MoDisco Framework [2] and allows creating SMM metrics models using graphic elements. The library structure is shown in the Table 1.

In Table 1 it is possible to see the structure of our metrics library. This library was developed with the objective to group a set of concern metrics. The library in contained inside the CC_MetricsLibrary.smm physical file, and contains the following elements: Model (the main element, that represents a SMM Model), Library (our concern metrics library), Measures (organized by Category, Characteristic or Scope), Operations (contains the OCL or XPath or XQuery code that will be applied in the target KDM Model). All these elements are useful when the engineer wants to search metrics or measurement results in a repository.

5   Tool Support

In this section we show how CMEE (Concern Metrics Execution Engine) works. To help in the understanding process, we have created an UML Activity Diagram with the flow to be executed that can be seen in Fig. 5. The flow starts when the Modernization Engineer (User) opens the CMEE Plugin on Eclipse IDE. In the first action, User needs to choose the .SMM Model file and one or more .KDM Model. If any of these models is not well-formed CMEE will detect and return to the first phase. Since all models are ready, the next step is choosing one measure to apply on KDM Model and choosing a directory to save the measurement results file.

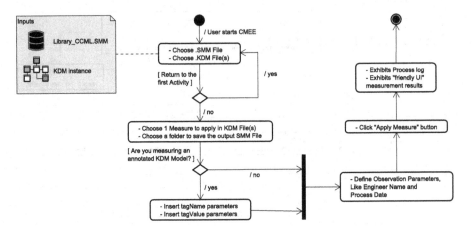

Fig. 5. Concern metrics execution engine – CMEE activity diagram

Then, User need to inform if the target KDM Model is an Annotated model (previously mining) or just a KDM Model, without annotations (See Fig. 6). If the KDM Model contains Annotations, it will be necessary to inform the parameters and CMEE will replace this information on the Operation Code, for instance: if the user had used a concern mining tool that annotated the KDM models with the following pattern "concern=concern_name" and the user is also using our parameterized metrics, it will be necessary to inform CMEE that the meta tag name is "tagName", the meta tag value is "tagValue", then, it will necessary to inform the tag name value, like "concern" and the concern name for tag value, like "persistence". The CMEE allow the inclusion of multiple patterns of annotations simply by clicking on the symbol with the add button.

Finally, the user needs to provide some information about the measuring process, like engineer name and date, then click on the button "Apply Measure" and see the results.

6   Execution Engine and Metrics Library Case Study

To validate and exemplify the use of the CMEE, we decide to measure KDM models of a system named CD Store. This system was written in Java and serves

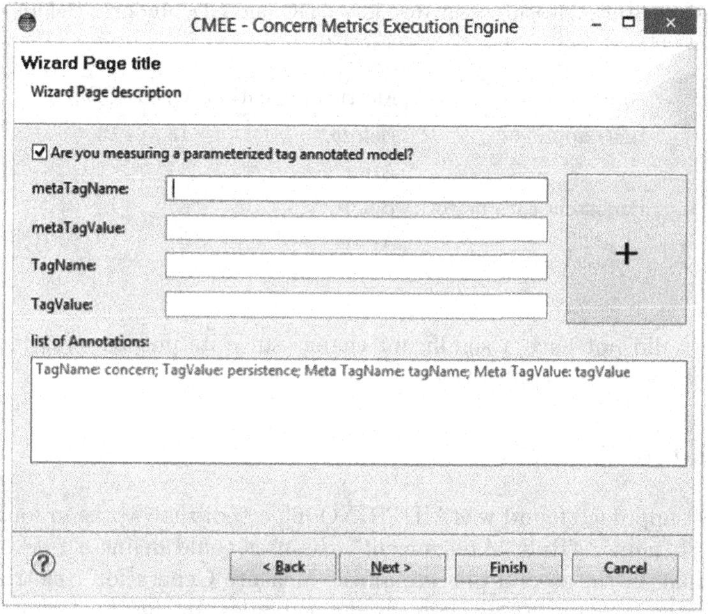

Fig. 6. CMEE screen – tag parametrization

to manage a store that sells CD/DVD. This case study has two parts. In the first part, we have applied the CDO and CDC metrics [9] on the legacy CD Store KDM Models and, in the second part, we have applied CDO and CDC Metrics in KDM-AO modernized models.

Legacy CD Store uses an Object-Oriented Framework to persist data on database. The problem is that a big number of classes in the application implements actions related to persistence. Therefore, the modernization aims to change this OO Persistence Framework for an AO Persistence Framework, in order to remove persistence implementation from the base application.

To discover where the crosscutting concern "persistence" is, we have used the CCKDM Tool [8] to mining concerns in our CD Store KDM and KDM-AO Models. Then we use our tool CMEE to measure the models using CDO and CDC. The CDO and CDC Indexes can be seen in Table 3. Note that before the modularity-oriented modernization process, the Base Application CD Store had a lot of persistence code in its classes and after these numbers decrease a lot, leaving only the Persistence AO Framework implementing the persistence of the application.

This kind of measurement helps the engineer to discover if the ADM modernization process was effective or not. In this case, the base app CD Store has been modernized successfully, because the diffusion of the concern "persistence" decreases from 13 to 1. But, if the engineer is not satisfied with the indexes, he can reapply the refactorings and then measure again. Notice that the Persistence

Table 3. Case Study Measurement Results - CDO and CDC Indexes Before and After Modernization

Application	Metric application	CDO	CDC
Base app	Before	13	13
	After	1	1
Persistence framework	Before	87	14
	After	87	19

Framework did not have a significant change since its purpose was to perform the persistence of the application.

7   Related Works

The oldest approach found was METRINO [6], a tool that works in four phases. In the first, named "Rule Management", the user could define a rule or use an existing rule. In the second phase, named "Measure Generation", metric models are generated based on the previously defined rules. In the third phase, named "Measure Management", it is possible to change the automatically generated metric models. Then, in the last phase, named "Measure Evaluation", METRINO applies the selected metrics (selected by the user) on the MOF-based target models.

Another related approach is Gra2Mol Motor [3]. The mechanism Gra2Mol receives as input metrics defined in a DSL (Domain Specific Language) named Medea and KDM files to apply the metrics. The tool has a translator that transforms Medea code in SMM Measures and then apply the selected measures in the KDM Model that represents the system.

And the last related approach found was MAMBA Framework (Measurement Architecture for Model-Based Analysis) [5]. MAMBA could receive both SMM and MDL Files. MDL (metrics definition language) is a DSL developed by MAMBA Team to facilitate the process of creating SMM Metrics files. As with other approaches, it is necessary to put a KDM File to measure and then the MAMBA Execution Engine starts the measurement process and generates an output SMM File.

It's important to emphasize that none of the related works can interpret aspect-oriented metrics and parameterized concern metrics.

8   Conclusion

By means of this research it is fairly evident that our approach fills a gap in the ADM context. Now, it is possible to measure Aspect-Oriented Software represented in KDM Models using Concern Metrics, like CDO and CDC.

We argue this approach is useful in modernization scenarios to improve the modularization of software systems, for instance, a modernization process that applies refactorings in order to modularize the persistence code which is scattered and tangled over operations, components and/or lines of code.

With our approach the Modernization Engineer could use SMM models with XPath Operations Code to collect data about crosscutting concerns and other metrics. Note that KDM model measurements is different to measurements in the source code. KDM models are versatile and can have multiple levels of abstraction, but cannot represent lines of code, for example.

We can also mention that measure crosscutting concerns is not something native on KDM, so it had to be extended (KDM-AO) and annotated by a crosscutting concern mining tool and then it could be measured.

This type of measurement (concern measurements) requires that the Operations of SMM metrics to be dynamic enough so that the user can specify which concern is required to be measured and how the mining tool annotate KDM models, that is, which annotation pattern the mining tool uses.

The CMEE tool supports multiple sets of parameters and can accept even one, two or more patterns of annotations in KDM target model. Thus, as a limitation for this research we can mention the need for prior concern mining of target models. To measure crosscutting concerns it is necessary to know where they are implemented. Therefore, mining techniques and tools should be used mandatory.

The dependence of the extension KDM-AO for representing aspect oriented software systems is another limitation for the reuse of metrics since our pre-defined parameterized metrics mention some terms like "AspectUnit" and "AdviceUnit" that is a particularity of our extension. Another limitation is the dependence of MoDisco tool to represent java source code, which so far does not have support for all KDM packages.

As a future work, we will perform a more in-depth evaluation of the approach and tool, involving real systems developed in different programming languages and software engineers from industry to evaluate whether the SMM instances are generic enough to measure different instances. Another future work is to enrich the SMM metrics library with other quality metrics and also to improve the output results in order to provide useful reports that could help software engineers in the decision making process.

Acknowledgements. This study was financed in part by the Coordenação de Aperfeiçoamento de Pessoal de Nível Superior - Brasil (CAPES) - Finance Code 001 and by FAPESP process number 2016/03104-0. We also would like to thank CONICYT PFCHA/DOCTORADO BECAS CHILE/2016 - 72170024.

References

1. Bruneliere, H., Cabot, J., Jouault, F., Madiot, F.: Modisco: a generic and extensible framework for model driven reverse engineering. In: Proceedings of the IEEE/ACM International Conference on Automated Software Engineering, ASE 2010, pp. 173–174. ACM, New York (2010). https://doi.org/10.1145/1858996.1859032

2. Brunelière, H., Cabot, J., Dupé, G., Madiot, F.: Modisco: a model driven reverse engineering framework. Inf. Softw. Technol. **56**(8), 1012–1032 (2014). https://doi.org/10.1016/j.infsof.2014.04.007

3. Canovas Izquierdo, J., Zapata, B., Molina, J.: Definición y ejecución de métricas en el contexto de adm. In: Taller sobre Desarrollo de Software Dirigido por Modelos (DSDM), pp. 1–10 (2009)

4. Durelli, R.S., et al.: A mapping study on architecture-driven modernization. In: Proceedings of the 2014 IEEE 15th International Conference on Information Reuse and Integration (IEEE IRI 2014), pp. 577–584, August 2014. https://doi.org/10.1109/IRI.2014.7051941

5. Frey, S., Hoorn, A., Jung, R., Kiel, B., Hasselbring, W.: MAMBA: model-based software analysis utilizing OMG's SMM. Softwaretechnik-Trends **32**(2), 49–50 (2012)

6. Hein, C., Engelhardt, M., Ritter, T., Wagner, M.: Generation of formal model metrics for MOF based domain specific languages. ECEASST **24** (2009). https://doi.org/10.14279/tuj.eceasst.24.339

7. Pérez-Castillo, R., de Guzmán, I.G.R., Piattini, M.: Knowledge discovery metamodel-ISO/IEC 19506: a standard to modernize legacy systems. Comput. Stand. Interfaces **33**(6), 519–532 (2011). https://doi.org/10.1016/j.csi.2011.02.007

8. San Martín Santibáñez, D., Durelli, R.S., Camargo, V.V.: A combined approach for concern identification in KDM models. J. Braz. Comput. Soc. **21**(1), 10 (2015). https://doi.org/10.1186/s13173-015-0030-3

9. Sant'anna, C., Garcia, A., Chavez, C., Lucena, C., von Staa, A.: On the reuse and maintenance of aspect-oriented software: an assessment framework. In: Proceedings XVII Brazilian Symposium on Software Engineering (2003). http://twiki.im.ufba.br/pub/Aside/NossasPublicacoes/sbes2003-135.PDF

10. Santos, B.M., de Guzmán, I.G., Camargo, V.V., Piattini, M., Ebert, C.: Software refactoring for system modernization. IEEE Softw. **35**(6), 62–67 (2018). https://doi.org/10.1109/MS.2018.4321236

11. Santos, B.M., de Landi, A.S., Santibáñez, D.S., Durelli, R.S., Camargo, V.V.: Evaluating the extension mechanisms of the knowledge discovery metamodel for aspect-oriented modernizations. J. Syst. Softw. **149**, 285–304 (2019). https://doi.org/10.1016/j.jss.2018.12.011

12. Visaggio, G.: Ageing of a data-intensive legacy system: symptoms and remedies. J. Softw. Maint. Evol.: Res. Pract. **13**(5), 281–308 (2001). https://doi.org/10.1002/smr.234

A Family of Domain-Specific Languages for Integrated Modular Avionics

Ricardo Alves[1], Vasco Amaral[1,2](✉), João Cintra[2], and Bruno Tavares[2]

[1] NOVA LINCS, Universidade Nova de Lisboa, Lisbon, Portugal
vasco.amaral@fct.unl.pt
[2] GMV, Madrid, Spain

Abstract. In the domain of avionics, we can find intricate software product lines constrained by both aircraft's hardware and conformance to strict standards. Existing general-purpose languages are complicated, as they do not hide unnecessary low level-details. This situation potentially leads to a lengthy process in the specification phase and the loss of control over the quality of the specification itself and possibly resulting in the generation of inconsistent products.

In Software development for avionics systems, the pressure of time-to-market is high. Additionally, the long time taken for systems certification of this sort of critical system pushes for the development of solutions that support specifications correct by construction. With that kind of solutions, we can release the burden of the software developer by positively constraining the configuration of the products. In this paper, we put into practice an in-house solution that implements the concept of Product Lines of Domain Specific Languages (DSLs). The solution allows generating dedicated DSLs for each sub-family/configuration in Modular avionics departing from the model of a given aircraft.

Keywords: Model-driven development · Family of languages ·
ARINC 653 · Integrated modular avionics DSL · Implementation reuse

1 Introduction

In the field of software development for avionics systems, the engineering life cycle of an aeroplane can reach up to almost a decade. Therefore, the pressure of time-to-market is very high. The long time taken for systems certification of this sort of critical system pushes for the development of solutions that support specifications correct by construction. They should also offer expressiveness at the level of abstraction of the problem domain instead of the technicalities of the solution domain. Domain-Specific Languages (DLS) [10], are known precisely for that, as they help to release the burden of the software developer by positively constraining the configuration of the products with less accidental complexity, and therefore increasing its productivity.

© Springer Nature Switzerland AG 2019
M. Piattini et al. (Eds.): QUATIC 2019, CCIS 1010, pp. 239–254, 2019.
https://doi.org/10.1007/978-3-030-29238-6_17

However, in Avionics, the variety of products can be vast (with sub-categories of families of products), with a broad set of configuration space possibilities at the configuration of partitions for Integrated Modular Avionics (IMA).

A problem to develop such DSLs is that to cover all products and keep versatile enough to capture the domain rules, it will have to become more general-purpose leading to the loss of control over the quality of the specification itself and bringing all the complexity again, and unnecessary details, found in lower levels of abstraction. With a vast design space, this situation might lead to the possible generation of inconsistent products, requiring elaborated Testing and Checking techniques. Ideally, there would be dedicated DSLs for each sub-family of products. However, the challenge of automating the process to generate different DSLs, like a common SPL, is still not a common practice, and it lacks successful examples in the bibliography.

This work presents an in-house solution for supporting product lines in the field of avionics (Sect. 3) of DSLs for the architecture of Integrated Modular Avionics (Sect. 2). We define our perspective of a family of DSLs, and we discuss its implication in the language design 4, including to configure and tailor different DSLs each of which will be destined to specify the set of possible applications for a given subfamily of products (partitions in a Real-Time Operating System). We then show our process and framework to generate the visual editors, validation rules and code generation templates from the input configuration models and the standard reference (Sect. 5). To complete the study, we evaluate (Sect. 6) the usability of the proposed framework that implies to analyse the configuration of the generated DSLs and to use them, comparing this solution to the previous approach. Finally, we discuss related work (Sect. 7) and conclude (Sect. 8).

2   Integrated Modular Avionics

IMA is an electronic architecture of an airborne system and consists of a network of physical computation modules which allow real-time processing. Each module supports the execution of multiple application with different critical levels. This means that a set of avionics functions that may be correctly executed, on the same hardware with guarantees of the external behaviour of each application, is the same as the one performed in specific dedicated hardware.

The communication between computation modules is usually achieved by using one shared high-speed network and regulated by a particular standard like ARINC 664 [2]. Most of the aircrafts flying today use a federated architecture, which is a proprietary architecture that uses specific hardware physically segregated for the execution of one avionic function. Plus, the federated architecture requires dedicated interconnection cables between each computer module.

The last generation of aircrafts have an IMA architecture which provides the following benefits: (1) Reduces aircrafts' global weight, with fewer cables and computation modules (so it can be used for more cargo or fuel); (2) Reduces energy consumption (to be used by other systems, requiring fewer batteries);

(3) Reduces complexity of the physical construction of the aircraft (less hardware); (4) Simplifies the development process of avionics software (the avionic application developers are focused on the high-level software layer).

Inside of each IMA computation module, it is installed a real-time operating system (RTOS). The standard ARINC 653 [1] specifies the application programming interface (API) between avionic application and operating system. Additionally, this standard restricts the answer of RTOS to the API invocations and provides time and space constraints for correct modules partitioning.

In Fig. 1 it is depicted the module architecture. The real-time operating systems run on the hardware, providing services to the avionics software hosted by several partitions. The avionics software makes calls to the API (denominated APEX) to use ARINC653 services.

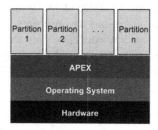

Fig. 1. ARINC 653 module architecture

3   Software Product Line (SPL) and DSL Families

A product belonging to a family of software products share a set of common characteristics in a specific way. Building a new product is mostly a process of selection of characteristics (integration of components), rather than exhaustive programming. This way, it is a level of indirection where the decision is made regarding features of a given product. Their features characterise a product that belongs to an SPL. The variability of those is usually analysed using the Feature-Oriented Domain Analysis (FODA) [7], mainly using Feature Models.

If we consider language models (metamodels) as a product, Fig. 2 shows an approach for defining a language product in the family. On the left-hand side, we present a feature model representing the variability of a particular representation of a Petri-Net. When it is required to build a new product, it is possible to choose between the existence or nonexistence of Tokens in the language. If it exists, the metamodel of the product will be composed by the part in the picture with the white and the grey background. If it does not exist, the metamodel of the product will only correspond to the part of the model with the white background.

This case is a simplified example of an SPL which has two variations and that the number of options is limited. To add new features not covered by the feature model presented, several significant changes will be necessary, i.e. you must change both the metamodel and the feature model.

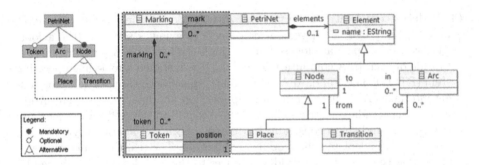

Fig. 2. Common SPL approach applied to metamodels (Adapted from [9])

At this point we can define a family of DSLs as a set of software languages (and corresponding artefacts) to specify products for a particular domain or task, sharing a common set of key concepts, but that is specifically tailored to meet the variability of the requirements and restrict the set of possible software products into a subfamily.

4   Languages Design

Domain-specific languages can be developed using model-driven development (MDD) in an incremental way. Underlying this paradigm are models [16] and model transformations [6,15]. One type of linguistic models are metamodels, and it defines the concrete and abstract syntax of a domain-specific language in the context. In this work, we mostly focus on the definition of the abstract syntax.

According to our DSL family definition, we will have a set of common and variable concepts represented in all generated target languages. On the one hand, some of those concepts are very rigid and are expressed in the same way in all generated languages' metamodels, on the other hand, some concepts are changed to achieve the particular configuration of each language. To better illustrate this concept of language SPL, we present Fig. 3, where we show the separation between common and specific configuration concepts and their metamodel representation. If these concepts are correctly separated, the development of metamodels can also be done separately. The idea behind this methodology is to develop the metamodel of common concepts and reuse in all languages, avoiding to do the same work repeatedly.

We use model merging [8]. This consists of joining the metamodels by sharing equivalent entities among them. This implies that if the name of the entity is the main attribute for the merging process, the elements of both metamodels having the same name are made the same (merged).

Figure 2 illustrates the resulting merged metamodel departing from the fragment metamodel represented in grey on the left together with the fragment in the right part (linked by "PetriNet" and "Place").

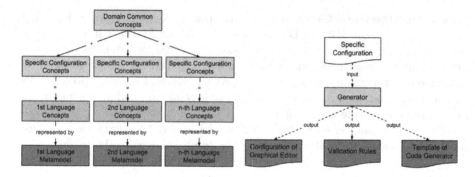

Fig. 3. Language concepts   **Fig. 4.** Generator module

The whole process of generating the family of DSLs was designed to be supported by a set of tools, called Languages Modelling Workbenches. These frameworks provide some essential features that facilitate the development and automatic generation of some artefacts and tools like the graphical language editor, and code generators.

After finishing the language's abstract syntax, and its concrete syntax mapping, it is necessary to generate the configuration of the graphical editor, the instance model validation rules and the code generator (shown in Fig. 4). If the DSL product line produces a possibly large set of DSLs, these tasks need to be done automatically, without any human intervention to be manageable.

For automatic generation of languages, we developed a generator capable of creating all the necessary artefacts.

Generating Configuration of a Graphical Editor - Some graphical editors are configurable by choosing user interaction features like: where we put toolbars, select buttons locations, rename our tools and other settings.

As our DSL family has languages with distinct concepts, it is essential to generate for each language the particular configuration of the graphical editor. This can be done by using a simple model-to-text transformation, responsible for generating the configuration in the target language automatically. The produced artefact will be read and interpreted by the external tool responsible for generating the graphical editor.

Generating Validation Rules - The validation rules of a domain-specific language provide additional guarantees of the well-formedness of the new DSL instance models. If two languages are different, then the set of validation rules will probably be different.

As we have different languages in the DSL family, we need to select and generate the specific validation rules tailored to this language. This is achieved by using a simple model-to-text transformation, which means to create the validation rules or assertions automatically, and write them to a file on a proper constraint language (like OCL, EVL, etc.) to be interpreted by the editor.

Generating the Code Generator - Sometimes, although not strictly following the principle of Model-Driven Development (MDD), we find that in practice the software development process based on models, the target artefacts of a given DSL is template code in a general purpose language (GPL), that is going to be completed by the software engineer to represent the final software product. To be able to do that, we need to generate the code template, and at this point, we are talking about code meta-generation.

This transformation is similar to the model-to-text transformation, but we are not generating the final artefact yet. The result is a new template able to be interpreted by the framework tool and then generate the proper end code.

5   DSL Family for IMA

Over the years the company GMV[1] has worked successfully, as part of its core business, in IMA projects and today is continuing to develop an Integrated Modular Avionics Development Environment (IMADE) [17]. The main objective is to provide a toolchain for the whole IMA development process while complying with the certification of the end product.

The development of avionics applications is an essential task and, considering this, a family of DSLs is being developed for IMADE. Each generated DSL allows specifying the code skeleton/template of new avionics applications according to the partition specification.

Using a DSL, we can get the benefits of this approach like the increase of the productivity, mainly if is used a graphical environment and improving the quality of the final product by generating some parts of code automatically.

It was observed that a solution based on a single DSL for all types of partition is not enough. The language would be too general, and it would be potentially error-prone, leading to the generation of inconsistent products. The envisaged solution was then the development of a new DSL for each partition configuration and then the creation of a family of DSLs. The main advantage of such an approach is the possibility of creating a different DSL according to the specific settings for each partition (subfamily). This means to constrain the expressiveness offered by the Avionics solution. This contributes to avoiding errors by construction in the early phases. For example, when using an API method regarding communication ports, the DSL user can select only the existing ports that can be correctly used under the partition configuration.

5.1   Languages Metamodeling Workbench

For the implementation of our solution, we used Eclipse Epsilon framework, as it presents several advantages, namely: (i) the possibility of integrating various plug-ins that provide extension capabilities, (ii) being multi-platform, (iv) open source, (vi) the availability of extensive online documentation, and (v) a large

---

[1] http://www.gmv.com.

community of users. Another important aspect is the fact that Eclipse is a platform very often used in the field of aviation, mainly due to its ability to integrate with various tools and ease to evolve.

5.2 DSLs generator module

This domain has common concepts like the application programming interface specified in ARINC 653 (see the fragment of the metamodel in Fig. 6a), but also has variable concepts like the specific configuration of one partition under development. This motivates the use of DSL families, and a DSL generator has been developed, as illustrated in Fig. 5.

The process of generating a new DSL of the family starts with an XML file containing an ARINC 653 configuration for a particular module (already produced by another tool outside the scope of this document). This file has all the additional information needed to generate the metamodel extension like the: number, type and other properties of the communication ports. Using the information in the XML file is possible to create the metamodel extension. Later this extension and the metamodel of common concepts are merged. This last metamodel has been developed at the same time as the tool and should never change in its lifetime.

With these two operations, two Ecore intermediate artefacts are also created: the extension metamodel; and, the abstract syntax metamodel. The first one is useful if we want to verify the particular configuration of one partition using the ecore formalism. The second one is helpful to generate the DSL and its corresponding graphics editor.

The generation of a graphical editor configuration is the next stage. This operation creates an EOL file (Epsilon Object Language is used), which is interpreted by the EuGENia tool and produces the graphical environment.

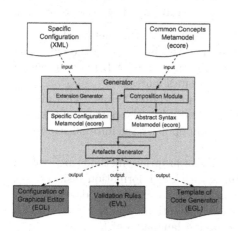

Fig. 5. IMADE generator module

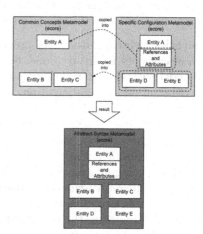

Fig. 6. Merging metamodels

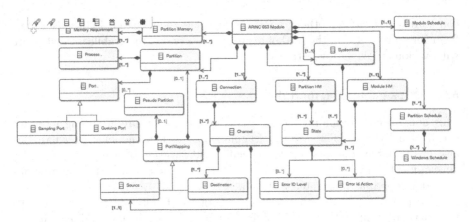

Fig. 7. Simplified fragment of the language metamodel (Ecore) visualised in Eclipse EcoreTools.

After that, also based on abstract syntax metamodel, it is created an EVL file. This file contains validation rules used by the graphical environment to verify the well-formedness of the instance models realised with the new language. These validations rules are written using the Epsilon Validation Language.

Finally, it is generated by the EGL file. This last artefact contains the template to create the final code in a GPL, and it is written using Epsilon Generation Language. After the generation of all artefacts, the EuGENia tool is invoked. Some of the artefacts, like the metamodel and the graphical editor configuration file, are only used at this stage to help to generate the graphical environment.

The validation rules (defined in an EVL file) and the code template (defined in an EGL file) are used at runtime by the graphical environment generated in the first stage. The first is used when it is necessary to validate the constructs produced by the programmer by using the language previously created. The second is used when the developer intends to generate code from the constructs.

Generating Metamodel - As previously mentioned, the metamodel of the common concepts is already done. So, the first step is to create the extension metamodel with the information that is coming from an XML file (containing the settings of all existing partitions on the avionics module).

To handle the XML file, it was developed a plug-in for Eclipse. This plug-in allows the DSL user to select the file location and select the partition he wants. Then the plug-in processes this information and populates the internal structures with the newly obtained information.

Later, when the information is required, the appropriate methods are evoked, and they should return the data structures with the information inside these. Thus, it becomes more modular, but also simpler, to realise and develop code. This approach improves the performance of the solution because we used JAVA to develop this plug-in instead of the interpreted languages of Epsilon.

The second step is to create the extension by using the same information obtained before. Using EOL, we create the EClass, EAttribute, EReference and other elements of the extension metamodel. These elements belong to the Ecore formalism used by Eclipse Epsilon to define metamodels. In Fig. 8 it is shown part of the code responsible for generating the extension. The *ExtensionMM* element is the extension metamodel (this element starts empty). Between line 3 to 9 is created the anchor entity and is also exists on the metamodel of common concepts. This entity will be used for merging both metamodels.

```
var package = ExtensionMM.resource.contents.first();
var mainEClass = new ExtensionMM!EClass;
mainEClass.name = "Process_Management";
mainEClass.abstract = true;
package.eClassifiers.add(mainEClass);
for(instructionName in getPortInstructions()){
    var portInstruction = new ExtensionMM!EClass;
        portInstruction.name = instructionName;
        portInstruction.eSuperTypes.add(mainEClass);
    var emfAnnotation = new ExtensionMM!EAnnotation;
    emfAnnotation.source = "gmf.node";
    var detail = new ExtensionMM!EStringToStringMapEntry;
    detail.key = "border.color";
    detail.value = "0,0,0";
    emfAnnotation.details.add(detail);
    portInstruction.eAnnotations.add(emfAnnotation);
    package.eClassifiers.add(portInstruction);
}
```

Fig. 8. Extension generation code

The loop condition has the *getSamplingPortInstructions()* method that returns the instructions taking into account the specific configuration of the partition. Between line 13 and 33, the entities responsible for representing the instructions in the metamodel are created.

While creating entities in the extension metamodel we also added the GMF annotations. These are necessary to generate the graphical environment with Eugenia. Code of lines 19 and 31 in Fig. 8 is responsible for that.

The third step is to merge the metamodel of common concepts with metamodel of specific configuration concept (extension metamodel created in the second step). This operation is illustrated in Fig. 6. It first identifies the entities that have common names in both metamodels. All attributes and references in each identified entity are copied from extension metamodel to the respective entity in metamodel of common concepts. All other entities are copied from the extension metamodel to the common concepts metamodel. Due to the internal representation of the ecore formalism, these two operations ensure the merger of the two metamodels.

Generating Configuration of Graphical Editor - The configuration of the Graphical Editor is defined using the EOL language. This configuration is stored in a file with the name of *"ECore2GMF.eol"*.

In general terms, it was defined as a template that contemplates the possible variations in the abstract syntax metamodel. This template generates only the configuration of the elements that are present in the metamodel and uses its attributes to produce the correct validation rules.

To implement the solution, we could have used instead of the EGL language included in Epsilon. This is a language tailored for model-to-text transformation (M2T) and can be used to transform models into textual artefacts like the code in multiple programming languages.

Our concern from the beginning was to use the same programming language to make the implementation more straightforward and to concentrate the code of the generator module without ever compromising its modularity. Therefore, we also used EOL language.

```
if(getPortInstructions().size() > 0){
    write("var toolGrp = new GmfTool!ToolGroup;");
    write("toolGrp.title = 'ARINC653: Interpartition';");
    write("toolGrp.collapsible = true;");
    write("palette.tools.add(toolGrp);");
}
```

Fig. 9. Generation of the configuration

```
var toolGrp = new GmfTool!ToolGroup;
toolGrp.title = 'ARINC653: Interpartition';
toolGrp.collapsible = true;
palette.tools.add(toolGrp);
```

Fig. 10. Result of the configuration

EOL is not appropriate to deal with model-to-text transformations because it cannot deal directly with text files. To tackle this limitation, we developed a plug-in that allows writing a file appropriately, i.e. to deal with opening and closing files and write the desired text in the correct position. In Fig. 9 it is shown some code which generates the configuration. The result of running this code is illustrated in Fig. 10. The write method allows writing directly in the text file. The code presented in Fig. 9 only writes the text in the file if there are instructions ARINC653 to handle communications.

In Fig. 10 is shown how to change the graphical environment, by creating a toolbar group with the name of *"ARINC653: Interpretation"*. Later on, the buttons can be added to the toolbar group.

Generating Validation Rules - A similar technique to the one described before was used in the same way to produce the validation rules. In this case, the target language is EVL.

The validation rule illustrated in Fig. 11 checks whether the *GET_ QUEUING_ PORT_ID* instruction has a defined port, otherwise a warning is shown. This rule and similar rules are produced if the configuration of the partition has at least one queuing port.

```
context GET_QUEUING_PORT_ID {
  constraint HavePort {
    check : self.port.isDefined()
    message : 'No port found'
  }
}
```

Fig. 11. Resulting validation rule

Generating the Code Generator - The code generator artefact is generated similarly to the previous artefacts. In this case, the final result is an EGL code template to be run in the Eclipse Epsilon framework.

Due to the use of EOL language to perform the model-to-text transformations (described in 5.2 it is now possible to produce EGL code more efficiently. Unfortunately, as a slight technology limitation and drawback, EGL does not cope well with embedded EGL code (for the purpose of being part of the generated rules) in the EGL template. In fact, it tries to interpret all the specified EGL code.

```
write("[%for(queuingPort in getQueuingPorts()) {");
write("var name = queuingPort.get('portname')%]");
write("CREATE_QUEUING_PORT('[%=name%]', ... );");
write("[%}%]");
```

Fig. 12. Generation of code generator

A short example of the code is illustrated in Fig. 12. The EGL code is written for a file. Later on, when the template is executed, the EGL code between characters *[%* and *%]* is executed. The final GPL code produced in Fig. 12 is *CREATE_QUEUING_PORT('<PORT NAME>', ...);* for each port present in the configuration file of partition.

6   Evaluating the Usability

A quasi-experiment was held to compare the newly generated DSLs and the previous programming experience with C was carried away to determine the degree of success of our approach in terms of usability. The steps were:

(1) Subject Recruitment - We looked for subjects proficient with programming in C and showing domain knowledge, including experience with previous projects where with ARINC 653. The universe of subjects was divided into a set of 4 medium experience and a set with 2 very experienced users. Finally, a seventh subject did not have any experience with ARINC 653.

(2) Task Preparation - We prepared several materials: slides for the training session; and, exercises for the final evaluation session. Two Desktops with the same hardware were installed with Microsoft Windows 7 Professional Software, with JAVA v1.7.0, Notepad++, CamStudio and the Eclipse framework with our DSL. The subjects were grouped into four groups: group 1 and group 2, with high experience (2 subjects each); group 3, medium experienced (2 subjects); and, group 4, with the non-ARINC 653 knowledge subject. Group 1 was evaluated while solving the exercise first using the DSL and C to introduce lines of code in the generated code, and after that, they produced their solution for the same problem just in C. The second group did the opposite, to minimise the bias. The third group and the 4th group (the inexperienced subject in ARINC) started with solving the problem with the DSL and C and then just C. All training and exercise sessions were monitored by the same person (project developer).

(3) Pilot Session - to avoid last minute problems, wasting time from the limited set of volunteers, we duly tested the material prepared. A champion for this technology in the company was asked to take the role of the subject and tested both the training material and the evaluation exercises. As expected, several errors and ambiguities were detected, as well as better strategies were designed to control timing.

(4) Training Session - This session was the first contact of the subjects with the DSL, and the subjects had the opportunity to try out some exercises and explore the language features. This session was video recorded for later analysis of the time taken to finish the tasks.

(5) Evaluation Session - Each subject had to participate in two sessions, the DSL with C and the session with just C (order in which this sequence occurred could be the reverse). The exercises were the same for both sessions. In the session with the DSL the C code skeleton that was generated in the model to code generation was used by the subject to introduce more lines of C code to complete the exercise. We have prepared three different exercises during the assessment. The first was meant for training, and the remaining two were used for the evaluation session. The degree of difficulty increased with each exercise in the sequence. At the end of each exercise, the subject would have a sophisticated avionics program, with communication between partitions and communication in between processes of the same partition.

As typical with in-house DSLs, the reduced number of subjects is a negative aspect of statistical evidence of the results. However, the mentioned seven subjects, with exception to occasional new recruited programmers, represent a majority of the whole universe of programmers that will make use of this solution in the company. The result of this assessment was positive. This information was also assessed via questionnaires at the end of the evaluation sessions. All users appreciated the tool since it improves their productivity by speeding up the process of producing the required repetitive code that is usually programmed manually. The subjects consider that the code resulting from the automatic model-to-code transformation is already well structured. It is well accepted that few lines of code have to be introduced to finalise the intended functionality.

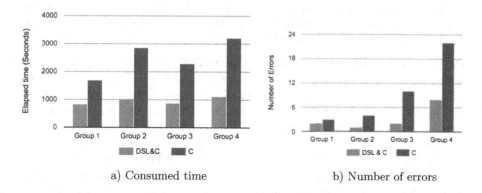

a) Consumed time   b) Number of errors

Fig. 13. Consumed time and errors with the exercises.

As observed in Fig. 13a, the estimated achievement, based on a mean value, is a gain of about 59,91% of the production of the predetermined avionic code.

Using just the C language, group 2 (experienced subjects), have taken more time than group 3 (moderately skilled). This fact can be explained (when looking at the video recorded sessions) because the users in group 2 took the time to comment correctly and indent code to be understandable and re-usable.

7   Related Work

Software Product Lines [13] and Domain-Specific Languages [10] are familiar concepts in both scientific and industrial communities. But, examples of the combination of the two concepts resulting in the particularisation of the family of DSLs are still very scarce. We next discuss MDD that inspired our solution.

Composition of DSLs - The first approach is to perform the composition of various DSLs, arising or not from different modelling aspects. One goal of this method is to create new languages to reduce the effort in the development of DSLs initially used in the composition. The composition of the new abstract syntax metamodel of the language is performed manually by engineers like a puzzle, reusing and adapting parts of metamodels. This process may be assisted by a feature model describing the concepts that are covered by each DSL, dependencies or conflicts between DSLs, and finally how the refinement of languages affects the coverage of the concepts [5]. This approach has several drawbacks. By definition a DSL is tightly coupled to the domain for which it was developed, which implies a reasonable effort from Language Engineers to compose languages from different domains [5]. This effort is due to the need to adapt to the reality of the concepts of the new language, and may ultimately be more appropriate to draw it from scratch. Another significant disadvantage of this process is related to the need for human intervention when it is necessary to generate a new DSL, which makes the time-consuming and error-prone process.

The repeated composition of the same DSL with other languages for specific domains is a practice used when we want to add an essential feature of a host language to a given hosted language [3, 12].

Positive Variability - An approach that uses the metamodel's positive variability of the language can be used to create a family of languages. It starts with a common minimum metamodel to all languages of the same family. Next, it is performed the composition with required extensions to achieve the desired language [11]. The extension process can be accomplished by using the model merging approach [8] or by weaving the models [14]. In both cases, extensions are anchored at pre-specified points through composition transformations.

It is possible to extend a language with the use of positive variability indefinitely. However, it is necessary that the composition of the two metamodels make sense (share the same base semantics) and belong to the same domain [8].

Negative Variability - In this approach, the complete metamodel of the language is initially defined completely. Afterwards, parts of the metamodel are removed, to obtain the desired configuration for the new member of the family of languages [11]. When the user wants to create a new DSL, selects the functionalities that are needed in the feature model. Removal and modification of metamodel elements are performed in an automated way using the predefined transformations. The last step is the language generation and its graphical environment [12].

The negative variability is suitable for use in situations where initially we have the full knowledge of the modelling domain [4]. It allows for the creation of a limited number of DSLs of the same family, according to the total number of combinations that we can select in the feature model.

Analysis of Alternative Development Approaches - We can find characteristics of automatic generation of a language and high extensibility in the technique that uses **positive variability** [14]. The merge of models became possible thanks to the contribution that explore the semantics of languages composition [8]. On the other hand, **negative variability** also has useful features, but initially requires the full metamodel of the language, which, in many areas, is difficult to obtain because it is too long or is always evolving. This aspect makes the extensibility limited because many additional changes are needed to extend the automatic generator of languages. This situation means that it would be required very frequently the manual intervention of a software engineer.

In conclusion, the positive variability presents the most appropriate approach for developing a DSL Family for IMA.

8 Conclusions

We report an in-house solution for the avionics software industry, that assists the IMA developers. It allows to produce more efficiently and error-prone code thanks to the automatic construction of languages that are part of a DSL family as an intermediate step, to help to constrain the software engineer's design space for the code generation. For that purpose, we used the Eclipse Epsilon and the positive variability technique. Thanks to our generator, it is now possible automatically produce all the required components/artefacts that make part of the new language IDE. For each DSL, we generate automatically, based on a configuration specification model of the standard ARINC 653 (prone to evolution): (i) the new language metamodel; (ii) the visual editor with the adequate concrete syntax; (iii) the corresponding well-formedness rules (in EVL); and (iv), code generator.

As future work, it will be necessary to work on the automatic generation/configuration of the dedicated set of properties to be checked in the new DSL instance models (supported by model checking tools).

Acknowledgments. NOVA LINCS (Ref. UID/CEC/04516/2019). FCT/MCTES: DSML4MAS (TUBITAK/ 0008/2014); 2018/2019(Proc. DAAD 441.00) "Social-Cyber-physical Systems modelling".

References

1. ARINC 653 Avionics Application Software Standard Interface, Part 1, Required Services. Annapolis, Maryland, USA (2003)
2. ARINC 664 Aircraft Data Network, Part 1, Systems Concepts and Overview. Annapolis, Maryland, USA (2006)
3. Barroca, B., Lúcio, L., Buchs, D., Amaral, V., Pedro, L.: DSL composition for model-based test generation. In: 3rd International Workshop on Multi-Paradigm Modelling: Concepts and Tools. No. 21 in Electronic Communications of the EASST (2009)
4. Huang, C., Kamei, Y., Yamashita, K., Ubayashi, N.: Using alloy to support feature-based DSL construction for mining software repositories. In: Proceedings of 17th International Software Product Line Conference Co-located Workshops. ACM (2013)
5. White, J., Hill, J., Tambe, S., Gokhale, A., Schmidt, D., Gray, J.: Improving domain-specific language reuse through software product-line configuration techniques. In: IEEE Software, vol. 26, no. 4 (2009)
6. Czarnecki, K., Helsen, S.: Feature-based survey of model transformation approaches. IBM Syst. J. **45**(3), 621–645 (2006)
7. Kang, K., Cohen, S., Hess, J., Novak, W., Peterson, A.: Feature-oriented domain analysis (FODA) feasibility study. Technical report CMU/SEI-90-TR-021, SEI (1990)
8. Pedro, L.: A Systematic Language Engineering Approach for Prototyping Domain Specific Modelling Languages. Ph.D. thesis, Université de Genève (2009)

9. Barbero, M., Jouault, F., Gray, J., Bézivin, J.: A practical approach to model extension. In: Akehurst, D.H., Vogel, R., Paige, R.F. (eds.) ECMDA-FA 2007. LNCS, vol. 4530, pp. 32–42. Springer, Heidelberg (2007). https://doi.org/10.1007/978-3-540-72901-3_3

10. Völter, M., et al.: DSL Engineering - Designing, Implementing and Using Domain-Specific Languages (2013). dslbook.org

11. Völter, M., Groher, I.: Product line implementation using aspect-oriented and model-driven software development. In: Proceedings of 11th International Software Product Line Conference, SPLC 2007. IEEE Computer Society, USA (2007)

12. Völter, M., Groher, I.: A family of languages for architecture description. In: Proceedings of 8th Workshop on Domain-Specific Modeling (2008)

13. Clements, P., Northrop, L.: Software Product Lines: Practices and Patterns. Addison-Wesley, Boston (2002)

14. Sanchez, P., et al.: VML*–a family of languages for variability management in software product lines. In: Proceedings of SLE. ACM Press (2009)

15. Sendall, S., Kozaczynski, W.: Model transformation: the heart and soul of model-driven software development (2003)

16. Kuhne, T.: What is a model? In: Bezivin, J., Heckel, R. (ed.) Language Engineering for Model-Driven Software Development. No. 04101 in Dagstuhl (2005)

17. Schoofs, T., et al.: An integrated modular avionics development environment. In: Proceedings of 28th Digital Avionics Systems Conference - DASC 2009. IEEE (2009)

ProFit – Performing Dynamic Analysis of Software Systems

Antonio García de la Barrera[(⊠)], María Ángeles Moraga,
Macario Polo, and Ignacio García-Rodríguez de Guzmán

Alarcos Research Group, Institute of Technologies and Information Systems,
University of Castilla-La Mancha, Ciudad Real, Spain
antonio.garcialabarrera@alu.uclm.es,
{mariaangeles.moraga,macario.polo,
ignacio.grodriguez}@uclm.es

Abstract. Dynamic analysis offers the possibility of studying software at runtime, documenting its internal behavior. This dynamic information about the software is very interesting for the purpose of identifying many aspects of its operation, such as detection of dead code, security problems, complexity, and so on. However, not all software systems have the capacity to generate detailed information about what happens at runtime. It is with that consideration in mind that in this work we present ProFit, an environment conceived to improve software with the capacity to generate dynamic information about its execution, thus complementing the static analysis that can be performed on it. ProFit implements two strategies for such purpose: (i) instrumentation of the source code, through the insertion of sentences that generate execution traces in log files, and (ii) automatic generation of aspects for the generation of execution traces. None of those strategies produces any alteration in the behavior of the software, so the information generated truly reflects what happens during the software execution. Finally, the execution logs are represented by means of a tree-like structure that makes it quite easy to implement several kinds of analysis on it.

Keywords: Dynamic analysis · Software maintenance · Execution trace ·
Instrumentation · Aspects

1 Introduction

The Quality of software can be assessed from multiple perspectives [1], obtaining measurements that determine the level of Quality in dimensions such as usability, maintainability, sustainability, performance, etc. [2].

Profiling (analysis of the behavior of the software at runtime) has thus been used not only as a tool to improve the understanding of the systems when performing reverse engineering, but also in the analysis of the energy consumption of the software [3], in the calculation of the degree of coverage in the processes of testing [4], in the detection of bottlenecks hindering the improvement of the performance [5] or in functionality identification of the System Under Analysis (SUA) [6].

© Springer Nature Switzerland AG 2019
M. Piattini et al. (Eds.): QUATIC 2019, CCIS 1010, pp. 255–262, 2019.
https://doi.org/10.1007/978-3-030-29238-6_18

In an effort to assess software system Quality in several dimensions, we are currently developing a toolbox for source code dynamic analysis, made up first of all of a tool (called ProFit) that makes it possible to generate an instrumented copy of a given System Under Analysis. The copy preserves the semantics of the original SUA but generates execution traces at runtime.

Secondly, we will implement a set of tools which will analyze the quality in several dimensions, using the traces left by the instrumented SUA in different executions as input, as illustrated in Fig. 1.

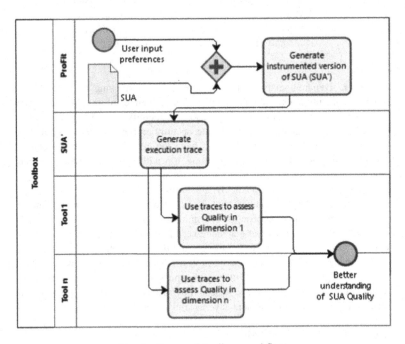

Fig. 1. Proposed toolbox workflow.

In this paper we present ProFit, a profiling tool for Java code that offers the researcher or developer the possibility to instrument the code automatically, allowing a choice of whether the instrumentation is done by the insertion of instructions in the source code, or through the addition of Aspect-oriented Programming (AOP). In addition, the tool enables the analysis options to be parameterized, making it possible to select which components of the system should be analyzed, and what information should be obtained from each one.

The paper is organized as follows: Sect. 2 sets out a general overview of the most important concerns; namely, code instrumentation, object-oriented aspect technique, and existing proposals; Sect. 3 presents the general view of the architecture of ProFit; finally, Sect. 4 outlines several conclusions and ideas as regards future work, as well providing details about the ongoing validation.

2 Background

This section will present the basics of ProFit (source code instrumentation and Aspect-oriented Programming).

2.1 Code Instrumentation

Instrumentation consists in the addition of instructions to the code of a system in such a way that, without modifying its behavior from a functional perspective, traces of execution can be obtained that inform the engineer in great detail of what is happening at any given time. There are many possible purposes for this instrumentation, such as to count the number of cache failures, to calculate the time (and/or energy) invested in a specific region of the code, to study the parameters given to a function, or the values that a variable contains throughout the execution, to name but a few examples [7].

2.2 Aspect-Oriented Programming

AOP has been used extensively to encapsulate non-business, transversal functionalities (like logging, authentication, transactions, etc.) which compromise several domain classes through different object-oriented modules.

"The main idea behind AOP is to consider these operations as crosscutting concerns and to group them into separate modules, which are automatically called by the system" [8]. In the previous state of the art, AOP has been found useful in software Quality assessment [9].

In regard to the present paper, AOP is used as a way of introducing code instructions in the SUA workflow without any direct modification of the source code, thus creating an alternative to direct source code insertions on profiling.

3 Architecture of the Proposal

In this section, the architecture and functionality of the technological framework will be discussed. Firstly, the overall structure will be presented, by a discussion of the different modules and the advantages of the architecture.

3.1 Overall Structure

The proposed architecture faces two challenges which are common to this kind of tools: the extensibility (of source code languages and techniques to instrument) and flexibility (the capacity to configure the instrumentation so as to produce customized execution information).

The main criterion behind the design is scalability. ProFit's design aims for a modularity that enables there to be consistent and ongoing addition of new instrumentation techniques or languages.

On one hand, in order to add the capability of analyzing systems in different languages, a new file for these must be implemented in the analyzer, instrumenter and aspectsGenerator modules, and some additions to the InstrumentationPerformer class need to be made. This is, however, limited to object-oriented languages.

On the other hand, in order to increment the number of instrumentation techniques that ProFit can perform, a new module must be developed. This module containing the technique logic, in conformity with existing interfaces, is placed alongside the already-existing ones.

The current version of ProFit deals with Java, as well as with two techniques to provide SUAs with the execution trace generation functionality: (i) source code insertion and (ii) Aspect-oriented Programming (Fig. 2).

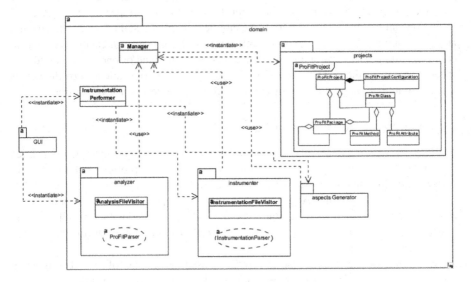

Fig. 2. ProFit overall architecture.

3.2   A Suitable Graphic User Interface

ProFit has a Graphic User Interface (GUI) that allows the user to select the SUA; it shows its structure through a dropdown tree, enabling the user to choose which parts are subject to analysis, as well as to determine a set of "pattern-*statements*". Any method whose name contains one of those *statements* will thus be automatically included in instrumentation.

The GUI also makes it possible for the user to select the parameters which will determine the nature of the instrumentation, namely:

- Regarding attribute operations traces: the user can either write the code to insert directly, or let it be autogenerated, choosing if parameter values are going to be included in the trace.
- Regarding method call traces: the user can either write the code to insert directly, or let it to be autogenerated, choosing if timestamps must be included.
- Regarding output format: the user can choose one or more of the following output formats: console output, .txt file, .csv file and serialized file.

3.3 Analyzer Module: Acquiring Knowledge from SUA

The first task in performing any instrumentation technique is to analyze the Legacy System architecture, so as to acquire the necessary knowledge for the subsequent actions.

For this purpose, ProFit first analyzes the SUA structure recursively, exploring its package and class composition. When a class is found, the system uses a modified parser to explore its code, obtaining the attributes and methods it contains.

Code 1 displays an example class, HelloWorld, designed to illustrate the output of the different instrumentation techniques discussed below.

```
public class HelloWorld {
        static String aString;
        public static void main( String args[] ) {
                salute();
        }
        private static void salute() {
                aString = "Hello world!";
                System.out.println(aString);
        }
}
```

Code 1. HelloWorld.java

3.4 First Strategy: Source Code Insertion

The direct source code insertion technique is based on the use of a second Java parser, created by extending the Java language grammar, as well as on a state machines module.

```
import traceWriter.TraceWriter;

public class HelloWorld {
        static String aString;
        public static void main( String args[] ) {
                salute();
        }
        private static void salute() {
TraceWriter.writeTxt( new MethodCallTrace( /*...*/);
TraceWriter.writeTxt( new FieldSetTrace( /*...*/);
                aString = "Hello world!";
TraceWriter.writeTxt( new FieldSetTrace( /*...*/ );
                System.out.println(aString);
TraceWriter.writeTxt( new MethodCallTrace( /*...*/);
        }
}
```

Code 2. Example class after code insertion.

The workflow is as follows: the parser reads a Java file and from a grammatical perspective identifies the parts of the code which are potentially subject to code insertions related to methods (also specific methods specified in the configuration of the execution trace). From a lexical perspective, those parts which are potentially subject to attribute modification-related code insertions are identified. Then the state machines build, if appropriate, the code line to be inserted.

3.5   Second Strategy: Aspect-Oriented Instrumentation

Aspect-oriented Programming allows cross-cutting functionalities to be added to an already existing system, without any modification to the original code. This is achieved by means of creating a new, autogenerated file, determining the interesting pointcuts in the original code, as well as the behavior when these are reached.

This is implemented by the execution of a grammar file, which, taking the SUA information and user's preferences as inputs, builds a file called *InstrumentationAspect. aj*, and inserts it into the SUA.

```
public aspect InstrumentationAspect {
        public pointcut DynamicMethodCall(Object object) : (
                        ( call(* HelloWorld.salute(..)) && target(object))
        );
        public pointcut AttributeOperation() : (
                        ( set(* HelloWorld.aString))
        );
        before(Object object) : DynamicMethodCall(object) {
                MethodCallTrace methodCall = new
        MethodCallTrace(/*...*/);
                        TraceWriter.writeTxt(methodCall);
        }
        // [...]
}
```

Code 3. Aspect file autogenerated for the example class.

The source code presented in **Code 3** displays an example of the generated file, taking as inputs the example file, HelloWorld.java, and the selection of the attribute "*String aString*" and the method "*void salute()*" by the user, who also determines the log to be stored as a.txt file.

3.6   Management of the Persistence of the Execution Traces

ProFit offers the user four different log output file types, namely: console output, .txt file, .csv file and serialized.txt.

The first three come in a more verbose, human-readable format, similar to JSON[1] (but without nested values, and thus incomplete). Serialized output is a non-human-readable, but recursive (and thus complete) format, designed to be loaded and visualized on a work-in-progress trace analysis system.

---

[1] https://www.json.org/.

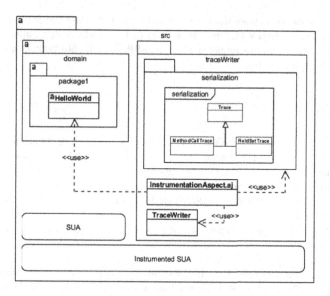

Fig. 3. SUA structure after aspect-oriented instrumentation.

In order to achieve this, a new package is inserted into the SUA, containing a class, called TraceWriter; this class, with a single instance, receives all the traces from the SUA and creates the files necessary to execute the persistence.

In the same package, moreover, a data structure is added, in order to represent the traces, as illustrated in Fig. 3.

4   Conclusions

This paper presents ProFit, a profiling tool to improve software systems developed in Java, with the capability of generating configurable execution traces. ProFit implements two strategies for profiling: (i) source code instrumentation and (ii) use of aspects. The result is a functionally equivalent software system that generates information about its execution in the form of log files when it runs.

This is verified by means of the instrumentation of a system with a 95.5% coverage test suite, and the execution of both the original system tests and those of the instrumented one, checking that the test results remain the same. The log created by the instrumented system during tests is also evaluated, verifying that it properly contains the required information about the system execution.

Regarding future (and ongoing) work, these traces will later be transformed into an execution tree that will be used to perform various types of analysis related to the measurement of some of the dimensions of Quality.

Case studies are currently being carried out both on open-source systems and on tools provided by companies, seeking to identify Quality defects that can be detected only at runtime.

Acknowledgements. This work has been funded by the TESTIMO and SOS projects (Consejería de Educación, Cultura y Deportes de la Junta de Comunidades de Castilla La Mancha, y Fondo Europeo de Desarrollo Regional FEDER, SBPLY/17/180501/000503 and SBPLY/17/180501/000364, respectively).

References

1. ISO: ISO/IEC 25000 - Requisitos y Evaluación de Calidad de Productos de Software (SQuaRE - System and Software Quality Requirements and Evaluation), International Organization for Standarization, Ginebra (2005)
2. ISO: ISO/IEC 25040. Systems and Software Engineering – Systems and software Quality Requirements and Evaluation (SQuaRE) – Evaluation Process, International Organization for Standarization, Ginebra (2011)
3. Jagroep, E.A., et al.: Software energy profiling: comparing releases of a software product. In: Proceedings of the 38th International Conference on Software Engineering Companion, New York, NY, USA, pp. 523–532 (2016)
4. Tikir, M.M., Hollingsworth, J.K.: Efficient instrumentation for code coverage testing. In: Proceedings of the 2002 ACM SIGSOFT International Symposium on Software Testing and Analysis, New York, NY, USA, pp. 86–96 (2002)
5. Shen, D., Luo, Q., Poshyvanyk, D., Grechanik, M.: Automating performance bottleneck detection using search-based application profiling. In: Proceedings of the 2015 International Symposium on Software Testing and Analysis, New York, NY, USA, pp. 270–281 (2015)
6. Del Grosso, C., Di Penta, M., de Guzman, I.G.-R.: An approach for mining services in database oriented applications, pp. 287–296 (2007)
7. Tirado-Ramos, A., et al.: Computational Science – ICCS 2009: 9th International Conference Baton Rouge, LA, USA, May 25-27, 2009 Proceedings, Part II, 1st edn. Springer, Heidelberg (2009). https://doi.org/10.1007/978-3-642-01973-9
8. Jacques Pasquier, P.F.: Mini-proceedings of the master seminar advanced software engineering topics: aspect oriented programming. University of Fribourg (2006)
9. Soni, G., Tomar, P., Upadhyay, A.: Analysis of software quality attributes through aspect-oriented programming (2013)

Code Smells Survival Analysis in Web Apps

Américo Rio[1,2(✉)] and Fernando Brito e Abreu[1]

[1] ISTAR-IUL, ISCTE-IUL, Lisbon, Portugal
{jaasr, fba}@iscte-iul.pt
[2] NOVAIMS, UNL, Lisbon, Portugal
americo.rio@novaims.unl.pt

Abstract. Web applications are heterogeneous, both in their target platform (split across client and server sides) and on the formalisms they are built with, usually a mixture of programming and formatting languages. This heterogeneity is perhaps an explanation why software evolution of web applications (apps) is a poorly addressed topic in the literature. In this paper we focus on web apps built with PHP, the most widely used server-side programming language.

We analyzed the evolution of 6 code smells in 4 web applications, using the survival analysis technique. Since code smells are symptoms of poor design, it is relevant to study their survival, that is, how long did it take from their introduction to their removal. It is obviously desirable to minimize their survival.

In our analysis we split code smells in two categories: scattered smells and localized smells, since we expect the former to be more harmful than the latter. Our results provide some evidence that the survival of PHP code smells depends on their spreadness.

We have also analyzed whether the survival curve varies in the long term, for the same web application. Due to the increasing awareness on the potential harmfulness of code smells, we expected to observe a reduction in the survival rate in the long term. The results show that there is indeed a change, for all applications except one, which lead us to consider that other factors should be analyzed in the future, to explain the phenomenon.

Keywords: Code smells · PHP · Software evolution · Survival analysis · Web apps

1 Motivation

This study is in the crossroads of Software Evolution [1, 2] and Web Engineering [3, 4] and is a follow-up of our preliminary work on the evolution of web systems/ applications, regarding maintainability and reliability problems [5, 6]. Web applications (web apps, for short) encompass a heterogeneity of target platforms, since they run both on a browser and a server, and a mix of programming and content formatting languages. That mix makes web apps a more complex target for software quality studies, either synchronic or diachronic (longitudinal), because those studies are often based on static analysis of source code, as is the case with code smells research. Indeed, for each language used (e.g. *JavaScript, HTML, CSS, PHP*) a different parser is

© Springer Nature Switzerland AG 2019
M. Piattini et al. (Eds.): QUATIC 2019, CCIS 1010, pp. 263–271, 2019.
https://doi.org/10.1007/978-3-030-29238-6_19

required, what may explain why software evolution of web apps is a poorly addressed topic in the literature, as we will see later.

Several perspectives can be adopted in longitudinal studies, were the evolution of software products or processes are analyzed, focusing on aspects such as software metrics, teams' activity, defects identification and correction, or time to release [7, 8]. This paper addresses the survival of code smells in web apps using PHP, the main server-side programming language, currently used in 79% of web apps[1]. Since code smells occurrences are symptoms of poor design and implementation choices, the Software Engineering community has been thriving to reduce their survival, i.e., how long does it take from when they were introduced to when they are removed, by proposing new detection techniques and tools [9, 10]. Despite this interest, there is a shortage of evolution studies on code smells in web apps, especially with PHP [11, 12].

The research described herein covers two factors: scope and period. Code smells effect can vary widely in spreadness. In localized ones, the scope is a method or a class (e.g. *Long Method, Long Parameter List, God Class*), while the influence of others may be scattered across large portions of a software system (e.g. *Shotgun Surgery, Deep Inheritance Hierarchies or Coupling Between Classes*). Since widespread code smells can cause more damage than localized ones, we expect their survival rates to be shorter. The other factor we are concerned with regards a superordinate temporal analysis. Since the topic of code smells has been addressed by researchers, taught at universities and discussed by practitioners over the last two decades, we want to investigate whether this had an impact on their survival. We expect that, in a long term, an increased awareness has caused a more proactive attitude towards code smells detection and removal (through refactoring actions), thus leading to shorter survival rates. Summing up, we aim at testing the following two null research hypotheses:

– H_{0X}: *Survival does not depend of the code smells scope.*
– H_{0Y}: *Survival of a given code smell does not change over time period.*

To test these hypotheses, we performed a longitudinal study encompassing 4 web apps, and 6 code smells, as surrogates of more scattered or localized scopes.

This paper is structured as follows: Sect. 2 introduces the study design; Sect. 3 describes the results of our data analysis; Sect. 4 overviews the related work and Sect. 5 outlines the major conclusions and identifies required future work.

2 Study Design

2.1 Aim of the Study

The aim of this work is to study the evolution/survival of code smells in web apps built with PHP in the server-side. We selected a set of applications from different domains, a set of 6 code smells, and collected data across all their stable development versions.

---

[1] https://w3techs.com/technologies/overview/programming_language/all (accessed: June 2019).

2.2   Applications Sampling

Inclusion criteria: (i) fully blown web apps taken from the GitHub top listings, (ii) programmed with object-oriented style[2], (iii) covering a diversity of application areas.

Exclusion criteria: (i) libraries, (ii) frameworks, (iii) web apps built using a framework (Table 1).

Table 1. Characterization of the target web apps

Web app	Purpose	Versions	Period	LOC	Classes
phpmyadmin	Database manager	158	Aug 2010–Jun 2018	89788	374
dukuwiki	Wiki solution	40	July 2005–Jan 2019	271514	402
opencart	Shopping cart solution	28	April 2013– April 2019	99052	760
phpbb	Forum/bulletin board solution	50	April 2012–Jan 2018	101556	846

2.3   Code Smells Sampling

We used PHPMD [13], the only open source tool, we are aware of, that is capable of detecting scattered and localized code smells in PHP. It supports 3 scattered code smells, so we chose the same number of localized ones, although more were available (Table 2).

Table 2. Characterization of the target code smells

Code Smell	Characterization	Type
ExcessiveMethodLength	The method does too much	Localized
ExcessiveClassLength	The class does too much	Localized
ExcessiveParameterList	The method has too many parameters	Localized
DepthOfInheritance	The class is too deep in the inheritance tree	Scattered
CouplingBetweenObjects	The class has too many dependencies	Scattered
NumberOfChildren	The class has too many descendants	Scattered

2.4   Design of the Study

The workflow of our study (see Fig. 1) was fully automated by means of batch and PHP scripts. First, all versions of the selected web apps were downloaded from *GitHub*, except the alpha, beta, release candidates and corrections for old versions. Then, using

---

[2] Note: PHP can be used in a pure procedural way.

the PHPMD tool, we extracted the location of the code smells from all versions and stored it in XML file format. After some format manipulation, the information on those XML files was stored in a database, to make it amenable for survival analysis. That includes the date when each code smell was first detected and, if that was the case, when it disappeared, either due to refactoring, or because the code where it was detected was (at least apparently) removed. Survival analysis took the input data from the database and stored the results in it too. Finally, a data completion step was performed, where results were exported to csv format, for interoperability with visualization tools.

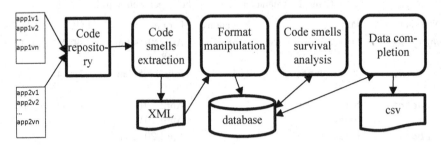

Fig. 1. Workflow of the study

2.5   Survival Analysis

Survival analysis encompasses a set of statistical approaches that investigate the time of interest for an event to occur [14]. The questions of interest can be the average survival time, and the probability of survival at a certain point in time. Also, we can calculate the Hazard function, the probability of the event to occur.

The Kaplan-Meier estimator is a non-parametric statistic that allows us to estimate the survival function and it gives the probability that a given code smell will subsist/exist past a time t. The log-rank test is used to compare survival curves of two groups, in our case two types of code smells. It tests the null hypothesis that survival curves of two populations do not differ by computing a p-value (statistical significance). In our analysis we will consider a confidence interval of 95%, corresponding to an observed significance level (known as p-value) of 0.05 for the test hypotheses.

Data Extraction and Processing, and Format for Survival Analysis

To apply survival data analysis, we transformed the collection of detected code smells instances for each version of each web app, to a table with the "life" of each instance, including the date of its first appearance, removal date (if occurred) and a censoring value, with the following meaning:

Censoring = 1 ⇒ the smell disappeared, usually due to a refactoring event;
Censoring = 0 ⇒ the code smell is still present at the end of the observation period.

For replication purposes, the collected dataset is made available for other researchers[3].

---

[3] https://github.com/americorio/articledata/.

3 Results and Data Analysis

To test the hypotheses, we used the R tool and the log-rank test [15]. We performed two kinds of studies, using the log-rank test and 2 different co-variables.

3.1 Comparing the Survival Curves for Different Types of Code Smells

For this study we divided the smells in "Localized Smells" and "Scattered Smells" (Table 3). We then fitted the Kaplan-Meier curves and performed the log-rank to compute the p-value.

Table 3. Code smells found, removed and survival in days (median and mean), by type.

Web app	Type	Found	Removed	Median(d)	Mean(d)
phpmyadmin	Localized smells	1067	846	707	744
	Scattered smells	34	23	324	424
dokuwiki	Localized smells	159	112	1381	2169
	Scattered smells	6	2	620	2779
opencart	Localized smells	798	393	1189	1281
	Scattered smells	12	0	NA	2172
phpbb	Localized smells	747	393	2512	2255
	Scattered smells	20	2	NA	2537

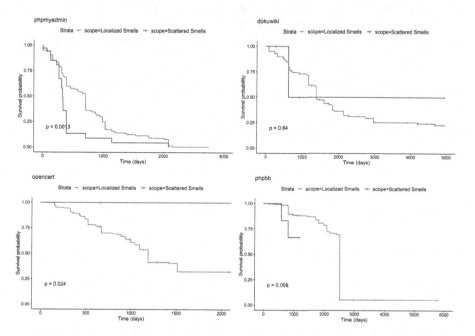

Fig. 2. Survival curves of localized and scattered code smells, by application.

For *phpMyAdmin* and *opencart*, the survival curves of scattered smells differ significantly from those of localized smells (see Fig. 2). For *phpbb*, the curves differ, but not with statistical significance (given the considered confidence interval). For *dokuwiki*, the study is inconclusive, since only 2 scattered code smells are removed. It is worth noticing that localized code smells are much more frequent targets for change than scattered code smells. This may be due to the lack of refactoring tools that support the automated removal of scattered code smells in PHP.

3.2   Comparing Code Smells Survival Curves for Different Time Frames

Here we used the log-rank test, and created a co-variate "timeframe", with two values 1 and 2, 1 being the first half of historic data, and 2 the second half. For the first half, we truncated the variables of the study as if it was a sub-study ending in this period. In other words, we considered two independent observation periods (Table 4).

Table 4. Code smells found, removed and survival in days (median and mean) by timeframe.

Web app	Timeframe	Found	Removed	Median(d)	Mean(d)
phpmyadmin	1 (<2014-07-01)	498	393	946	787
	2 (≥2014-07-01)	603	371	451	473
dokuwiki	1 (<2012-04-03)	94	53	2139	1582
	2 (≥2012-04-03)	71	52	1381	1352
opencart	1 (<2016-03-31)	496	276	1016	794
	2 (≥2016-03-31)	314	35	NA	966
phpbb	1 (<2015-02-15)	685	79	NA	986
	2 (≥2015-02-15)	82	1	NA	952

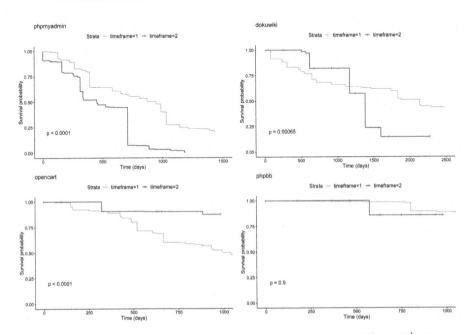

Fig. 3. Code smells survival curves in two consecutive timeframes (1st and 2nd half)

For all projects except *phpbb*, the survival curves of the 1st timeframe differ significantly from the 2nd one (see Fig. 3). In *phpMyAdmin* and *dokuwiki* the area under the code smells survival curves is smaller in the 2nd timeframe, what seems to corroborates our expectation that, due to the increasing awareness on the potential harmfulness of code smells, we would observe a reduction in the code smells survival rate in the long term. However, for *opencart* and *phpbb*, we cannot draw the same conclusion, probably because the number of detected and removed code smells is much smaller.

4   Related Work

In [11], the authors study five web apps in PHP, the aspects of their history, unused code, the removal of functions, the use of libraries, the stability of interfaces, migration to object-orientation and the evolution of complexity. They found these systems undergo systematic maintenance.

In [12], the authors analyze 30 PHP projects for their metrics, to examine if the Lehman's laws of evolution are maintained in an web app, and found that not all of them stand true for this kind of projects.

In [16], the authors analyze two Java open source systems and four code smells, in a longitudinal study with versions. They study the evolution of code smells, including their persistence, and do survival analysis to find the average time of persistence.

In [17], after a survey to developers, the authors analyze when test smells occur in source code, what their survivability is, and whether their presence is associated with the presence of design problems in production code (code smells). They found, among other conclusions, relationships between test and code smells. They extracted data from a Git repository from 3 ecosystems making a total of 152 projects. They employ, among other techniques, survival analysis to study the longevity of test smells.

In [18] the authors address the faults in the releases of five JavaScript projects (1 framework, 2 libraries and 2 command line programs) and try to relate them to 12 types of code smells. They employ survival analysis for the faults.

The techniques used to extract the code for further analysis are divided in mining software repositories and getting full versions or mining Git repositories for the changes. However, to compute scattered code smells, we had to deal with the full code. For smells based only on metrics for the file, the Git extraction is simpler to automate.

5   Conclusions

As far as we know, this is the first study analyzing code smells in PHP web apps. We studied the evolution of 6 groups of code smells, in 4 web applications built with PHP.

For the first hypothesis we found that the code smells survival curves indeed vary with the type of code smell, localized or scattered. We also found that the insertion and removal events are much lower for the scattered code smells. Nevertheless, for PHP web apps developed with object-oriented paradigm, it is not enough to study localized smells in the file scope, but we also must address the smells that are scattered across the system, since the latter are potentially more harmful.

For the second hypothesis results, in 3 of the applications the survival curve varies between timeframes, but for one (*phpbb*) we do not observe this variance. This can be explained by the low relative removal of code smells compared to the other applications. We cannot fully sustain that the long-term reduction in survival rate of code smells in PHP web apps is due to the awareness on potential code smells harmfulness. Other factors should be analyzed in the future, to explain the phenomenon.

The biggest validity threats are: there should be a bigger number of apps and smells studied; perceive if applications that implemented OOP gradually, impact the study.

In Memoriam Acknowledgment. We are grateful to the late Professor Rui Menezes (deceased 14 May 2019), whose contribution to this work was of great significance. He encouraged and supported us on the usage of survival analysis techniques and inspired us with his enthusiasm.

References

1. Mens, T., Demeyer, S. (eds.): Software Evolution. Springer, Heidelberg (2006)
2. Madhavji, N.H. et al.: Software evolution and feedback. Wiley Online Library (2006)
3. Rossi, G., Pastor, O., Schwabe, D., Olsina, L.: Web Engineering: Modelling and Implementing Web Applications. Springer, London (2007). https://doi.org/10.1007/978-1-84628-923-1
4. Mendes, E., Mosley, N.: Web Engineering. Springer, Heidelberg (2006). https://doi.org/10.1007/3-540-28218-1
5. Rio, A., Brito e Abreu, F.: Analyzing web applications quality evolution. In: Iberian Conference on Information Systems and Technologies, CISTI, pp. 1–4. IEEE (2017)
6. Rio, A., Brito e Abreu, F.: Web systems quality evolution. In: QUATIC, pp. 248–253. IEEE (2016)
7. Herraiz, I., Rodriguez, D., Robles, G., Gonzalez-Barahona, J.M.: The evolution of the laws of software evolution: a discussion based on a systematic literature review. ACM Comput. Surv. **46**, 28 (2013)
8. Radjenović, D., Heričko, M., Torkar, R., Živkovič, A.: Software fault prediction metrics: a systematic literature review. Inf. Softw. Technol. **55**, 1397–1418 (2013)
9. Zhang, M., Hall, T., Baddoo, N.: Code bad smells: a review of current knowledge. J. Softw. Maint. Evol. Res. Pract. **23**, 179–202 (2011)
10. Fernandes, E., Oliveira, J., Vale, G., Paiva, T., Figueiredo, E.: A review-based comparative study of bad smell detection tools. In: Proceedings of the 20th International Conference on Evaluation and Assessment in Software Engineering, p. 18. ACM (2016)
11. Kyriakakis, P., Chatzigeorgiou, A.: Maintenance patterns of large-scale PHP web applications. In: 2014 IEEE International Conference on Software Maintenance and Evolution, pp. 381–390 (2014). https://doi.org/10.1109/icsme.2014.60
12. Amanatidis, T., Chatzigeorgiou, A.: Studying the evolution of PHP web applications. Inf. Softw. Technol. **72**, 48–67 (2016). https://doi.org/10.1016/j.infsof.2015.11.009
13. Tufano, M., et al.: When and why your code starts to smell bad (2015)
14. Clark, T.G., Bradburn, M.J., Love, S.B., Altman, D.G.: Survival analysis part I: basic concepts and first analyses. Br. J. Cancer **89**, 232 (2003)

15. Schuette, D.: Survival analysis in R tutorial (article) – DataCamp. https://www.datacamp.com/community/tutorials/survival-analysis-R
16. Chatzigeorgiou, A., Manakos, A.: Investigating the evolution of bad smells in object-oriented code. In: 2010 Seventh International Conference on the Quality of Information and Communications Technology (QUATIC), pp. 106–115. IEEE (2010)
17. Tufano, M., et al.: An empirical investigation into the nature of test smells. In: 2016 31st IEEE/ACM International Conference on Automated Software Engineering (ASE), pp. 4–15 (2016)
18. Saboury, A., Musavi, P., Khomh, F., Antoniol, G.: An empirical study of code smells in JavaScript projects. In: 2017 IEEE 24th International Conference on Software Analysis, Evolution and Reengineering (SANER), pp. 294–305 (2017)

Data Science and Services

Evaluation of Maritime Event Detection Against Missing Data

Maximilian Zocholl[1(✉)], Clément Iphar[1], Manolis Pitsikalis[2(✉)], Anne-Laure Jousselme[1(✉)], Alexander Artikis[2,3(✉)], and Cyril Ray[4(✉)]

[1] NATO STO Centre for Maritime Research and Experimentation,
La Spezia, Italy
{maximilian.zocholl,clement.iphar,anne-laure.jousselme}@cmre.nato.int
[2] NCSR Demokritos, Athens, Greece
manospits@iit.demokritos.gr
[3] University of Piraeus, Piraeus, Greece
a.artikis@unipi.gr
[4] Naval Academy Research Institute, Brest, France
cyril.ray@ecole-navale.fr

Abstract. Detecting and preventing maritime events like collisions or unusual behaviour of vessels are of high importance for maritime safety and security. As the trust of human operators in automated maritime event detection and prediction depends on the quality of the corresponding algorithms, the evaluation methodology becomes a driving force for the future development of maritime event detection and forecasting methods. The main contribution of this article consists in the development of an evaluation methodology and its application to a selected set of maritime event detectors. The approach links a reference dataset, controlled data variations, maritime event detection algorithms with internal parameters, and performance criteria. Among pre-established possible input data variations applied to a reference Automatic Identification System (AIS) dataset, the article focuses on the evaluation of detection accuracy of maritime event detectors implemented with the Event Calculus logical language against variable amounts of missing data, as a frequently observable type of AIS data degradation. Twelve maritime event pattern detectors are evaluated and most of them are found to vary very little in performance while only one detector shows an unexpected strong performance drop giving insights into how to improve the detection method. Results are provided on a real AIS data enriched with specific simulated events.

Keywords: Evaluation methodology · Maritime event detection · Event Calculus · Datasets creation · Missing data · Data veracity

1 Introduction

In the maritime domain Automatic Identification Systems (AIS) installed on vessels transmit periodically position, speed and other information about the

© Springer Nature Switzerland AG 2019
M. Piattini et al. (Eds.): QUATIC 2019, CCIS 1010, pp. 275–288, 2019.
https://doi.org/10.1007/978-3-030-29238-6_20

vessel [6]. Primarily designed for collision avoidance purposes, AIS data became important for a broad range of detection, prediction and forecasting applications. For the beneficial exploitation of the large amount of AIS data received by base stations and satellites, scalable data processing solutions are required that increase and speed up the maritime situational awareness of human operators.

As operators trust only on antecedent data processing units that yield high data quality, their evaluation requires a meaningful methodological basis. Existing evaluation methods underline the importance of considering imprecise real-world conditions [11]. A comparison of evaluation methods is proposed by [9]. Based on uncertainty representations, the impact of different imputation strategies on the retrieval performance on incomplete data is characterised in [7]. An evaluation method for classifiers used on classes with strongly varying occurrence probabilities and costs for misclassifications is presented in [10]. While the creation of training and testing datasets is always expensive due to manual labelling work, the creation of maritime training and testing datasets requires subject matter experts and additionally has to rely on assumptions. This is necessary as scarce maritime events are only partially observable via AIS data, which has unknown quality and can be incomplete. The evaluation of computer vision based maritime event detectors using synthetic track generation with position and speed information is proposed by [4]. An evaluation method for maritime event visualisation proposes [14].

The article proposes an evaluation method using missing data mechanisms, as initially classified by [16], and applies them to AIS messages. The main contribution of the presented work is the meaningful combination and articulation of data variation method and evaluation methods and criteria. The article is divided in three parts, firstly maritime situational indicators are presented as a list of maritime events of interest, followed by a description of an implementation of a subset of detectors of these indicators. The second section describes the data variation methodology for the systematic and reproducible creation of testing or training data with known veracity variation, here performed as a reduction of AIS messages for each vessel. The third section presents and discusses the results obtained. Future perspectives and a summary conclude the contribution to the use of AIS data for the evaluation of maritime events detection.

2   Maritime Events

For operators in a maritime surveillance mission maritime events are typically observable only indirectly via a collection of incomplete data which comes from different sources and has different values of veracity. The interpretation of the data in the maritime context results in a maritime situational awareness. As different sources can possibly give different, even contradicting information, the distinction between a type of maritime event, introduced in the following under the notion of maritime situational indicators (MSI) and its subsequently presented implementation is crucial.

2.1   Maritime Situational Indicators (MSI)

Maritime situational indicators (MSI) are intended to alert an operator observing a maritime situation about important changes, hence to filter information and to drive the operators attention to a specific location in the surveillance area.

Table 1. List of maritime situational indicators.

#	Maritime situational indicator	#	Maritime situational indicator
1	Close to critical infrastructure	15	No AIS reception
2	Within a given area	16	AIS reception interrupted
3	On a maritime route	17	Change in AIS static information
4	Proximity to other vessels	18	AIS error detection
5	In stationary area	19	Under way
6	Null speed	20	At anchor or moored
7	Change of speed	21	Movement ability affected
8	Mismatch speed area	22	Aground
9	Mismatch speed vessel type	23	Engaged in fishing
10	Mismatch speed vessel history	24	Tugging
11	Mismatch speed user defined value	25	In Search And Rescue (SAR) operation
12	Change of course	26	Loitering
13	Mismatch course vessel destination	27	Dead in water, drifting
14	Mismatch course user defined value	28	Rendez-vous

The list of MSIs shown in Table 1 is a synthesis of outcomes of workshops gathering user's elicitation and reported in the literature e.g. [1, 15]. These MSIs have then been filtered according to their ability to be automatically detected or predicted through the processing of AIS data. For instance, any MSI referring to visual sighting has been excluded from this list. In this paper the implementation of detectors for the MSIs 2, 6, 7, 8, 9, 16, 19, 21 as well as five speed related building blocks are evaluated.

2.2   Complex Event Recognition with RTEC

The 'Event Calculus for Run-Time reasoning' (RTEC) [2,3] is an open-source Prolog implementation of the Event Calculus [8], designed to compute continuous narrative assimilation queries for pattern matching on data streams. RTEC has a formal, declarative semantics—complex patterns are (locally) stratified logic programs [12]. Moreover, RTEC includes optimisation techniques for efficient pattern matching, such as 'windowing', whereby all input events that took place prior to the current window are discarded/'forgotten'. Details about the reasoning algorithms of RTEC, including a complexity analysis, may be found in [3].

Table 2. Main predicates of RTEC. '$F = V$' denotes that fluent F has value V.

Predicate	Meaning
happensAt(E, T)	Event E occurs at time T
holdsAt($F = V, T$)	The value of fluent F is V at time T
holdsFor($F = V, I$)	I is the list of the maximal intervals for which $F = V$ holds continuously
initiatedAt($F = V, T$)	At time T a period of time for which $F = V$ is initiated
terminatedAt($F = V, T$)	At time T a period of time for which $F = V$ is terminated
union_all(L, I)	I is the list of maximal intervals produced by the union of the lists of maximal intervals of list L
intersect_all(L, I)	I is the list of maximal intervals produced by the intersection of the lists of maximal intervals of list L
relative_complement_all(I', L, I)	I is the list of maximal intervals produced by the relative complement of the list of maximal intervals I' with respect to every list of maximal intervals of list L

The time model in RTEC is linear and includes integer time-points. An *event description* includes rules that define the event instances with the use of the happensAt predicate, the effects of events on *fluents*—time-varying properties—with the use of the initiatedAt and terminatedAt predicates, and the values of the fluents with the use of the holdsAt and holdsFor predicates. Table 2 summarises the main predicates of RTEC.

Fluents are 'simple' or 'statically determined'. In brief, simple fluents are defined by means of initiatedAt and terminatedAt rules, while statically determined fluents are defined by means of application-dependent holdsFor rules, along with the interval manipulation constructs of RTEC: union_all, intersect_all and relative_complement_all. See Table 2 for a brief explanation of these constructs and Fig. 1 for an example visualisation. Complex events/activities are typically durative; thus the task generally is to compute the maximal intervals for which a fluent expressing a complex activity has a particular value continuously.

3   Dataset Variations

3.1   Notations

The generation of pseudo-synthetic datasets requires an original AIS dataset to which is applied a series of modifications that will be presented in Sect. 3.2.

In the remaining of this paper, let us denote by D the set of datasets. As to provide a common frame for the data pseudo-synthesis functions, let us denote by

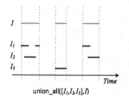 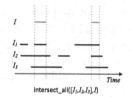 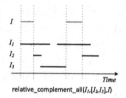

Fig. 1. A visual illustration of the interval manipulation constructs of RTEC. In these examples, there are three input streams, I_1, I_2 and I_3, coloured black. The output of each interval manipulation construct I is coloured light blue. (Color figure online)

X_n^m a dataset containing n rows and m columns. Original datasets are denoted by $\bar{X}$, and synthetic datasets are denoted by $\widehat{X}$.

All operations performed on those datasets in this paper are presented by a series of functions $f_k : D \rightarrow D$. We denote by x_i^j the value of the jth column of the ith entry.

3.2 Data Variation Functions of Interest

Three Families of Functions

Three main families of data pseudo-synthesis functions are distinguished: the data improvement, the degradation and the event injection [5]. Data improvement increases the data veracity level, by the addition of attributes (add columns by labelling operation) or the addition of contacts (add rows that were sent but not received by the antenna). Data degradation lowers the data veracity level, by removing whole data attributes (columns), whole contacts (rows) or adding noise in data (field values are blurred in accordance with a chosen probabilistic model). The removal can be targeted on a trajectory or follow a law (linear decrease with the distance or uniform for instance). Event injection modifies the "story" that the data tells, by contact addition. This addition can consist of either the injection of a spatio-temporal shift of a trajectory already existing in the dataset or the targeted injection of synthetic data directly in the existing fields. The injection of synthetic events consists in the synthesis of specifically designed contacts in order to create maritime events depending on a handful of parameters and providing a high flexibility in the precise modelling of a wanted situation.

Assign Function

The assign function is an event injection function having, in our case, the purpose to better fit existing data to a given scenario. This function takes a given data field and changes its value, either by applying a given offset to the previously existing value, or by replacing the value by a fixed value.

The parameters that can be set in this function are: the mode μ (μ_o in case of offset, μ_v in case of fixed value assignment), the value V to be used as assigned value or offset, the data field (column) of application c, the set of messages A

(rows) to which this assignment must be performed. The nature of the value V depends on the nature of the data within the field c, as numeric fields must be assigned numeric values and categorical data must be assigned valid categories. The set of messages A which are processed can be a list of id number of messages, a list of MMSI number (unique ship identifier) of interest or a random subsample of such.

$$f_a(\mu, c, A, V) : \ \bar{X}_n^m \mapsto \widehat{X}_n^m \tag{1}$$

where $\bar{X}_n^m = X_{Card(A)}^{\prime m} \frown X_{n-Card(A)}^{\prime\prime m}$ and $\widehat{X}_n^m = \widehat{X}_{Card(A)}^{\prime m} \frown X_{n-Card(A)}^{\prime\prime m}$, where $\frown$ denotes the append operation.

The operation from $X_{Card(A)}^{\prime m}$ to $\widehat{X}_{Card(A)}^{\prime m}$ is described as such: $x_{i \in A}^{j=c} \mapsto \widehat{x}_{i \in A}^{j=c}$ where $\forall i \in A \ \widehat{x}_i^c = V$ if $\mu = \mu_v$ and $\widehat{x}_i^c = x_i^c + V$ if $\mu = \mu_o$.

Event function
The event function is an event creation function, of which the purpose is to synthesise new entries in the dataset in order to generate a given event of interest. Currently, the events available are the collision, the near-collision and the rendezvous, the latter being the voluntary meeting of two vessels at sea defined in three steps: the approach, the co-location (with variable duration) and the separation. The addition of such events, rare in the real world, is crucial in the understanding of maritime behaviours and maritime security.

The main parameters here are the number n and the kind of event E wanted. Then, according to the kind of event, other specific parameters p can be set, for instance for targeting a specific point of real data, choosing the angle of approach, the angle of departure or the time of rendezvousing.

As of today, $E \in \{C, NC, R\}$, respectively standing for Collision, Near-Collision and Rendezvous, with specific parameters associated p_C, p_{NC} and p_R. For instance, p_C is a table of k specific parameters (currently five: targeted point, angle of approach, speed of approach, identity and nature of synthetic vessel) each being a vector of n values, *i.e.* one for each of the events created.

$$f_e(n, E, p) : \ \bar{X}_n^m \mapsto \widehat{X}_{n+Card(E)}^m \tag{2}$$

where $\widehat{X}_{n+Card(E)}^m = \bar{X}_n^m \frown \widehat{X}_{Card(E)}^m$, $\widehat{X}_{Card(E)}^m$ standing for the newly created event data. $Card(E)$ is not a fixed number, and it varies accordingly with the number, nature and specific local conditions of the created events.

Remove Function
The remove function is a data degradation function, the purpose of which is to decrease the dataset size by removing entire rows of data.

The parameters to define are the subset of interest α, the nature of data to be removed A (following the same rules that the one from assign function) and the nature N of the removal. This nature N can define the grounds on which data is removed, *i.e.* either totally at random (MCAR) or based on the simulation of a natural process (MAR, such as the distance to the receiving station in the case of a reception simulation), or targeting on the base of some data fields values

(MNAR, e.g. remove messages of speed inferior to a given threshold). In our case, $A = A_p$ is a set of messages defined by the percentage p of data not to remove.

$$f_\rho(\alpha, A_p, N) : \bar{X}^m_n \mapsto \widehat{X}^m_{n-Card(A_p)} \tag{3}$$

where $\bar{X}^m_n = \widehat{X}^m_{n-Card(A_p)} \frown X'^m_{Card(A_p)}$, from which $X'^m_{Card(A_p)}$ dataset has been removed. N is user-defined and $Card(A_p)$ is defined with respect to α such as $\forall j \in [1, J]$, L_j is one MMSI in the list L of all MMSI in α, $Card(A_p) = \sum_{j=1}^J \lceil p * Card(L_j) \rceil$, p being the parameter defined for A, as described above.

3.3   Dataset Generation

Let us denote by X_α the source dataset, consisting of two subsets X_β and X_γ such as $X_\alpha = X_\beta \frown X_\gamma$. X_β and X_γ each consist of 30 min of recorded data excerpted from a source AIS dataset [13]. Each dataset contains rows (AIS messages) and columns (parameters). X_β action takes place in the Brest roadstead while X_γ is located in the Four channel, off the Brittany coast, in France, as shown in Fig. 3.

In this section, let us simplify the notation of datasets by removing the number of rows and columns: $\widehat{X}^m_n = \widehat{X}$. Across this paper, no column modification is made and the value remains constant at $m = 11$. Rows modifications occur at several stages, and the value taken by n is indicated in Fig. 3 and Table 3.

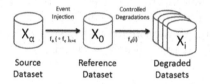

Fig. 2. Datasets generation workflow

This source dataset was then enriched by a total of four events, with one rendezvous, one collision and two near-collisions, as well as a series of data assignment on speed values to preexisting data so that the presented scenario is consistent. Les us denote by X_0 the resulting dataset, generated such as:

$$\widehat{X}_0 = \left(f_a(\mu_v, speed, A, V) \circ f_e(2, NC, p_{NC}) \circ f_e(1, R, p_R) \circ f_e(1, C, p_C)\right)(X_\alpha) \tag{4}$$

where A is the subset of interest for specific speed modification (in order to better fit preexisting data to the scenario created by the event injection), V is a vector of those assigned speeds, p_{NC}, p_R and p_C the parameters of the event functions, not explicitly described here and $n_{(\widehat{X}_0)} = n_{(X_\alpha)} + \sum_{i=1}^4 Card(E_i)$.

From now on, $\widehat{X}_0$ will be considered as the reference dataset. The data within this dataset is presented in Fig. 3. From this reference dataset, a series of

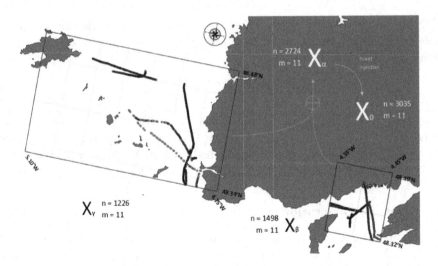

Fig. 3. The $\widehat{X}_0$ reference dataset, with the two boundary boxes of the areas from which X_β and X_γ are excerpted. Each point is a contact, either original ($\in X_\alpha$) or synthetic ($\in \widehat{X}_0 \backslash X_\alpha$). Each colour stands for a unique MMSI value in each box. For each dataset, m and n stand for the number of columns and rows (Colour figure online).

degraded datasets will be generated, using the remove function. Three levels of degradation are performed on data: the removal of 10, 20 and 30% of data from each unique MMSI number. A total of five datasets for each level of degradation are produced. All generated datasets are different because of the random nature of the data removal process random draw of $\lceil p * Card(n_{MMSI}) \rceil$ values amongst the n_{MMSI} messages sent by each unique MMSI.

Table 3. List of degraded datasets

Name	i	X	p	k	m	n	Name	i	X	p	k	m	n	Name	i	X	p	k	m	n
$\widehat{X}_1$	1	$\widehat{X}_0$	90	1	11	2729	$\widehat{X}_6$	6	$\widehat{X}_0$	80	1	11	2428	$\widehat{X}_{11}$	11	$\widehat{X}_0$	70	1	11	2125
$\widehat{X}_2$	2	$\widehat{X}_0$	90	2	11	2729	$\widehat{X}_7$	7	$\widehat{X}_0$	80	2	11	2428	$\widehat{X}_{12}$	12	$\widehat{X}_0$	70	2	11	2125
$\widehat{X}_3$	3	$\widehat{X}_0$	90	3	11	2729	$\widehat{X}_8$	8	$\widehat{X}_0$	80	3	11	2428	$\widehat{X}_{13}$	13	$\widehat{X}_0$	70	3	11	2125
$\widehat{X}_4$	4	$\widehat{X}_0$	90	4	11	2729	$\widehat{X}_9$	9	$\widehat{X}_0$	80	4	11	2428	$\widehat{X}_{14}$	14	$\widehat{X}_0$	70	4	11	2125
$\widehat{X}_5$	5	$\widehat{X}_0$	90	5	11	2729	$\widehat{X}_{10}$	10	$\widehat{X}_0$	80	5	11	2428	$\widehat{X}_{15}$	15	$\widehat{X}_0$	70	5	11	2125

The list of generated datasets $\widehat{X}_i$ is presented in Table 3 (in which p is the removal rate, k the identifier of the dataset linked to the p value, m the number of columns and n the number of lines), $\forall i \in [\![1, 15]\!]$, i referring to the corresponding line in Table 3, the synthetic datasets, computed using the function described in Sect. 3.2 are:

$$\widehat{X}_i = f_\rho(source_i, A_{p_i}, MCAR) \tag{5}$$

As a consequence, $\forall i \in [\![1,5]\!]$, $\widehat{X}_i$ are the dataset with a rate of removal of 10%, 20% $\forall i \in [\![6.10]\!]$ and 30% $\forall i \in [\![11,15]\!]$. Those datasets, alongside with $\widehat{X}_0$, are used in the assessments, the results of which are presented in Sect. 4.

4   Evaluation of MSI Detection with Data Removal

The proposed evaluation method depicted in Fig. 4 includes the following elements and their exemplary instantiations: The workflow starts from a **Real world phenomenon** that triggers data variations. Here, the variation of AIS reception probability is chosen. The reception probability diminishes non-linearly with increasing distances between transmitter and receiver. In order to make the results applicable to different AIS receivers, the data is varied linearly. The **Varied Data** is the outcome of the process described in Sect. 3, specified by three data removal rates. As an example for a **Detector** RTEC is chosen, as presented in Sect. 2.2. The output of the detector is then evaluated with the **Evaluation Criteria** and measures. As one of many possible instantiations, the metrics used for measuring the accuracy are the number of true positives (TP), false positives (FP) and the derived metrics recall, equal to the TPs per number of all actual positives (P) and precision, equal to the TPs per number of all assumed positives which are the sum of TPs and FPs, and F1-score. The variation of these metrics relative to the amount of removed data is depicted and possible reasons for the observed differences in the variations between different MSI detections are discussed. The **Interpretation** of the evaluation of the linear data variation for a specific receiver requires the chaining of a specific receiver function f_ρ : Distance $\rightarrow$ Reception Probability and the detector function f_d : Reception Probability $\rightarrow$ Accuracy as $f_d(f_\rho)$. Similarly, the interpretation is meant to contain application specific cost functions for a weighting of different types of misclassification.

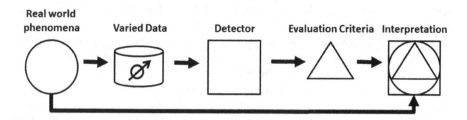

Fig. 4. Evaluation workflow

4.1   Variations of MSI Detections on Data Removal

In this experiment, the evaluation reference is provided by RTEC detections on the dataset X_0. This allows for a quantitative analysis of the variation in accuracy of MSI detectors to the lack of data. It does not state that the detections on the non-degraded dataset are correct in the first place. In order to evaluate the accuracy of detections on X_0, an expert is suitable to provide a more complete assessment of the MSI detectors.

The sensitivity analysis investigates the impact of veracity variations on the performance of RTEC. In the context of AIS, a typical example of a reduced veracity is the lack of transmitted or received AIS messages. Hence, the following analysis examines the impact of data removal on the performance of RTEC.

Experiment Description

From the data degradation methods described in Sect. 3.2, the data removal method is used for removing randomly 10, 20 and 30% of the messages of each vessel from the non-degraded dataset. Thus, random 90, 80 and 70% of the original dataset are kept and processed by RTEC. The data removal process was repeated 5 times leading to 5 different datasets for each data removal rate. The same datasets were used as input for all event detections. As a selection of MSIs presented in Sect. 2.1 MSIs 2, 6, 7, 8, 9, 16, 19, 21 as well as five speed related building blocks were evaluated. For each event results are shown as average, minimum and maximum of the 5 different datasets.

Discussion of Results

As expected, for most events detected by RTEC, the larger the data degradation, the lower Recall, Precision and F1. Remarkably is that most of the events detected show only relatively small variation in performance with respect to the large amounts of removed data, as shown in Table 4. The range of performance variations is shown in Fig. 5a with the smallest variations by the event "high speed near coast" and the largest variations of "movement ability affected" in Fig. 5b.

In the group of events with small performance variations a reduction of 30% leads to a reduction of less than 3% of the F1-score for "movingSpeed", "tuggingSpeed", "underway" and "withinArea", ca. 4% for "lowSpeed" and ca. 7% for "unusualSpeed". A behaviour which is still mitigating the effect of data removal is observed for "changingSpeed" and "gap" for which a data reduction of 30% leads only to a reduction of less than 20% in F1 score.

A linear and strong variation of performance due to the data removal is shown by the event "stopped", for which 30% of data removal lead to ca. 37% of reduction in F1-score; Similar for "SAR course".

The largest variation in performance is observed for the event "movement ability affected". Here, the removal of 20% of the data leads to an indulgent behaviour while the removal of additional 10% of the data leads to a factual collapse of Recall and Precision, implied by the fact that no TP detections are made in the 5 differently degraded datasets. The primary reason for the strong variability in performance is due to the fact that only one event is detected in X_0. But MSIs with strong variations in performance do not necessarily have a small number of detections in the non-degraded dataset X_0. The accuracy of the "stopped" event detector is also varying strongly while the number of detections in X_0 reaches 4,364 detections. This is a larger number of detections than other MSIs which vary much less, e.g. "high speed near coast" with 1,925

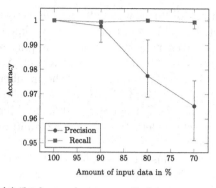

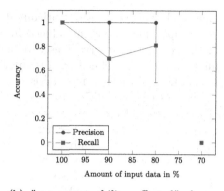

(a) "high speed near coast" shows small variations

(b) "movement ability affected" shows large variations

Fig. 5. Impact of data removal on accuracy measured by mean, minimum and maximum precision and recall over 5 datasets.

detections in X_0. Hence, the variability of the performance is not necessarily uniquely dependent on the number of samples.

Table 4. Mean values for Precision, Recall and F1-score for detection of maritime event patterns on 90, 80 and 70% of data from the reference dataset X_0.

MSI#	Pattern	90%			80%			70%		
		Prec.	Rec.	F1	Prec.	Rec.	F1	Prec.	Rec.	F1
7	changing speed	0.974	0.908	0.939	0.949	0.836	0.888	0.899	0.748	0.815
16	gap	0.899	0.999	0.946	0.795	0.997	0.885	0.695	0.969	0.809
8	high speed nc	0.998	0.999	0.999	0.977	1	0.9886	0.965	0.999	0.982
11	low speed	0.995	0.989	0.992	0.99	0.976	0.983	0.957	0.963	0.96
21	maa	1	0.700	0.8	1	0.811	0.876	0	0	-
19a	movingSpeed	0.995	0.998	0.996	0.992	0.997	0.995	0.961	0.994	0.976
25a	SAR Course	1	0.901	0.934	0.8	0.751	0.835	0.6	0.834	0.89
6	stopped	0.953	0.878	0.911	0.844	0.755	0.795	0.612	0.65	0.63
24a	tugging speed	0.996	0.996	0.996	0.989	0.989	0.989	0.961	0.983	0.971
19	under way	0.997	0.997	0.997	0.99	0.989	0.989	0.967	0.985	0.975
9	unusual speed	0.988	0.975	0.981	0.968	0.947	0.957	0.948	0.919	0.933
2	within area	0.975	1.0	0.987	0.96	1	0.979	0.951	0.997	0.974

As the data removal process is aleatoric, the repeated removal of the event of interest due to the removal of the same AIS messages is highly unlikely for "movement ability affected". This may indicate that the design of the detection pattern is also depending on a higher level of data availability and veracity than other detectors.

An obvious difference between this detector with strongly varying accuracy and the other detectors that could provide an explanation is the fact that "movement ability affected" is a 'statically determined' fluent while all other detectors are 'simple' fluents, as introduced in Sect. 2.2. This could point to a weakness in the concept of interval based detectors, given that they typically require a minimum length, defined by a temporal threshold, in order to be detected. An argument against this hypothesis as unique cause is the fact that the number of TP and FP vary differently. While the number of TP decreases the number of FP increases from an average of 324.2 to 395.8 FP from 80 to 70%. Another reason for the drop of "movement ability affected" detections might be found in "gap", as this event terminates all other events.

Also surprising is the difference between "unusual speed" and "stopped". Despite their conceptual similarity, the variation of detection accuracy of "unusual speed" in Fig. 6b is significantly smaller than the variations for the "stopped" event depicted in Fig. 6a vary significantly stronger.

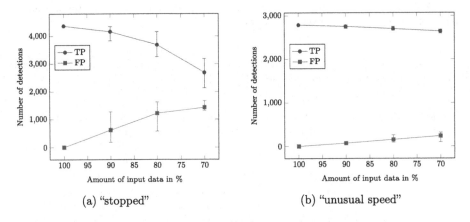

(a) "stopped"   (b) "unusual speed"

Fig. 6. Two speed related events with different accuracy variations measured by mean, minimum and maximum True Positive (TP) and False Positive (FP).

For all events FPs are detected. For some events this behaviour is intuitive. As an example, the event "changingSpeed" is based on the reported or calculated speed of a vessel and a changing speed can be represented simplified as a unit step function where a number of messages imply a low speed followed by a number of messages implying a higher speed. The removal of the message on the limit between the two speed levels does not impact on the reported speed before and after the removed message, hence it can be assumed that the data removal leads only to a shift in the detection, creating a FP as the new limit between the two speed levels does not correspond to the old limit. For other events such as "stopped" depicted in Fig. 6a and similarly for "underway" or "withinArea" FP detections are not expected as the removal of one AIS message is not changing the speed of another AIS message to zero or the removal of one AIS message inside a specific area is not impacting on the position of other AIS messages. These observations reveal perspectives for further analysis.

It seems possible, that events which occur less often in the dataset give a smaller variation of the response to data removal as the small number of 5 repetitions under represents unlikely events. The development of a specialised data removal method which is capable of removing targeted AIS messages known to be P detections in the reference dataset would allow for a better comparison of response behaviour of differently distributed events. While this approach would improve the comparability between events with similar detectors, e.g. "low speed" and "stopped", it potentially creates new inequalities between time point and interval based detectors. Another potential direction for future works is the development of a detector- or task-related metric. On the example of "changing speed" it becomes clear that a removal of an AIS message leads to a shift in the detection, thus both a FN and a FP. From an operational point of view this double-penalised behaviour might be still preferable in many cases before a missed detection which is not shifted in time and which does not create a FP.

5   Conclusions

The article summarises the development of an evaluation method that uses replicable data variation methods for the creation of pseudo-synthetic AIS datasets. For each vessel in the original dataset these degraded datasets contain a known and reduced number of AIS messages, which makes the detection of maritime events more difficult. The degraded datasets are then ingested into RTEC, an implementation of Event Calculus for maritime event pattern detection.

The detections obtained on degraded datasets are compared for each AIS message with the detections on the original dataset in order to derive True and False Positives as well as Recall and Precision for 90, 80 and 70% of the original dataset. The major part of the 12 evaluated maritime event patterns show a robust or even very robust behaviour, given that a data removal of 30% results only in a performance reduction of less than 20% for 9 patterns and for 6 of those only to a reduction of less than 4%. The performance reduction of 2 patterns is slightly over-proportional with respect to the amount of data removed. Only for 1 pattern the reduction of 30% leads to a complete non-detectability.

Acknowledgement. This work was supported by project datAcron, which has received funding from the European Union's Horizon 2020 research and innovation programme under grant agreement No. 687591. The authors wish to thank the NATO Allied Command Transformation (NATO-ACT) for supporting the CMRE project on Data Knowledge and Operational Effectiveness (DKOE).

References

1. Andler, S., Fredin, M., Gustafsson, F., van Laere, J., Nilsson, M., Svenson, P.: SMARTracIn - a concept for spoof resistant tracking of vessel and detection of adverse intentions. In: SPIE Defense, Security, and Sensing, Orlando, FL (2009)
2. Artikis, A., Sergot, M.J.: Executable specification of open multi-agent systems. Logic J. IGPL **18**(1), 31–65 (2010)

3. Artikis, A., Sergot, M.J., Paliouras, G.: An event calculus for event recognition. IEEE Trans. Knowl. Data Eng. **27**(4), 895–908 (2015)
4. Auslander, B., Gupta, K.M., Aha, D.W.: A comparative evaluation of anomaly detection algorithms for maritime video surveillance. In: Sensors, and Command, Control, Communications, and Intelligence (C3I) Technologies for Homeland Security and Homeland Defense X, vol. 8019, p. 801907. SPIE (2011)
5. Iphar, C., Jousselme, A.L., Ray, C.: Pseudo-synthetic datasets in support to maritime surveillance algorithms assessment. In: Proceedings of the VERITA Workshop, 19ieme Journées Francophones Extraction et Gestion des Connaissances (EGC 2019), January 2019
6. ITU: Technical characteristics for an automatic identification system using time-division multiple access in the VHF maritime mobile band (2010)
7. Jousselme, A.L., Maupin, P.: Comparison of uncertainty representations for missing data in information retrieval. In: Proceedings of the 16th International Conference on Information Fusion, pp. 1902–1909. IEEE (2013)
8. Kowalski, R.A., Sergot, M.J.: A logic-based calculus of events. New Gener. Comput. **4**(1), 67–95 (1986)
9. Lavesson, N., Davidsson, P.: Evaluating learning algorithms and classifiers. Int. J. Intell. Inf. Database Syst. **1**(1), 37–52 (2007)
10. Margineantu, D.D., Dietterich, T.G., et al.: Bootstrap methods for the cost-sensitive evaluation of classifiers (2000)
11. Provost, F., Fawcett, T.: Robust classification for imprecise environments. Mach. Learn. **42**(3), 203–231 (2001)
12. Przymusinski, T.: On the declarative semantics of stratified deductive databases and logic programs. In: Foundations of Deductive Databases and Logic Programming. Morgan (1987)
13. Ray, C., Dréo, R., Camossi, E., Jousselme, A.L., Iphar, C.: Heterogeneous integrated dataset for maritime intelligence, surveillance, and reconnaissance. Data Brief (2019, in Press). https://doi.org/10.1016/j.dib.2019.104141
14. Riveiro, M., Falkman, G.: Supporting the analytical reasoning process in maritime anomaly detection: evaluation and experimental design. In: 2010 14th International Conference Information Visualisation, pp. 170–178. IEEE (2010)
15. Roy, J., Davenport, M.: Exploitation of maritime domain ontologies for anomaly detection and threat analysis. In: Proceedings of the IEEE international Waterside Security Conference (WSS) (2010)
16. Rubin, D.B.: Inference and missing data. Biometrika **63**(3), 581–592 (1976)

Toward the Measure of Credibility of Hospital Administrative Datasets in the Context of DRG Classification

Diana Pimenta[1] , Julio Souza[1,2(✉)] , Ismael Caballero[3] ,
and Alberto Freitas[1,2]

[1] MEDCIDS – Department of Community Medicine,
Information and Health Decision Sciences, Faculty of Medicine,
University of Porto, Alameda Prof. Hernâni Monteiro, 4200-319 Porto, Portugal
juliobsouza@gmail.com
[2] CINTESIS – Center for Health Technology and Services Research,
R. Dr. Plácido da Costa, 4200-450 Porto, Portugal
[3] University of Castilla-La Mancha, Ciudad Real, Spain

Abstract. Poor quality of coded clinical data in hospital administrative databases may negatively affect decision making, clinical and health care services research and billing. In this paper, we assessed the level of credibility of a nationwide Portuguese inpatient database concerning the codification of pneumonia, with a special emphasis on identifying suspicious cases of upcoding affecting proper APR-DRG (All-Patient Refined Diagnosis-Related Groups) classification and hospital funding. Using data on pneumonia-related hospitalizations from 2015, we compared six hospitals with similar complexity regarding the frequency of all pneumonia-related diagnosis codes in order to identify codes that were significantly overreported in a given facility relatively to its peers. To verify whether the discrepant codes could be related to upcoding, we built Support Vector Machine (SVM) models to simulate the APR-DRG system and assess its response to each discrepant code. Findings demonstrate that hospitals significantly differed in coding six pneumonia conditions, with five of them playing a major role in increasing APR-DRG complexity, being thus suspicious cases of upcoding. However, those comprised a minority of cases and the overall credibility concerning upcoding of pneumonia was above 99% for all evaluated hospitals. Our findings can not only be relevant for planning future audit processes by signalizing errors impacting APR-DRG classification, but also for discussing credibility of administrative data, keeping in mind their impact on hospital financing. Hence, the main contribution of this paper is a reproducible method that can be employed to monitor the credibility and to promote data quality management in administrative databases.

Keywords: Data quality · All Patient-Refined Diagnosis-Related Groups · Clinical coding · Hospital administration · Data quality management · Data governance

© Springer Nature Switzerland AG 2019
M. Piattini et al. (Eds.): QUATIC 2019, CCIS 1010, pp. 289–296, 2019.
https://doi.org/10.1007/978-3-030-29238-6_21

1 Introduction

The Diagnosis Related Groups (DRGs) classification system is currently employed in several countries worldwide and was developed to group hospital cases into specific clusters of patients (DRGs) with similar resource use and costs [1, 2]. The DRG system heavily relies on the quality of the data held in administrative databases, mainly regarding standard codes representing diagnoses and inpatient procedures [3]. Portugal's hospital financing system currently uses a more refined version of the DRG system, the All Patient-Refined Diagnosis-Related Groups (APR-DRG) version 31 [4]. From the point of view of data, the APR-DRG system can be understood as Master Data Repository, where the data model should be aligned to a standardized data model or vocabulary, and the collected values corresponding to codes of medical diagnoses and procedures should be aligned to a set of reference data. Codes representing the principal (hospitalization cause) or secondary (additional) diagnoses and inpatient procedures are captured by using the corresponding standard code from the ICD-9-CM (The International Classification of Diseases, Ninth Revision, Clinical Modification) classification system. Each APR-DRG represents the patient's reason for hospital admission, either in terms of disease or procedure performed [5].

In Portugal, data used for APR-DRG grouping purposes is acquired from hospital administrative databases, which were originally extracted and translated from largely unstructured patient records, diagnostic exams, pathology reports and discharge summaries by trained medical coders. According to Strong et al. [6], the subjective generation of these values when interpreting the diagnoses can lead to data quality problems, namely loss of objectivity and credibility of the data. In the context of APR-DRG classification, this usually happens when coding errors occurs. At this point, it is necessary to recall that the Portuguese government pays hospitals according to an established list of prices that are linked to each APR-DRG. Therefore, failures in the data representing codes of diseases and procedures will undoubtedly have an economic impact to hospitals.

There are several data quality problems related to medical coding errors that could negatively impact hospital funding. One the most common examples is denominated in the literature as upcoding, which is the practice of miscoding patient data to receive higher reimbursements [7]. Upcoding occurs when coders purposely choose more complex codes than the reality in order to classify patients into higher-complexity APR-DRGs, which in turn will result in more money to the hospitals [8]. That can happen when a hospital coder tries to explore the medical records to extract the most lucrative codes, including changes between the principal and secondary diagnosis, look for reimbursable conditions and exaggerate the choice of codes without supportive evidence in the patient's record, such as adding more diagnoses [9].

Consequently, it is paramount to watch the levels of quality of the APR-DRG data. In this paper, we aimed at assessing the credibility of administrative data regarding coding issues that can potentially impact APR-DRG classification, with emphasis on upcoding. As a pilot for the methodology, we limited our study to inpatient episodes due pneumonia. We assessed the quality of data concerning pneumonia-related diagnoses, which are key codes for properly grouping hospital cases into APR-DRGs in respiratory diseases.

The main contribution of this paper is to describe how to assess the credibility of the dataset used for APR-DRG classification, as we were particularly interested in the degree to which a set of attributes representing diagnosis codes are believable by users, namely hospital providers and managers, regarded as true and how much they represent the reality. In our context, we can attribute low-credibility data when possible upcoding cases are flagged.

2 Methods

2.1 Data Sources

As previously said, data used for this study was extracted from Portugal's National DRG database, which is a nationwide inpatient database containing coded clinical data provided by all public hospitals from the National Health System (NHS) in mainland Portugal. We analyzed data from 2015, which was the last year in which Portugal used the ICD-9-CM to code all episodes. In 2016 onwards, episodes were either coded in ICD-9-CM or in the newest tenth revision, so we opted to avoid further bias related to the transition of ICD versions. We selected all cases with a principal or secondary diagnosis from the ICD-9-CM codes comprised in the interval 480–488, which corresponds to Pneumonia and Influenza diagnoses [10]. All variables required for APR-DRG grouping were collected, namely principal diagnosis, up to 30 secondary diagnoses, up to 30 inpatient procedures, discharge status, sex and age.

Since inpatient data used in this study was completely anonymized and only contained the discharge year, diagnosis and procedure codes, sex, age, discharge status and an arbitrary episode identification number, there was no need for ethical approval.

2.2 Developing the Mechanisms to Measure the Credibility of a Record

To identify abnormal frequencies of APR-DRGs across hospitals, Chi-square test with Bonferroni correction for multiple comparisons was firstly employed. For each discrepant APR-DRG, the same statistical test was employed to compare hospitals regarding the frequency of pneumonia-related diagnosis codes among cases grouped into the discrepant APR-DRGs. Our hypothesis was that patients with the same APR-DRG should not significantly differ in the frequencies of these codes as they present the same hospitalization causes. Following this analysis, all pneumonia codes that accounted for a significantly higher-than-expected frequency in at least one hospital were targeted, as they might lead to suspicious upcoding cases. In order to minimize the bias introduced by differences in the complexity of the patients treated by each hospital, we restricted our analyses to six hospitals with similar capacity based on a standard categorization defined by the Portuguese NHS [11].

To investigate whether the targeted codes could be associated with an upcoding case, we employed Support Vector Machine (SVM) [12] to simulate APR-DRG classification. The main advantage of using SVM is that it can overcome high dimensionality issues [13], which is the case of the APR-DRG classification problem.

We built two SVM-based classification models: (1) one for predicting any APR-DRG related to a disease or disorder of the respiratory system, based upon 17 different APR-DRGs defined in version 31 [5]; and (2) another one to determine the Severity of Illness (SOI) level, which is a score to be added to the APR-DRG, always ranging from 1 to 4 (1 – minor; 2 – moderate; 3 – major; 4 – extreme). The full APR-DRG classification includes both, the APR-DRG itself and the SOI level. We trained the SVM models on two thirds of the inpatient data for the period 2011–2015 and tested their performance on the remaining third. A total of 487,156 cases were used for training and testing the SVM models. As evaluation metrics of the goodness of the model, we considered precision, recall and the percentage of correctly classified cases. We further tested the models on data from the year of 2016 in order to add critical validation to the models and assess their capacity of generalization.

Using the constructed SVM models, we performed a sensitivity analysis to discover the individual role of each discrepant pneumonia code on APR-DRG classification by removing the code from the original dataset and assessing APR-DRG changes. If the exclusion of the code alone moves the episode to a lower intensity APR-DRG, then the episode is labeled as a suspicious case of upcoding. Finally, we estimated the levels of credibility. We define the measure "level of credibility" as the difference of the percentage of possible cases of pneumonia-related upcoding in a given facility from the total number of inpatient episodes in that same facility.

Data processing, training and testing phases of SVM were performed using Java code in combination with a Weka open source library for Java [14], version 3.8.0.

3 Results

Significantly different frequencies of APR-DRG 137 (Major respiratory infections and inflammations) and APR-DRG 139 (Other pneumonia) were found across hospitals. The diagnosis codes that presented a significantly higher-than-expected frequency in at least one hospital were: 482.42 - Methicillin resistant pneumonia due to Staphylococcus aureus (Hospital F), 480.9 - Viral pneumonia, unspecified (Hospital E), 481 - Pneumococcal pneumonia (Hospitals A, C and E), 482.9 - Bacterial pneumonia, unspecified (Hospital A), 485 - Bronchopneumonia, organism unspecified (Hospital B) and 486 - Pneumonia, organism unspecified (Hospitals B, E and F).

Regarding the performance of the SVM-based models, considering the first level (APR-DRG without the SOI level), weighted recall and precision were both 0.994 and the percentage of correctly classified cases were 99.4%. Considering the SOI determination, overall weighted recall and precision were both 0.893, with a percentage of correctly classified cases of 89.3%. When tested in data from 2016 (92475 episodes), we verified that the SVM presented a high capacity of generalization, with a percentage of correctly classified cases of 88.4%.

Table 1 summarizes the sensitivity analysis results by indicating how many episodes were driven to a given APR-DRG by each targeted code. For instance, from 7059 episodes it occurred, code 486 alone was responsible for allocating 6826 episodes to APR-DRG 139 and 1 episode to APR-DRG 137 when coded as principal diagnosis, whereas it accounted for placing 185 episodes (out of 540) once it was coded as secondary diagnosis. In 222 episodes (out of 760), five codes were alone responsible for allocating the episodes into APR-DRG 137 when they are reported as secondary diagnosis rather than principal diagnosis.

Table 1. Individual effects of each discrepant pneumonia-related diagnosis codes on APR-DRG classification

	APR-DRG 137	APR-DRG 139	Total episodes
Principal diagnosis			
482.42	0	0	102
480.9	0	53	54
481	1	483	509
482.9	1	466	488
485	0	449	455
486	1	6926	7059
Total	3	8377	8667
Secondary diagnosis			
482.42	3	0	64
480.9	0	0	5
481	5	0	34
482.9	26	0	78
485	3	0	39
486	185	0	540
Total	222	0	760

Table 2 below shows, for each hospital, the number of hospitalizations flagged as suspicious cases of upcoding and the respective credibility levels. Hospital D was the only one that did not present an abnormal frequency of a pneumonia code. The occurrence of upcoding related to pneumonia was proportionally small, not reaching 1% of the cases in any of the evaluated hospitals. Moreover, the credibility levels across the hospital databases were very high, with values higher than 99%.

Table 2. Levels of credibility concerning upcoding cases in pneumonia

Hospital	Number of suspicious cases of upcoding	Total number of episodes	Credibility level
Hospital A	7 (0.1% of the total)	3884	99.8
Hospital B	51 (0.94% of the total)	5408	99.1
Hospital C	1 (0.05% of the total)	2205	99.9
Hospital E	21 (0.55% of the total)	3846	99.5
Hospital F	49 (0.73% of the total)	6676	99.3

4 Discussion

The credibility of coded clinical data in administrative databases is a critical issue in the context of health care funding, research, decision making and quality of care assessment. The emphasis of this article was to measure the credibility of data concerning upcoding of pneumonia, a condition that already has found to be manipulated in hospital datasets to alter the complexity of hospitalizations in order to increase reimbursements [15–17].

From the clinical point of view, a total of five out of six discrepant codes presented similar effects on APR-DRG grouping as they drove the classification into the APR-DRG 139 as principal diagnosis. The exclusion of these five pneumonia codes would shift these episodes to APR-DRG 137 in nearly all episodes they occurred (8377 out of 8667 episodes, see Table 1), which is an APR-DRG with a higher weight and reimbursement rates [18]. Moreover, in some cases (222 out of 760 episodes, see Table 1), switching these conditions from principal to secondary diagnosis alone would result in more financial compensation to hospitals, as it could prevent episodes from being assigned to APR-DRG 139 and move them to APR-DRG 137 instead. These cases should be watched more closely as they could be an indicator of upcoding practices.

The number of cases flagged as upcoding by our method was proportionally small and the credibility of the data concerning upcoding of pneumonia was very high. The magnitude of upcoding observed in our findings appear to be in line with a systematic literature search conducted by Lüngen and Lauterbach [19], who estimated that upcoding was related with up to 1% of the inpatient care payments in Germany [19]. However, this value is quite lower than the rates identified in a 1995–1996 coding audit in Australia, which revealed that an estimated of 5.2% of the medical records were upcoded [9]. In the United States, it was found that one-third and one-half of the case-mix increase occurred due to upcoding in the periods 1986–87 and 1987–88, respectively [20, 21]. In Portugal, Barros and Braun analyzed the same Portuguese DRG database used in this study and found that upcoding has been occurring in public hospitals to increase their budgets, but the impact was quantitatively small [17].

As a limitation of our study, we mention that flagging possible upcoding cases was based upon results obtained with the direct application of the SVM algorithm. Therefore, existing errors or shortcomings associated with the SVM models might have influenced or been replicated in our results. Furthermore, we only evaluated credibility related to coding the six conditions in which at least one hospital presented a significantly higher-than-expected frequency of cases, and not consider possible coding issues related to other diagnoses or procedures.

5 Conclusion and Future Work

We described and applied a method for monitoring possible upcoding cases related to pneumonia diagnoses. Overall credibility levels of clinical were high and only a few proportions of suspicious cases were flagged by our method. Hospitals significantly differed on reporting six pneumonia conditions that drove the classification to APR-DRG 139 when coded as principal diagnosis, though the episode would move to a higher paying APR-DRG (APR-DRG 137) once these codes are reported as secondary diagnosis. We employed a generic and reproducible method that can be useful for discovering relevant APR-DRG relations and thus to filter cases for audit planning. Future works include the refinement of the machine learning models, including testing different algorithms and approaches, the extension of the proposed methodology to measure other data quality dimensions and other disease domains, automate some part of the process and establish a relationship between the levels of credibility and the amount of reimbursement affected by that.

Acknowledgements. The authors would like to thank the Central Authority for Health Services, I.P. (ACSS) for providing access to the data. We would also like to thank to project GEMA: Generation and Evaluation of Models for Data Quality (Ref.: SBPLY/17/180501/000293) and the Master Programme in Medical Informatics of the Faculties of Medicine and Sciences of the University of Porto for financial support.

References

1. Aiello, F.A., Roddy, S.P.: Inpatient coding and the diagnosis-related groups. J. Vasc. Surg. **66**(5), 1621–1623 (2017)
2. Mathauer, I., Wittenbecher, F.: Hospital payment systems based on diagnosis-related groups: experiences in low- and middle-income countries. Bull. World Health Organ. **91**(10), 746–756 (2013)
3. Cheng, P., Gilchrist, A., Robinson, K.M., Paul, L.: The risk and consequences of clinical miscoding due to inadequate medical documentation: a case study of the impact on health services funding. Health Inf. Manag. J. **38**, 35–46 (2009)
4. Agrupador de GDH All Patient Refined DRG. http://www2.acss.min-saude.pt/Portals/0/CN22.pdf. Accessed 22 May 2019
5. All Patient Refined Diagnosis Related Groups Methodology Overview 3M Health Information Systems. https://www.hcup-us.ahrq.gov/db/nation/nis/grp031_aprdrg_meth_ovrview.pdf. Accessed 22 May 2019
6. Strong, D.M., Lee, Y.W., Wang, R.Y., Strong, D., Lee, Y.W., Wang, R.: 10 potholes in the road to information quality. IEEE Comput. **30**, 38–46 (1997)
7. Dafny, L.S.: How do hospitals respond to price changes. Am. Econ. Rev. **95**, 1525–1547 (2005)
8. Silverman, E., Skinner, J.: Medicare upcoding and hospital ownership. J Health Econ. **23**, 369–389 (2004)
9. Pongpirul, K., Robinson, C.: Hospital manipulations in the DRG system: 755 a systematic scoping review. Asian Biomed. **7**, 301–310 (2013)
10. International Classification of Diseases, Ninth Revision, Clinical Modification (ICD-9-CM). https://www.cdc.gov/nchs/icd/icd9cm.htm. Accessed 22 May 2019
11. Administração Central do Sistema de Saúde. Grupos e Instituições. http://benchmarking.acss.min-saude.pt/BH_Enquadramento/GrupoInstituicoes. Accessed 22 May 2019
12. Chu, A., et al.: A decision support system to facilitate management of patients with acute gastrointestinal bleeding. Artif. Intell. Med. **42**, 247–259 (2008)
13. Verplancke, T., et al.: Support vector machine versus logistic regression modeling for prediction of hospital mortality in critically ill patients with haematological malignancies. BMC Med. Inform. Decis. Mak. **8**, 56 (2008)

14. University of Waikato Weka 3: Data Mining Software in Java. https://www.cs.waikato.ac. nz/ml/weka/index.html. Accessed 28 June 2019
15. Sjoding, M.W., Iwashyna, T.J., Dimick, J.B., Cooke, C.R.: Gaming hospital-level pneumonia 30-day mortality and readmission measures by legitimate changes to diagnostic coding. Crit. Care Med. **43**(5), 989–995 (2015)
16. Hebert, P.L., McBean, A.M., Kane, R.L.: Explaining trends in hospitalizations for pneumonia and influenza in the elderly. Med Care Res Rev. **62**(5), 560–582 (2005)
17. Barros, P.P., Braun, G.: Upcoding in a national health service: the evidence from Portugal. Health Econ. **26**, 600–618 (2017)
18. Diário 777 da República. Diário da República, Portaria No. 207/2017 778 de 11 de julho de 2017. http://www.acss.min-saude.pt/wp-content/uploads/2016/12/Portaria_207_2017-1.pdf. Accessed 27 June 2016
19. Lungen, M., Lauterbach, K.W.: Upcoding—a risk for the use of diagnosis-related groups. Dtsch. Med. Wochenschr. **125**, 852–856 (2000)
20. Carter, G.M., Newhouse, J.P., Relles, D.A.: How much change in the case mix index is DRG creep. J. Health Econ. **9**, 411–428 (1990)
21. Carter, G.M., Newhouse, J.P., Relles, D.A.: Has DRG Creep Crept Up? Decomposing the Case Mix Index Change Between 1987 and 1988. RAND Corporation, Santa Monica (1991)

RETORCH: Resource-Aware End-to-End Test Orchestration

Cristian Augusto[1]($\boxtimes$) , Jesús Morán[1] , Antonia Bertolino[2] ,
Claudio de la Riva[1] , and Javier Tuya[1]

[1] Computer Science Department, University of Oviedo, Gijón, Spain
{augustocristian, moranjesus, claudio, tuya}@uniovi.es
[2] ISTI-CNR, Consiglio Nazionale Delle Ricerche, Pisa, Italy
antonia.bertolino@isti.cnr.it

Abstract. Continuous integration practices introduce incremental changes in the code to both improve the quality and add new functionality. These changes can introduce faults that can be timely detected through continuous testing by automating the test cases and re-executing them at each code change. However, re-executing all test cases at each change may not be always feasible, especially for those test cases that make heavy use of resources thoroughly like End-to-End test cases that need a complex test infrastructure. This paper is focused on optimizing the usage of the resources employed during End-to-End testing (e.g., storage, memory, web servers or tables of a database, among others) through a resource-aware test orchestration technique in the context of continuous integration in the cloud. In order to optimize both the cost/usage of resources and the execution time, the approach proposes to (i) identify the resources required by the End-to-End test cases, (ii) group together those tests that need the same resources, (iii) deploy the tests in both dependency isolated and elastic environments, and (iv) schedule their parallel execution in several machines.

Keywords: Software testing · Continuous integration · Continuous testing · Testing in the cloud · End-to-End testing · Test orchestration

1 Introduction

Continuous integration practices and methodologies are based on incremental changes of the code to improve quality or add new functionalities [1]. However, while introducing new features in the code, new faults can be introduced as well, which as a consequence can destabilize even code that was successfully tested in the past. To ensure that the modifications and the new code do not endanger the existing functionality, regression testing [2] is standard practice. In modern agile processes, though, in which new versions of software are continuously and frequently delivered within very short cycles, regression testing may face many challenges.

One emerging practice to shorten the validation of newly released version is *continuous testing* [3]: it consists of automating the test cases and re-executing them before any new release in the source code repository. However, a well-known problem is that as the number of tests increases, re-executing all of them at each frequent change

© Springer Nature Switzerland AG 2019
M. Piattini et al. (Eds.): QUATIC 2019, CCIS 1010, pp. 297–310, 2019.
https://doi.org/10.1007/978-3-030-29238-6_22

may not be possible due to the extent of resources employed like the computational cost of execution, time required, or the number of virtual instances needed. As a solution to partially address this problem, many test minimization and prioritization techniques [2] have been proposed to identify a minimal subset of test cases or optimize their order of execution, respectively. The objective of these techniques is to look for a tradeoff between the probability of discovering the faults potentially added with a modification and the resources employed for regression testing. The prioritization techniques permute the execution order of the test cases aimed to firstly execute the relevant tests, but the whole execution of the test suite remains expensive unless the tester decides to execute only a subset of the more relevant tests through a minimization technique. The latter techniques reduce the usage of resources by not re-executing all tests, but they neither optimize the resources of the test executed nor alleviate the thoroughly use of resources in the whole test suite.

One of the testing stages that require a large amount of physical-logical-computational resources is End-to-End testing (from now onwards referred to as E2E), i.e., the test of the whole flow from start to end of the user interaction with the system. In E2E testing, the application of techniques such as parallelization, minimization or reduction may not be effective for cost reduction: this type of tests usually requires large amounts of resources in the broadest sense, including the high execution time, the cost of replicating resources, the resources to be made available, among others. In addition, the set-up of the testing environment acquires great importance. Thus, if this set-up requires a large amount of time compared with that employed in test execution, parallelizing the test cases in separate instances without a proper strategy would not solve the problem: for those tests sharing the usage of heavy resources, parallelization would be inefficient and a best solution would be to set up the test environment once and execute them in sequential way. Therefore, to optimize the cost of E2E testing, detecting the dependencies between the tests and the resources they require is a crucial aspect.

Moving the testing to the Cloud [4] is commonly acknowledged as a solution to reduce the cost of testing, especially to exploit the potential of unlimited resources and scalability delivered on demand. ElasTest [5] is an open source platform aimed to support Cloud testing and simplify the E2E test process. It avoids several testing dependence problems by providing dependency isolation through the containerized execution of the tests. This is done through the TJobs that are the tests together with the Docker containerized system under test (SUT), customized to provide not only the production environment, but also utilities to execute, monitor and collect testing information.

Containerization has provided new advantages in the virtualization field, reducing the amount of both resources and time required to deploy a service in an isolated environment. The SUT instantiation can take advantage of the containerization in order to be deployed several times in the same machine, avoiding common problems like dependencies. However, in the current version, the ElasTest containerized execution presents the problem that it needs the instantiation of the resources required for each container causing underusage of those resources. Our proposal is intended to reduce the number of resources used in the containerized execution of the test during E2E testing and it could be integrated into the ElasTest platform to support resource-aware Cloud testing orchestration. We call the approach RETORCH (**R**esource-aware **E2E** Test **ORCH**estration).

We present the concept behind the RETORCH approach and show an example of its application to a demonstrator from the ElasTest project. Precisely, this paper includes the following contributions:

1. A motivation and description of the RETORCH framework through which to perform the E2E resource identification, the test grouping and scheduling.
2. An illustrative example scenario of RETORCH usage.

The rest of the paper is organized as follows. Section 2 describes the related work. Section 3 introduces the orchestration approach proposed and defines its terminology. Section 4 describes a working example related to a teaching online service (Full Teaching application using the OpenVidu Streaming Engine). Finally, the conclusions and future work are in Sect. 5.

2   Related Work

RETORCH is motivated by the Multi Objective Regression Test Optimization approach presented by Harman in [6]. He discussed several cost and value-based objectives for testing, supporting the new point of view that testing optimization should be performed by considering in combined way the several different types of resources needed.

Despite the recent advances in the efficient and effective use of resources during testing, there remain several open challenges [7] to be addressed when performing test prioritization, selection, and minimization. Several authors have studied approaches to optimize these techniques considering both cost and rate of fault detection [8–10]. Our proposal has some aspects in common with prioritization techniques [2], as we schedule the test cases aiming at improving one metric of the tests contained on the suite (in our case resource efficiency).

To make test suite prioritization, test dependencies are an important aspect to take into account. Some authors have proposed techniques and tools to detect dependencies between test cases. Bell et al. [11] provide a dependency detection tool (Electrictest), and compare it to other state of the art tools, getting a similar fault detection rate with lower slowdown. Gyori et al. [12] introduce formally the concept of test Pollution problem and present a technique (called POLDET) that detects in execution time the "polluting" tests. Another technique that addresses the test dependence problem is in [13], where Gambi et al. provide an evolution of their prior approach (ElectricTest), and test it empirically with good results: they discover the known dependences and find another one that previous tests and tools did not discover.

Test resource optimization has been widely treated in the literature. In [14] Gambi et al. provide a solution that allows the developer to choose between different resource optimization parameters, as time, cost or a mix of both. In [15] Sundar et al. address the test execution optimization problem considering the cost, and present the concept of test plan derivation. Test plan derivation is composed by three processes of test resources partition that redistribute the tests to ease test parallelization. In another work by

Yu et al. [16], the resource optimization problem is addressed by performing a clustering of test cases with resources. Unlike those works, we understand as a resource a wide range of terms beyond time or cost, and aim to optimize the testing depending on several aspects. A similar aim is pursued by García et al. [17], who propose to orchestrate test cases (essentially to find a proper selection and sequencing) depending on the outcome of test execution (verdict-driven) or on the produced output (data-driven).

In the field of Cloud services, several approaches have been proposed to face similar problems, e.g. Esfahani et al. in [18], expose the Cloud build infrastructure of Microsoft (so-called CloudBuild). This infrastructure presents similar dependences issues, which they address by extracting dependence graphs and deriving the dependencies on them automatically. We propose a future line of work that aims at a similar automated detection of the test resources into the containers.

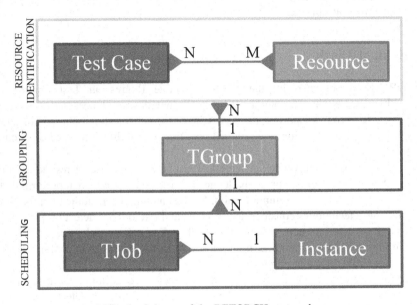

Fig. 1. Scheme of the RETORCH approach

3   Approach

The RETORCH framework aims at optimizing the cost/usage of resources orchestrating the E2E test cases in different machines based on the resources needed to execute each test. Figure 1 depicts the core concept of the orchestration starting from the E2E test cases to their execution in several machines/instances grouping those tests that use homogeneous resources in order to optimize both resources and execution time.

As first step, the resources used by each test case are identified to detect those tests that require the same resources (Resource identification). According to the resources identified, some tests can be executed together while others cannot because of incompatibilities in their allocated resources or in the way in which they access these resources. Then, those test cases that can be executed together are grouped to arrange their execution and reuse their resources to optimize their cost (Grouping). These groups of tests are called TGroups. Test cases that belong to different TGroups can be executed independently because the resources they employ are different. Finally, each TGroup may be split and allocated in several instances (Scheduling) to optimize both the cost/usage of resources and the test execution time. The test cases of these TGroups are split in several subsets of test cases, which are called TJobs, that contain not only the code of the test, but also the environment with the dependencies isolated in a container that allows easy deployment of the test in a cloud instance.

In the following subsections the above key concepts are detailed. Subsection 3.1 below defines the resources and their attributes. These resources can be used in different ways by the E2E test cases considering the access mode (Subsect 3.2) and the properties (Subsect 3.3). Finally, the processes that orchestrate the E2E test cases are defined in Subsect 3.4.

3.1   Definition of Resources and Test Jobs/Groups

The core of RETORCH is based on three main concepts defined below: the resources required by the test cases, the groups of test cases that use homogeneous resources (TGroups) and a partitioning of these TGroups so to isolate the dependencies in elastic environment and optimize resource usage through scheduling (TJobs).

1. **Resource**: Physical, logical and/or computational entities required by the execution of one or more test cases, for example, a web server requested by a test case or a table of database queried by the test case. The resources are characterized by the following attributes:
   a. **Elasticity**: A resource is elastic when it can be instantiated and made available for the tests cases on the fly (e.g. a database running in a container, a software simulator). Conversely, a resource is not elastic when only a fixed maximum number of instances is available (e.g. a sensor, a camera, a hardware emulator).
   b. **Hierarchy/partitioning:** A resource may contain sub-resources or partitions that also are resources (e.g. a database may be partitioned into several tables or sets, of tables).
   c. **Sharing:** Shared resources may be used simultaneously by more than one test case without interfering into the test result.
   d. **Lifecycle:** All resources have a lifecycle composed of three phases: set up of resource, test execution using the resource and disposal of the resource. In the Set-up phase, the resources are deployed and initialized according to the test data (e.g. initial load of the database, configuration data). Once the resources are ready, the tests use these resources in the test execution phase according to the proposal. After finishing the test execution, the resources are disposed and released, making them available for other test cases.
2. **TGroup (Test Group)**: is a set of test cases that use homogeneous resources and can be deployed together in the same environment. For example, a TGroup can contain the test cases that query the same database with the same initial load and

without modifying the information. These test cases can use the same database set-up in the same instance. In contrast, two test cases that both query and modify the database information can cause wrong test execution, and then these two test cases must be in different TGroups and deployed in different instances/environments. Each TGroup settles the environment needed by the test execution in the whole system or also considering scaffolding and test harness through the mocks, stubs or other simulators that can alleviate the cost of resources that are not mainly needed for the tests of the TGroup. The test cases of the TGroup can be also divided to not only optimize the cost/usage of resources but also the execution time through a distributed scheduling.

3. **TJob (Test Job):** is a partitioning of a TGroup containing several test cases inside a Docker container that also deploys the system under test isolating the dependencies and is customized to provide utilities to execute, monitor and collect testing information. Then one TGroup can be split into several TJobs and these can be scheduled them in different instances of the cloud, so to reduce the execution time by executing more TJobs in parallel thanks to the isolation of dependencies.

Example 1: Air Traffic Management (ATM). When testing the operations that an air traffic controller makes to manage their assigned flights, we need a resource that is the Control Working Position (CWP), which is itself a complex system, so as, it is not elastic. The CWP may become a shared resource if we partition the flight area into hierarchical clusters of sectors, provided that each test case will manage only flights belonging to a cluster. Moreover, when testing a transfer of flights between controllers will need two CWP, either exclusive or shared. This resource also has his own life-cycle, with a set-up (prepare all the CWP and flight plans), a test phase and finally a release and disposal.

3.2   Resource Access Modes

In order to group the test cases in TGroups and then schedule them in TJobs, RETORCH considers how the test cases must use the resources. Each test case can perform different kind of operations over the allocated resources. These operations can have two properties: **safety** and **idempotency.** Safe operations are those whose execution does not modify the resource, for example, a SELECT operation in a database query because it does not change the information of the database and does not introduce dependencies between test cases. Idempotent operations are those that can be performed several times consecutively producing the same result.

Different test cases may have different usage patterns when sharing the same resource. Each pair of test case and resource is associated according to an access mode that determines if the operations performed during the test execution modify the resource or not, and how. The access modes are enumerated below:

- **Read-only:** the test case performs both safe and idempotent operations allowing other test cases read the resource at the same time (e.g. a test case that queries the master tables of a database without any change, allows that other test cases query the same resource).

- **Read-write:** the test case performs operations that are neither safe nor idempotent. Then, other test cases may not use this resource simultaneously to avoid unexpected erroneous executions (e.g., a communication channel, if we are not doing performance-related testing).
- **Write-only:** the test case performs operations that are neither safe nor idempotent similar to those "read-write", but allows that more than one test case update the resource simultaneously, restricting reads to only assertions that check the expected results (e.g., a centralized log system may be used simultaneously by several test cases, provided that, if we need to check the logs, there is a mechanism that allows identifying the logs produced by each test case).
- **Dynamic:** the test case performs operations that are safe but not idempotent. The resource is partitioned on the fly allowing that each test case create and access each partition independently from other test cases (e.g., when testing several test cases that issue orders, more than one test can place an order at the same time, but in dynamic access each test case must only use the orders that it has created).
- **No access:** This access mode is banally safe because the operations of the test case do not make use of any resource (e.g., when using a simple mock that does not requires any resource).

Example 2: In ATM, the Flight plans in an Air Traffic simulator are usually a shared dynamic resource, because they are created on fly as needed when the test is performed. On the other hand, the operation logs that are kept for legal requirements, are a write-only resource because they do not use it for anything other than saving the different usage traceback.

3.3 Resource Properties

The test cases can be grouped according to their access modes in the resources, but the test orchestration also considers other properties that allow the deployment and proper monitorization of both test cases and resources needed. Each pair of test case and resource is characterized by the following properties:

- **Allocated:** Location of each resource must be known to make possible their identification (e.g., the instances over where is deployed). Allocation is crucial when an effective use and measure of the resource performance during testing is considered.
- **Measurable:** Each resource must have indicators to allow measuring how many of them are deployed and their performance (e.g. RAM, processor usage or heartbeat latency received by a sensor network).
- **Traceability**: Each resource must be always traceable, allowing to know its state at every time of the test execution (e.g. ready, running, disposing of, or testing over it).
- **Elasticity Cost:** The elasticity cost measures the expenses incurred during the resource life cycle. This cost may be a combination of money, time, processing power, memory, energy, among others.

- **Test Environment:** The resources and test cases must be deployed in an environment that isolates the dependencies and avoids wrong executions/accesses with a properly set up. The whole environment can be encapsulated in a Docker container to be easily deployed in a cloud instance.

3.4   Processes

The behavior of RETORCH is organized around three different processes, namely Resource Identification, Grouping and Scheduling. Resource identification provides a first view of the resources required by the test cases. Then, a grouping is performed for later, optimizing the execution of those tests in a proper scheduling process. These processes, schematically represented in Fig. 2 are described below:

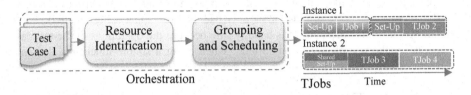

Fig. 2.   Scheme of the main RETORCH processes

1. **Resource Identification:** In this process the resources that each test case needs to be executed properly are identified. To determine how the test case uses the resource, each association of a resource and test case is labeled with an access mode and the properties required by the test (Subsects 3.2 and 3.3). With the information about the resources, we can calculate the elasticity cost of the resources.
2. **Grouping:** To arrange the test cases according the resource usage, several groups are formed. The goal is to arrange the execution of the test cases based on their associated resources. For example, if two tests perform a safe access mode they can be grouped together. However, if two test cases perform a non-safe operation on the same resource, they are candidate to be placed in the same or separate groups depending on the access mode. The result of this grouping is a set of test cases put together with all scaffolding required for the execution. The objective of these groups is to avoid instantiation of a resource with more features than required and hence underutilized.
3. **Scheduling:** Although grouping achieves some optimization on the resource usage, the whole test process may be further optimized by ordering and splitting the TGroups taking into account the available infrastructure. For instance, TGroups may be distributed in parallel to achieve better use of the test infrastructure and reduce the execution time. Not all schedules are aimed to minimize both execution time and the resource usage (one possible objective may be to maximize the usage of several instances, minimizing the idle time or another possible objective may be minimizing the execution time using more resources).

4   Working Example

To illustrate the RETORCH approach, we present an example of its application on a real-world open-source application called FullTeaching [19]. FullTeaching is an educational platform that provides teachers with many features for organizing the teaching material, scheduling courses, and structuring classes; it provides also means for interacting with students, e.g., calendars, dashboards, forums. FullTeaching is a complex application involving several resources, including the OpenVidu Server [20], the Kurento Media Server [21], and the MySQL DBMS. In particular, for online teaching FullTeaching includes features enabling real-time video conferencing that are supported by OpenVidu via W3C Web-RTC [22] open source api. For the purpose of E2E testing such functionality, testers should take into account the underlying infrastructure and the resource usage by OpenVidu.

For the several test cases that concern the OpenVidu Engine, deploying one instance for every TJob may be too expensive in terms of resource usage due to heavy resources for storage and graphical processing evolved by video streaming. For this reason, we divide the server in three types of resources with different usage rates exposed as follows:

1. **Minimal OpenVidu Server**: This type of server is a little mock that just provides a random number as session id, whenever any client requires it. Precisely, this resource has a No-Access mode meaning that the requests from the test do not access the real resource, it is a simple mock. It is used in those TJobs that only require this type of interaction with the OpenVidu Server,
2. **Medium OpenVidu Server:** The medium server is a light implementation of the service, with only basic functionalities and without any storage to record the session. This service will be employed in those test that require to check any functionality that needs a classroom or a simple chat between users.
3. **Heavy OpenVidu Server:** The heavy server provides all the functionalities of the OpenVidu Server, beside several video lessons recorded. This will be used in those test cases that require these video streaming recording functions or require all the functionality of the engine for his execution.

Using these three types of resources we proceed to classify all the test cases available depending on their resource usage requirements. For this we use the three phases of RETORCH, beginning with the resource identification, next the grouping and finally the scheduling.

Resource Identification: In this stage we detect which type of OpenVidu engine is required for each test case. After collecting this information, we can proceed with the grouping phase.

Test cases assigned to a Light OpenVidu are the cheapest in term of elasticity cost: they can be available for testing on the fly and can be shared between multiple tests. The lifecycle of this resource is composed of the three usual phases, being the only without any cost.

Test cases assigned to a Medium OpenVidu Server require deploying a simple container that consumes a small amount of resources in terms of elasticity cost and allows sharing between multiple tests (although with some performance penalty). In this case, the set-up/dispose lifecycle phases do have a cost, so us the grouping performed later will try to share this set-up between several tests. Test on this resource has a Read-Write access mode.

Last, test cases assigned to Heavy OpenVidu Server should be executed in a sequential way due to the high elasticity cost that does not allow for deploying more than an instance. This resource has a read-write access mode because they employ and create the video into the resource.

Grouping: As described before, the next stage is to group those test cases that are compatible and can be executed with the same resource set up into TGroups. The deployment of the proposed RETORCH application for E2E testing of FullTeaching considering the OpenVidu resource is depicted in Fig. 3: we classify the Test Cases in heavy (Fig. 3 black color) medium (Fig. 3 red color) and light (Fig. 3 blue color).

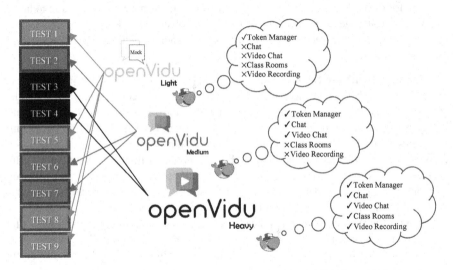

Fig. 3. Resource dependencies and grouping process (Color figure online)

Let suppose that we have nine test cases and determine three TGroups as indicated below:

TGroup 1 (Light OpenVidu): Test case 1, 5, 8 and 9
TGroup 2 (Medium OpenVidu): Test case 2, 6 and 7
TGroup 3 (Heavy OpenVidu): Test case 3 and 4

In the most basic grouping, an instance is used by each TGroup to deploy the TJobs of the three types created in the scheduling phase (each type in one isolate instance). The TGroups include the test cases with their different scaffolding, avoiding the underutilization of a streaming server with more resources than needed.

Scheduling: Once the grouping is done we proceed to schedule the different TGroups to optimize the resource usage, execution time and execution cost. In this case, in Fig. 4 we give four different examples of schedules, for each type of TGroups (assigned to a Light, Medium and Heavy resource):

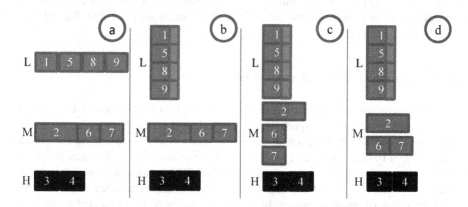

Fig. 4. Different TJob Scheduling examples depending on the objective

1. Figure 4(a) represents a sequential execution of Light, Medium and Heavy Open-Vidu servers. This scheduling provides a baseline, giving the worst execution time, but using the minimal number of instances required to keep the TGroups isolated. All TGroups are deployed in separate instances sharing the same set-up between them.

2. Figure 4(b) depicts a similar configuration to the previous one concerning the Medium and Heavy OpenVidu server and instead the parallel execution in one instance of the Light one. The difference with the previous resides in lower execution time of the Light instances in addition to a small reduction of the time employed to execute all tests regarding the Scheduling represented in Fig. 4(a). Each Light OpenVidu TJob employs more time in the individual execution due to the overload caused by the concurrent access, but in this case, it is not relevant because the critical execution time corresponds with the Medium TJobs that mark the final execution of the Test phase.

3. In Fig. 4(c) Medium TJobs are deployed in a parallel way into three instances because they cannot share the same instance. The performance of this scheduling is limited by the execution time of the heavy TJobs, and requires the high amount of resources represented in the figure. This type of scheduling improves the execution time of the test cases whereas it reduces the idle time of the instances which deploy light and heavy TJobs.

4. Last, Fig. 4(d) depicts a parallelization of the Medium TJobs in two separated instances. With this scheduling, the number of instances required by the TJobs are the lowest, providing a similar execution time due to the time employed by the execution of the Heavy TJobs. This is suitable when the execution time is the most

valuable resource to improve and it depends on whether the elasticity cost of performing one extra instance of this type can be assumed.

As shown in this working example, there are several features and constraints that need to be considered for optimizing test scheduling based on resource usage. The critical step is the proper identification of which resources are needed by the test cases and their dependencies.

5   Conclusions and Future Work

This paper introduces a resource-aware E2E test orchestration proposal through: the identification of resources required to run an E2E test case, the grouping of the test cases based on the minimization of the resources to be deployed and on the parallel scheduling of the tests in several machines in order to optimize the resource usage and execution time. The framework proposed, RETORCH, is intended to be used with the ElasTest platform for Cloud test automation, to optimize the execution of the E2E test cases in terms of resource usage. In the paper, we provide a practical example to illustrate the different type of E2E test cases and potential scheduling that can be put in place with them. RETORCH is still under development and we will make it available when more mature. We expect that the several concepts we defined can improve the efficiency of E2E testing by achieving significant savings of resources usage.

There are several open questions that we can summarize in two main lines for future work. The first one is concerned with the resource identification process: we would like to automate the process allowing the detection of the dependencies between resources and test cases. This would require a comprehensive evaluation of these dependencies through tools or resource specification files. Last, the second line of work is focused on the development of one new orchestration method based on Grouping and Scheduling process to optimize in automatic way the resources employed in the E2E tests.

Acknowledgments. This work was supported in part by the Spanish Ministry of Economy and Competitiveness under TestEAMoS (TIN2016-76956-C3-1-R) project and ERDF funds, and by the European Project ElasTest in the Horizon 2020 research and innovation program (GA No. 731535).

References

1. Meyer, M.: Continuous integration and its tools. IEEE Softw. **31**, 14–16 (2014). https://doi.org/10.1109/MS.2014.58
2. Yoo, S., Harman, M.: Regression Testing Minimisation, Selection and Prioritisation: A Survey, p. 60 (2007)
3. Fitzgerald, B., Stol, K.-J.: Continuous software engineering: a roadmap and agenda. J. Syst. Softw. **123**, 176–189 (2017). https://doi.org/10.1016/j.jss.2015.06.063

4. Bertolino, A., et al.: A systematic review on cloud testing. ACM Comput. Surv. (2019, to appear)
5. Bertolino, A., Calabró, A., De Angelis, G., Gallego, M., García, B., Gortázar, F.: When the testing gets tough, the tough get ElasTest. In: Proceedings of the 40th International Conference on Software Engineering: Companion Proceeedings, pp. 17–20. ACM, New York (2018). https://doi.org/10.1145/3183440.3183497
6. Harman, M.: Making the case for MORTO: multi objective regression test optimization. In: 2011 IEEE Fourth International Conference on Software Testing, Verification and Validation Workshops, pp. 111–114. IEEE, Berlin (2011). https://doi.org/10.1109/ICSTW.2011.60
7. Bertolino, A.: Software testing research: achievements, challenges, dreams. In: 2007 Future of Software Engineering, pp. 85–103. IEEE Computer Society, Washington, DC (2007). https://doi.org/10.1109/FOSE.2007.25
8. Rothermel, G., Harrold, M.J., von Ronne, J., Hong, C.: Empirical studies of test-suite reduction. Softw. Test. Verif. Reliab. **12**, 219–249 (2002). https://doi.org/10.1002/stvr.256
9. Wong, W.E., Horgan, J.R., London, S., Mathur, A.: Effect of test set minimization on fault detection effectiveness. In: Proceedings - International Conference on Software Engineering, p. 41 (1995). https://doi.org/10.1002/(SICI)1097-024X(19980410)28:4%3c347::AID-SPE145%3e3.0.CO;2-L
10. Engström, E., Skoglund, M., Runeson, P.: Empirical evaluations of regression test selection techniques: a systematic review. In: ESEM 2008: Proceedings of the 2008 ACM-IEEE International Symposium on Empirical Software Engineering and Measurement, pp. 22–31 (2008). https://doi.org/10.1145/1414004.1414011
11. Bell, J., Kaiser, G., Melski, E., Dattatreya, M.: Efficient dependency detection for safe java test acceleration. In: Proceedings of the 2015 10th Joint Meeting on Foundations of Software Engineering, pp. 770–781. ACM, New York (2015). https://doi.org/10.1145/2786805.2786823
12. Gyori, A., Shi, A., Hariri, F., Marinov, D.: Reliable testing: detecting state-polluting tests to prevent test dependency. In: Proceedings of the 2015 International Symposium on Software Testing and Analysis, p. 223. ACM, New York (2015). https://doi.org/10.1145/2771783.2771793
13. Gambi, A., Bell, J., Zeller, A.: Practical test dependency detection. In: 2018 IEEE 11th International Conference on Software Testing, Verification and Validation (ICST), pp. 1–11 (2018). https://doi.org/10.1109/ICST.2018.00011
14. Gambi, A., Gorla, A., Zeller, A.: O!Snap: cost-efficient testing in the cloud. In: 2017 IEEE International Conference on Software Testing, Verification and Validation (ICST), pp. 454–459 (2017). https://doi.org/10.1109/ICST.2017.51
15. Chakraborty, S.S., Shah, V.: Towards an approach and framework for test-execution plan derivation. In: 2011 26th IEEE/ACM International Conference on Automated Software Engineering (ASE 2011), pp. 488–491 (2011). https://doi.org/10.1109/ASE.2011.6100106
16. Yu, L., Su, Y., Wang, Q.: Scheduling test execution of WBEM applications. In: Proceedings - Asia-Pacific Software Engineering Conference, APSEC, pp. 323–330 (2009). https://doi.org/10.1109/APSEC.2009.27
17. García, B., et al.: A proposal to orchestrate test cases. In: 2018 11th International Conference on the Quality of Information and Communications Technology (QUATIC), pp. 38–46 (2018). https://doi.org/10.1109/QUATIC.2018.00016
18. Esfahani, H., et al.: CloudBuild: Microsoft's distributed and caching build service. In: Proceedings of the 38th International Conference on Software Engineering Companion, pp. 11–20. ACM, New York (2016). https://doi.org/10.1145/2889160.2889222

19. Pérez, P.F.: A web application to make teaching online easy. Contribute to pabloFuente/full-teaching development by creating an account on GitHub (2019)
20. OpenVidu. https://openvidu.io/
21. Kurento. https://www.kurento.org/
22. WebRTC Home | WebRTC. https://webrtc.org/

Verification and Validation

Android Testing Crawler

Jorge Ferreira[1] and Ana C. R. Paiva[1,2(✉)]

[1] Faculty of Engineering of the University of Porto, Porto, Portugal
{up201207133,apaiva}@fe.up.pt
[2] INESC TEC, Porto, Portugal

Abstract. Smartphones are becoming more important in our every-day lives and it is increasingly common to perform critical tasks on these devices, such as making payments. For this reason, ensuring the quality of these applications is an important task. One way to do this is through software testing. However, the testing of these applications presents major challenges due to the wide variety of devices available in the market. In this context, automated testing gains more relevance. There are dynamic test approaches for testing mobile applications, but there are some challenges that need to be overcome for good results, such as, being able to explore the complete behaviour of the application (e.g., overcoming blocking points); choosing appropriate input data; testing dynamic behaviour; testing specific characteristics of mobile applications, such as specific forms of interaction, e.g., long press, and so on. This paper presents a dynamic exploration approach of Android mobile applications that aims to overcome some of the problems identified. During the exploration process, the algorithm builds a Finite State Machine where states are traversed screens and transitions between states describe events that allow moving from one screen to another. This approach is implemented as an extension of the iMPAcT tool. The approach is validated over real Google Play apps and the test coverage results achieved are presented, compared and discussed.

Keywords: Software crawler · Mobile exploration ·
Reverse engineering · Dynamic exploration · Mobile testing

1 Introduction

At the beginning of November 2018, the number of mobile applications available on the Google Play Store was over 2.5 million[1], and in 2017 there were approximately 178.1 billion mobile downloads[2], which shows the importance of smartphones in the daily lives of the world's population. The growing number of existing mobile applications as well as the existence of critical applications makes it very important to ensure that they work the best they can.

---

[1] https://www.appbrain.com/stats/number-of-android-apps.
[2] https://www.statista.com/statistics/271644/worldwide-free-and-paid-mobile-app-store-downloads/.

© Springer Nature Switzerland AG 2019
M. Piattini et al. (Eds.): QUATIC 2019, CCIS 1010, pp. 313–326, 2019.
https://doi.org/10.1007/978-3-030-29238-6_23

One way to increase confidence in the quality of the software is through testing. However, testing mobile applications manually in all the diversity of existing devices may be unfeasible. So, software test automation acquires more relevance in this context.

The simplest way to automatically test a mobile application is through fuzz testing, also known as monkey testing. However, these test techniques have several problems, one of their main being the redundant event generation due to their randomness. Another problem is that tracing suspicious paths to find possible failures is more difficult than in systematic approaches [5].

Model-based testing is a technique that facilitates the automatic exploration of the application under test based on a model that describes its system. The construction of the required model may be based on a reverse engineering process (either static or dynamic) of the target mobile application. However, due to the dynamic and event-based nature of mobile applications, dynamic reverse engineering techniques are more appropriate than static ones [10].

With the increasing concern about testing mobile applications, both official and unofficial test frameworks have emerged, such as Espresso[3], UI Automator[4], Robotium[5] and Appium[6], that provide a set of APIs for creating user interface tests and interacting with the application and with other services dynamically. These frameworks are the basis of many existing mobile application testing tools.

This paper introduces a new dynamic exploration algorithm to test Android mobile applications simulating the typical user behaviour in the application interface. During the process, a Finite State Machine (FSM) is constructed where each state represents a screen and each transition an executed event.

The next section presents motivational examples illustrating common problems in an exploration process; Sect. 3 presents related work and Sect. 4 the iMPAcT tool; the new exploration algorithm is described in Sect. 5; Sect. 6 presents a case study performed over some applications available on the Google Play Store; Finally, the conclusions and future work are presented in Sect. 7.

2   Motivational Examples

Black-box dynamic exploration of mobile applications may be a challenge due to infinite behaviour, blocking points and new forms of interaction.

Mobile applications, due to their dynamic nature, may have an infinite number of events on a screen, causing the automatic exploration process to stay stuck on that screen.

Figures 1 and 2 illustrate cases where there is a multitude of events to run on the same screen. In Fig. 1, whenever an item is added to the list ("New item"), a new GUI element appears immediately below. So, the list of options may grow infinitely (or until some limit is reached). Figure 2 represents a calendar widget,

---

[3] https://developer.android.com/training/testing/espresso.

[4] https://developer.android.com/training/testing/ui-automator.

[5] https://github.com/RobotiumTech/robotium.

[6] https://appium.io.

Fig. 1. Omni Notes screen with dynamic behaviour

Fig. 2. Omni Notes screen that contains a widget with infinite events

with an infinity of events (dates). However, interacting with all these possible dates does not help increase knowledge about the application. Also, applications like YouTube that allow scrolling through a huge list of videos are examples of applications with a huge number of possible events that are impossible to exercise completely.

Identifying different screens may also be a problem because it is not possible to know dynamically when the application reaches a new screen. Thus, to classify two screens as different, some heuristics may be defined. They may classify two screens as different when screen elements are different or by using more complex heuristics that are not sensitive to small changes on the GUI elements. There are already studies that show the importance of the correct distinction of different screens in model-based GUI testing. An example is [5].

Another challenge is the existence of blocking points, such as authentication mechanisms. A login screen may prevent the exploration from accessing private parts of the application. In this case, if correct authentication data is not used, the exploration process will not be able to exercise the entire application.

Finally, the constant evolution of the mobile applications world can bring new forms of interaction. In addition, certain parts of the application may only be accessed through specific gestures. For this reason, a dynamic exploration algorithm should be updated in order to execute all the possible forms of interaction.

3   State of the Art

In the last years, various testing tools for Android mobile applications have been created with the objective of automatically discovering faults. These tools attempt to achieve a high percentage of code coverage in order to increase confidence in the tests performed on the application. Dynamic interface exploration (crawlers) techniques are widely used in the context of mobile applications because of their event-based nature. These techniques can support reverse engineering processes or test processes to these same applications. The dynamic exploration approaches of a mobile application may follow different strategies:

- Random – Random events are generated at the application's interfaces;
- Heuristic – The decision of the event to be executed is made based on heuristics that guide all the exploration process;
- Active Learning – The model is built as the application is tested. Based on this model, it is decided which event should be executed next.

Monkey[7] is a Google tool built into the Android SDK. This tool is capable of automatically generating sequences of pseudorandom events in the interface of an Android application. The main objective of Monkey is to detect crashes in the test application.

Dynodroid [3, 7] is a random testing tool that works with the unmodified binaries of the application under test. This tool can generate events in the interface elements and system events. The authors recognized the importance of human intervention in the exploration and, for this reason, it is possible for the user to manually execute events into the application interface. This type of exploration, as mentioned previously, can generate redundant inputs on the application due to their random nature.

There are also several model-based testing tools where an application model is created. This model is the basis for the event generation process in the application interface. Amalfitano *et al.* [1] have created AndroidRipper that dynamically builds the Android application model following a depth-first exploration strategy. By 2015, this approach has been improved, resulting in a new tool named MobiGUITAR [2]. SwiftHand [16] is a test technique that uses active learning to build the application model during the tests and, based on the learned model, it generates events that try to reach states not yet explored in the application. The new data obtained during the exploration helps to improve the application model. PUMA [6] is a programmable framework that incorporates, in its dynamic analysis, the basic exploration strategy of Monkey that can be configurable to guide the exploration. This tool provides the application model in the form of a finite state machine.

---

[7] https://developer.android.com/studio/test/monkey/.

There are also testing tools that infer the set of events to be executed through static analysis [4,15,17].

As far as we know, there is no crawler that deals with applications that have screens with a growing number of events due to the dynamic addition of GUI elements.

4 iMPAcT Tool

The iMPAcT tool [8,11] automates the testing of recurring behaviour, also known as UI Patterns, present in Android mobile applications. The approach implemented in the tool is based on an iterative process (Fig. 3) of three phases [12]:

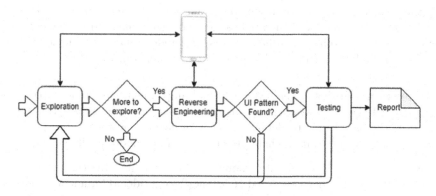

Fig. 3. The iMPAcT tool iterative process.

1. **Exploration of the application under test** - At this phase, a recursive reading of all elements present on the current screen is performed, which represents the current state of the application. After reading the screen, all the events that can be executed are identified. Finally, the event to be executed is selected and executed. The events implemented in the tool associated with the elements of the user interface are: click, check, long click, edit and scroll. For edit events, the tool only supports number and text inputs.
2. **UI Patterns identification** - After the event execution, the current screen is analysed to try to identify possible recurring behaviour (UI Patterns). All the patterns analysed are available in the tool's patterns catalogue.
3. **UI Patterns testing** - If UI Patterns are detected in the previous phase, the Test Patterns associated with each pattern found are applied. Like UI Patterns, Test Patterns are present in the tool's patterns catalogue.

All the patterns present in the tool's catalogue can be formally defined as a tuple <Goal, V, A, C, P> [9,13], where the Goal represents the pattern identification, V is the set of pairs <variable, value> that relates the input data with the variables involved, A defines the sequence of actions to perform, C represents the set of checks to be performed after the actions are executed and P is the precondition indicating whether or not the pattern should be applied.

The patterns currently present in the tool's catalogue, which are based on guidelines provided by Google[8] on how to develop and test Android mobile applications, are: Side Drawer Pattern, Orientation Pattern, Resource Dependency Pattern, Tabs Pattern, Back Pattern, Background Pattern [14], UP Pattern and Action Bar Pattern [12].

The iterative process of the exploration can be terminated by two situations: (1) Manually, with the user pressing the home button on the mobile device; (2) Automatically, when the home screen of the device appears, after pressing the back button in an attempt to return to the previous screen.

At the end of the exploration process, two main artefacts are created [12]: (1) the exploration report, which contains the execution log and the test results, and (2) the application model, represented as a finite state machine where each state symbolizes a new screen of the application and each transition the execution of an event. These artefacts can help the user to understand the behaviour of the application and the results of the tests that were performed.

Exploration Modes. The iMPAcT tool implements different exploration modes to get the set of available events on a screen during its exploration phase. For this, the user needs to define, in the interface of the tool, the exploration mode that he wants to use. There are currently four modes available [12]:

1. **Execute once** – Each event can only be executed once. In other words, if an event has already been executed, it will not be considered for a new execution.
2. **Priority to not executed** – This mode gives priority to events that have not yet been executed. However, if all available events have already been executed, there is the possibility of running some of these events if they lead to states that are not yet fully explored. In this exploration mode, there is also a limit of executions for each event in order to avoid cycles.
3. **Priority to not executed and list items** – This strategy is similar to the previous one and aims to better explore the content of the current screen before switching to a new screen. This way, the events that belong to a list have higher priority than the other events. Furthermore, the "click on the App button" event is only selected when there are no more events to execute.
4. **All events** – This exploration mode is a mode without restrictions. Thus, there is no priority on the events to be executed.

The number of events identified and the total time of exploration depend on the exploration mode initially configured by the user [10].

5   iMPAcT Tool Crawler

Automatically exploring a mobile application is a process that simulates user events in the application interface. This process can help to uncover faults that

---

[8] https://developer.android.com/docs/quality-guidelines/core-app-quality.

would be very costly to find if a manual exploration was performed. Algorithm 1 contains the pseudocode that illustrates the new exploration approach presented in this paper.

The exploration of the application can terminate automatically or manually, and the variable that controls the end of the iterative process is the *finishExploration*. At this moment, there are three stop execution conditions:

- The screens identified are all explored;
- The exploration time limit has been reached;
- The user pressed the home button on the device.

The iterative process starts by reading the structure of the current screen and checking if it is part of the already detected screens (i.e., if it belongs to the list of already identified screens) based on a defined heuristic to compare screens (similar to the ones presented in [11]). If the screen already exists in that list, its inner elements are updated based on the current screen structure; otherwise, the screen is added to the list. In the situation of an already detected screen, it may be necessary to add GUI elements to the screen structure because of the dynamic behaviour. In this case, in order to avoid situations like the one illustrated in Fig. 1, there is a limit of times such screen structure may be updated. In other words, if there are new events added because of new GUI elements, after some upper limit, they will not be added to the screen and not considered in future explorations of the same screen. This upper limit value can be configured by the user.

Next, all the events that are still valid on the current screen are collected (in the *getPossibleEvents*() function). An event is considered valid if:

- Has not yet been executed;
- It has already been executed, but its execution has given rise to new events that have not yet been fully exercised.

The second case is necessary because, due to the dynamic nature of various applications, new elements may appear on the screen as a result of the first event execution (depicted in Fig. 4). If the new elements disappear during exploration and the first event is not executed again, these elements will never be reached again.

Fig. 4. Appearance of new elements on the same screen after clicking on the search button

If there are still valid events, the event to fire next is selected randomly; otherwise, the current screen is marked as explored and another screen not yet explored must be exercised. For this, the algorithm selects the first one present in the list with events to execute. Then, based on the Finite State Machine built during the exploration process, it calculates the shortest sequence of events between the current screen and the screen to be explored using the Dijkstra algorithm.

If such path does not exist, the back event is executed to try to return to the previous screen. After this, if the application closes, it is restarted and the target screen marked as explored. If there is a path, the sequence of events is executed (function *executePath()* in Algorithm 2). Due to the dynamic nature of a mobile application, an already executed event may no longer exist on the screen or the execution of that event may lead to a screen that was not expected. For these reasons, the *executePath()* function checks if the event exists and whether the screen reached is or not the expected one.

The exit situations are dealt in the *dealWithOutOfApp()* function. There are three types of exit considered:

1. Application Crashes – In this situation, the action taken is to close the dialogue associated with the crash and restart the application;
2. User Permissions Requests – The allow button of the dialogue is pressed (required from Android 6);
3. Another type of exit, such as the click on a link that opens another app – The back event is executed to return to the application under test.

5.1   Exploration Modes

At this stage, there are two possible modes of exploration based on the priority of events that can be configured by the user:

– No Priority Mode (Crawling) – All the valid events on a screen can be executed;
– Priority mode (Crawling with priority) – Event priority is as follows: life cycle events > events associated with new elements that appeared on the screen (Fig. 4) > events related to elements of *EditText* or *CheckBox* type > all others events. Events of *EditText* and *CheckBox* elements have priority over the other elements so that, in the exploration process, if a login screen appears, these fields are filled in and only then the button to advance clicked.

5.2   Supported Event Types

Running multiple event types makes it possible to reach more application states and, thus, achieve higher coverage of the application that we are testing. The events implemented in the approach associated with the components present in the user interface are: click, long click, check, edit, scroll, swipe, pinch and drag. In addition, there is a specific event to cover Android life cycle methods.

Algorithm 1. Exploration algorithm

```
 1: finishExploration ← false
 2: while !finishExploration do
 3:     dealWithOutOfApp()
 4:     currentScreen ← readScreen()
 5:     currentScreenOnList ← updateScreen(currentScreen)
 6:     if executedEvent then
 7:         executedEvent.setNextScreen(currentScreenOnList)
 8:     end if
 9:     events ← currentScreen.getPossivelEvents()
10:     if events then
11:         executedEvent ← chooseAndFireEvent(events)
12:     else
13:         currentScreenOnList.setExplored(true)
14:         destScreen ← getNextScreenNotExplored(screens)
15:         eventsPath ← shortestPath(currentScreenOnList, destScreen, screens)
16:         if eventsPath then
17:             executedEvent ← executePath(eventsPath)
18:         else
19:             executedEvent ← new Event(BACK)
20:             executeEvent(executedEvent)
21:             if isOutOfTheApplication() then
22:                 startApplication()
23:                 destScreen.setExplored(true)
24:             end if
25:         end if
26:     end if
27:     if allScreensExplored(screens) or timeExpired() or homePressed() then
28:         finishExploration ← true
29:     end if
30: end while
```

The implemented approach can also detect several input types of an *EditText* element such as *password, email, email subject, phone number, address, time, date, number, signed number, person name, URI, text,* among others.

Although the exploration exercises the scroll event, it is only executed once per element on each screen to prevent execution from being stuck on an infinite scroll screen.

5.3 Configuration File

To assist in the exploration process, the user can configure some data in a configuration file. This data can be divided into two types:

- Exploration data – includes the maximum execution time and the maximum number of updates (upper limit) that can be made to a screen already found;

Algorithm 2. Execute an event path

```
 1: procedure EXECUTEPATH(eventPath)
 2:     for i ← 0 to eventPath.size() - 1 do
 3:         event ← eventPath.get(i)
 4:         screen ← readScreen()
 5:         events ← screen.getAllEvents()
 6:         if !events.contains(event) then
 7:             event.setAvailable(false)
 8:             return null
 9:         end if
10:         executeEvent(event)
11:         expectedScreen ← event.getNextScreen()
12:         screen ← readScreen()
13:         if expectedScreen.isDifferent(screen) then
14:             return event
15:         end if
16:     end for
17:     return null
18: end procedure
```

- Input type data – contains the multiple input types detectable by the algorithm (e.g., *password*) and the value that the user wants to be entered associated with each type.

If the configuration file is not provided, the tool will use default values.

6 Case Study

This case study was performed over mobile applications available in the Google Play Store. These applications were chosen according to the following criteria:

- Must be available in the Google Play Store;
- Number of downloads over 10.000;
- Minimum rating of 4.0;
- Open source;
- Use Gradle to simplify its build;
- Must have a user interface;
- Use a Western European language.

The final set of applications used in this case study is presented in Table 1.

The quality of the exploration process may be assessed by coverage analysis. This analyses may be code based or event based. Code coverage is a measure that indicates how much application code was executed during exploration. This analysis includes several types of coverage, such as classes, methods, lines, among others. Event coverage is a measure that indicates the number of events that were found and exercised during the tests. This technique is particularly useful when validating dynamic analysis techniques of mobile applications.

Table 1. Applications selected.

Application	Version	Number of statements
Omni Notes	6.0.0 Beta 9	38.325
aMetro - World Subway Maps	2.0.1.6	19.681
Easy xkcd	7.3.2	28.483

In this case study, code coverage measures statement coverage, and event coverage measures the events exercised over the ones detected. The goal is to compare the results of three different exploration algorithms:

- priority to not executed and list items,
- crawling and
- crawling with priority.

The first exploration algorithm was already present in the iMPAcT tool and was chosen because, according to the author [10], it provides a more complete exploration identifying more events and executing a higher event percentage. The last two algorithms are the new ones presented in this paper. The execution of these last algorithms was performed using the default values for the different input types of the *EditText* elements and the value 5 for the limit of times that a screen may be updated.

Tables 2 and 3 present the results obtained after exploring the selected applications. In these tables, the following data is analysed:

- Exploration algorithm: the executed algorithm;
- Execution time: the average execution time of the executions;
- Events identified: maximum number of events identified by the executions of the algorithm;
- % events: the average percentage of executed events over identified events;
- % events over max: the average percentage of executed events over the maximum number of events identified in the algorithm executions;
- % events over max all: the average percentage of executed events over the maximum number of events identified by all algorithms;
- % statement coverage: the average percentage of statements covered by the executions of the algorithm.

Each of the exploration algorithms was executed three times due to the randomness associated with the choice of event to be executed. The values present in the tables are the average of all executions. By analysing the results of Table 2, it is possible to verify that:

- Algorithms B and C have a higher percentage of statement coverage than Algorithm A, except for the "Easy xkcd" application, where only Algorithm C has a higher coverage percentage than Algorithm A;

- Algorithms B and C identify a higher number of events in the applications "Omni Notes" and "Easy xkcd";
- In the "aMetro" application, although Algorithms B and C identify fewer events, they have a higher percentage of events executed than Algorithm A, slightly increasing the application statement coverage;
- Algorithm A always ends when the maximum exploration time is reached;
- Algorithm C always execute a higher percentage of events.

The results show that Algorithm C is able to explore better the application, executing more events than the other algorithms. In addition, this algorithm has, on average, a higher percentage of statement coverage.

Table 2. Results obtained when applying the three different exploration algorithms with a 30 min time limit

Exploration algorithm	Execution time	Events identified	% events	% events over max	% events over max all	% statement coverage
Omni Notes						
A - Priority to not executed and list items	30 min 9s 669ms	228	70.4	64.0	39.2	27.0
B - Crawling	27 min 5 s 830 ms	356	69.8	65.7	62.9	35.9
C - Crawling with priority	30 min 6 s 712 ms	372	80.7	72.9	72.9	33.8
aMetro - World Subway Maps						
A - Priority to not executed and list items	30 min 13 s 422 ms	275	41.8	27.2	27.2	62.4
B - Crawling	8 min 36 s 742 ms	133	63.6	55.1	26.7	67.3
C - Crawling with priority	12 min 46 s 968 ms	126	82.4	79.4	36.4	66.6
Easy xkcd						
A - Priority to not executed and list items	30 min 7 s 72 ms	253	68.7	66.8	59.5	50.2
B - Crawling	30 min 3 s 351 ms	299	64.6	55.9	55.9	49.5
C - Crawling with priority	30 min 5 s 581 ms	292	73.4	69.7	68.1	52.9

To analyse the effect of the maximum time on the exploration process, an execution was performed with each of the algorithms in the "Omni Notes" application for a maximum time of 50 min. The results are presented in Table 3 and, by analysing them, it is possible to verify that:

- Algorithm C executes a higher percentage of events than the others;
- With the increase of the maximum time, the statement coverage percentage increases more in Algorithms B and C that in Algorithm A;
- Algorithm B was the only one finishing before the time limit.

Table 3. Results obtained when applying the three different exploration algorithms on the "Omni Notes" application with a 50 min time limit

Exploration algorithm	Execution time	Events identified	% events	% events over max	% events over max all	% statement coverage
A - Priority to not executed and list items	50 min 16 s 601 ms	229	66.9	61.1	27.7	28.1
B - Crawling	43 min 8 s 618 ms	497	68.4	65.9	64.7	39.8
C - Crawling with priority	50 min 5 s 213 ms	506	83.9	72.9	72.9	43.4

The difference in the results obtained between Algorithm A and Algorithms B and C, when increasing the maximum time, show that the latter two modes allow better exploration of the application under test, covering a higher statement percentage and detecting and executing a higher number of events.

7 Conclusions and Future Work

This paper presented a new algorithm to explore Android mobile applications. It was developed as an extension to iMPAcT tool (a mobile testing tool).

It presented motivational examples from real applications that illustrate challenges in black-box dynamic exploration: dynamic behaviour, distinguish screens, exercise all new possible interactions and blocking points.

The goal of this work was to develop strategies to overcome the challenges identified. The algorithm was presented and the strategies used described.

The overall approach was validated through a case study performed over three apps. This is a small set which may be considered a threat to validity. However, in order to mitigate this issue, the subjects were randomly selected over real freely available apps on Google Play Store. The results were analysed in terms of black (events exercised) and white box (statement coverage) coverage.

The experiments performed showed that our crawler is better than the previous existing algorithms on iMPAcT tool. In particular, when we explored during 50 min, our crawler was able to exercise more ~15% of the code.

In the future, we want to compare our crawler with others available on the state of the art, such as Dynodroid [7].

References

1. Amalfitano, D., Fasolino, A., Tramontana, P., De Carmine, S., Memon, A.: Using GUI ripping for automated testing of Android applications. In: 2012 27th IEEE/ACM International Conference on Automated Software Engineering, pp. 258–261. IEEE (2012)
2. Amalfitano, D., Fasolino, A., Tramontana, P., Ta, B., Memon, A.: MobiGUITAR: automated model-based testing of mobile apps. IEEE Softw. **32**(5), 53–59 (2015)

3. Anand, S., Naik, M., Harrold, M.J., Yang, H.: Automated concolic testing of smartphone apps. In: 20th ACM SIGSOFT International Symposium on the Foundations of Software Engineering, pp. 599–609. ACM (2012)

4. Azim, T., Neamtiu, I.: Targeted and depth-first exploration for systematic testing of Android apps. In: 2013 28th ACM SIGPLAN Conference on Object-Oriented Programming, Systems, Languages, and Applications, pp. 641–660. ACM (2013)

5. Baek, Y.M., Bae, D.H.: Automated model-based Android GUI testing using multi-level GUI comparison criteria. In: 2016 31st IEEE/ACM International Conference on Automated Software Engineering, pp. 238–249. ACM (2016)

6. Hao, S., Liu, B., Nath, S., Halfond, W.G.J., Govindan, R.: PUMA: programmable UI-automation for large-scale dynamic analysis of mobile apps. In: Proceedings of the 12th Annual International Conference on Mobile Systems, Applications, and Services, pp. 204–217. ACM (2014)

7. Machiry, A., Tahiliani, R., Naik, M.: Dynodroid: an input generation system for Android apps. In: 2013 9th Joint Meeting of the European Software Engineering Conference and the ACM SIGSOFT Symposium on the Foundations of Software Engineering, pp. 224–234. ACM (2013)

8. Morgado, I.C., Paiva, A.C.R., Faria, J.P.: Automated pattern-based testing of mobile applications. In: 2014 9th International Conference on the Quality of Information and Communications Technology, pp. 294–299. IEEE (2014)

9. Morgado, I., Paiva, A.: The iMPAcT tool: testing UI patterns on mobile applications. In: Proceedings - 2015 30th IEEE/ACM International Conference on Automated Software Engineering, pp. 876–881. IEEE (2015)

10. Morgado, I., Paiva, A.: Impact of execution modes on finding android failures. Procedia Comput. Sci. **83**, 284–291 (2016)

11. Morgado, I., Paiva, A.: Mobile GUI testing. Software Qual. J. **26**(4), 1553–1570 (2018)

12. Morgado, I.C., Paiva, A.C.R.: The iMPAcT tool for Android testing. Proc. ACM Hum.-Comput. Interact. (EICS) **3**, 4:1–4:23 (2019)

13. Morgado, I.C., Paiva, A.C.: Testing approach for mobile applications through reverse engineering of UI patterns. In: Proceedings - 2015 30th IEEE/ACM International Conference on Automated Software Engineering Workshops, pp. 42–49. IEEE (2015)

14. Paiva, A.C.R., Gouveia, J.M.E.P., Elizabeth, J., Delamaro, M.E.: Testing when mobile apps go to background and come back to foreground. In: 2019 IEEE International Conference on Software Testing, Verification and Validation Workshops, pp. 102–111 (2019)

15. Salihu, I.A., Ibrahim, R., Ahmed, B.S., Zamli, K.Z., Usman, A.: AMOGA: a static-dynamic model generation strategy for mobile apps testing. IEEE Access **7**, 17158–17173 (2019)

16. Choi, W., Necula, G., Sen, K.: Guided GUI testing of Android apps with minimal restart and approximate learning. ACM SIGPLAN Not. **48**(10), 623–639 (2013)

17. Yang, W., Prasad, M.R., Xie, T.: A grey-box approach for automated GUI-model generation of mobile applications. In: Cortellessa, V., Varró, D. (eds.) FASE 2013. LNCS, vol. 7793, pp. 250–265. Springer, Heidelberg (2013). https://doi.org/10.1007/978-3-642-37057-1_19

Local Observability and Controllability Enforcement in Distributed Testing

Bruno Lima[1,2]([⊠]) [iD], João Pascoal Faria[1,2] [iD], and Robert Hierons[3] [iD]

[1] Faculty of Engineering of the University of Porto, Porto, Portugal
{bruno.lima,jpf}@fe.up.pt
[2] INESC TEC, Porto, Portugal
[3] The University of Sheffield, Sheffield, UK
robert.hierons@gmail.com

Abstract. To ensure interoperability and the correct end-to-end behavior of heterogenous distributed systems, it is important to conduct integration tests that verify the interactions with the environment and between the system components in key scenarios. The automation of such integration tests requires that test components are also distributed, with local testers deployed close to the system components, coordinated by a central tester. In such a test architecture, it is important to maximize the autonomy of the local testers to minimize the communication overhead and maximize the fault detection capability. A test scenario is called locally observable and locally controllable, if conformance errors can be detected locally and test inputs can be decided locally, respectively, by the local testers, without the need for exchanging coordination messages between the test components during test execution (i.e., without any communication overhead). For test scenarios specified by means of UML sequence diagrams that don't exhibit those properties, we present in this paper an approach with tool support to automatically find coordination messages that, added to the given scenario, make it locally controllable and locally observable.

Keywords: Model-based testing · Observability · Controllability · Integration testing · Distributed systems · UML

1 Introduction

Due to the increasing ubiquity, complexity and need for assurance of software-based systems [1], testing is a fundamental but challenging lifecycle activity, with a huge economic impact if not performed adequately [12]. Test automation is particularly challenging for the end-to-end services that are being proposed in several domains (e-health, smart cities, etc.), based on the integration of multiple devices and applications from different vendors, forming distributed and heterogeneous systems or systems of systems, often subject to timing requirements [9]. To ensure interoperability and the correct end-to-end behavior of such systems,

© Springer Nature Switzerland AG 2019
M. Piattini et al. (Eds.): QUATIC 2019, CCIS 1010, pp. 327–338, 2019.
https://doi.org/10.1007/978-3-030-29238-6_24

it is important to conduct integration tests that verify not only the interactions with the environment but also between the system components in key scenarios.

Integration test scenarios for that purpose may be conveniently specified by means of UML Sequence Diagrams [11] (SDs), because they are an industry standard well suited for describing and visualizing the interactions that occur between the components and actors of a distributed system, and may be enriched with control flow variants and time constraints.

In order to be able to check the interactions with the environment (actors) and between the system components, *local testers* have to be deployed close to the system components, coordinated by a *central tester* (Fig. 1). Besides observing the messages sent and received by each component (acting as *test monitors*), local testers may also inject test inputs, simulating actors (as *test drivers*) or even system components (as *test stubs*). To cope with non-determinism, test inputs may have to be decided at runtime in an adaptive way, based on the observed execution events and the behavioral specification.

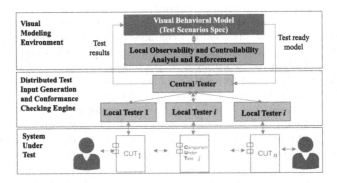

Fig. 1. Test architecture for the model-based integration testing of distributed systems.

In such a test architecture, it is important to minimize the communication overhead between test components during test execution, particularly in the presence of time constraints, and detect errors as early as possible, to facilitate fault localization. Ideally, after the central tester initiates the local testers, no communication between test components occurs during test execution, and the central tester only needs to receive a verdict from each local tester at the end of successful execution or as soon as an error is detected.

A test scenario is called locally observable and locally controllable, if conformance errors can be detected locally and test inputs can be decided locally, respectively, by the local testers, without the need for exchanging coordination messages between the test components during test execution. Procedures for checking if a test scenario specified by a UML SD is locally controllable and locally observable, pinpointing violations to those properties, were presented in [8]. However, approaches to refine scenarios that don't exhibit those properties, in order to make them locally observable and locally controllable, were not addressed, as we intend to do in this paper.

Hence, the main contributions of this paper are:

- an algorithm, with tool support, to automatically suggest coordination messages to add to an integration test scenario of a distributed system, described by a UML SD, in order to make it locally observable and locally controllable;
- examples of test scenarios that exhibit different combinations of local observability and local controllability properties, illustrating common causes of local observability and local controllability problems, and ways to overcome them by adding coordination messages.

To our knowledge, although observability and controllability have been addressed by other authors in the context of distributed systems testing, previous work did not address the automatic generation of coordination messages to enforce the properties of local observability and controllability in the context of integration testing with control flow variants and time constraints.

The rest of the paper is organized as follows: Sect. 2 provides some motivating examples; Sect. 3 presents the algorithm to automatically enforce local observability and controllability; implementation and evaluation is described in Sect. 4; related work is presented in Sect. 5 and conclusions and future work are presented in Sect. 6.

2   Motivating Examples

Figure 2 shows examples of simple scenarios to illustrate local observability and controllability problems and ways to overcome them.

Scenario (a) illustrates a local controllability problem caused by a race condition. Based on local knowledge only, lifeline $L1$ doesn't know when to send z to ensure that it arrives at $L3$ after y, so it may generate invalid (*unintended*) traces with $?z$ before $?y$. On the right, are illustrated the way to overcome this problem. The solution is add a *coordination message* c from $L3$ to $L1$, so that $L1$ knows when to safely send z. From a testing perspective, assuming that $L1$ is simulated by a local tester (test driver) and $L3$ is monitored by another local tester, the coordination message would be exchanged between the local testers (without affecting the SUT). The communication overhead of this solution (1 message) is much smaller than the overhead incurred by a centralized testing approach, in which the events observed by the local testers are constantly communicated to the central tester (4 messages from the local testers at $L2$ and $L3$ to the central tester), that decides and communicates back to the local testers the next test inputs (2 messages from the central tester to the local tester at $L1$).

Scenario (b) illustrates a local observability problem caused by an optional message without a corresponding acknowledgment message. If message x is lost (i.e., is sent by $L1$ but does not arrive at $L2$), the problem will go unnoticed at $L2$, because not receiving any message is also a valid behavior. In other words, the invalid trace $[!x]$ is *locally uncheckable*. This problem may be overcome by adding a coordination (acknowledgment) message c, as illustrated on the

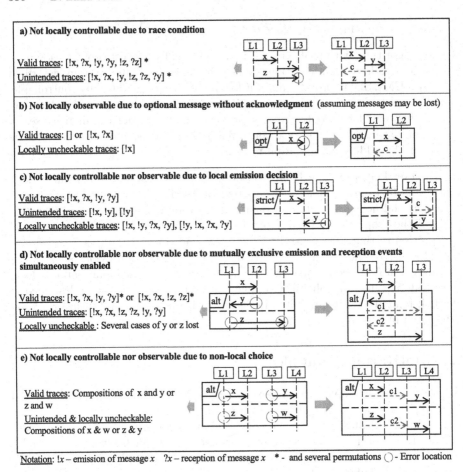

Fig. 2. Interaction fragments with local observability and controllability problems and possible refinements.

right; now, if x is lost, that will be noticed at $L1$. The coordination message need only be exchanged between the local testers. Again, the communication overhead of this solution (1 message) is smaller than the overhead of a centralized testing approach, in which the events observed by the local testers are constantly communicated to the central tester for conformance checking (2 messages from the local testers at $L1$ and $L2$ to the central tester).

Scenario (c) illustrates a local observability and local controllability problem caused by a local emission decision. Based on local knowledge only, lifeline $L3$ does not know when to send y to ensure that this is done only after x has reached $L2$ (the `strict` interaction operator requires that all events in one interaction operand occur before all the events in the next interaction operand). The early emission of y can then lead to invalid (*unintended*) traces with $!y$ before $?x$. On the other hand, the above error is not locally observable, since, based on local knowledge only, the invalid execution trace $[!x, !y, ?x, ?y]$ is *locally uncheckable*. As described on the right, to solve this problem we need to add a coordinating message c between $L2$ and $L3$, so that $L3$ knows when it can send message y. The communication overhead of this solution (1 message) is smaller than the overhead of a centralized testing approach, in which the events observed by the local testers are constantly communicated to the central tester (4 messages from the local testers at $L1$, $L2$ and $L3$ to the central tester), that decides and communicates back to the local testers the next test inputs (2 messages from the central tester to the local testers at $L1$ and $L3$).

Scenario (d) illustrates a local observability and local controllability problem caused by mutually exclusive emission and reception events simultaneously enabled. In this case, $L1$ and $L2$ do not have local information that allows them to determine which alternative should be executed; this can lead to the invalid (*unintended*) traces with $!y$ and $!z$ (in the same execution trace). The scenario is also *locally uncheckable*, since the loss of messages y or z will not be detected by the lifelines $L1$ and $L3$, because the non-receipt of these messages is a locally valid trace. In order to overcome this problem we need to add a coordinating message $c1$ between $L1$ and $L3$ and a coordinating message $c2$ between $L2$ and $L1$; with this, $!z$ will only be executed if $!c$ occurs. The communication overhead of this solution (2 messages) is, again, smaller than the overhead of a centralized testing approach.

Scenario (e) illustrates a local observability and local controllability problem due to a non-local choice. In this case, and based only on local information, $L3$ does not know in which situations it should send y or w, leading to invalid (*unintended*) traces with combinations of x & w and z & y. Locally this error is also not detectable, since for $L2$ and $L4$, reception of x or z and y or w is always locally valid. In order to solve this problem (as shown on the right), two coordination messages ($c1$ and $c2$) are required between $L1$ and $L2$. With these coordination messages, $L3$ becomes able to know locally which message to send in order to ensure correct execution. Once again, the communication overhead of this solution (2 messages) is smaller than the overhead of a centralized testing approach.

In all cases, the scenarios on the right are *refinements* of the scenario on the left, in the sense that execution traces valid for the latter are also valid for the former (with coordination messages removed), although the opposite may not be true (the semantics is narrowed for the sake of implementability and testability).

All the violations (unintended and locally uncheckable traces) and the recommendation of the coordination messages are determined automatically by our tool. The process of how to automatically check if an integration test scenario is locally observable and locally controllable, pinpointing any violations (locally uncheckable and unintended traces, respectively) was previously described by [8]. In the rest of the paper we show how to automatically determine the coordination messages to enforce local observability and controllability.

3   Algorithm to Search for Coordination Messages

For the case of interactions (UML SDs) that are not locally observable or locally controllable, we present in this section an algorithm to search for coordination messages (one or more) to be added to the given interaction, in order to enforce local observability and local controllability, whilst preserving the traces valid locally at each lifeline.

Several heuristics are used to guide the search. The first heuristic, used when searching for single message solutions, is based on the intuition that the locations of local observability and local controllability problems (locations where the locally uncheckable or unintended traces deviate from valid traces), might suggest points where coordination messages need to be inserted. When a single message solution is not found, multiple message solutions are searched in an incremental way, inspecting first messages that contribute to a higher reduction of the number of problematic traces (locally uncheckable and/or unintended traces).

Algorithm 1 (Search for coordination messages). Finds a set of coordination messages to enforce local observability and local controllability of a test scenario specified by an interaction (UML SD) ι, in the following steps:

1. Determine the set V of valid traces defined by ι, following the procedure described in [8];
2. Determine the set U of unintended and/or locally uncheckable traces of ι (problematic traces), following the procedures described in [8];
3. Determine a set S of *suspicious* lifeline locations in ι (locations where coordination messages might need to be inserted), as follows:
   (a) Truncate on error the traces in U, obtaining a set T of truncated traces, proceeding as follows for each trace $u \in U$:
      i. in case u is a valid partial trace (i.e., $\exists v \in V \cdot u \in prefixes(v)$), we consider that it is already truncated on error (notice that u cannot be a valid complete trace (i.e., $u \notin V$), by the definition of U);
      ii. otherwise, select the prefix t of u such that t is not a valid partial trace, but $t_{1,...,|t|-1}$ (with the last event removed) is;
   (b) Determine the set $\mathcal{E}$ of missing or erroneous events in the traces in T, proceeding as follows for each trace $t \in T$:
      i. in case t is a valid partial trace, select all the valid next events, i.e., select the set $\{e | t \frown [e] \in prefixes(V)\}$ (missing events);
      ii. otherwise, select the last event in t (erroneous event);
   (c) Determine the set S of lifeline locations where the events in $\mathcal{E}$ occur (notice that each event corresponds to the emission or reception of a message);
4. Determine a set C of candidate coordination messages, according to the following criteria:
   – candidate messages can start in any location in any lifeline (before/after an emission event, a reception event, a boundary of a combined fragment or a boundary of an interaction operand);

- candidate messages cannot cross boundaries of interaction operands, and, inside an interaction operand, can only be exchanged between participating lifelines;
- candidate messages can terminate in any lifeline, different from the start lifeline, in the earliest possible location;
- candidate messages that are received immediately before another reception event are discarded, to avoid introducing a race condition;

5. Rank the candidate messages in C based on their proximity to the suspicious locations in S, and obtain a sorted set C' of candidates, filtering out candidates below a certain threshold (e.g., to exclude candidates that do not touch any suspicious lifeline);

6. Search for single message solutions, proceeding as follows for each candidate c (message with emission and reception locations) in C', by the defined order:

   (a) insert the message into the selected locations in ι, obtaining an augmented interaction ι';

   (b) determine the set $\mathcal{V}'$ of valid traces defined by ι';

   (c) check if the projections of $\mathcal{V}$ and $\mathcal{V}'$ (with coordination events removed) onto each lifeline of ι coincide (i.e., the traces valid locally at each lifeline are preserved); if they don't coincide, discard this candidate;

   (d) determine the set $\mathcal{U}'$ of unintended and/or locally uncheckable traces of ι'; if such set is empty, terminate and return this candidate c; otherwise, if $\#\mathcal{U}'$ (with coordination events removed) is not smaller than $\#\mathcal{U}$, discard this candidate;

7. If a single message solution was not found in the previous step, search for multiple message solutions as follows:

   (a) pick the candidate messages in C that were not discarded in steps 6c or 6d, and re-rank them by decreasing values of $\#\mathcal{U} - \#\mathcal{U}'$ (with coordination events removed), i.e., based on how many invalid traces each candidate eliminates, producing a new ordered set C'' of candidates;

   (b) for each candidate message $c \in C''$, by the defined order, insert c onto ι and execute recursively this same algorithm (with the calculations of steps 1–2 already performed); if a solution is found, return the inserted coordination messages;

8. If no single or multiple message solution was found in steps 6 or 7, fail.

By construction (built-in checks in steps 6c and 6d), when the above algorithm finds a solution, it is always a valid (admissible) solution, in the sense that the augmented interaction is locally observable and locally controllable, and traces valid locally at each lifeline are preserved.

Although variants (with higher processing time) of the algorithm could be considered to ensure that the solution found is of minimum size, the presented algorithm doesn't give such a guarantee in the case of multiple message solutions. Nevertheless, it is structured in a way that tends to minimize the size of the solution.

Depending on the threshold used in step 5, the algorithm might be unable to find a solution when a solution exists, but the user may relax the threshold (or it may be relaxed automatically).

Several variants of the above algorithm may be considered: different thresholds can be considered to filter out candidates in step 5; instead of searching for one solution, one can search for all solutions up to a given size; in the case of time constrained interactions, one can work with time constrained traces (pairs of traces and associated time constraints), instead of simple traces; instead of enforcing both local observability and local controllability, one might want to enforce just one of these properties (local controllability is usually the most relevant).

In any case, the solution produced by the algorithm should be regarded as a recommendation (quick fix) that the user may accept or not.

4   Implementation and Evaluation

We specified, at a high level of abstraction, the algorithm described in the previous section and auxiliary operations in the VDM++ formal specification language [3]. Specifications in VDM++ can be directly executed with the Overture [7] tool and translated to Java code ready for execution and integration with other code (namely for importing UML diagrams).

To test the implemented algorithms regarding efficiency and effectiveness, we used the examples presented in Fig. 2. The results obtained can be observed in Table 1. The experiment was conducted in an Intel Core i7 machine running Windows 10 Professional at 2.20 GHz with 16 GB RAM.

Table 1. Execution results of the implemented algorithm for the examples in Fig. 2.

SD	Number of valid traces	Number of unintended traces	Number of locally uncheckable traces	Running time	Size of the solution (number of coordination messages)	Number of candidate solutions inspected
(a)	4	6	0	0.5 s	1	1
(b)	2	0	1	0.3 s	1	1
(c)	1	2	2	0.5 s	1	2
(d)	4	7	11	2.7 s	2	10
(e)	12	8	12	3.6 s	2	5

In all cases, the solution found (with one or two coordination messages) coincides with the expected solution (of minimal size) as described in Fig. 2.

The effectiveness of the heuristics used to guide the search can be assessed based on the number of candidate solutions inspected, 1 being the optimal value. In the case of single message solutions, for this set of examples, the heuristic was quite effective, because the number of candidates inspected is equal or close to 1, whilst the number of possible candidates is quite larger (e.g., 6 candidates are generated in case a). In the case of multiple message solutions, because the algorithm first tries to inspect all promising coordination messages individually, the number of candidate solutions inspected increases, but is still much smaller than the number of all possible pairs.

Regarding the time efficiency, the running time is higher to find multiple message solutions, as one would expect.

In order to validate the algorithm in an industrial scenario, we conducted an evaluation experiment with a real world test scenario from an industrial partner who is currently developing a solution for automatic incident detection on motorways. We asked our partner to describe the system interactions (including temporal constraints) using UML SDs. Figure 3 shows one of the scenarios that was provided (without the coordination message in red). The scenario contains some time constraints between pairs of events, denoted {min..max}, representing the minimum and maximum time elapsed between the events, in some time scale (seconds, in this case).

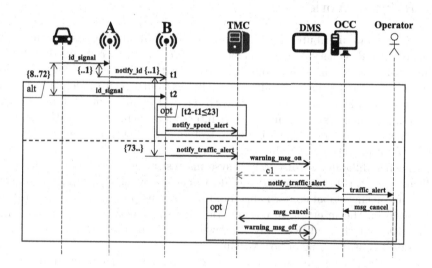

Fig. 3. Motorway incident detection scenario. (Color figure online)

The scenario involves 3 alternatives. In the first case, a vehicle circulating on the motorway is detected by sensors A and B, situated 1 km apart, in a time interval between 24 s and 72 s (indicating that the vehicle circulates at a speed between 50 and 150 km/h). In this case the system does not need to take any action. In the second case, the vehicle is detected by sensors A and B in a time interval less then 23 s, which corresponds to a speed above 150 km/h. In this case the system sends a speed alert to the Traffic Management Controller (TMC). In the last case, a vehicle is detected by sensor A but is not detected by sensor B in the next 72 s, meaning that something may have occurred with the vehicle and it may be immobilized on the road. In this case, the system informs the TMC that automatically sends a message to be presented to the other drivers through the DMS and informs the Operational Coordination Center (OCC). In the OCC the operator visualizes the alert and can optionally cancel the alert which is done through the TMC that removes the message from the DMS.

We analyzed the provided test scenario with our tool and we detected unintended traces, corresponding to situations in which the warning_msg_off message reaches the DMS lifeline before the warning_msg_on message. In 3.4 s our tool was able to suggest the insertion of a coordination message c1 (indicated in red in Fig. 3), in order to make the scenario locally controllable.

Although our validation focused only on one industrial scenario, our approach is scaleable for large systems because what matters is the size of each test scenario. From our experience, even in large ecosystems, test scenarios tend to be of small to moderate size (with dozens but not thousands of messages). In bigger systems we will have a larger number of diagrams to analyze.

5   Related Work

One difficulty in distributed systems testing is observability, because communication delays and the lack of a global clock limit the conformance faults detectable. Three test architectures have been proposed, with different conformance relations and fault detection capabilities: purely distributed, with independent local testers communicating synchronously with the SUT components [13]; purely centralized, in which a single central tester interacts asynchronously with the SUT components [5]; hybrid, combining local testers and a central tester to achieve a higher fault detection capability [5].

Another difficulty in distributed systems testing is controllability, i.e., the difficulty for the local testers to decide when and what test inputs to inject, without causing global conformance faults. Solutions proposed in the literature are based on the insertion of coordination messages between test components [2,4,6,10], but they address only the "when" and not the "what" aspect (i.e., they don't consider control flow variants).

In [4], the authors investigate the use of coordination messages to overcome controllability problems when testing from an input/output transition system and give an algorithm for introducing sufficient messages; however, the approach is focused on system testing only, and not integration testing. In [10], the author discusses the problems related to race conditions in scenarios described through MSCs or UML SDs, and presents solutions to these problems; however, control flow variants are not taken into consideration. In [2], the authors propose algorithms to extend test scenarios for distributed systems represented by MSCs or UML SDs, in order to obtain race-free scenarios suitable for test implementation, by inserting coordination messages between test components and quiescence observation events in each test component; however, in their work, only the interactions with the environment are modeled.

A common limitation of the above works is that they only consider the messages exchanged with the environment (system testing), represented by a single input or output event, and not the messages exchanged between system components (integration testing), that need to be represented by pairs of events.

More recently, observability and controllability in the context of integration testing of distributed systems based on UML SDs were analyzed in [8]. However, they did not address the automatic generation of coordination messages to overcome local observability or local controllability problems, as we do here.

6   Conclusions and Future Work

Given the growing importance of distributed systems testing and the need to minimize the communication overhead during test execution, we address in this paper the problem of local observability and controllability enforcement in model-based integration testing of distributed systems, with test scenarios specified by means of UML SDs. In order to solve the problem we have created an algorithm that automatically suggests where coordination messages must be inserted in order to guarantee these properties. All the algorithms were formalized in an executable specification language (VDM++), translatable to Java, and validated with several test scenarios. To validate the algorithms in an industrial setting, we conducted an evaluation experiment with a real world test scenario from an industrial partner. In that experiment, our tool was able to correctly locate local controllability issues, and suggest a corresponding fix.

As future work, we intend to integrate the developed algorithms in a tool chain for integration testing of time-constrained distributed systems and to explore the possibility of resolving controllability and observability problems by adding time constraints instead of just coordination messages.

References

1. Boehm, B.: Some future software engineering opportunities and challenges. In: Nanz, S. (ed.) The Future of Software Engineering, pp. 1–32. Springer, Berlin (2011). https://doi.org/10.1007/978-3-642-15187-3_1
2. Boroday, S., Petrenko, A., Ulrich, A.: Implementing MSC tests with quiescence observation. In: Núñez, M., Baker, P., Merayo, M.G. (eds.) FATES/TestCom - 2009. LNCS, vol. 5826, pp. 49–65. Springer, Heidelberg (2009). https://doi.org/10.1007/978-3-642-05031-2_4
3. Durr, E., Van Katwijk, J.: VDM++, a formal specification language for object-oriented designs. In: CompEuro 1992. Proceedings of Computer Systems and Software Engineering, pp. 214–219. IEEE (1992)
4. Hierons, R.M.: Overcoming controllability problems in distributed testing from an input output transition system. Distrib. Comput. **25**(1), 63–81 (2012). https://doi.org/10.1007/s00446-011-0153-5
5. Hierons, R.M.: Combining centralised and distributed testing. ACM Trans. Softw. Eng. Methodol. **24**(1), 5:1–5:29 (2014). https://doi.org/10.1145/2661296
6. Hierons, R.M., Merayo, M.G., Núñez, M.: Using time to add order to distributed testing. In: Giannakopoulou, D., Méry, D. (eds.) FM 2012. LNCS, vol. 7436, pp. 232–246. Springer, Heidelberg (2012). https://doi.org/10.1007/978-3-642-32759-9_20

7. Larsen, P.G., et al.: VDM-10 language manual. Technical report (2016)
8. Lima, B.M.C., Faria, J.C.P.: Towards decentralized conformance checking in model-based testing of distributed systems. In: 2017 IEEE International Conference on Software Testing, Verification and Validation Workshops (ICSTW), pp. 356–365, March 2017. https://doi.org/10.1109/ICSTW.2017.64
9. Lima, B., Faria, J.P.: Automated testing of distributed and heterogeneous systems based on UML sequence diagrams. In: Lorenz, P., Cardoso, J., Maciaszek, L.A., van Sinderen, M. (eds.) ICSOFT 2015. CCIS, vol. 586, pp. 380–396. Springer, Cham (2016). https://doi.org/10.1007/978-3-319-30142-6_21
10. Mitchell, B.: Resolving race conditions in asynchronous partial order scenarios. IEEE Trans. Softw. Eng. **31**(9), 767–784 (2005). https://doi.org/10.1109/TSE.2005.104
11. OMG: OMG Unified Modeling Language TM (OMG UML) Version 2.5. Technical report, Object Management Group (2015)
12. Tassey, G.: The economic impacts of inadequate infrastructure for software testing. National Institute of Standards and Technology, RTI Project 7007(011) (2002)
13. Ulrich, A., König, H.: Architectures for testing distributed systems. In: Csopaki, G., Dibuz, S., Tarnay, K. (eds.) Testing of Communicating Systems. ITIFIP, vol. 21, pp. 93–108. Springer, Boston (1999). https://doi.org/10.1007/978-0-387-35567-2_7

Mutation-Based Web Test Case Generation

Sérgio Almeida[1], Ana C. R. Paiva[1,2](✉), and André Restivo[1]

[1] Faculty of Engineering, University of Porto, Porto, Portugal
{up201403074,apaiva,arestivo}@fe.up.pt
[2] INESC TEC, Porto, Portugal

Abstract. Regression testing is of paramount importance to ensure that the quality of software does not suffer when code changes are implemented. However, having a large set of tests is mostly done by hand and is time-consuming. Regression tests are written to test functionality that is already implemented and thus are a prime target for automatic test generation. Mutation testing is a technique that evaluates the quality of tests by applying simple changes to source code and checking if any test detects those changes. This paper presents an approach focused on GUI Testing that takes the idea behind mutation testing and applies it, not to the source code, but the actual tests. Generated tests are then analyzed, and those that generate different outcomes are chosen. The set of initial test cases is obtained from the interactions of the actual users of the service under analysis. In the end, an evaluation of the approach is presented.

Keywords: Software testing · Mutation testing · Test case generation · Web testing

1 Introduction

Software development is challenging, and evolving a system that is already in production is even harder. Source code changes in one place can have repercussions in a different area. To make things easier, we usually rely on regression tests to make sure code changes are not breaking parts that were previously working.

Testing Graphical User Interfaces (GUIs) is a challenge on its own. One of the reasons for this is that the number of possible interactions users can perform is extremely large, and the number of different combinations of those interactions if even higher. This means that selecting meaningful interactions is crucial in creating a good test suite without an explosion in the number of test cases.

Our approach uses real test cases provided by web usage information that has been captured using a web analytics tool. We start by using the most commonly performed user interaction paths calculated by the tool as regression tests. But we argue that these can be improved by generating more test cases that exercise other aspects of the application under test.

© Springer Nature Switzerland AG 2019
M. Piattini et al. (Eds.): QUATIC 2019, CCIS 1010, pp. 339–346, 2019.
https://doi.org/10.1007/978-3-030-29238-6_25

Mutation testing is a testing technique which injects mutations in source code and checks if a test suite can detect them. This is a common way to assess the quality of a test suite. The goal of this work is to apply mutations over existing test cases (most frequent paths of user interaction over a web application) and check which ones produce different results from the original tests when exercising the website. The mutations, applied directly in the test cases instead of in the source code, try to change the original test case in order to detect some additional problems as will be explained in Sect. 3.

This paper is organized as follows: Sect. 2 presents the state of the art; Sect. 3 describes the structure of the initial test cases, which problems we want to detect and which mutations to apply; Sect. 4 presents a case study to illustrate the presented approach and the results; Sect. 5 presents conclusions and future work.

2   State of the Art

GUIs are an essential part of software systems as it is through them that users interact with the system. It is crucial that the behavior of the program corresponds to the user's expectations.

Testing GUIs manually is a very hard and a costly task [8]. Currently, GUIs are becoming more sophisticated and with lots of controls, so manual testing is becoming unfeasible. Automating this task will allow the detection of faults earlier and provide a superior product.

Besides random testing, there are three main techniques to automate GUI tests: *model-based testing, capture & replay* and *scripting*. There is a lot of research in model-based testing, which is a technique to generate test cases from a model based on software requirements [3]. Barbosa et al. proposed an approach for model-based testing of graphical user interfaces from task models [1].

Capture & replay is a technique which records user interactions from the software under test and converts them into test cases [5]. These test cases are scripts which are executed automatically to simulate the user interactions within the application.

Scripting is when testers write a script with test instructions using one of the languages supported by the test framework such as Selenium, which is the framework used in this work.

Automated web testing has been explored and there are some approaches which generate test cases from web usage information. *REQAnalytics* is a recommendation system [2] that collects information from web usage information and makes recommendations to change the requirements. An extension was developed that generates test cases from this information, an approach proposed in [9].

There is also an approach proposed by Koroglu et al. which injects mutations in test cases instead of in the source code [4]. Some other testing tools, like Sapienz [7], apply mutations directly into test cases. EvoDroid [6] uses evolutionary testing through genetic algorithms to generate new test cases based on the original test suite.

3   Test Case Generation

3.1   Generation and Execution

The initial test cases were collected by a *JavaScript* script running on the client side and saving the collected data into a graph database: Neo4j. Each sequence on the database corresponds to a test case, ordered by execution step (`elementPos`) and grouped by session (`session`). Once they are stored, it is possible, through the tool, to download and save each test case on a JSON file. The structure of each JSON file is an array of JSON objects, in which each object represents a step. Each step is the action performed in a web element and contains the necessary information to reproduce it. Listing 1.1 shows the structure of an example JSON file containing a test case which contains two steps: an *input* and a *click* which represent a simple search on the website.

Listing 1.1. JSON structure of a test case

```
[
  {
    "path": "id(\"search\")/input[@class=\"text\"]",
    "session": "dfdf5a5d-98a4-d90d-334d-094fb7180d80",
    "actionId": 3,
    "action": "input",
    "pathId": 5,
    "elementPos": 1,
    "value": [
      "char",
      "char",
      "char",
      "Enter"
    ],
    "url": "http://www.ipvc.pt/"
  },
  {
    "path": "id(\"searchbutton\")",
    "session": "dfdf5a5d-98a4-d90d-334d-094fb7180d80",
    "actionId": 1,
    "action": "click",
    "pathId": 7,
    "elementPos": 2,
    "url": "http://www.ipvc.pt/"
  }
]
```

From these JSON files, it is possible to generate test scripts written in Java and the Selenium framework and reproduce them whenever desired. This generation process is made by identifying the element selected by the provided XPath and applying the corresponding action. Selenium provides a lot of ways to identify the elements: by id, class name, tag name, name, link text, partial link text, CSS and XPath. XPath stands for XML Path Language and uses a non-XML syntax to point to different parts of an XML document [1]. It is used to navigate through the DOM of the web page using its structure. This may be a better way to find an element than using its *id*, because the *id* may be dynamic or non-existent.

In order to protect sensitive and personal information, the input data is not recorded and it is necessary to use random data to reproduce these type of actions. The information stored about the input data is the `value` field. It contains the word 'char' as many times as the user presses a key. It also distinguishes numbers and some keys such as tab, delete, backspace, and space. If the input data is made by a 'copy-paste', the 'String' word appears in this field. The tool contains a random data generator which can be easily updated to provide data according to the software under test.

The tool allows reproducing 5 types of actions: click, input, drag and drop, back and forward. These are the main supported actions by the Selenium [2] framework. In the drag and drop action, the `value` field contains the *XPath* of the second object. This object corresponds to the place where the first object (pointed by the `path` field) will be dropped. The drag and drop action is not supported in HTML5, so a JavaScript file is used to perform this action. It is also possible to execute the generated tests in two browsers: *Google Chrome* and *Mozilla Firefox*.

At the end of the execution, a report will be generated. The report includes the result of each test case and, in the end, the number of passed and failed tests.

3.2   Mutations

The goal of this work is to extend these generated test cases with mutations to detect specific additional problems. Some different operators were created in order to detect this problems and modify the test cases:

1. **Remove Step.** Exercise situations when user skips interaction with mandatory fields. This problem can be detected by injecting a mutation which removes the mandatory step and so the generated test case will have a different behaviour. The Remove Step mutation is the operator which removes a specific step from the total steps of the test case.
2. **Add Step.** Check if the verification of some fields is correctly done. For example, on a registration form, there is usually one field to insert the password and another field to confirm the password. If the password check is made only on the second step, another input in the first field will not be validated and the program will not be able to catch this error. To detect this problem, it is possible to inject a mutation by adding an input in the first field, after the second one. The Add Step mutation operator receives two input fields as parameter. It adds another input step in the first input field after the execution of the two inputs.

---

[1] XPath - Documentation, https://developer.mozilla.org/en-US/docs/Web/XPath.
[2] Selenium - Documentation, https://www.seleniumhq.org/docs/03webdriver.jsp.

3. **Change Step Order.** Another way to detect the problem above is to swap the execution order of these steps. Change Step Order mutation is the operator which changes the order of two input fields.

4. **Data Generator.** The tool is also capable of checking the behaviour of the system with different input data. The tool is prepared to add data generators, such as name generators, address generators, that can be used to test the software with different data. This is made by adding a tag to the `value` field which identifies the desired generator. This mutation calculates all the possible combinations among the number of available inputs and generates test cases with different tags, resulting in different types of data. For example, if there are 3 input fields {A, B, C}, there will be new 7 test cases with the following inputs with different data = {A, B, C, AB, AC, BC, ABC}.

5. **Add Back Action.** To check if buttons are still working or if sensitive data is not available after a page change. After a click, the browser's 'back' button is pressed to navigate to the previous page. After this, the click is performed again and a check is done to see if we achieved the same result. It also checks if the password fields are not filled. The Add Back Action mutation is the operator which applies a back after a click and tries to click the same object.

The mutation operators "Remove Step", "Add Step", "Change Step Order", "Data Generator" are applied only when the input actions occur one next to the other or when they have just another action in between.

For the Add Back Action mutation operator, there is no pre processing: it is applied just on a click action.

The tool provides an interface which allows the user to choose which mutations will be applied. It also asks the number of mutations to be applied: from 1 to the maximum number of possible mutations. The input can also be a directory with tests and the same rule will be applied for all of them.

After all the mutation operators are applied, a report is created. The report's name is also the timestamp. Each report contains the type of mutation injected and the name of the original test case.

The tool contains a script which runs the original test and the mutated test cases. It generates a report with the results and identifying which tests produced a different result from the original. The number of these tests and the ones which have the same behaviour are also reported. The tool also excludes test cases that have the same behavior as the original.

4   Case Study

A simple website was used that simulates a registration form as shown in Fig. 1. When the 'Sign Up' button is pressed, after the form is complete, another simple page is shown to the user (as can be seen in Fig. 2). This simple website contains 5 input fields about personal information, all of them are required. The 'Sign up' button only works if all the input fields are filled in and if the two password fields match. The verification of these two fields is made just on the second one. The second website is just a page to be redirected when clicking with success on 'Sign up' button.

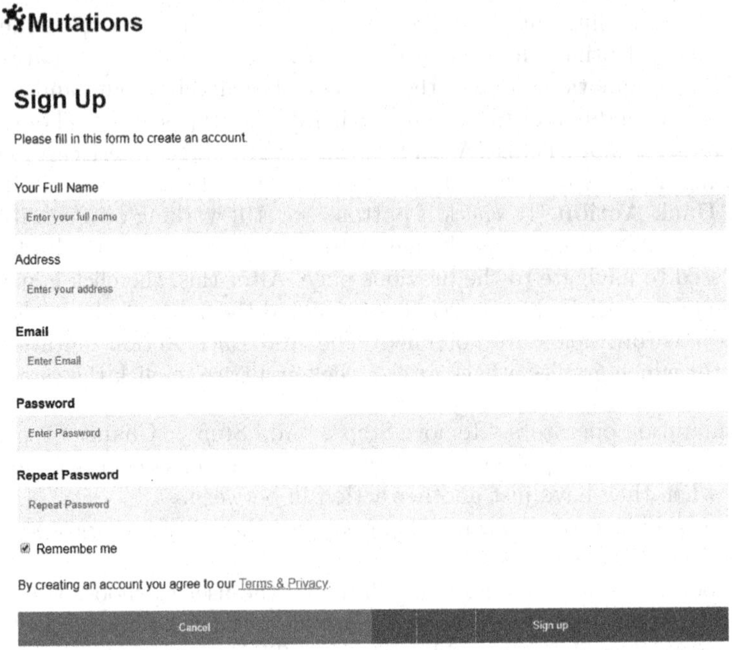

Fig. 1. Simple example website

The recorded example test case is composed by 13 steps:

1. Click on input name field
2. Write the name
3. Click on input address field
4. Write the address
5. Click on input email field
6. Write the email
7. Click on input password field
8. Write the password
9. Click on input repeat password field
10. Write again the password
11. Click on 'Sign up' button
12. Click on Link
13. Click on Link

From this test case, 58 mutations were generated. The generation time was about 1 s. The following mutation operators were selected: 'Add Back Action', 'Add Step', 'Remove Step', 'Change Step Order' and 'Data Generator'.

After the generation, the test cases were executed to check if the result obtained through Selenium was different from the result of the original test case. This execution time was about 9 min. Between each step of the test and between

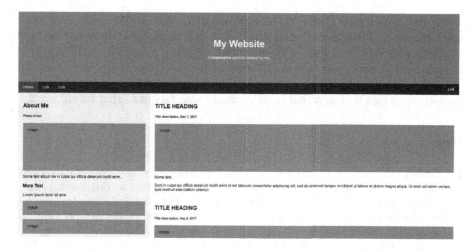

Fig. 2. Simple example website 2

each key pressed, there is a delay of 300 ms to be perceptible during executing. Of the 58 mutated tests, 17 test cases were irrelevant, which means that they have the same behaviour as the original test case and 41 test cases have different behaviour from the original one. 40 of them had the same result because they could not find an element on the second website, once they could not click on 'Sign up' button successfully. The other one could not find an element after a Back mutation.

In this case, about 70% of the generated test cases have different behaviour of the original test case. One of the reasons for this is, for example, the specific behavior related to the password and repeat password. In this particular case, we need the same input data for both fields. So, when we apply the 'Data Generator' mutation operator we get several test cases with different input values for password and repeat password which may fail because values are different or because one of them is not filled in. At this point in time we are not able to tell the reason for such failure because we only consider the results obtained by Selenium, which is "element not found", i.e., we were not able to reach the second screen since the registration failed.

5 Conclusions and Future Work

In this research work, we developed a tool that is able to automatically execute real test cases previously recorded or, if desired, manually written. The tool is also able to generate mutations on real test cases and return those which have a different behaviour than the original ones.

As future work, we want to create more mutation operators to inject in order to detect more types of errors. The data generation could be improved to get more useful data. It would also be important to have some more information about the web elements such as the type of input, allowing us to get even more adequate data. The generation of input data is a challenging field in this type of research as real data cannot be captured for privacy reasons. In future, it is intended to evaluate the result of each test with more metrics, i.e., an adaptation of the *Levenshtein* algorithm to assess similarity among generated test cases. The evaluation of this tool in a real context would also be interesting future work.

References

1. Barbosa, A., Paiva, A.C.R., Campos, J.C.: Test case generation from mutated task models. In: Proceedings of the 3rd ACM SIGCHI Symposium on Engineering Inter-active Computing Systems (EICS 2011), pp. 175–184 (2011). https://doi.org/10.1145/1996461.1996516. http://portal.acm.org/citation.cfm?doid=1996461.1996516
2. Garcia, J.E., Paiva, A.C.R.: Manage software requirements specification using web analytics data. In: Rocha, Á., Adeli, H., Reis, L.P., Costanzo, S. (eds.) WorldCIST 2018. AISC, vol. 746, pp. 257–266. Springer, Cham (2018). https://doi.org/10.1007/978-3-319-77712-2_25
3. Highway, B.A.: Model base testing: a review. Int. J. Adv. Sci. Res. **2**(3), 44–51 (2017)
4. Koroglu, Y., Sen, A.: TCM: test case mutation to improve crash detection in Android. In: Russo, A., Schürr, A. (eds.) FASE 2018. LNCS, vol. 10802, pp. 264–280. Springer, Cham (2018). https://doi.org/10.1007/978-3-319-89363-1_15
5. Liu, C.H., Lu, C.Y., Cheng, S.J., Chang, K.Y., Hsiao, Y.C.: Capture-replay testing for Android applications (2014). https://doi.org/10.1109/IS3C.2014.293
6. Mahmood, R., Mirzaei, N., Malek, S.: EvoDroid: segmented evolutionary testing of Android apps. In: Proceedings of the 22nd ACM SIGSOFT International Sympo-sium on Foundations of Software Engineering, FSE 2014, pp. 599–609. ACM, New York (2014). https://doi.org/10.1145/2635868.2635896
7. Mao, K., Harman, M., Jia, Y.: Sapienz: multi-objective automated testing for Android applications. In: Proceedings of the 25th International Symposium on Software Testing and Analysis, ISSTA 2016, pp. 94–105. ACM, New York (2016). https://doi.org/10.1145/2931037.2931054
8. Moreira, R.M., Paiva, A.C., Nabuco, M., Memon, A.: Pattern-based GUI testing: bridging the gap between design and quality assurance. Softw. Test. Verif. Reliab. **27**(3), e1629 (2017). https://doi.org/10.1002/stvr.1629
9. Silva, P., Paiva, A.C.R., Garcia, J.E., Restivo, A.: Automatic test case generation from usage information. In: 11th International Conference on the Quality of Infor-mation and Communications Technology (QUATIC) (2018)

Author Index

Printed in the United States
By Bookmasters